PERSPECTIVES ON UNITED STATES HISTORY

FROM RECONSTRUCTION THROUGH THE NEW MILLENNIUM

JACK D. ANDERSEN

Bassim Hamadeh, CEO and Publisher
Mazin Hassan, Acquisitions Editor
Michelle Piehl, Senior Project Editor
Christian Berk, Associate Production Editor
Stephanie Kohl, Licensing Associate
Natalie Piccotti, Director of Marketing
Kassie Graves, Vice President of Editorial
Jamie Giganti, Director of Academic Publishing

Cover image copyright © 2010 Depositphotos/rabbit75_dep.

Printed in the United States of America.

ISBN: 978-1-5165-3473-9 (pbk) / 978-1-5165-3474-6 (br)

PERSPECTIVES ON UNITED STATES HISTORY

FROM RECONSTRUCTION THROUGH THE NEW MILLENNIUM

CONTENTS

INTRODUCTION

Many years ago, one of my professors opined to his young undergraduates that United States history has become one of those subjects that students are reluctant to engage in. Whether or not that professor wished to find some common ground with his students on the first day of class, the opinion stuck with us. He was more correct than we thought at the time. For much of our academic lives, history has been a litany of dates, names, and places that students need to memorize for the next standardized exam. Such trivia are sometimes crammed over late-night study sessions with flash cards and coffee. The lesson that is thus unfortunately reinforced to students is that history is not something that is relevant. It is an unpleasant class that students must get through to check off on the list for graduation.

This should not be the case. History is, after all, a story about human beings. All facets of history reveal the complex depth of the human experience. The facts do not change, but the interpretations of those facts do. And it is up to historians to communicate those facts and interpretations in ways people can understand and appreciate. When history is revealed as a story about people, it becomes relevant across generations. And we crave stories about ourselves. See the numerous magazines in the grocery store's checkout lanes, the celebrity gossip tabloids and news feeds, or even the multitudes of websites about the lives of even fictitious characters in popular culture. History is not so different and is relevant to peoples' daily lives, if approached properly.

Communicating history is similar to preparing a meal; a few ingredients are needed if it is to be done properly. Objectivity is important. An honest assessment of the facts, documentation, and tone are critical. Historians are not supposed to simply make things up out of whole cloth. As historians, we do not reject anything that can honestly inform us of the past, even if the facts conflict with preconceived notions. Today, we live in an economic and political context that did not exist in the past. But you still need the facts to be able to interpret and communicate that past to people.

To that end, the articles in this reader offer a look at how major historians have interpreted key events in United States history. These scholars address major events that have shaped the United States as the country transformed from a divided nation into a continental, then a global power. As the United States transformed over the centuries, so did the experiences of those who lived under the Stars and Stripes. These experiences differed from person to person and were interpreted through individual experience. Historians in turn interpret these stories in their own ways and filter them through their own experiences. Some of these opinions might be controversial, while others may be less so. As you examine these articles, look at what the authors are trying to argue. Ask yourself if these arguments about people in United States history are based in facts, interpretations of the facts, or without basis in facts. As you do this, you will develop your critical thinking skills, traits that will serve you very well in life long after you complete this course. The discussion questions offered with each chapter are by no means comprehensive; they are intended as guides to start you on the road to understanding.

I hope this reader helps you learn new viewpoints of the history of the United States. If your class lecture provides the "forest," this reader will offer the "trees." Your journey through history can be a very personal one, and the interpretations offered to you in this reader will help you form your own perspective on United States history.

Jack D. Andersen, Ph.D.
Collin College

CHAPTER I

SLAVERY, THE CIVIL WAR, AND RECONSTRUCTION

OBJECTIVES

- Analyze the evolving historical interpretations of slavery, the American Civil War, and Reconstruction.
- Explain why historians evolved their interpretations over time.

PREWRITING

- What do you already know about the Civil War and Reconstruction eras? How are these topics typically presented to Americans today?

Slavery, The Civil War, and Reconstruction

ERIC FONER

N o period of our nation's history has proved as perennially fascinating to Americans as the era of the Civil War And in the past generation, none has been the subject of so outstanding a body of new historical writing. Like their counterparts studying other periods of American history, Civil War scholars have devoted increasing attention to the everyday lives of ordinary Americans. Under the impact of this redefinition of the study of history, old questions about the period have yielded new answers; and new concerns such as regional variations in the institution of slavery, the impact of the Civil War upon nonslaveholding whites, and the role of blacks in the sectional crisis have come to the forefront of scholarship. If new research seems at times to fragment history into the diverse experiences of individual groups, and historians continue to differ on key points of interpretation, a synthesis is now emerging that sees slavery as the most crucial problem of antebellum American life and the fundamental cause of the Civil War, and the myriad consequences of emancipation as the central themes of the war and Reconstruction.

SLAVERY AND THE ORIGINS OF THE CIVIL WAR

Arguably the finest body of literature produced by American historians since 1960 has been the work reappraising the South's "peculiar institution." But before new views could take hold, the traditional interpretation that had dominated the field until the mid-1950s had to be swept away. Shaped by the assumption that slavery was a civilizing institution made necessary by the racial inferiority of Afro-Americans, previous histories sketched a congenial portrait of plantation life: decent living conditions for all, only the lightest of punishments, and a general system of give-and-take between master and slave. In this view, slavery—usually unprofitable —was maintained for racial and cultural reasons, rather than economic self-interest, and might well have died out peacefully had the Civil War not intervened.

Not until the era of the modern civil rights movement, which profoundly affected the ways historians viewed race relations in the past, did a full-scale refutation of the traditional interpretation appear. This was provided by Kenneth M. Stampp, who perceived that once one abandoned the notion that slaves were an inferior race in need of civilizing influences, the entire edifice of the traditional viewpoint must fall to the ground. Stampp depicted the plantation as an arena of persistent conflict between masters concerned mainly with maximizing their income and slaves in a constant state of semirebellion.

If Stampp cleared away old delusions about slavery, it was Stanley Elkins who drew attention to his generation's major concern—the nature of the slave experience itself. Impressed by studies arguing that other societies that had known slavery, such as Brazil, were marked by significantly less racial prejudice than the United States (an argument subsequently challenged by other scholars), Elkins asserted that bondage in this country had taken a particularly oppressive form, for which the best analogy was the Nazi concentration camp. A more devastating critique of American slavery could hardly be imagined, but Elkins was less concerned with the physical conditions of slave life than with the psychological impact of "total institutions" upon their victims, whether white or black. He concluded that the culture and self-respect of the slave had been stripped away, leaving an "infantilized" personality incapable of rebellion and psychologically dependent upon the master.

More than any other scholar, Elkins redefined the *problématique* (to borrow a term from the French philosopher Louis Althusser) of historians of slavery: that is, the underlying preoccupations that shape the questions scholars ask. His comparative approach inspired subsequent historians to place the South's peculiar institution within the broad context of the hemisphere as a whole, thus counteracting the insular

"American exceptional-ism" that underpins so many accounts of this nation's history. At the same time, comparative analysis has underscored the unique qualities of the old South's slave society in which, unlike that of the Caribbean, the white population considerably outnumbered the black. But most strikingly, even though few subsequent writers agreed entirely with his conclusions, Elkins pushed to the forefront the issue of "slave culture," which has dominated scholarship ever since. A generation of historians set out to demonstrate that rather than being transformed into "Sambos" entirely dependent upon their masters, slaves had created a viable, semiautonomous culture among themselves. Scholars delved into sources hitherto largely ignored— slave songs, spirituals, folklore, narratives written by fugitives, the reminiscences of ex-slaves interviewed during the 1930s by the Works Projects Administration (WPA), marriage registers dating from just after emancipation—to demonstrate that slaves possessed their own values, aspirations, and sense of identity. Their work formed a major component of the broader effort in the 1960s and 1970s to rewrite American history "from the bottom up." The study of slave culture continued to dominate writing on slavery in the 1980s, although Peter Kolchin, in a work comparing American slavery with Russian serfdom, argues that scholars must not lose sight of the authority that planters exercised over every aspect of the slaves' lives, and the obstacles to the creation of real independence within the slave community.

Two institutions of slave life have attracted the most intense scrutiny—the church and the family. The vitality, outlook, and distinctive patterns of worship of slave religion underscore the resiliency of the African inheritance and the degree to which blacks managed to resist the dehumanizing implications of the South's peculiar institution. Blacks rejected the interpretation of Christianity promoted by their masters, which emphasized obedience, humility, and release from suffering in an afterlife rather than in this world. Instead, they came to see themselves as a chosen people akin to the Children of Israel, their bondage and eventual freedom parts of a preordained divine plan. From the Bible they drew favorite images of those who had overcome adversity: Daniel escaping the lions' den, David slaying Goliath, and especially Moses leading his people to a promised land of freedom. In religion blacks found a vehicle for surviving the experience of enslavement with their dignity intact, and in the church an arena for developing a leadership independent of white control. Preachers were key organizers of the nineteenth century's major slave conspiracies, those of Gabriel Prosser (1800), Denmark Vesey (1822), and the religious exhorter Nat Turner (1831). Simultaneously, studies of folktales emphasized the slaves' imaginative reversal of everyday power relations: in the Brer Rabbit stories, for example, weaker creatures get the better of the strong by relying upon their wits. In black religion and folkways, scholars have found solid evidence that slaves understood their own exploitation and believed in the inevitability of their release from bondage.

Similarly, studies of the slave family have shown that an institution once thought to have been destroyed by enslavement not only survived but did so with a set of distinctive values, demonstrating again the partial autonomy of the slave community. Herbert G. Gutman, who has produced the most comprehensive investigation of this subject, acknowledges that black family life faced the constant threat of disruption because of the frequent sale of slaves. Yet he also presents convincing evidence that most slaves lived in "traditional" two-parent families, that many slave marriages were of long duration, and that naming patterns revealed an awareness of family ties going back one or two generations. Subsequent scholars have brought the insights of women's history to bear upon the slave family. Investigating the "internal economy" of slave life—how slaves managed their own time when not at work for their masters—they have discovered a sexual division of labor in which women were generally assigned the tasks of child rearing, cooking, and cleaning, while men hunted, fished, and did outdoor chores. Rather than being the "matriarchy" described in much traditional literature, the slave family was as much influenced by tendencies toward male primacy as the white families around it.

Most recently, historians have moved beyond broad generalizations about the South as a whole to explore the regional variations that gave rise to distinctive forms of antebellum slavery. It has long been recognized that slavery in the cities, where many bondsmen worked as skilled artisans and enjoyed considerable independence from white supervision, differed substantially from the institution in the countryside. But only lately have scholars investigated in detail how rural slavery outside the Cotton Kingdom produced distinct ways of organizing labor, affecting the lives of white and black alike. In the sugar and rice regions, where agriculture required enormous capital investment to support elaborate irrigation systems and grinding and threshing machinery, there arose planter elites whose wealth placed them at the apex of antebellum society. And in both, slaves enjoyed a modicum of day-to-day autonomy: those in the rice fields set their own work pace under a system of individual tasks rather than gang labor; on the sugar plantations, as in the West Indies, black families were allotted individual garden plots. In both cases, slaves used their free time to grow and market crops of their own and were able to accumulate personal property, thus developing a far greater familiarity with the marketplace than those in the cotton region could acquire. In the upper South, moreover, a shift from tobacco to wheat production lessened the need for a resident year-round labor force, leading to the manumission of increasing numbers of slaves. In Maryland, for example, half the black population was already free by 1860.

Attention to regional diversity has also enriched our understanding of the South's free black population. Those in the upper South, employed primarily as agricultural workers or unskilled urban laborers and often linked by family ties to persons in bondage, found their lives closely intertwined with the slave community. Far different was the situation in the port cities of the deep South, particularly Charleston and New Orleans, where there arose a prosperous group of light-skinned free persons of color. Occupying a middle ground between slave and free, black and white, they created a flourishing network of schools, churches, and other institutions and had little in common with the slaves around them. But this free elite would come to play a major role in the turbulent politics of the Civil War and Reconstruction.

Initially, the new focus on the social and cultural aspects of plantation life was accompanied by a neglect of nonslaveholding whites, the majority of the region's population. To a considerable extent, geographical divisions within the old South paralleled those of class and race, and in the predominantly white upcountry a society developed that was distinct in many respects from that of the Black Belt, where most planters and slaves resided. Only recently have historians begun to illuminate this world. The work of Steven Hahn depicts a largely self-sufficient white yeomanry owning few or no slaves, living on the periphery of the market economy, and seeking to preserve the autonomy of their small, local communities. Among other things, Hahn's book adds a new dimension to the continuing discussion of the degree of difference and similarity between northern and southern societies. The world of these yeomen differed profoundly from that of the market-oriented farmers of the Middle West, suggesting that commercial values had penetrated antebellum southern society far less fully than the contemporary North.

The view that slavery was the foundation of an economic and social order differing in fundamental respects from that of the antebellum North can be found in most sophisticated form in the writings of Eugene D. Genovese, his generation's most influential interpreter of the old South. Genovese argued that slavery, although embedded within a capitalist world economy, spawned a unique form of social relations. More than simply an economic investment, it served as the foundation of a distinct way of life, which grew increasingly separate from that of the North as time went on. Slavery gave rise to a hierarchical society based on paternalism, an ideology linking dominant and subordinate classes in a complex pattern of mutual responsibilities and obligations. The slaveholders' outlook differed profoundly from the competitive individualism and acquisitiveness so powerful in the contemporary North. They saw themselves as responsible for the well-being of an extended "family" of dependents, including not only slaves but white women and children on the plantations. The recent work of Elizabeth Fox-Genovese shows that planters' wives accepted and reinforced these paternalist, familial values.

The portrait of the old South as a social and economic backwater reminiscent of the semifeudal European periphery did not, however, win universal assent. An entirely different point of view was adopted by historians who believed that the antebellum

South adhered to, rather than diverged from, the main trends of nineteenth-century development. This interpretation was most closely associated with the work of "cliometricians" Robert Fogel and Stanley Engerman, whose writings embodied two major departures in historical methodology: the computerized analysis of quantitative evidence, and the application of modern neoclassical economic theory to historical problems. The first greatly expanded the possibilities for finding definitive answers to statistical questions (Fogel and Engerman demonstrated, for example, that slavery was a profitable institution, which was not likely to disappear for economic reasons). The second reduced the distinctiveness of the old South to a nonproblem by assuming that slave society functioned according to the same market assumptions as those that prevailed in the North.

Inferring the values and motives of blacks and whites alike from the aggregate economic data, Fogel and Engerman concluded that planters and slaves behaved toward one another in terms of rational calculation: the former concerned primarily with maximizing production, efficiency, and profit; the latter, equally imbued with the capitalist ethic, aspiring to social mobility within the slave system (for example, the ability to rise from field hand to driver). Other historians argued that antebellum North and South shared not only a common value structure but also the common experiences of territorial expansion and (for whites) political democratization. This emphasis on shared values made the Civil War itself rather difficult to explain, but the actual degree of southern distinctiveness remains a point of continuing debate.

No scholar has yet succeeded in synthesizing the new insights into a coherent account of American slavery's historical evolution from the colonial period through the era of "King Cotton." Nonetheless, the cumulative impact of the recent literature has been enormous. For one thing, it leaves little doubt as to the centrality of slavery to the course of nineteenth-century American history. Scholars of slavery were among the first to challenge the consensus interpretation of the American experience that dominated writing in the 1950s but which, as its leading practitioner Richard Hofstadter later acknowledged, could hardly encompass the stark reality of the Civil War. It is no longer possible to view the peculiar institution as some kind of aberration, existing outside the mainstream of American development. Rather, slavery was intimately bound up with the settlement of the Western Hemisphere, the economic development of the antebellum nation, and the structure of national politics. And as Lincoln observed in his second inaugural address, everyone who lived through that era understood that slavery was "somehow" the cause of the war.

Not all historians, however, agree with Lincoln's assertion. For example, the Republican party's rise to power, which provided the immediate cause of secession and war, has inspired sharp differences of interpretation concerning the importance of antislavery within northern politics and culture. Paralleling, in a sense, the emphasis some writers placed on the basic similarities between the two sections, a number of historians have insisted that the slavery issue had little impact on the decisions of northern voters. Practitioners of the "new" political history, such as Michael Holt, have argued that the cultural clash between competing ethnic and religious groups, rather than diverse ideological positions on national issues, formed the basis of grass-roots northern voting alignments. In this view, the Republican party appears as the instrument whereby New England reformers sought to impose their cultural norms (including temperance and opposition to immigration and Catholicism as much as antislavery) upon the nation as a whole, while the Democratic party united those—including southern slaveholders and northern immigrants—committed to maintaining local autonomy and resisting the cultural encroachment of New England Puritanism.

Those historians who, by contrast, see slavery as the foundation of a society funda-mentally distinct from that of the contemporary North, tend also to view Republicans as carriers of an antislavery ideology deeply rooted in the small-town and rural North. This "free-labor ideology" affirmed the superiority of northern society to the "backward" slave South, and viewed the expansion of slavery as a threat to northern laborers' prospects for achieving the economic independence that was ostensibly a right for all members of "free society." Lincoln's own critique of slavery rested firmly on a free-labor ideology, for he saw the institution as violating the right of workers to the fruits of their toil and denying them the opportunity to improve their condition in life through hard work. For the "new" political historians, Lincoln's election in 1860 posed no real threat to the South, and secession resulted from an irrational "crisis of fear." Those who stress the ideological conflict of two fundamentally different societies see in secession the reflection of a reasoned appraisal of the dangers posed by the coming to power of a political party hostile to the South's way of life.

THE CIVIL WAR

Apart from works primarily military in orientation, recent studies of the Civil War carry forward themes dominant in the new interpretation of antebellum history. If slavery was central to prewar American life, it is now clear that emancipation transformed the nature of the war itself. Attention to the experience of slaves, nonslaveholding whites, and free blacks has altered our understanding of the war's course and impact. Moreover, historians are increasingly aware of how the war transformed the warring sections internally, deepening existing divisions and inspiring new social conflicts. Although the terms "North" and "South" continue to be employed as an unavoidable shorthand, it is no longer possible to describe either the Union or the Confederacy as unified monoliths.

The steps by which Congress and President Lincoln moved from an initial policy devoted entirely to the preservation of the Union to embracing the end of slavery as a war aim have often been chronicled. Most Americans, of course, identify the end of slavery almost entirely with the Emancipation Proclamation of January 1, 1863. But it is now clear that the proclamation only confirmed what was already happening on farms and plantations throughout the South. Whatever politicians and military commanders might decree, blacks from the outset saw the Civil War as heralding the long-awaited end to their bondage, and the strength of the community forged under slavery enabled them to seize the opportunities for freedom that now presented themselves. As the Union Army occupied territory first on the Confederacy's periphery and then in its heartland, slaves by the thousands abandoned their owners and headed for the Union lines. Some who escaped then made the hazardous journey "home" to lead their families away. Reports of "demoralized" and "insubordinate" behavior on the plantations mounted, especially after the arrival of Union troops in a neighborhood. Slavery, wrote a northern reporter in November 1862, "is forever destroyed and worthless, no matter what Mr. Lincoln or anyone else may say on the subject."

In many ways, nonetheless, the Emancipation Proclamation, rather than the battles of Gettysburg and Vicksburg, marked the war's turning-point, for it transformed a struggle of armies into a combat of societies, affirming that Union victory would result in a social revolution within the South. In such a struggle, compromise was impossible; the war had to continue until the unconditional surrender of one side or another. Moreover, the proclamation authorized for the first time the large-scale enlistment of black soldiers. By the war's end some 180,000 blacks had served in the Union army—over one-fifth of the black male population of the United States between the ages of eighteen and forty-five. As demonstrated in a remarkable documentary collection edited by a group of scholars headed by Ira Berlin, the enrollment of black troops breathed life into the promise of emancipation. This development was especially significant in Maryland, Kentucky, and Missouri, which remained in the Union and were therefore unaffected by the Emancipation Proclamation; there, enlistment for a time constituted the blacks' only route to freedom.

Within the army, blacks were anything but equal to white soldiers. They served in separate units, initially received less pay than white recruits, were generally assigned to fatigue duties, and suffered abuse from white officers. Yet by the end of the war their service had transformed the nation's treatment of blacks, and blacks' conception of themselves. For the first time in American history, large numbers of blacks had been treated as equals before the law—if only military law—and former slaves had for the first time seen the impersonal sovereignty of the law supersede the personal authority of their masters. It was in military service that large numbers of freedmen first learned to read and write, and out of the army would come many of the articulate leaders of black politics during Reconstruction.

If the war severed the bonds that had connected master and slave, it also widened divisions within southern white society. As in the case of the antebellum South, the experience of nonslaveholding whites during the Civil War has only recently been chronicled in detail. There is little doubt, however, that increasing discontent among upcountry yeomen fatally undermined the Confederate war effort. From the outset, disloyalty was rife in the southern mountains. A region of self-sufficient farmers cut off from the rest of Virginia by the Blue Ridge Mountains, seceded from the state in 1861 to become West Virginia, and the yeomen of eastern Tennessee likewise remained loyal to the Union. Elsewhere, the impact of the war and Confederate policies awakened antiwar sentiment and social conflict. With slavery increasingly weakened by black actions, the Confederate government molded its policies to protect the interests of the planter class, and these policies in turn sundered white society.

Many nonslaveholding whites became convinced that they bore an unfair share of taxation, especially direct impressment of goods by the army and the hated tax-in-kind, which undermined the ability of upcountry small farmers to feed their families. Above all, the conscription law convinced many yeomen that this was "a rich man's war and a poor man's fight." Provisions that a draftee could avoid service by producing a substitute and that one able-bodied white male would be exempted for every twenty slaves were deeply resented in the upcountry. The result, by 1863, was widespread draft resistance and desertion—a virtual civil war within the Civil War, which sapped the military power of the Confederacy and hastened its defeat. Moreover, as portions of the upcountry lying at the war's strategic crossroads were laid waste by the march of opposing armies or by marauding bands of deserters, the war experience redrew the economic and political map of the white South. Much of the upcountry was plunged into poverty, thereby threatening the yeomanry's economic independence and opening the door to the postwar spread of tenancy. And counties in areas such as eastern Tennessee and western North Carolina would defy southern voting patterns for decades, remaining Republican long after the rest of the white South had united within the Democratic party.

For the Union as well as the Confederacy, the war was a time of change. Although historians differ as to the conflict's precise impact on economic growth, there is no question that most branches of industry prospered, and that agriculture flourished as farm machinery replaced rural laborers drawn into the army. Even more important, however, the war tied the fortunes of an emerging class of industrialists to the Republican party and a national state whose power had been greatly enhanced by the conflict. The economic policies of the Lincoln administration—high protective tariffs, a transcontinental railroad, a national currency (the "greenbacks"), and a new national banking system—shifted the terms of trade against agriculture in favor of industry and centralized control of credit in the hands of leading New York banks. As in the South, however, wartime policies also galvanized opposition that threatened to disrupt the war effort. The enrichment of industrialists and bondholders appeared unfair to workers, who saw their real income devastated by inflation. The expanding powers of the federal government clashed with cherished traditions of local autonomy. And the vast changes in race relations implied by emancipation stirred ugly counterattacks by proponents of white supremacy.

Although not as widespread as in the South, these elements of opposition to the war and its consequences came together for a few terrifying days in July 1863 in the New York City draft riots, the largest civil insurrection in American history apart from the South's rebellion itself. Originating in resentment against conscription (the Union draft, too, allowed individuals to buy their way out of military service), the riot quickly developed into a wholesale assault upon all the symbols of the new order being created by the Republican party and the Civil War. Its targets included government officials—especially draft officers and policemen—factories, docks, the homes of wealthy Republicans, and above all, the city's black population, uncounted numbers of whom were lynched or driven out of the city.

The riots revealed the class and racial tensions lying just below the surface of northern life and raised troubling questions about the war's ultimate meaning. Could a society in which racial hatred ran so deep secure a modicum of justice for the former slaves? This issue acquired new urgency as the end of the war approached. Recent writings emphasize the impact of black military service on Republicans' evolving racial attitudes and locate the origins of the party's Reconstruction commitment to black civil rights in the closing months of the Civil War. But it was not the actions of Congress or the president that forced black suffrage to the center stage of politics at this time. That was accomplished by the political mobilization of the free blacks of New Orleans, who compelled the nation's political leaders to grapple with the question when Louisiana, under a reconstructed government organized at Lincoln's behest, sought readmission to the Union.

If before the war Louisiana's free blacks had thought of themselves as having little in common with the slaves, developments in 1864 propelled them down a radical road. They were shocked by the refusal of Louisiana's Constitutional Convention of 1864, which abolished slavery in the state, to extend political rights to the free black community. And they resented the labor system established by the Union's General Nathaniel Banks, which coerced freedmen into signing labor contracts on the plantations and made no distinction between free blacks and former slaves in applying new "vagrancy" statutes. Increasingly, the free black leadership of New Orleans demanded that the right to vote be given to both free blacks and the new freedmen.

Their complaints against the Louisiana government received a sympathetic hearing in Washington. Black suffrage became a live issue in the Congress that assembled in December 1864. When Congress adjourned in March, the issue remained unresolved. But the impasse led Lincoln, in his last speech, for the first time to call publicly for suffrage for black soldiers and "the very intelligent." Hardly a ringing endorsement of black rights, the speech nonetheless suggested that blacks would have a role to play in shaping the political course of the Reconstruction South. With Lincoln's death and the accession of Andrew Johnson, affairs took a very different course. Indeed, the most recent study, by LaWanda Cox, of Lincoln's attitude toward slavery and race during his presidency refutes the familiar claim that the two presidents' plans for Reconstruction were essentially the same (a notion that originated with Johnson himself, although he never showed the same flexibility on the question of blacks' rights as Lincoln).

Historians today are less inclined to regard the Civil War as the settlement of the issues that had divided Americans than to emphasize that the conflict's most significant achievements—the preservation of the Union and the abolition of slavery—bequeathed to the postwar world a host of unanswered questions. They also stress that the wartime corollaries of these accomplishments, a more powerful national state and a growing sense that blacks were entitled to a still-to-be-defined measure of civil equality, produced their own opposing tendencies. In both North and South, the war's end left continuing conflict over the legacy of emancipation.

RECONSTRUCTION

No period in American history has undergone a more complete reevaluation since 1960 than Reconstruction. As with slavery, scholars began by dismantling a long-dominant one-dimensional view and then proceeded to create new and increasingly sophisticated interpretations. According to the portrait that originated with nineteenth-century opponents of black suffrage and achieved scholarly legitimacy early in this century, the turbulent years after the Civil War were a period of unrelieved sordidness in political and social life. Sabotaging Andrew Johnson's attempt to readmit the southern states to full participation in the Union immediately, Radical Republicans fastened black supremacy upon the defeated Confederacy. An orgy of corruption and misgovernment followed, presided over by unscrupulous carpetbaggers (northerners who ventured South to reap the spoils of office), scalawags (southern whites who cooperated with the new governments for personal gain), and ignorant and childlike freedmen who were incapable of responsibly exercising the political power that had been thrust upon them. After much needless suffering, the South's white communities banded together to overthrow these "black" governments and restore "home rule" (their euphemism for white supremacy).

Resting on the assumption that black suffrage was the gravest error of the entire Civil War period, this traditional interpretation survived for decades because it accorded with firmly entrenched American political and social realities—the disfranchisement and segregation of blacks, and the solid Democratic South. But the "Second Reconstruction"—the civil rights movement—inspired a new conception of the first among historians, and as with the study of slavery, a revisionist wave broke over the field in the 1960s. In rapid succession virtually every assumption of the old viewpoint was dismantled. Andrew Johnson, yesterday's high-minded defender of constitutional principles, was revealed as a racist politician too stubborn to compromise with his critics. By creating an impasse with Congress that Lincoln surely would have avoided, Johnson effectively destroyed his own presidency. Radical Republicans, acquitted of vindictive motives, emerged as idealists in the best nineteenth-century reform tradition. Their leaders, Charles Sumner and Thaddeus Stevens, had worked for black rights long before any conceivable political benefit could have flowed from such a commitment. Their Reconstruction policies were based on principle, not mere political advantage or personal gain. And rather than being the concern of a small band of extremists, the commitment to protecting the civil rights of the freedmen—the central issue dividing Congress and the president—enjoyed broad support within the Republican party.

At the same time, the period of "Black Reconstruction" after 1867 was portrayed as a time of extraordinary progress in the South. The rebuilding of war-shattered public institutions, the establishment of the region's first public school systems, the effort to construct an interracial political democracy on the ashes of slavery—all these were commendable achievements, not elements of the "tragic era" described by earlier historians.

The villains and heroes of the traditional morality play came in for revised treatment. Former slaves did enjoy a real measure of political power, but "black supremacy" never existed: outside of South Carolina blacks held only a small fraction of Reconstruction offices. Rather than unscrupulous adventurers, most carpetbaggers were former Union soldiers seeking economic opportunity in the postwar South. The scalawags were an amalgam of "Old Line" Whigs who had opposed secession in the first place and poorer whites who had long resented the planters' domination of the region's life and saw in Reconstruction a chance to recast southern society along more democratic lines. As for corruption, the malfeasance of Reconstruction governments was dwarfed by contemporary scandals in the North (this was the era of Boss Tweed, Credit Mobilier, and the Whiskey Ring) and could hardly be blamed on the former slaves. Finally, the Ku Klux Klan, whose campaign of violence against black and white Republicans had been minimized or excused by earlier historians, was revealed as a terrorist organization that beat and killed its political opponents to deprive blacks of their newly won rights.

By the end of the 1960s the old interpretation had been completely reversed. Most historians agreed that if Reconstruction was a "tragic" era, it was so because change did not go far enough; it fell short especially in the failure to distribute land to the former slaves and thereby provide an economic base for their newly acquired political rights. Indeed, by the 1970s this stress on the "conservative" character of Radical Reconstruction was a prevailing theme of many studies. The Civil War did not signal the eclipse of the old planter class and the coming to power of a new entrepreneurial elite, for example. Social histories of communities scattered across the South demonstrated that planters survived the war with their landholdings and social prestige more or less intact.

The denial of substantive change, however, failed to provide a compelling interpretation of an era whose participants believed themselves living through a social and political revolution. And the most recent work on Reconstruction, while fully cognizant of what was not accomplished, has tended to view the period as one of broad changes in southern and national life. In the first modern, comprehensive account of the period, Eric Foner portrays Reconstruction as part of a prolonged struggle over the new system of labor, racial, and political relations that would replace the South's peculiar institution. As in the study of slavery, moreover, some scholars of Reconstruction have sought to place this country's adjustment to emancipation in the broad context of international patterns of development, and to delineate what was and was not unique about the American response. Neither slavery nor emancipation was unique to the United States, but Reconstruction was; it stands as a dramatic experiment, the only instance in which blacks, within a few years of freedom, achieved universal manhood suffrage and exercised a real measure of political power.

Like recent studies of slavery and the Civil War, current writing. on Reconstruction is informed by a recognition of the extent to which blacks themselves helped shape the contours of change. In a kaleidoscopic evocation of black response to the end of slavery, Leon Litwack has shown that freedmen sought to obtain the greatest possible autonomy in every area of their day-to-day lives. Institutions that had existed under slavery, such as the church and family, were strengthened, and new ones sprang into existence. The freedmen made remarkable efforts to locate loved ones from whom they had been separated under slavery. Many black women, preferring to devote more time to their families, refused to work any longer in the fields, thus contributing to the postwar "labor shortage." Continuing resistance to planters' efforts to tie black children to long periods of involuntary labor through court-ordered "apprenticeships" revealed that control over family life was a major preoccupation of the freedmen. Blacks withdrew almost entirely from white-controlled churches, establishing independent religious institutions of their own; and a diverse panoply of fraternal, benevolent, and mutual aid societies also sprang into existence. And though aided by northern reform societies and the federal government, the freedmen often took the initiative in establishing schools. Nor was black suffrage thrust upon an indifferent black population, for in 1865 and 1866 black conventions gathered throughout the South to demand civil equality and the right to vote.

As in every society that abolished slavery, emancipation was followed by a comprehensive struggle over the shaping of a new labor system to replace it. The conflict between former masters aiming to recreate a disciplined labor force and blacks seeking to carve out the greatest degree of economic autonomy profoundly affected economics, politics, and race relations in the Reconstruction South. Planters were convinced that their own survival and the region's prosperity depended upon their ability to resume production using disciplined gang labor, as under slavery. To this end, the governments established by President Johnson in 1865 established a comprehensive system of vagrancy laws, criminal penalties for breach of contract, and other measures known collectively as the "Black Codes" and designed to force the freedmen back to work on the plantations. As Dan T. Carter shows in a study of Presidential Reconstruction, the inability of the leaders of the white South's "self-Reconstruction" to accept the implications of emancipation aroused resentment in the North, fatally weakened support for the president's policies, and made Radical Reconstruction inevitable.

Out of the conflict on the plantations, new systems of labor emerged in the different regions of the South. Sharecropping came to dominate the cotton South. In this compromise between the blacks' desire for land and the planters' for labor discipline, each black family worked its own plot of land, dividing the crop with the landlord at the end of the year. In the rice-growing areas, with planters unable to attract the outside capital needed to repair wartime destruction and blacks clinging tenaciously to land they had occupied in 1865, the great plantations fell to pieces, and blacks were able to acquire title to small plots and take up self-sufficient farming. And in the sugar region, gang labor survived the end of slavery. In all cases, blacks' economic opportunities were limited by whites' control of credit and by the vagaries of a world market in which the price of agricultural goods suffered a prolonged decline. Nevertheless, the degree to which planters could control the day-to-day lives of their labor force was radically altered by the end of slavery.

The sweeping social changes that followed the Civil War were also reflected in the history of the white yeomanry. Wartime devastation set in motion a train of events that permanently altered these farmers' self-sufficient way of life. Plunged into poverty by the war, ravaged by war casualties, they saw their plight exacerbated by successive crop failures in the early Reconstruction years. In the face of this economic disaster, yeomen clung tenaciously to their farms. But needing to borrow money for the seed, implements, and livestock required to resume farming, many became mired in debt and were forced to abandon self-sufficient farming for the growing of cotton. A region in which a majority of white farmers had once owned their own land was increasingly trapped in a cycle of tenancy and cotton overproduction and became unable to feed itself.

The South's postwar economic transformation profoundly affected the course of Reconstruction politics. As the Black Codes illustrated, state governments could play a vital role in defining the property rights and restricting the bargaining power of planters and laborers. Not surprisingly, when Republicans came to power—largely on the basis of the black vote—they swept away measures designed to bolster plantation discipline and sought to enhance the status of sharecroppers by giving them a first claim on the growing crop. They also launched an ambitious program of aid to railroads, hoping to transform the region into a diversified, modernizing society with enhanced opportunities for white and black alike. But as Mark Summers has shown in an investigation of the program, railroad aid not only failed to achieve its economic aims but produced a sharp increase in taxes, thus exacerbating the economic plight of the yeomanry (attracted in some measure to Reconstruction in its early days by the promise of debtor relief) and preventing the Republican party from broadening its base of white support. Railroad aid also generated most of the corruption that undermined the legitimacy of the Reconstruction governments in the eyes of southern opponents and northern allies alike.

To blacks, however, Reconstruction represented the first time they had ever had a voice in public affairs, and the first time southern governments had even attempted to serve their interests. Recent studies of black politics have stressed both the ways black leaders tried to serve the needs of their constituents and the obstacles that impeded them from doing so effectively. The signal contribution of this new literature has been to reject the idea that Reconstruction politics was simply a matter of black and white. In a broad reevaluation of South Carolina politics, Thomas Holt has argued that many statewide leaders derived from the old Charleston free elite, whose conservative economic outlook rendered them unresponsive to the freedmen's desire for land; studies of Louisiana politics have reached similar conclusions. Free blacks, at the cutting edge of demands for civil and political equality during the Civil War and Reconstruction, failed to find ways of combatting the freedmen's economic plight.

At the local level, however, most black officeholders were former slaves. Although the arduous task of analyzing the local politics of Reconstruction has barely begun, it appears that men who had achieved some special status as slaves—such as ministers and artisans—formed the bulk of black officials. Their ranks were augmented by the little-studied "black carpetbaggers," who looked to the Reconstruction South for opportunities denied them in the North. The presence of sympathetic local officials often made a real difference in the day-to-day lives of the freedmen, ensuring that those accused of crimes would be tried before juries of their peers, and enforcing fairness in such prosaic aspects of local government as road repair, tax assessment, and poor relief. All in all, southern Reconstruction represented a remarkable moment in which the old white elite was stripped of its accustomed political power. It is hardly surprising that its opponents responded not only with criticism but with widespread violence, or that local Republican officials were often the first victims of the Klan and kindred groups.

Recent scholars, indeed, have not only emphasized the role of pervasive violence in the eventual overthrow of Reconstruction but have shown how the problem of law enforcement exposed growing resistance to the expanded federal powers generated by the Civil War. In the war's immediate aftermath Republicans altered the nature of federal–state relations, defining for the first time—in the Civil Rights Law of 1866 and the Fourteenth Amendment—a national citizenship and a national principle of equality before the law, and investing the federal government with the authority to enforce the civil rights of citizens against violations by the states. Then the Fifteenth Amendment prohibited states from infringing upon the right of suffrage for racial reasons, and the Enforcement Acts of 1870–71 gave the federal government the power to protect the civil and political rights of the former slaves against acts of violence.

These were profound changes in a federal system in which the states had traditionally determined and protected the rights of citizens. Yet Reconstruction failed to establish effective means for securing its lofty precepts. The burden of enforcing the new concept of equality before the law was placed upon the federal courts, and it was unrealistic to assume that the courts—even when supplemented on occasion by federal marshals and the army—could bear the major burden of putting down violence in the South. By the 1870s, moreover, many Republicans were retreating from both the racial egalitarianism and the broad definition of federal power spawned by the Civil War. As localism, laissez-faire, and racism—persistent themes of nineteenth-century American history—reasserted themselves, the federal government progressively abandoned efforts to enforce civil rights in the South.

Thus, a complex dialectic of continuity and change affected the ways Americans, black and white, responded to the nation's most profound period of crisis. By the end of the period, slavery was dead, the Union preserved, and both North and South transformed. The social structure populated by masters, slaves, and self-sufficient yeomen was evolving into a world of landlords, merchants, and sharecroppers, both black and white. Also fading into the past was Lincoln's America—a world dominated by the small shop and family farm—as a rapidly industrializing economy took hold in the North. Yet the aspiration galvanized by the Civil War for a society purged of racial injustice had yet to be fulfilled. The end of Reconstruction thrust former slaves into a no-man's-land between slavery and freedom that made a mockery of the ideal of equal citizenship. Scholars, indeed, have yet to assess fully the significance of Reconstruction's failure. That it was a catastrophe for black America is clear, but it also affected the entire structure of American politics, creating a solid Democratic South whose representatives increasingly aligned with northern conservatives to oppose every effort at social change.

It is hardly likely that recent writing represents the final word on slavery, the Civil War, or Reconstruction, for that era raised the decisive questions of America's national existence: the relations between local and national authority, the definition of citizenship, the meaning of equality and freedom. As long as these issues remain central to American life, scholars are certain to return to the Civil War period, bringing to bear the constantly evolving methods and concerns of the study of history.

BIBLIOGRAPHY

SLAVERY, THE OLD SOUTH, AND THE COMING OF THE CIVIL WAR

Berlin, Ira. *Slaves without Masters: The Free Negro in the Antebellum South.* New York: Pantheon Books, 1974.

Blassingame, John. *The Slave Community: Plantation Life in the Antebellum South.* Rev. ed. New York: Oxford University Press, 1979.

Clinton, Catherine. *The Plantation Mistress: Woman's World in the Old South.* New York: Pantheon Books, 1982.

Elkins, Stanley. *Slavery.* Chicago: University of Chicago Press, 1959.

Fields, Barbara J. *Slavery and Freedom on the Middle Ground: Maryland during the Nineteenth Century.* New Haven, Conn.: Yale University Press, 1985.

Fogel, Robert, and Stanley Engerman. *Time on the Cross: The Economics of American Negro Slavery.* Boston: Little, Brown, 1974.

Foner, Eric. *Free Soil, Free Labor, Free Men: The Ideology of the Republican Party before the Civil War.* New York: Oxford University Press, 1970.

Fox-Genovese, Elizabeth. *Within the Plantation Household: Black and White Women of the Old South.* Chapel Hill: University of North Carolina Press, 1988.

Genovese, Eugene D. *The Political Economy of Slavery.* New York: Pantheon Books, 1965.

———. *Roll, Jordan, Roll: The World the Slaves Made.* New York: Pantheon Books, 1974.

Gienapp, William E. *The Origins of the Republican Party, 1852–1856.* New York: Oxford University Press, 1987.

Gutman, Herbert G. *The Black Family in Slavery and Freedom, 1750–1925.* New York: Pantheon Books, 1976.

Hahn, Steven. *The Roots of Southern Populism: Yeoman Farmers and the Transformation of the Georgia Upcountry, 1850-1890.* New York: Oxford University Press, 1983.

Harding, Vincent. *There Is a River: The Black Struggle for Freedom in America.* New York: Harcourt. Brace Jovanovich, 1981.

Harris, J. William. *Plain Folk and Gentry in a Slave Society: White Liberty and Black Slavery in Augusta's Hinterlands.* Middletown, Conn.: Wesleyan University Press, 1985.

Holt, Michael. *The Political Crisis of the 1850s.* New York: Wiley, 1978.

Jones, Jacqueline. *Labor of Love, Labor of Sorrow: Black Women, Work, and the Family from Slavery to the Present.* New York: Basic Books, 1985.

Joyner, Charles. *Down by the Riverside: A South Carolina Slave Community.* Urbana: University of Illinois Press, 1984.

Kolchin, Peter. *Unfree Labor: American Slavery and Russian Serfdom.* Cambridge, Mass.: Harvard University Press, 1987.

Levine, Lawrence W. *Black Culture and Black Consciousness: Afro-American Folk Thought from Slavery to Freedom.* New York: Oxford University Press, 1977.

Potter, David M. *The Impending Crisis, 1848–1861.* New York: Harper & Row, 1976.

Silbey, Joel H. *The Partisan Imperative: The Dynamics of American Politics before the Civil War.* New York: Oxford University Press, 1985.

Stampp, Kenneth M. *The Peculiar Institution: Slavery in the Antebellum South.* New York: Knopf, 1956.

White, Deborah G. *Ar'n't I a Woman? Female Slaves in the Plantation South.* New York: Norton, 1985.

THE CIVIL WAR

Berlin, Ira, et al., eds. *Freedom: A Documentary History of Emancipation.* New York: Cambridge University Press, 1982– .

Bernstein, Iver. *The New York City Draft Riots: Their Significance for American Society and Politics in the Age of the Civil War.* New York: Oxford University Press, 1989.

Berry, Mary F. *Military Necessity and Civil Rights Policy: Black Citizenship and the Constitution, 1861–1868.* Port Washington, N.Y.: Kennikat Press, 1977.

Cox, LaWanda. *Lincoln and Black Freedom: A Study in Presidential Leadership.* Columbia: University of South Carolina Press, 1981.

Escott, Paul D. *After Secession: Jefferson Davis and the Failure of Southern Nationalism.* Baton Rouge: Louisiana State University Press, 1978.

McPherson, James M. *Battle Cry of Freedom: The Civil War Era.* New York: Oxford University Press, 1988.

Montgomery, David. *Beyond Equality: Labor and the Radical Republicans, 1862–1872.* New York: Knopf, 1967.

Paludan, Philip S. *A People's Contest: The Union and the Civil War.* New York: Harper & Row, 1989.

Thomas, Emory M. *The Confederate Nation, 1861–1865.* New York: Harper & Row, 1979.

RECONSTRUCTION

Benedict, Michael L. *A Compromise of Principle: Congressional Republicans and Reconstruction, 1863–1869.* New York: Norton, 1974.

Brock, W. R. *An American Crisis.* New York: Harper & Row, 1963.

Carter, Dan T. *When the War Was Over: The Failure of Self-Reconstruction in the South, 1865–1867.* Baton Rouge: Louisiana State University Press, 1985.

Foner, Eric. *Nothing but Freedom: Emancipation and Its Legacy.* Baton Rouge: Louisiana State University Press, 1983.

———. *Reconstruction: America's Unfinished Revolution, 1863–1877*. New York: Harper & Row, 1988.

———. *A Short History of Reconstruction*. New York: Harper & Row, 1990.

Gillette, William. *Retreat from Reconstruction, 1869–1879*. Baton Rouge: Louisiana State University Press, 1979.

Holt, Thomas. *Black over White: Negro Political Leadership in South Carolina during Reconstruction*. Urbana: University of Illinois Press, 1977.

Jaynes, Gerald. *Branches without Roots: Genesis of the Black Working Class in the American South, 1862–1882*. New York: Oxford University Press, 1986.

Litwack, Leon F. *Been in the Storm So Long: The Aftermath of Slavery*, New York: Knopf, 1979.

Perman, Michael. *The Road to Redemption: Southern Politics, 1869–1879*. Chapel Hill: University of North Carolina Press, 1984.

Rabinowitz, Howard N. *Race Relations in the Urban South, 1865–1890*. New York: Oxford University Press, 1978.

Rable, George C. *But There Was No Peace: The Role of Violence in the Politics of Reconstruction*. Athens: University of Georgia Press, 1984.

Ransom, Roger L., and Richard Sutch. *One Kind of Freedom: The Economic Consequences of Emancipation*. New York: Cambridge University Press, 1977.

Summers, Mark W. *Railroads, Reconstruction, and the Gospel of Prosperity: Aid under the Radical Republicans, 1865–1877*. Princeton, N.J.: Princeton University Press, *1984*.

Trefousse, Hans L. *The Radical Republicans: Lincoln's Vanguard for Racial Justice*. New York: Knopf, 1969.

Wiener, Jonathan M. *Social Origins of the New South: Alabama, 1860–1885*. Baton Rouge: Louisiana State University Press, 1978.

Williamson, Joel. *After Slavery: The Negro in South Carolina during Reconstruction, 1861–1877*. Chapel Hill: University of North Carolina Press, 1965.

DISCUSSION QUESTIONS

- According to Foner, how did American historians treat issues of slavery, the Civil War, and Reconstruction over time?

- According to Foner, why did American historians change their arguments?

- How do the evolving interpretations of slavery, the Civil War, and Reconstruction relate to current affairs?

CHAPTER II

THE AFTERMATH OF 'REDEMPTION'

OBJECTIVES

- Analyze the effects of "Redemption" on the South.
- Describe the various transformative changes that Southerners (black and white) underwent during Redemption.

PREWRITING

- Why did Southern Democrats return to power so quickly after the American Civil War?
- What cultural and political factors in the South encouraged the rise of the "Redeemers?"

The Aftermath of 'Redemption'

JOHN HOPE FRANKLIN AND MICHAEL W. FITZGERALD

The peaceful inauguration of Rutherford B. Hayes on March 4, 1877, as the nineteenth President of the United States marked the formal end of reconstruction, but not the final solution of the problems created by the war and its aftermath. At last the former Confederate states were back in the Union under conditions favorable to those who had led the secession movement and fought the Civil War. But their political position was actually no better than it had been in 1860. The South had made more permanent than ever its distinctive minority status, and its intransigence might well give it greater unity but hardly an opportunity for greater power and influence on the national scene. Meanwhile, within the states themselves, the Redeemers, the self-styled saviors of the South, in order to secure their position, resorted to ruse, conspiracy, and violations of the Fourteenth and Fifteenth Amendments. These practices further dulled whatever sense of political integrity remained.

Politically, then, the South retreated further from democracy and pro-ceeded to institutionalize and make permanent the redemption policies by which it had overthrown reconstruction. African Americans could still vote and hold office after 1877, but it became increasingly difficult—almost impossible—for them to discharge their responsibilities of citizenship. While their participation in politics declined sharply toward the end of reconstruction, blacks as a political issue in Southern politics tended to gain in importance as the years passed. "Waving the bloody shirt" was abandoned by the Republicans, but the Redeemers never tired of warning their fellows of the dangers of a recurrence of "Negro domination." Their consequent determination to maintain their own powerful position led not only to incredible schemes to disfranchise blacks but also to the decline of white manhood suffrage. Last-minute changes in polling places, long, complicated ballots, and even literacy tests could hardly have been calculated to encourage the common white populace to exercise the franchise. Effective political power therefore remained where it had been before the war—with an oligarchy, a small ruling clique that wielded power far out of proportion to its numerical strength.

Nor did the end of reconstruction usher in an entirely new era in the economic life of the South. Agriculture, having made a dramatic recovery, continued to dominate the scene not only as a way of making a living but as a way of life. By 1880 the planting aristocracy had settled down to habits not unlike those that characterized it in 1860. Contrary to the widely held view, there was no significant breakup of the plantation system during and after reconstruction. Day labor, renting, and sharecropping were innovations, to be sure, but those occupying such lowly positions bore a relationship to the planter that, while it was not slavery, was nevertheless one of due subordination in every conceivable way. The role of the planter remained that of paternal despot, controlling the destiny of his many wards and determining the social position of all, including those having little or no connection with agriculture.

There was more industry in the South in 1880 than there had ever been before. This fact, however, was not so much a measure of progress as it was an indication of the South's industrial backwardness in earlier years. Most Southern states had increased their railroad mileage between 1870 and 1880, but the significant increases were just beginning. By 1880 iron furnaces were being fired in Alabama, Tennessee, and Virginia, and the patenting of the first cigarette machine in that year merely suggested the possibilities that lay in the processing of tobacco products. Already, by 1880, the Southern cotton textile industry was rapidly gaining ground, but the mills of the Carolinas and Georgia were not yet within sight of those of New England. Everywhere, however, the young, aggressive spokesmen began to speak confidently of a "New South," implying that their faces were turned resolutely toward the future with no serious desire to keep more than one foot planted in the past.

Whether the spokesmen wanted to or not, the South, even as it moved haltingly toward industrialization, did more than look over its shoulder to the past that had been. It bathed itself in glorious memories and retained much that was a part of that past. Its values continued to be those of a plantation society; and the aspirations even of some of those whose opportunities lay in the new industrialization were geared to an agrarian way of life. The most highly respected member of society in 1880, and indeed the most powerful in many ways, was still the planter. He was still the lord of the manor, setting the tone and the values of all others and occupying a position of respectability if not of affluence to which even the young industrialist aspired.

Where there was industrialization, the similarities between the Old South and the New South were striking. For one thing urbanization in the South increased only slowly in the first two decades following the war. The older towns showed almost no signs of growth, while the new ones crept painfully beyond the stage of hamlets. Unlike the bustling industrial cities of the North, the Southern communities where the cotton mills were built remained relatively small towns for decades. The general atmosphere was bucolic, and the influence of farms and plantations could everywhere be seen.

Despite Southern pride that stimulated local support for the new industries, much of the substantial capital came from the outside. By 1880 Northern capitalists were investing heavily in Southern lands. Northerners, as Paul Gates has observed, controlled the best pine and cypress lands, and they were to reap the benefit by taking most of the profits from the rising lumber industry. Likewise, the railroad boom that was well under way by 1880 was stimulated by Northern capital and directed from New York. Already, with more than $150,000,000 being invested in Southern railroads by Northern and foreign capitalists between 1879 and 1881, the foundation was being laid for the building of the great Morgan empire in the South that came with the consolidations of the 1890's. In minerals the story was essentially the same. New Englanders dominated coal mining in Alabama. When the iron industry emerged there and elsewhere, it was Northern capital that gave it the first big push. If Southerners gave greater support to the cotton textile industry, it was because mills could more easily assimilate small investments. Indeed, the multiplicity of them, scattered over the Southern countryside, captured the imagination of those prideful Southerners who could find a few dollars to invest. Before the war Thomas Kettell had complained that the enormous resources of the South were being turned into profits which only the North enjoyed, while Hinton Rowan Helper had asserted that the South was dependent on the North for almost everything except a few staples. If, by 1880, the South was producing more commodities than at any previous time, it remained a favorite place for Northern investors to reap handsome profits. Real economic independence had not yet come to the South.

And what of the human elements that had played a large part in the drama of the previous decade or so? African Americans who watched political developments began to entertain serious doubts about the Republican party. Those who had fought for effective civil rights legislation in 1874 and 1875 were not satisfied with the law that was finally passed. They were even more disturbed by how some of their friends seemed to be tiring of the fight. When Hayes withdrew the last troops from the South and toured about befriending the former Confederates, some African Americans felt that the party of Lincoln had deserted them. "The party of great moral ideas," said the editor T. Thomas Fortune, "relinquished its right to the respect and confidence of mankind when, in 1876, it abandoned all effort to enforce the provisions of the war amendments…. The black man, who was betrayed by his party and murdered by the opponents of his party, is absolved of all allegiance which *gratitude* may have dictated."

Perhaps few blacks were prepared to condemn the Republican party as unequivocally as Fortune did, but all of them had good reason to be unhappy about their condition at the end of the reconstruction era. Wholesale intimidation and obstructions left them without the ballot to give them a share in making the policies affecting them. Not only had the federal government done almost nothing to protect them from bodily harm, but it now entered upon a course of action committing it to do even less. The Civil Rights Act of 1875 was a dead letter from the day of its enactment, and white Southerners boasted that it was not being enforced and could not be enforced anywhere in the South. With no active political support and with no federal officials willing to enforce the constitutional amendments and the laws that protected them, blacks had reason to despair for their own future.

Their economic condition was no better than their political status. Some blacks, of course, had made significant strides during reconstruction. The great mass of them, however, remained impoverished, with only their labor to sell under conditions peculiarly disadvantageous to them. In the rural areas most remained in the employ of planters or entered into a sharecropping relationship that was hardly better. And the convict-lease system provided black labor for many whites who needed such labor. In the towns and cities they were barred from employment in the new industries that were rising. Persistent myths about their inability to handle machinery and a determination to maintain racial peace kept them in the position of unskilled, untrained menials. Capital and management in the New South placed them in that lowly position; white labor unions and inferior, segregated education would keep them there.

The African American's severe political and economic disabilities insured his continued social degradation. They had not "died out" in freedom, as some Southerners had confidently predicted in 1865. In 1860 there had been 4,441,000 blacks in the United States. By 1880 the number had increased to 6,580,000. But, if anything, population growth increased their troubles. They migrated from place to place; some moved from the country to the towns, others from one part of the South to another. Already, a small number, disgusted with their lot and pessimistic about the future, began to migrate to other sections of the country. In communities where the black population was numerically dominant, the machinery to maintain its due subordination was strengthened. This was a gradual process not perfected until the turn of the century, but it had its beginnings in the early post-reconstruction years. In every important social relationship African Americans were kept at a "safe distance." The result was that in education, religion, social welfare, and the like, they had to build institutions completely separate from those of the whites. The response to the existence of a white world to which blacks were denied entrance, these institutions contributed to the emergence of a black world with all the trappings of an entirely separate community. Suspicion and distrust were the inevitable byproducts of such racial division.

As for the whites, particularly the Redeemers, they had outdone themselves. They had overthrown the reconstruction governments, and they were rapidly rising in the national councils of their party and, indeed, of the federal government. By 1880 they had attained a respectability that had all but obliterated their earlier identification with secession—their war for independence. Presidential pardons and acts of amnesty had brought them back into full citizenship, and they had made the most of it. With a determination equaled only by their energy, they had worked diligently to regain their former positions of influence. Robert E. Lee felt "honored" to pay a courtesy visit to President Grant at the White House on May 1, 1869. On slightly lower levels other former Confederates sought to establish with other parts of the country lines of contact which might prove useful in the future.

The Redeemers' move toward acceptance and respectability precluded by its very nature a move toward democracy. In the reforms they instituted upon their return to power they displayed a singular distrust of the masses, black *and* white. In North Carolina, where they feared that blacks might enjoy some power in counties where they outnumbered whites, they passed the County Government Act in 1876. Among other things this Act empowered the legislature to name the county justices of the peace who, in turn, would name the county commissioners. In some other states where conditions were different, the Redeemers were inclined to limit the power of the legislature. In Texas, for example, the constitution of 1876 severely limited the powers of the legislature and favored the greater concentration of power in the executive. The Louisiana constitution of 1879 is an eloquent expression of "no confidence" in the legislature. In a lengthy section entitled "Limitation of Legislative Powers" the constitution, among other things, enjoins the legislature from contracting any debt or issuing any bonds except to raise money to repel an invasion or suppress an insurrection.

The Redeemers made much of the alleged corruption and extravagance of the reconstruction governments and based their claims to office on their promise to deal sternly with offenders and to eliminate any such dishonest practices in the future. Once in office, they did deal sternly with offenders, although the Redeemers themselves had frequently shared the spoils with former Republican officeholders. The elimination of dishonest practices, however, was another matter. The Redeemers in power clearly proved that the Republicans had no monopoly on perfidy and that both sides had a share in the apparently universal public immorality. In 1879 several officials in Georgia, including the state treasurer, the comptroller-general, and the commissioner of agriculture, resigned under fire or were impeached for scandals and irregularities in the conduct of their offices. In 1873 the state treasurer of Virginia was indicted for embezzlement and escaped trial only on a plea of insanity. In 1883 the treasurers of Tennessee and Virginia disappeared with more than $400,000 and $200,000, respectively. Each was a Confederate veteran who had been active in the movement to restore honesty in government. There were similar defalcations in Arkansas, Kentucky, Mississippi, and Louisiana. For all their professions and promises and for all the claims that were to be made in their behalf, the Redeemers failed to provide the South with governments free of the faults they had laid at the door of the Radicals.

Reconstruction was over. The South was back in the Union, with a leadership strikingly like that of the South which had seceded in 1860. The period had brought changes, to be sure, but most of them had taken place in the North. The section that had expressed deep feelings about slavery and human degradation and had gone to war to preserve the Union had itself been transformed. It was now an industrial colossus with new values, new leadership, and new aspirations. No longer was it interested in activities that might distract or disturb its phenomenal growth and expansion. The South, having changed much less, was more than ever attached to the values and outlook that had shaped its history. Even its once-belligerent adversary was now conciliatory. On the points most important to the white South the North was willing to yield; and on the points most important to the North the white South was willing to yield. In a sense, then, both sides were pleased with the outcome of reconstruction. In another sense, however, both sides suffered an ignoble defeat. The Union had been preserved and human slavery had been abolished; but these were achievements of the war. In the postwar years the Union had not made the achievements of the war a foundation for the healthy advancement of the political, social, and economic life of the United States.

DISCUSSION QUESTIONS

- According to Fitzgerald, what were the effects of Redemption on black Southerners? Could they fulfill their roles as full citizens in the United States in a "Redeemed" state? Was the "American Dream" something most black Southerners could aspire to in a "Redeemed" state?

- Was the South during Redemption truly different than the Old South? If so, how was the South different politically, culturally, and economically?

CHAPTER III

ACCULTURATION UNDER DURESS, 1876-1920

OBJECTIVES

- Explain the ways that Native Americans were subjected to acculturation in the United States after the American Civil War.
- Analyze the effects of federal assimilation efforts on Native Americans in the late nineteenth century.

PREWRITING

- Why was the United States in conflict with the Native American tribes in the nineteenth century?
- Was the conflict between the United States and the Native Americans based on cultural differences? Land and resource disputes? Was it uniquely American?

Acculturation Under Duress, 1876–1920

WILLIAM T. HAGAN AND DANIEL M. COBB

From the mid-nineteenth century forward, proposals for the transformation of American Indians were many. Most were old standbys—Christianize, educate, and introduce private property. The variable factor was the condition under which these policies would be applied. The 1850s saw the concept of a permanent Indian Country shattered by a rapidly growing white population and the railroad net devised to serve it. Then large reservations came under attack and the tribal land base was further whittled down. Until the 1880s proposals to concentrate Native peoples in Indian Territory and a comparable area in the North had strong supporters. During this period at least twenty-five tribes were located in what is now Oklahoma, and many others were shifted to new locations. Quite apt was the barbed question of Spotted Tail, a Lakota, who asked, "Why does not the Great Father put his red children on wheels, so he can move them as he will?" With businessmen happy to part with as much as $20,000 to secure the contract to ration tribes during removal one reason for its popularity is obvious. It took well-publicized condemnations of the traumatic experiences endured by the Cheyenne, Ponca, and Nez Percé during their forced migrations to Indian Territory for the policy to be abandoned.

Like the Nez Percé discussed in the previous chapter, the Poncas, a small northern Plains tribe, suffered illness and death during their two-month forced removal. Their exodus carried them first from Nebraska to Kansas in 1877 and then to Indian Territory the following year. The Northern Cheyennes, who had fought in dozens of military engagements with the United States between 1854 and 1879, were relocated in Indian Territory only to be decimated by malarial fevers. A shortage of medicine and food complicated their situation. Of the meat rationed to them their agent could only say, "it was not grossly bad." Concluding that to remain in the South meant a slow death, Cheyennes under Dull Knife and Little Wolf elected defiance and made their way back home. Thousands of troops hounded the small band of about three hundred; only about one in five were warriors. In the face of steadily mounting odds the party fought its way north, leaving a trail of the dead, wounded, and debilitated. Dull Knife ultimately surrendered, only to flee once more. Little Wolf's party wintered in Wyoming, relented, and remained in the North.

Tales such as these fell on more and more sympathetic ears. Parts of the West that clamored for blood in 1865 had passed through the frontier stage by 1880 and developed a humanitarian interest. But the rule enunciated by Senator Plumb of Kansas that sympathy for Indians increased proportionally to distance from them still seemed to apply. Typical of the attitude of most Westerners was an Iowan's comment on the local reservation Indians, "They are as worthless as so many tamed wolves." The center of agitation in behalf of Indians continued to be the East.

Before the Civil War interest in Indian rights ran a distant second to concerns over slavery. The postwar period continued to be one of lassitude and apathy on the part of reformers. In the wake of Reconstruction, the general public seemed to be in no mood to launch new crusades. One agent campaigned for reform by displaying gunshot and knife wounds he received during the 1873 Modoc War, only to be regarded as a crackpot by Americans intent upon their pursuit of the almighty dollar.

Prodded by the frightful reports of Indian and white battle losses and the high attrition rates among Native populations, the consciences of reformers slowly awakened. Recitation of the wrongs inflicted on the Poncas recruited the vitriolic pen of Helen Hunt Jackson. Critics damned her lack of balance, even suppression of facts that did not fit her preconceptions, but in *A Century of Dishonor* and *Ramona* she publicized the abuse of Native rights as it had never been publicized before.

Around 1880 the growing interest in Indian welfare produced several organizations. One, the National Indian Association, was promoted primarily by women. From its headquarters in Philadelphia it sponsored missions and its state chapters bombarded Washington with petitions. Another, the Indian Citizenship Committee of Boston, was a by-product of the Ponca fiasco and labored to secure political rights. Most influential was the Indian Rights Association organized in Philadelphia by Herbert Welsh and Henry S. Pancoast. From the beginning it earned respectful attention by its on-the-spot investigations which it publicized in hundreds of pamphlets and letters. Officials who ignored them were made aware of the association's objectives by a lobbyist maintained in Washington.

In a class by itself was the National Indian Defense Association founded by Dr. T. A. Bland, publisher of the *Council Fire*. Bland and his associates opposed policies which would rush acculturation. Alone among the reformers they looked askance at attempts to detribalize Native Americans and emasculate the chiefs. Red Cloud, a leader among the Oglala Lakota, inspired and was inspired by Bland.

The Lake Mohonk Conference served as an unofficial coordinating agency for the reformers. From 1883 until his death in 1912, Quaker educator and Board of Indian Commissioners member Albert K. Smiley sponsored annually a conference at his resort that attracted government officials, congressmen, and reformers. Out of their sessions came programs that subsequently inspired much criticism. At the time, however, they represented majority thinking of those styled as "friends of the Indian." The policies they recommended guided the administration of Indian affairs during the next quarter century.

Regardless of the policies devised, in the final analysis their efficacy depended upon their administrators. And Indian Service personnel too seldom were both honest and able. Grant's Quaker policy and his brief experiment with army officers recruited many honest and well-intentioned agents, but too frequently they were totally ignorant of the culture of the people they were supposed to administer. The folly of selecting agents from among people who had never seen an Indian seems not to have been understood. A much more essential qualification in the eyes of those who made the appointments was the political lineage of the appointee. One successful applicant for the Blackfeet agency proved so worthless that a party leader pronounced the ultimate in condemnations: "His character is such that he ought not to hold office even if a Republican." The Democrats were less guilty only in that they were seldom in a position to make appointments. Such criteria provided instructors in agriculture who had never farmed, clerks who couldn't write, and teachers too dissolute or incompetent to hold positions in other schools. But it is perhaps unrealistic to expect better appointments at the lower levels when the average term for commissioners of Indian affairs seldom exceeded two years.

One might well wonder at the attraction the agency positions seemed to hold. Top pay in the 1880s was about $1,500 a year for service in some remote spot under obvious disadvantages with every expectation of brief tenure. Yet there was never a shortage of applicants. The answer can perhaps be found in the commonly held belief that a few years as an Indian agent would guarantee the fortune of anyone not overly burdened with scruples. In an era of United States history when the acquisitive instinct reached perhaps its highest development, as seen in the careers of the Daniel Drews, John D. Rockefellers, William Marcy Tweeds, and Roscoe Conklings, the Indian Service opened vistas of opportunity. The devices employed to defraud Indians, or to manipulate services to further financial interests of certain parties, ranged from crude theft to refined questions of ethics.

Did the location of agencies with an eye to profiting certain communities rather than benefiting Indians constitute corruption? Obviously many businessmen, bulwarks of respectability in their communities, did not think so. When the issue of transferring an agency from Camp Apache to San Carlos arose, it was damned as a conspiracy to replace New Mexican contractors with Arizonans and Californians. The issue was discussed as though the principal consideration was the profit to be made from supplying the reservation.

There was no room for doubt about the ethics of some of the practices on reservations. At San Carlos the agent had been devoting his time and effort to mining operations which he partially supported by food and materials diverted from the agency warehouses. The agent not only escaped prosecution but sold a mine to the inspector sent to check on him. The inspector in turn involved the son of the commissioner of Indian affairs in his mining venture.

Another agent sent to guide the Apaches toward acculturation stocked his ranch with government cattle and sold to local farmers the blankets and other supplies designated for the needy Apaches. He also permitted considerable latitude to his subordinates. The agency blacksmith and carpenter spent much of their time on private projects, the former even charging for shoeing the mounts of government scouts.

Contracting to supply an Indian reservation was a lucrative business. Collusion between contractor and agent provided "steel chopping knives made of cast iron; best brogans with paper soles; blankets made of shoddy and glue, which fell to pieces when wet … forty dozen elastics … when there was not a stocking in the tribe." Collusion between ranchers and lumbermen on the one hand and agents on the other resulted in herds fattening on Indian grass and contracts being filled with Indian timber. Honest mistakes were as damaging. Sawmills were erected miles from any timber; bakeries were built which Indians declined to patronize; agency farms were opened where drought was a chronic condition.

In the light of such blundering or outright fraud, Indian resistance to the feeble missionary activities is understandable. Although the expenditures of church groups increased over what they had been in the early nineteenth century, the record was still quite spotty. The idea of a Chinese person on the banks of the Yangtze remained more romantic and challenging than an Indian sitting in the dust of an allotment. When the reservations were parceled out for missionary activity, some of the tribes were completely neglected by the denominations to which they had been assigned. Former Commissioner of Indian Affairs George W. Manypenny protested that Americans were expending millions of dollars on foreign missions while the total budget for Indian work did not exceed $10,000 a year.

In contrast to tribes that attracted no missionaries, there were tribes that had too many. At one time the Lakota at the Rosebud Agency were the subjects of a tug of war between Roman Catholics and Episcopalians that resulted in the ouster of a priest by the agency police. Frequently the sect to be indulged depended upon the affiliation of the agent and this was particularly true during the Quaker policy era.

For Indians the whole business must have been amusing. A change in agency administration might also result in the substitution of an Episcopalian for a Roman Catholic, or a Baptist for a Presbyterian. Moreover, the doctrinal disagreements in which they seemed to delight were bewildering. Chief Joseph refused to countenance missionary work among his band, charging, "They will teach us to quarrel about God as the Catholics and Protestants do on the reservation. … We may quarrel with men sometimes about things on this earth, but we never quarrel about God. We do not want to learn that."

Whether Baptist, Roman Catholic, or Presbyterian, missionaries suffered certain common handicaps. Some Christian concepts, such as penance and baptism, were totally alien to tribal belief systems. There was also a general tendency for the missionaries to extend their operations beyond spiritual needs. They did not feel their mission accomplished unless Indian men not only accepted Christianity, but also gave up hunting and raiding, shed their blankets, and settled down to farm an allotment. One denomination demonstrated this by explaining its lack of success at an agency in terms of such mundane matters as frosts, droughts, and caterpillars.

Some of the missionaries' failures could be attributed to faulty technique and poorly chosen personnel. As one Quaker remarked, "To reach the full-blooded Indian send after him a full-blooded Christian." And even these rare creatures would be more effective if they knew the people they were trying to save. Some missionaries worked among a tribe for years without troubling to acquaint themselves with the Native belief systems they were trying to supplant. Religious bigots made little headway with Indians unimpressed by the quality of the Christianity to which they were exposed. As one Indian reportedly responded to a missionary's injunction against drunkenness and adultery, "My father, it is your people, who you say have the Great Spirit's book, who bring us the fire-water. It is your white men who corrupt our daughters. Go teach them to do right, and then come to us and I will believe you."

Where Christianity made its greatest inroads, it depended upon the services of Native pastors who blended old teachings with new, as Christianity had once absorbed pagan practices. Among the Creeks, hymns were translated into the Muskogee language, social customs found expression in camp meetings lasting days, and traditional values showed up in Christian garb. Sermons employing tribal stories to make a point were much more meaningful than those dependent upon parables based on an alien culture.

Among the important Indian religious movements to appear in the late nineteenth century were peyotism and the Ghost Dance. Peyotism centered upon the consumption of a nonaddictive narcotic found in a type of cactus. The mild, colorful hallucinations induced by peyote provided the setting for singing, prayer, and testimonials. Most peyote groups grafted this onto Christianity; others did not. In both forms it spread rapidly from the Southwest, worrying agency officials and missionaries but providing its participants with an opportunity to commune with the sacred, a path to right living, and peace of mind.

The Ghost Dance emerged from the teachings of a Paiute named Wovoka during the 1880s. It quickly spread across the northern and southern Plains. Like the Delawares of the 1760s and Senecas of the early 1800s, Plains peoples faced tremendous adversity. The buffalo, an animal upon which they had based their whole way of life, had virtually disappeared. Rather than enjoying the excitement of buffalo hunts and horse-stealing expeditions, they had been threatened and cajoled to embrace the drudgery of the plow and the hoe. Amidst poverty, poor health, and extreme deprivation, the world Plains people once knew had fallen apart. When reports of Wovoka's revelations made their way into their communities, many embraced his vision.

Plains tribes had produced prophets like Isatai (Comanche), Pautapety (Kiowa), and Paingya (Kiowa) who promised the return of the buffalo, the annihilation of all whites and nonbelievers, and the revival of the old ways. But it was Wovoka whose message spread like a prairie fire. Also known as Jack Wilson, the Paiute prophet received a vision when he fell seriously ill in 1888. On recovery he reported that while unconscious he had received a message for his people. Similar to the teachings of an older Paiute who may have been his father, Wovoka predicted the Plains would again support millions of buffalo and the whites and all their ways would disappear. The Paiute did not claim divinity, nor did he incite Indians to drive the intruders from the land. He deplored resort to force and instead prescribed dances and songs which would hasten the great day.

By the summer of 1890 word of Wovoka filtered onto the Great Plains and roused thousands from despair. The rumor among the southern tribes was that a new Christ had appeared, one dispatched to the Indians—not the whites, who had killed theirs. The Arapahoes were particularly intrigued and sent two of their policemen to verify the story. They returned without having personally seen the messiah but were convinced of his existence. In some of the camps all work stopped, and Indians gave themselves over completely to the Ghost Dance, as non-Natives termed the ceremony prescribed by Wovoka. The military was alerted to expect trouble on the southern Plains, but close surveillance failed to reveal any cause for armed intervention and the excitement gradually subsided.

In the north the fever was higher. The Ghost Dance attracted thousands of converts in a matter of weeks. The agency officials in some instances allowed themselves to be stampeded. Wovoka's chief apostle among the Lakota was Kicking Bear, who together with others journeyed a long way to see him. The agent at Standing Rock dispatched police to arrest Kicking Bear for stirring up Sitting Bull's band. The police returned without him and too dazed and confused to explain their failure. The power of the Ghost Dance was also attested to by many of the converts who recovered from unconsciousness brought on by fasting and dancing to describe visits with deceased loved ones who spoke of returning. Warriors also began to prepare shirts bearing symbols that could turn aside bullets. Such developments increased the uneasiness of white settlers and some of the military and Indian Service personnel. When soldiers began to concentrate in the vicinity of the centers of the Ghost Dance, some of the enthusiasm for it began to wane.

At the Standing Rock Agency, Sitting Bull's band, which had returned from Canada in 1881, provided a flurry of excitement. The agent had been at odds with the Lakota leader for years and the Ghost Dance movement only aggravated the situation. Using as a pretext reports that Sitting Bull was preparing to leave the reservation, the agent sent a detachment of Indian police to arrest him. Although the Indian police were employed on this mission in the hope that they would arouse less antagonism than troops, the ill feeling between the conservatives and the upholders of white authority may only have worsened a bad situation. The attempt to take Sitting Bull into custody precipitated a burst of violence that resulted in a number of deaths, including Sitting Bull's.

One band of Ghost Dancers left their agency during the excitement, despite orders to the contrary. To prevent them from joining forces with dissidents at the Pine Ridge Agency, troops were sent to intercept them. When overtaken by Custer's old regiment, the Seventh Cavalry, the Lakotas were ordered to turn in all weapons. During a moment of confusion, the soldiers opened fire on the entire band. The result was the Massacre at Wounded Knee. Hotchkiss guns hurled shells into the terrified camp, and the troops fired their rifles indiscriminately. Approximately three hundred Lakotas, perhaps half of them women and children, and twenty-five troops lost their lives.

Ironically, one of the bulwarks of the acculturation policy—schools—had facilitated the spread of the Ghost Dance. English learned in mission or government schools was the means of communication used to overcome the tribal language barriers. Indeed, non-Indians first learned of the magnitude of the movement from a Native postmaster who had been asked to read letters addressed to illiterates. It was a curious product for a policy upon which all reformers agreed.

Despite general acceptance of schools, little progress had been made since the first ones were instituted before the Civil War. The average agency school was an unknown quantity, many of them un-inspected for years. The teacher frequently was the wife or other relative of the agent and if he or she was competent, it was a coincidence. Even able instructors found it difficult to maintain any enthusiasm. The reports of teachers abound in instances of semesters begun with rooms full of eager youths only to have the attendance drop sharply once the novelty wore off.

Until 1870 federal aid for the schools was limited to half-hearted attempts to fulfill treaty stipulations and sporadic efforts to satisfy the reformers. Most of the funds appropriated for acculturation went into pattern farms, mills, and salaries for sundry agency employees. In 1870 Congress appropriated the first sum specifically for the purpose of education. By 1899 over $2.5 million was being expended annually on 148 boarding schools and 225 day schools with almost 20,000 children in attendance. Nevertheless, about half of the children still were not enrolled.

The off-reservation boarding school was most popular in the last quarter of the nineteenth century. Reformers and Indian Service personnel generally agreed that a complete break with the home environment was desirable. Schools like the Carlisle Indian Industrial School in Pennsylvania were the temporary homes of thousands of Indian children. There the youths were encouraged to shed their tribal culture as a relic of the past. With the best of intentions the school administrators did a poor job. Forced to increase enrollment to secure enough federal subsidy to operate, the crowded institutions trained the girls in home economics and the domestic arts. The boys became adept at handling farm machinery and adjusting furnaces. These vocational skills often had little application to the type of lives they would lead when they returned home. While some returned students adjusted, others did not. By 1900, every reservation had former boarding school students who struggled to find a place in their communities. In one extreme example, a young man named Plenty Horses (Lakota) sought to regain status by murdering an army officer during the Ghost Dance controversy.

It was another army officer, Captain Richard H. Pratt, who in 1879 established Carlisle, the best known of the boarding schools. In charge of Apache prisoners in Florida, he was impressed by their adaptability and helped secure admission for some of them to Hampton Institute, a private school for African Americans. At Carlisle, which was supported entirely by federal funds, Pratt introduced the outing system. Coming at the end of their stay at Carlisle, this involved placing mature students for a period of as much as three years with one of the rural families near Carlisle. Pratt was a strong advocate of acculturation and a bitter critic of contract schools maintained by church groups with government subsidy. The captain maintained that the churches always wanted to return students to the reservation to do church work, whereas Pratt's greatest ambition was to see reservations abolished and Indians completely integrated into the dominant society. "In Indian civilization I am a Baptist," he once told an audience,

Figure 3.1 Non-Native policy makers intended off-reservation boarding schools to be a means of destroying tribalism. Students, such as the children in this late-nineteenth-century photograph of the Riverside Indian School in southwestern Oklahoma, invested the boarding school experience with different meanings that often produced unintended consequences. Frank Phillips Collection #436-A, Western History Collections, University of Oklahoma Libraries.

"because I believe in immersing the Indians in our civilization and when we get them under holding them there until they are throughly [sic] soaked."

In the 1890s the popularity of the day schools increased. Members of Congress preferred them because they were cheaper than the boarding schools, particularly those that were located off-reservation, like Carlisle. It was also argued that day schools did not separate children from their families and served as a little nucleus of civilization within tribes. Westerners appreciated it for a different reason but one familiar to anyone who has seen a community mixing God and Mammon in its efforts to attract eleemosynary institutions for the money they bring to the area.

While the boarding school was reaching its peak of popularity, some changes had been introduced into the Indian schools which improved their overall performance. Uniform textbooks and methods, together with a merit system for teachers, ended some of the grosser inequities among the day schools. The strictly tribal boarding and day schools were brought into the federal system. Some people applauded the government's decision, because of the separation of church and state issue, to cease subsidizing church schools. Others were pleased by the plans to move Indian children into the public school system as rapidly as possible.

Recruiting students for any type of school proved to be a challenge. Indian parents were understandably reluctant to lose their children for months—or permanently: the death rate among the students was abnormally high. Stories of corporal punishment, of school jails, and of young warriors shorn of their long hair heightened the unpopularity of the institutions. To fill the rosters a practice for many years was to deny rations to uncooperative parents or, infrequently, even to imprison them. If this tactic seems harsh, it would be well to note that a contemporary commissioner of Indian affairs could defend the requirement on the use of English in the schools by citing as precedent German practices in Alsace and Lorraine. Little wonder that agency police were used virtually to kidnap children for the schools and to guard against truancy. On one reservation the rounding up of students for the agency school provoked such outrage that cavalry had to be summoned.

Native youths' experiences were as diverse as the students themselves. Many of them endured severe hardships that included physical violence, such as being beaten for speaking Native languages. The violence could be cultural or psychological, as well. At Carlisle, teachers forced Daklugie, an Apache student, to take the name "Asa." As an adult he rejected the name and all that it represented. His memoir, *Indeh: An Apache Odyssey*, recounts feelings of utter despair. "There, desperate to the extent that we did not care whether we lived or died," he recalled, "we were thrust into a vicious and hostile world that we both hated and feared." In confirmation of this observation, Carl-isle's school paper regularly included stories about students who ran away, sometimes with tragic consequences. And yet, Indian youths also found it possible to carve out places for themselves. They formed friendships and fell in love, played in school marching bands, and took to the diamond or gridiron as athletes. Some graduates went on to work in their home communities or the Indian Bureau. A few attained renown as artists, professional athletes, writers, medical doctors, and performers.

The Indian police and the Courts of Indian Offenses were attempts to employ law not only for the purpose of maintaining order and protecting property, but also as an active agent in the acculturation process. When, in 1878, Congress first appropriated funds for agency police, there was ample precedent for their action. The Light Horse, a tribal police force, had appeared among the Creeks before their removal. Among Plains Indians soldier societies combined police and military functions, particularly during buffalo hunts. Several agents, John P. Clum being the best example, had evolved their own answer to questions of law and order by recruiting private police forces.

Within six years police forces had been established at forty-eight of sixty agencies. Some officials were critical of the policy and made little use of the police. Many agents, however, came to depend on them for a variety of services. Indian police not only served as truant officers; they also ran down rustlers and bootleggers, acted as messengers, cleaned out irrigation ditches, and took the census. The quality of the personnel varied greatly from reservation to reservation, but as the Quapaw agent summed it up, "They are not perfect, but we could not get along without them at all."

The police were active agents of the acculturation process also. They provided the agent a counter to the influence of conservative chiefs, as Sitting Bull learned at the cost of his life. Policemen were expected to set an example by wearing white man's attire when out of uniform, cutting their hair, practicing monogamy, and taking an allotment after their tribe was introduced to severalty—individual as opposed to communal ownership of land.

For obvious reasons culturally conservative factions disliked the police. Their duties included such onerous tasks as determining whether members of the tribal community were working hard enough to merit their sugar, coffee, and tobacco rations. "The police are looked upon as a common foe, and the multitude are bitterly opposed to them," reported one agent. Being saddled in 1883 with the additional duty of judges on the newly established Courts of Indian Offenses did not ease their situation.

The Courts of Indian Offenses were the answer to complaints about the persistence of "heathenish dances," polygamy, and the influence of "medicine men." Originally police were to serve as judges without additional compensation, playing the roles of both prosecutor and arbiter. On a few reservations they even shared in the fines they levied, an equally dubious practice. Eventually Congress appropriated money to pay the judges salaries not exceeding eight dollars a month, grossly inadequate even by reservation standards.

Like the policemen, the judges were supposed to exhibit proper cultural characteristics indicative of acculturation. The headmen who could command respect as judges, however, frequently were cultural conservatives. And even those individuals commonly referred to as progressives occasionally had flaws. Quanah Parker, the former Comanche war chief who became a collaborator after surrendering in 1875, was eventually relieved of his judicial position for a serious lapse. Quanah had too many wives—"five undisputed facts" as his agent referred to them in 1890.

Quanah Parker and his colleagues relieved the agent of many burdens as community peacemaker, although the agent reserved the right to review their decisions. From non-Native viewpoints the courts were an asset in eliminating vestiges of the old ways. Whether or not individual Indians approved depended upon the value they set upon the practices of their ancestors. Even those considered most progressive, however, often found it difficult to accept the principle that crimes against persons were crimes

Figure 3.2 Quanah Parker, standing at the far left with other members of his council, led the Comanche people through a period of war, reservation making, assimilation, and allotment. After initially refusing to sign the Treaty of Medicine Lodge in 1867, he served on the tribal council and court and became a leading advocate of ranching and peyotism. Jay Hargett Collection, #11, Western History Collections, University of Oklahoma Libraries.

against society as well and could not be compromised by a gift to an individual. At the other extreme were Indians who tried to control the court to advance their interests.

Both tribal police and judges declined in number and importance as allotment destroyed the closed reservation and regular law enforcement agencies took over. The elimination of the reservation, this "City of Destruction" as Captain Pratt termed it, was just one of the results of the severalty policy which had been advocated for so long. As noted in chapter two, American officials early discerned the advantages of private property. Provisions for severalty were written into a number of treaties following 1850. As with Christianity and education, severalty had almost unanimous support. Scholars were cited to prove that private property had always been the basis of civilization. Local officials urged it to undercut the power of the chiefs. One commissioner of Indian affairs, apparently impressed by the activities of the anarchists and labor agitators, emphasized the conservative influence of private property as a counterweight to the "heresies in the social and political world." The familiar argument was employed by a governor of Dakota Territory that a "reasonable quantity of land held … by direct grant would not become such an object of complaint or greed as enormous tracts occupied by tribes and claimed by no definite individual." A corollary to this, and a powerful argument for severalty, was the assumption that it would lead to the breakup of the reservations and the sale to whites of the surplus acres after Indians had received their allotments. The Indians' new neighbors were envisioned as examples worthy of emulation.

Severalty was that rare policy on which Helen Hunt Jackson and the most rabid Indian haters could agree, although for different reasons. Some of its advocates waxed absolutely lyrical. A Sioux agent in 1886 was inspired to visualize an Indian on his allotment, singing as he worked:

> We'll have a little farm, a horse, a pig, and cow.
> And she will mind the dairy and I will guide the plow.

Critics of the policy were few. One senator suggested that perhaps the true principle was not private property but rather that the individual should "own just so much of his mother earth as he can make useful to himself." Smacking of Henry George's philosophy, this view had little support. Captain Pratt's reasons for supporting severalty were similarly unpopular, but the captain must be given credit for his honesty. He urged it on the assumption that Indians would soon squander their holdings and then be forced to go to work. There was evidence available that previous experiences with severalty had resulted in something quite like this. Of 1,735 Anishinaabeg granted allotments about 1871, five-sixths of them had sold their lands or been defrauded of them by unscrupulous whites by 1878.

Despite this, the Dawes Severalty Act of 1887 enshrined as general policy what had been taking place piecemeal for years. The law provided that at his discretion the president could allot reservation land to Indians, the title to be held in trust by the United States for twenty-five years. Full citizenship would accompany the allotment. Heads of families were to receive 160 acres with smaller amounts going to other adults, children, and orphans. The surplus, after all of the allotments had been assigned, was to go on the market. As written in 1887, the act did not apply to the Chickasaws, Choctaws, Seminoles, Cherokees, and Creeks and several smaller Indian nations.

Native people did not join in the general rejoicing over the passage of the act. Even among non-Indians there were a few lingering doubts. Henry L. Dawes, the Massachusetts senator for whom the bill was named, was not enthusiastic. A few months before the passage of the bill he defended it lamely as an attempt to salvage something for Indians who might otherwise lose all their land to voracious whites. Grover Cleveland signed the bill, but only after remarking that he agreed with Dawes that the "hunger and thirst of the white man for the Indian's land is almost equal to his hunger and thirst after righteousness." The president promised to be careful to

Tribal Lands 1860-1890

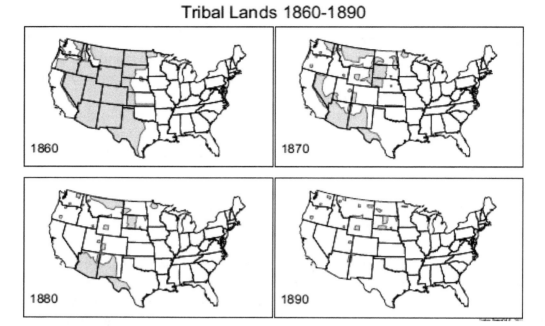

Figure 3.3 As this map illustrates, the tribal land base west of the Mississippi River diminished rapidly during the last half of the nineteenth century. The process continued in the wake of the General Allotment Act of 1887. Between its passage and 1934, approximately 100 more million acres of the tribal domain were lost to non-Indians. Map courtesy of Joshua A. Sutterfield.

appoint officials who would protect the interests of Indians in carrying out the severalty policy.

A concerted act of opposition to the Dawes Act was expressed by delegates at a convention of representatives from nineteen of the tribes in Indian Territory. Others opted for subtler means of resistance, such as refusing to sign the government's census rolls or by taking contiguous allotments that preserved extended kinship relations. The Cherokees, Creeks, Seminoles, Chickasaws, and Choctaws put up the most effective resistance to severalty. They were alert to congressional developments and lobbied in Washington. One Cherokee delegation denied to Congress that their tribe practiced communism. "The only difference between your land system and ours," the Cherokees insisted, "is that the unoccupied [land] … is not a chattel to be sold and speculated in by men who do not use it. … As it is, so long as one acre of our domain is unoccupied," the delegation continued, "any Cherokee who wishes to cultivate it can do so, and make a home, which is his." They predicted that if severalty were forced upon them, a few would monopolize the land.

In contrast, advocates of severalty painted sordid pictures of a few sophisticated Indians engrossing the best land under the tribal system. But there was occasional testimony by whites to the contrary. In 1886 the Senate Committee on Indian Affairs

Figure 3.4 Cherokees who did not remove to the Indian Territory between 1838 and 1839 either accepted individual allotments or became landless. After the Civil War, they secured a reservation, known as the Qualla Boundary, and incorporated as the Eastern Band of Cherokee Indians. As this photograph dated 1888 to single and 1893 shows, families endured despite difficult circumstances. In 2010, the Eastern Band reported more than twelve thousand citizens. National Anthropological Archives, Smithsonian Institution (06212100).

reported, "The entire absence of pauperism amongst these tribes and the general thrift of the people are most powerful arguments in favor of their system of landhold-ing." But the momentum of the severalty movement was too great. In 1893 a sena-torial commission came to Indian Territory, and after carefully choosing its witnesses, submitted a report which laid the groundwork for the introduction of severalty there.

That the severalty policy was a terrible mistake was apparent shortly after its gen-eral application. Some reformers who had pushed it assumed that their job was done and turned to other interests, much as the abolitionists had abandoned emancipated slaves after the Civil War. Despite Cleveland's pessimism about the ability of Indians to succeed at agriculture when experienced white farmers were retreating to the cities, neither he nor his successors reversed the policy. Reservation after reservation was surveyed and allotted, even some where insufficient rainfall made agriculture risky. One is reminded of the Kiowa Chief Little Mountain's sarcastic suggestion that if the president wished corn raised by Indians he should send them land fit for corn produc-tion. Where the land was sufficiently undesirable to whites, as in the desert country of the Southwest, Indians were not pressured into severalty and there was little change in their pattern of land tenure.

Prior to its passage, the Creek Chief Pleasant Porter had doubted that Americans were sufficiently virtuous not to use the Dawes Act to their own advantage. Twenty years later Oklahoma editors were justifying the pillaging of Indians by such state-ments as "Sympathy and sentiment never stand in the way of the onward march of empire" and "If they don't learn the value of property and how to adjust themselves to surroundings, they will be 'grafted' out of it—that is one of the unchangeable laws of God and the constitution of man." "Grafted" out of it they were, by tactics that ranged from deceit and duplicity to murder. Had it not resembled what had been happening for three centuries whenever Indian property aroused white cupidity, one would have concluded that some tragic deterioration of American character had taken place.

The first loophole whites exploited was the act permitting Indians to lease their allot-ments. Unaware of the worth of their holdings and in need of what small income might be generated, Indians leased their land at ridiculously low figures. When members of the Creeks, Choctaws, Seminoles, Cherokees, and Chickasaws finally received their allotments, real estate agents assisted them in selecting their land and then leased it. The real estate agent made his profit by subletting the property, at a much higher rate, to a white farmer. Most sought after were leases on timber land which could be stripped and, coached by whites, Indians sought many such allotments. What could not be done by conforming to the letter of the law, whites tried to do by circumventing it. On one reservation a gang of illegal leasers defied the police to evict them.

Leasing had been defended as exposing Indians to beneficial contacts with in-dustrious white farmers. Guardianship, another technique for looting, was offered as a device to protect the interests of minors or incompetents who had received allotments. Enterprising non-Indians with the proper connections would secure ap-pointment as guardians of incompetent adults, or orphans, or obtain waivers from a child's parents. Thus in control of the property they would manipulate it to their own advantage. Outright embezzlement and forgery were not as popular as excessive fees and exorbitant purchases which profited guardians and their business associates. One non-Native tried unsuccessfully to secure guardianship of a group of 161 children whose allotments he had planned to select so as to cover a valuable tract of timber.

One particularly underhanded tactic was to inveigle Indians into writing wills which would assign most of their property to their white friends. This practice perhaps explains a suspicious increase in the number of Indian deaths from undetermined causes. In a few cases murder was definitely proved, the most reprehensible being the bombing of two sleeping children. Kidnapping was yet another weapon in the unprin-cipled speculator's arsenal. It was sometimes used to facilitate the marriage of a minor, thus qualifying the newly wed boy or girl to sign over the allotment immediately. The wife or husband supplied by the speculator would then disappear.

Several attempts were made to protect Indians by amending the Dawes Act. The Burke Act of 1906, for example, withheld citizenship until the trust period expired and gave the Secretary of Interior more latitude in handling competency and heirship problems. But as rapidly as Indian Service personnel closed one loophole, grafters would discover another. And the apparently limitless possibilities corrupted government officials as well. Judges furthered their careers by selecting the proper guardians; agency officials accepted bribes to expedite allotments which non-Indians hoped to exploit; even the members of the Dawes Commission and executives in the Interior Department were stockholders in companies which dealt in Indian lands. Severalty may not have civilized Indians, but it definitely corrupted most of the non-Indians who had any contact with it.

Honest administrators, and there were some, found the heirship problem a maze of frustrations. As allottees died intestate, their tracts were assigned to their several heirs, with each death complicating the situation. By 1920 there were allotments shared by over fifty heirs, by 1950 by over a hundred. And any use of the property required the consent of each heir. Countless hours were expended just trying to apportion the income from leases on such property. Certainly Native people receiving several checks, some for only a few cents, were not profiting greatly from the situation. One way out of the imbroglio was to sell the land, but even this could be done only if all of the heirs consented.

Ironically, among the first people to impress allottees with their new status were tax collectors. In some areas Indians were assessed at excessive rates for all personal property as well as improvements on their farms. The net effect was actually to drive some of them from the community. Far from being a stimulus, severalty seemed to penalize Indians for changing. Unfamiliar with new farming methods, without the credit to purchase the tools and livestock necessary to do the job effectively, and harassed by tax collectors, the allottees often failed as farmers. They had difficulty realizing why they should join school children in celebrating the anniversary of the signing of the Dawes Act.

A small minority did well by severalty. And there were others who captured publicity during the twenties, when their allotments sprouted oil drilling rigs. They, too, became targets for salesmen and swindlers. But for every allotment containing oil, there were a score that could not produce enough wealth to sustain the families that depended on them. Restricted to unsought allotments, they often lost the land as soon as alienation became possible.

Alienation was facilitated by the previously mentioned Burke Act and two additional pieces of legislation. The Burke Act gave the Secretary of the Interior authority to reduce the period of wardship for Indians judged competent to handle their business affairs. They, in turn, secured full title to their allotments. The Dead Indian Act of 1902 also hastened the loss of land by permitting heirs to sell lands they inherited, and the Non-Competent Indian Act of 1907 authorized individuals so designated to sell portions of their allotments to obtain the capital necessary to develop their remaining lands.

Those three acts significantly accelerated the transfer of land from Indians to non-Indians. Between 1887 and 1934 Indians were separated from an estimated eighty-six million of a total of 138 million acres. Most of that remaining was desert or semidesert: worthless to the white population. Bishop Hare had remarked at the time of the passage of the Dawes Act, "Time will show whether the world or the Church will be more on the alert to take advantage of the occasion." By 1920 the verdict was in. Worldly interests had demonstrated what can happen to a democratic society when the balance of power militated against effective political action.

Administrators were loath to recognize the failure of severalty and the other techniques for acculturation they were trying to apply. As former Commissioner of Indian Affairs Francis E. Leupp summed it up in 1919, "The Indian problem has now reached a stage where its solution is almost wholly a matter of administration." What Leupp and the others found difficult to believe was that Indians could possibly be better off as members of tribal societies than as members of the dominant society. They also failed to take into account cultural diversity among the tribes. Even in the interest of uniform administration it is hard to defend blanket orders to reservation officials to slash food and clothing rations so as to force tribes to support themselves. Native people did what they had always done—shared what they had even if that meant they would also go hungry together later. Equally indefensible was the order from Washington that all male Indians should cut their hair. Some tribes believed that long hair had spiritual significance, or that they would be in peril if their clipped hair fell into the hands of their enemies. Agents, for their part, regarded long hair as the symbol of resistance to acculturation. An agent to the Shoshones referred to it as the Gordian knot. On at least one reservation those who did not submit were shackled so that the hair-cutting order might be carried out.

Amidst these trying circumstances, Native people turned to wage labor, ranching, and farming. For years, tribes like the Pawnee furnished scouts for the United States troop columns combing the Plains. Late in the nineteenth century this practice was regularized, and several all-Indian units were recruited. Long after the fighting had ended, Sitting Bull and many of his contemporaries performed in Buffalo Bill's Wild West shows. They ambushed stagecoaches in stirring finales all over the United States and in a number of European countries. Many of them enjoyed the traveling and the parts they played, and they were able to use the money they earned to support their families and to gain status in their communities. In the Pacific Northwest, migrant labor in the hop fields offered similar opportunities to get away from the reservation, interact with extended kin groups, and earn money. Kwakwaka'wakw used the income to host potlatches or giveaways that enabled them to reaffirm or establish social status in their communities. In New York state, Iroquois men earned reputations for being among the best high-steel workers in the world. They built many of the city's skyscrapers, including the Empire State Building.

Still, the self-styled Friends of the Indian who were willing to face the facts must have been at their wit's end by the 1920s. Policies undertaken in the nineteenth century with sublime assurance of their ultimate success no longer appeared efficacious, even with good administration. The death rate was exceeding the birth rate, and economic conditions were clearly worsening. When tribal identities appeared less prominent, the reformers considered one of their great objectives accomplished. But Native people refused to assimilate. Instead, they blended their communities' traditions with values and practices borrowed from other tribes and non-Natives. As with the peyote way which generated the Native American Church, so with songs, dances, and craft s. Intertribal contacts in the boarding schools and the crowding together of tribes into smaller areas led to considerable cultural exchange. On the Plains, formerly inveterate enemies visited each other's settlements. Taken together these movements and exchanges contributed to the rise of supratribal identities and pan-Indian political movements.

The most prominent organization to emerge during the early twentieth century was the Society of American Indians (SAI). Founded in Columbus, Ohio, on October 12, 1911, the SAI drew leadership primarily from Native men and women who went through the boarding school experience and became professionals in their own right. Not unlike constituents of the National Association for the Advancement of Colored People (NAACP), SAI members styled themselves as an elite segment or "Talented Tenth" of their people. Led by individuals such as the Dakota physician Charles Eastman, Seneca ethnologist Arthur C. Parker, Dakota writer Zitkala Sa, Yavapai physician Carlos Montezuma, Reverend Sherman Coolidge (Arapaho), and Omaha lawyer Thomas Sloan, the SAI debated the major issues of the day. Their publication, *The Quarterly Journal* (later renamed the *American Indian Magazine*), published statements on education, treaty rights, and the status of health services. Prominent issues included access to the Court of Claims, US citizenship, and whether to abolish or reform the Bureau of Indian Affairs.

World War I (1914–18), which the United States entered in 1917, shaped the reform movement and dramatically affected the lives of Native people. On the home front, men and women sought work in war industries, contributed to the Red Cross, and raised money to buy liberty bonds. Meanwhile, approximately sixteen thousand Indians served in various branches of the military, a figure estimated to be 20 to 30 percent of the adult male population. Although most served in integrated units, racism affected the form their contributions took and how the military reported it to the public. For instance, Indians were disproportionately selected to serve as scouts due to their supposedly innate sense of direction or ordered to lead attacks given their cultural predisposition for warfare. In typical fashion, the army's *Stars and Stripes* wrote glowingly of "Indian buck privates," a "species of American fighter" that struck fear into the Germans by "yelling and whooping" during bayonet charges "in true woodsman style."

Despite the prevalence of racist imagery, Indians made important contributions to the war effort. A unique area involved the cryptographic use of Native languages. This occurred formally, as in the case of Choctaws in Company E of the 142nd and 143rd Infantry Regiment who developed a system of coded words to use in the field. In addition, Cherokee, Cheyenne, Comanche, Osage, and Dakota soldiers used their languages incidentally or informally. Though the use of code talking would be much more expansive in World War II, Native languages played an important role in sending telephone and radio transmissions when the Germans intercepted other modes of communication.

Throughout the war and after, the Society of American Indians capitalized on the war effort to push for reform. Its members pointed to both the high rate of voluntarism and draft registration to demand respect for treaty rights, the settlement of outstanding claims, and legislation to extend citizenship universally to all Indian people. "Loving liberty as he does, he will fight for it," Arthur C. Parker argued. "Knowing the tragedy of 'broken treaties,' he will fight that there be not more treaties broken." In an essay entitled "Democracy and Not Wardship for the Indians," Carlos Montezuma added that "the great object of the war" was to "redeem the oppressed of all nations and thus place the world on a basis of justice." By this time, Montezuma had a radical proponent of abolishing the BIA. In the pages of his new journal *Wassaja*, he explained his position in no uncertain terms, "The U.S. government considers an Indian man enough to go over to France and lay down his life for freedom, but is not entitled to freedom at home. 'How long, oh how long! will the people of the United States keep us under the bondage of the Indian Bureau?' comes the anguishing appeal from the Indian race."

Not all Native people shared Montezuma's position. Some looked instead to President Woodrow Wilson's Fourteen Points to defend treaty rights and to demand that Indians be accepted among the family of nations. Though supporters of citizenship, Arthur Parker, Charles Eastman, and Zitkala Sa also invoked Wilson's support for "little peoples" or small nations seeking self-determination. Crow leader Robert Yellowtail and Deskaheh, a First Nations Cayuga, pushed the connection to international law even farther. During a congressional hearing in 1919, Yellowtail reminded legislators that the Crows were a "separate semisovereign nation" and that "the history of all nations tells us that they have grown only better in proportion as they have grown free." When Canada threatened Iroquois rights during the early 1920s, Deskaheh went so far as to seek an audience at the newly established League of Nations in Geneva, Switzerland.

Neither overt resistance nor creative adaptation—whether cultural or political in nature—sat well with non-Native reformers. Rather than being overwhelmed by modernity, Native people had adjusted to it. The elaborate pompadour hairstyles and long dresses of Seminole women, for instance, were not ancient tribal customs but rather selective appropriations of the Gibson girl style of the turn of the century. Photographs of Geronimo sitting in a 1905 Locomobile Model C did not represent a contradiction between tribalism and modernity but Native engagement with new technologies. Boarding school educations did not annihilate Indian identities but instead equipped people such as Delos Lone Wolf (Kiowa), Fred Mahone (Hualapai), and Albert Hensley (Ho-Chunk) with skills they used to defend their community's rights to the land and religious freedom. In still another example, the poetry and short stories written by D'Arcy McNickle, an aspiring young Native writer, about Montana, New York City, and the Flathead Reservation did not convey a search for identity "between Indian and white worlds" but expressions of the many places he knew as home.

These examples were of small comfort to reformers or administrators, because they led to the conclusion that the policy of acculturation under duress was a failure. Unsatisfied with merely modifying traditional ideas and practices, they actually sought nothing less than complete assimilation. In their minds, progress equated to the total loss of a separate identity—the substitution of one way of life (white) for another (Indian). Wedded to a host of untenable binary oppositions, they could not fathom the idea that Native people could exist as Native people in the contemporary world. To their dismay, tribal cultures did not vanish but instead proved quite durable. Friends of the Indian, therefore, could not agree with the observer who designated the first decades of the twentieth century as "the beginning of the end of the Indian problem."

DISCUSSION QUESTIONS

- According to Cobb, what were the major motivations for the United States to bring Native Americans into American society? How did the Native Americans react to these policies?

- Did the stereotypes of Native Americans in the minds of Americans change over time after the Civil War? If so, analyze these changes.

- Did the Native Americans have groups that advocated on their behalf for reform in the assimilation process? If so, how effective were these efforts?

- Based on the moral and ethical standards of the late nineteenth century, was there any reasonable alternative to the United States government's policy of acculturation?

CHAPTER IV

FACTORIES, RAILROADS, AND ROTARY EGGBEATERS

FROM FARM TO TABLE

OBJECTIVES

- Analyze the effects of industrialization and railroads on American agriculture in the late nineteenth century.
- Analyze how industrialized agriculture transformed Americans' approach to the acquisition and consumption of food at the turn of the century.

PREWRITING

- Why was the United States undergoing such rapid technological and industrial changes in the nineteenth century? How did those developments in production affect how people ate?

Factories, Railroads, and Rotary Eggbeaters
From Farm to Table

KATHERINE LEONARD TURNER

INDUSTRIALIZED AGRICULTURE AND THE TRIUMPH OVER SEASONALITY

The American foodscape was transformed in the late nineteenth and early twentieth centuries. The industrialization of agriculture changed the size and nature of American farms, which were becoming larger, more efficient "factory farms" that required enormous inputs in the form of machinery and chemical fertilizers. Improvements in transportation changed the way food was bought and sold and lowered its price. Perhaps most importantly, the combined effects of industrialization and transportation worked together to reduce seasonality.

These structural changes profoundly affected working-class diets by lowering food prices and making the purchase of out-of-season foods at least possible. These changes allowed everyone, including working-class people, to eat more like wealthy people of the past, with more access to high-status foods like meat and white sugar and access to a larger variety of produce throughout the year. In fact, twentieth-century advertisers and promoters seized on this idea, crowing that industrialization made it possible for a poor man to eat like a king. However, these changes to the food system occurred at the same time that America's "second industrial revolution" concentrated new immigrants and American rural migrants into crowded industrial cities. Despite the long-term movement toward lower food prices, frequent industrial depressions and job insecurity meant that working-class city dwellers frequently had trouble stretching their food dollars to feed the family. Eating like a king was still a dream rather than a reality for most.

The triumph over seasonality was probably the biggest revolution in food of the time. For the whole of human history, the food supply had been limited by the annual cycle: plants will grow only during certain times of the year, and animals follow a seasonal reproduction cycle. To be eaten out of season, food had to be preserved; for example, pigs slaughtered in the fall were salted and apples gathered at the same time were dried so that they could be eaten, in altered form, throughout the year. Food could be grown in controlled environments, such as greenhouses, or transported to areas where it was not in season, but until the twentieth century, these options were both impractical and expensive. Prior to the twentieth century, people ate fresh foods only in season, and they ate preserved food or did without during the rest of the year. Although foodies today advocate a more seasonal way of eating (both for better taste and better sustainability), for those without a choice, seasonality seemed like a curse. It meant long stretches of dull food and poor nutrition through the winter and early spring. The decrease in seasonality would eventually transform the American diet entirely from its nineteenth-century format.[1] Like other technological changes, the increased availability of fresh food regardless of season carried moral and social implications as well. Working-class people, like other Americans, would have to decide whether the novelty and variety offered by out-of-season food was worth the extra cost.

In the 1870s foods were already becoming available outside their traditional times of year through improved transportation and new technologies in farming and food processing. Faster transportation effectively shortened distances, so that ripe fruit could be brought from southern or western states or even from other countries and sold before it rotted.[2] Refrigerated train cars meant that animals could be slaughtered and their meat shipped at any time of year, not just in the cold months, as before. New farming technologies could also reduce seasonality. For example, chickens normally lay fewer eggs in winter, meaning higher prices for eggs in the cold months. If they are exposed to a source of artificial light, however, hens can produce more eggs year-round. Improvements in food processing, such as canning, also made preserved food seem fresher. Canned food was much closer in taste and texture to fresh foods than dried or salted foods were, so the improved availability of canned foods represented an impressive reduction of seasonality.

The industrialization of agriculture also helped smooth out seasonal variations and pressures on the prices of staples and grains. Industrialized agriculture was more like factory production than traditional farming, with increased use of mechanization, increased dependence on capital and credit, economies of scale, and market special-ization. America had more land available for plowing: in the thirty years after 1870, farmers began to flood into the Great Plains, which were previously considered a use-less desert.[3] More land under cultivation meant a larger supply of food on the market and lower prices, especially for grains and meat. Farmers changed their tools as well. Innovations such as mechanical planters, reapers, and binders (tools that still used horses as the motive power rather than steam or gasoline) increased the amount of crop farmers could produce with less labor. Wheat production increased 250 percent in the last quarter of the century.[4] Farmers needed significant capital to farm in the West in order to pay for the now-critical inputs of mechanized tools and fertilizer, leading to increased dependence on banks. Larger farms resulted in lower commodity prices, which in turn made it even harder for small farmers to compete.[5] These changes in American farming combined to bring a greater variety of food into American markets and, at least for a while, lowered prices for food as well. The urban working class, who bought all of their food and needed to count their pennies, benefited from these changes, destructive as they were to the traditional American small farm.

Railroad transportation and related technological changes altered the nature of food as a commodity. First, railroad transportation decreased food prices. As historian William Cronon argues, Chicago's growth as an entrepôt of grain sales and the use of grain elevators combined to encourage standardized grain grading systems. Instead of being hauled into the city by farmers in their wagons and sold as bags of grain from a single source, grain was increasingly brought in by railroad and classified by grade, such as number two spring wheat. Graded grain could be bought and sold in any quantity or traded as futures. The commodification of grain increased its supply and lowered its price by streamlining its transport and sale.[6] Secondly, the railroads transformed food by increasing the supply radius. Food could be transported quite cheaply over long distances, which both lowered prices and increased the variety of food available. By the 1880s, the use of refrigerated railroad cars was beginning to transform agriculture, as fruits, vegetables, meat, and other perishable goods could be shipped long distances. In some instances, the railroad system transformed entire industries.

The development of the refrigerated railroad car made it possible to develop a centralized meat-processing center in Chicago. In the 1850s, cattle from Texas were herded through Kansas and into Chicago by rail. From Chicago the cattle would be shipped, still "on the hoof," to slaughterhouses throughout the East. In the 1870s, Gustavus Swift built a more efficient system, shipping chilled butchered meat rather the entire living cow. His plan required refrigerated cars that would chill the meat with-out damaging it; icehouses along the way to refresh the car refrigeration; and butchers who would consent to sell "chilled beef" instead of beef that they had butchered themselves. Once Swift was able to perfect this system, other packers followed suit. As this "western beef" flooded the market in the last quarter of the nineteenth century, prices for beef dropped considerably, as much as 30 percent between 1882 and 1893.[7] Meat, traditionally a scarce item in working-class diets, became vastly cheaper. Americans could now eat fresh meat instead of preserved meat, and replace salt pork with fresh beef. The changes in the meat industry affected individual neighborhoods as well: local slaughterhouses disappeared, and retailers concentrated on selling the most desirable cuts rather than having to dispose of all the parts of a locally slaughtered animal.[8]

In tandem with the increasing availability of fresh packed beef and pork, wild game and shellfish declined in numbers due to overhunting. By 1900, for example, Americans living in New York, Philadelphia, and Baltimore could easily buy inexpensive beef butchered and packed in Chicago, but the ducks, oysters, and crabs that were once plentiful in the Chesapeake Bay were becoming scarce.[9] The decline in seasonality went hand in hand with a more centralized food system in which more food poured out of fewer processing locations.

The milk supply was also drastically altered by the railroads. Until the 1870s, city dwellers drank milk from cows kept right in the city in locations derided as "swill dairies," where the cows ate discarded distillery and brewery mash and were penned in small, filthy stalls. The milk traveled only a short distance to customers, but it tasted sour and was often dirty. In the late nineteenth century, "milk trains" carried milk from large rural dairies into the city. As "country fresh" milk became more widely available, demand increased; city dwellers drank more fresh milk and fed it to their babies instead of breast-feeding them. However, railroads increased the distance and time that milk could travel between cow and consumer, and bacterial contamination plagued urban milk supplies until pasteurization became widespread in the 1910s.[10]

The railroads had possibly their greatest effect on produce. Seasonal fruits and vegetables were being shipped from the warm South into colder northern cities even before the Civil War, but by the 1870s this had increased considerably. Southern states like Florida, Georgia, and South Carolina, with their longer growing seasons, specialized in fruits and vegetables that were shipped to New York and other northern cities. The use of refrigerated railroad cars made it easier to ship perishable produce. Historian Richard Hooker notes that after 1878, "cities near sea or rail transportation … had, even in winter, fresh tomatoes, radishes, cucumbers, spinach, cauliflowers, eggplants, Valencia onions, and salad greens, all but spinach from the Deep South."[11] Fresh produce was shipped not only from the South to the Northeast and Midwest, but all the way from California to the cities of the East. The first carload of fresh fruit reached the East Coast from California in 1869, and the California agricultural economy boomed in the last quarter of the nineteenth century, as refrigerated cars could ship produce almost anywhere in the country without significant damage—especially after sturdy varieties like iceberg lettuce were specially developed for long transport.[12]

This meant that city dwellers, even in cold northern states, could enjoy locally out-of-season fruits and vegetables. Americans in much of the country were able to benefit from the long southern and western growing seasons instead of being limited to what was locally available. Cooking teacher and home economist Maria Parloa, in an 1880 cookbook, wrote about the temptations of supplementing Northeast produce with southern items, warning of their higher cost: "The railroads and steamers connect the climes so closely that one hardly knows whether he is eating fruits or vegetables in or out of season. The provider, however, realizes that it takes a long purse to buy fresh produce at the North while the ground is yet frozen."[13]

Cold-storage warehouses attached to the railroad network also extended foods' seasonal range. Home freezers were not common until the 1950s, but cold-storage warehouses, cooled by mechanical refrigeration, were common at the turn of the twentieth century. Refrigerated food could be sold as fresh, helping to eliminate seasonality long before the mass retailing of frozen food. In 1891 *Harper's Weekly* reported that large cold-storage warehouses in New York and Chicago were keeping eggs, meats, and other items fresh for weeks or months out of their seasons. The buying public was often suspicious of cold-storage foods: the food seemed unnaturally fresh though months old, and the cold could conceal spoilage.[14] For *Harper's*, however, cold storage promised a "peaceful revolution" in which eggs would sell for the same low price year-round, spring lamb would be available any time, and "people of very small incomes will be able to enjoy a bill of fare such as the richest man was unable to procure within the memory of the reader."[15] The changes in food distribution promised a sort of "democracy of goods" in which even poor people would be able to buy plenty of fresh, luxurious food. Whether or not this promise was achieved, most Americans did benefit from the wider seasonal availability of food. Anthropomorphic measurements (height and weight) indicate that until the widespread adoption of refrigeration, many groups of Americans were perennially underfed. The better nutrition from refrigerated meat and dairy allowed everyone to grow a little taller and heavier.[16]

After the turn of the twentieth century, working-class people in cities could afford a bit more variety in produce than previously, able to purchase produce perhaps a few weeks earlier or later than it would be available locally. In 1893 William T. Elsing, an activist minister on New York's Lower East Side, thought that even the poor in New York could afford early or late-season produce "raised in hot-houses, or sent from Southern markets" at "reasonable prices."[17] The rural population, who lived far from railroad terminals or shipping ports, did not benefit from this new transportation technology, of course; they were still largely limited to produce that grew locally or could survive longer, slower hauls. Out-of-season produce was mostly an urban phenomenon.

INDUSTRIAL FOOD PROCESSING

Beginning in the late nineteenth century, food-processing industries worked along with transportation to change Americans' experience of food. There were two major sets of changes to American food processing. First, traditional processes such as cheese making, brewing, bread baking, and meat curing were accelerated and converted from small-batch, artisan production to continuous factory production. Second, new processes such as canning and breakfast cereal manufacture created new processed foods that had the potential to radically change American eating habits. These changes came to fruition during the 1920s. Working-class people incorporated processed foods into their diets very slowly during this period, but the growth in processed food changed the American diet more generally.

Traditional food-processing techniques changed slowly but steadily throughout the nineteenth century. To use cheese as an example: by the 1870s, most cheese was produced in large cheese factories rather than small farmhouses. Newly available laboratory-produced rennet (the enzymes that separate milk into curds and whey) was more reliable than that extracted on farms from calves' stomachs. In the early twentieth century, food science researchers at land-grant colleges and state experimental stations attempted to "rationalize" cheese making, instituting the use of pure milk with a precise butterfat content and replacing naturally occurring bacteria with precise inoculations of the correct cultures. Processed cheese, which did away with troublesome natural variations, was being sold by 1916.[18] By the 1930s, the cheese that Americans ate was likely to be prepared in large batches under sterile, standardized conditions. This was true of bread, beer, ham, pasta, and other traditional foods as well.[19]

Canned food was the processed food most commonly eaten by working-class people in this period. Food had been canned since the early 1800s, but for most of the nineteenth century canned food was an expensive luxury, often sold to travelers and those who wanted to enjoy out-of-season or rare delicacies. In the 1850s, a small can of oysters, salmon, lobsters, tomatoes, corn, or peas might cost fifty cents in an Eastern grocery store.[20] (At that time a skilled mason working on the Erie Canal earned about $1.50 each week.)[21] After the Civil War, canned food was often sold to miners and others on the far western frontier. In "boom" areas where few vegetables were yet cultivated for sale, canned fruits and vegetables were sometimes the only ones available at any price. Newly rich miners in California lavished money on canned delicacies, paying exorbitant prices for exotic "prepared" foods like turtle soup and lobster salad in cans.[22] In the late nineteenth century, the industry expanded and canned food's retail price dropped as manufacturers found ways to eliminate costly human labor:

Figure 4.1 Sociologist and photographer Lewis Hine devoted his career to exposing and eliminating child labor in the United States with the National Child Labor Committee. This photograph, taken in July 1909 near Baltimore, Maryland, shows women and small children stringing beans before they are canned. Photograph by Lewis Hine for the National Child Labor Committee, July 1909. Library of Congress, Prints and Photographs Division, National Child Labor Committee Collection, LOT 7475, v. 1, no. 0855. Reproduction Number: LC-DIG-nclc-00031.

that of the skilled tinsmiths who made and soldered the cans, as well as that of the unskilled, low-paid women and children who prepared the food to be canned.[23]

Canned food finally became affordable for the middle classes in the 1880s, and for most people around 1900. Technological advances and the elimination of high labor costs lowered the prices of common canned foods, especially tomatoes, corn, and peas, to within the reach of the working class. By 1900 middle-class cooks were already accustomed to using canned fruits and vegetables when fresh ones were seasonally unavailable.[24] In Fannie Farmer's 1905 cookbook, aimed at the urban middle class, a recipe for "Green Peas" began, "Open one can of peas."[25] Even poor working-class families used a small amount of canned food. At about the same time as Fannie Farmer's cookbook was published, working-class New York City families that spent only $10 per week for food regularly spent 10 cents for a can of tomatoes.[26] Americans' consumption of canned foods increased steadily through the 1910s and 1920s, as the foods available now included convenient prepared dishes such as canned soup and spaghetti. By 1930 Americans consumed twice as many canned vegetables and four times as much canned fruit as they had in 1910.[27] Canned food joined abundant meat and out-of-season produce as former luxuries that were now everyday foods available to the working class.

There was, however, some continuing resistance to canned food. Some recent immigrants, especially those from less industrialized parts of Europe, refused to use canned foods. Italians in particular made a point of seeking out and, if necessary, creating local sources of fresh vegetables.[28] Even native-born Americans believed that canned food was a necessary evil. In a 1926 Department of Commerce study, the consumers polled overwhelmingly preferred fresh food to canned in terms of flavor, and more than half believed that fresh food was more nutritious.[29] The reality of canned food hadn't lived up to the canners' extravagant promises of a bounty of flavor.

The path food took from farm to kitchen had changed almost beyond recognition. Farms were larger, food traveled faster and farther to market, and some food was transformed along the way into a growing selection of packaged and processed foods. The kitchens where this food was processed for the last time before it was eaten had changed too. In working-class kitchens the economic and political food system met the private world of individual decisions, preferences, and cooking ability. The types of tools and utilities available to working-class people, and the shape and character of their kitchens, dictated how food was cooked.

WORKING-CLASS KITCHENS: THE WORKPLACE AT THE HEART OF THE HOME

In the late nineteenth century, working-class and middle-class people thought about kitchens in very different ways and used them for different purposes. Among the middle class, the kitchen was a separate, clearly defined room that reflected the family's orderly social life. Well-designed homes had kitchens whose activities would not be seen, heard, or smelled by anyone else in the house, especially guests. At a time when most middle-class people could afford to hire one or two servants, the kitchen was a place for cooks and maids to work unobtrusively. Ideally, the heat, noises, and smells of cooking would be completely blocked from the semipublic social areas of the home, such as the parlor or sitting room.

After the turn of the twentieth century, architects and "domestic feminists" (reformers who wanted to redesign the home to improve women's work in it) planned kitchens that used new technologies to lighten household work. By the early twentieth century, it had become more socially acceptable for middle-class women to "do their own work" with few or no servants, partly because their kitchens were now clean, light, and well designed.[30] Even in these modern kitchens, middle-class women preferred to screen off the dirt, smells, and labor of the kitchen from the rest of their family's life.

In contrast, working-class kitchens were not isolated, specialized spaces. The kitchen was the center of the home, busy with activities such as eating, bathing, socializing, and working. The kitchen might be a small or large room, or it might simply be one area of a large room where the stove, sink, and table were located. Anecdotal and photographic evidence shows stoves, sinks, and kitchen tables in the midst of family activities. On dark evenings and during cold winters, families huddled around the stove, a source of heat and light. In summer, people tried to use the stove as little as possible or used small tabletop gasoline or oil stoves to save fuel and reduce heat in their living and working area.[31] For present-day observers, the most striking feature of working-class kitchens as shown in many photographs is the presence of a bed or other seemingly out-of-place furniture or objects, as well as the lack of a formal dining space. People slept in the kitchen if that was the most comfortable room, or if there was no other space. They ate wherever it was convenient and comfortable: near the stove in winter, near the open door or windows in summer.

This lack of specialized functions and formal spaces was the primary characteristic that differentiated a working-class home from a middle-class one. The difference, however, was only partly due to a lack of space and resources; it was equally the result of a choice that working people made about their living spaces. Historian Lizabeth Cohen explains that there were both material and cultural reasons that working people simply were not interested in clearly differentiated home spaces. Working-class homes, whether apartments or houses, were generally small and full of people, with little in the way of built-in storage or single-function rooms. Practically speaking, working-class people could not afford to light and heat several rooms of the home at once, so it made sense to huddle together around the source of heat and light, or to work on piecework in the same room where the children played and slept.

Working-class people were accustomed to sharing their living and working spaces closely with others. While middle-class women believed their homes should be a refuge from the economic world, working-class women constantly performed wage-earning work there, keeping boarders, doing piecework, or working in the adjoining family business. The kitchen space was functional and social, not symbolically separated, as it was in middle-class homes. Working-class families would no doubt have appreciated larger functional spaces, and the ability to separate messy tasks like laundry and food processing from the family's living space. (Whenever the weather and access permitted it, they took messy tasks outside.) But they didn't seem to want to wall off the kitchen from the rest of the home, even if it was possible. The material culture evidence shows

Figure 4.2 This Hine photograph from the National Child Labor Committee shows a nine-year-old girl named Jennie Rizzandi performing piecework sewing with her parents rather than attending school—but it also offers a glimpse of the interior decoration of a working-class tenement apartment in New York City in 1913. Photograph by Lewis Hine for the National Child Labor Committee, January 1913. Library of Congress, Prints and Photographs Division, National Child Labor Committee Collection, LOT 7481, no. 3256. Reproduction Number: LC-DIG-nclc-04306.

that although working-class people were constrained by cramped living spaces and a lack of storage, they still sought to arrange and adorn their living spaces according to their own preferences, and they often refused to rearrange their lives according to middle-class ideas of propriety.

Even when working-class families had more room, they retained the practice of eating, living, and working in the same room. If there was a separate dining room in the home (a rarity), it was kept for "company" or for other purposes, not for family dining.[32] Margaret Byington, who studied steelworkers' families in Homestead (a mill town just outside Pittsburgh) as part of the Pittsburgh Survey, reported, "Though a full set of dining room furniture, sideboard, table, and dining chair, are usually in evidence, they are rarely used at meals. The family sewing is done there . . . but rarely is the room used for breakfast, dinner, or supper."[33]

Although their homes were small and crowded, working-class people worked hard to decorate their homes. Nearly every photograph of a working-class home shows embellishment of some kind. Families that had a steady income or a sudden windfall bought the largest, grandest furniture they could afford (often purchased on install-ments), and they were particularly fond of luxurious-looking items like plush furniture, drapes, lace curtains, and mirrors.[34] Kitchens and dining rooms were festooned with extensive lace or paper lambrequins (decorative short, stiff drapes) on every shelf, with deep ruffles of fabric around sinks and stoves.[35] The ruffles decorated, but did not attempt to hide, the utilitarian appliances. Sideboards and cupboards displayed stacks of ceramics and rows of glassware. Walls were adorned with colorful chromo-lithographs, advertisements, religious images, and calendars. Working people in cities clearly intended to live in and enjoy their kitchens rather than isolate the space from their family and social life or hide its productive capacity.

UTILITIES

Despite the curtains, mirrors, and lambrequins, kitchens were also workplaces. The utilities and tools in working-class kitchens were usually older and less efficient than those in middle-class kitchens, which made the women's work demonstrably more difficult. As historian Susan Strasser writes, "Well into the twentieth century, indoor plumbing remained a matter of class: the rich had it, the poor did not."[36] In the late nineteenth century, most working-class people had to haul water, either from a single sink in their apartment building or from a pump in the backyard or on the corner. In Homestead, Pennsylvania, in 1907, only about half of families of mill workers lived in buildings with running water, even including those few who owned their homes.[37] Plumbing was expensive to install, and landlords who rented to working-class people avoided installing it until required by law. For instance, a 1902 Chicago city ordinance required that every new tenement have one sink with running water on each floor of the building. Older buildings were required to have a sink with running water in a lo-cation easily accessible to each apartment, which usually meant the hallway.[38] Hallway sinks were common in city apartment buildings well into the twentieth century; in some cities, a sink with running water in each dwelling was still not required as late as 1920.[39] The authors of *Middletown* estimated that one out of four residents of Muncie, Indiana, lacked running water in 1924.[40]

By the 1930s almost all working-class housing, even the most dilapidated, had running water. This water, however, might still have to be carried to the stove to be heated. Throughout this period utilities that had been installed grudgingly to satisfy the letter of the city law were not always kept in good working order. Tenants re-peatedly suffered from backed-up toilets and drains, which landlords ignored. In the hallway sinks of some New York tenements in 1911, the *Daily People* reported, "the pressure is insufficient, and it is necessary for tenants on each floor to pump the water after turning on the spigot."[41]

In some places the lack of utilities was a function of the physical location of working-class neighborhoods and their lack of municipal clout. In Pittsburgh, the mills on the river flats used so much water that those living in the surrounding hills had no water pressure. As Susan J. Kleinberg writes, "During the summer, many neighborhoods in the largest industrial section of the city (the South Side) had no water from seven in the morning until six at night when the mills operated."[42] Women had to carefully plan their working days around the mills' schedules, scheduling the heavy work of laundry and cleaning for the very early morning or evening hours. Kleinberg argues that this directly affected the efficiency of working-class women's work: "Her washing and cleaning chores, made difficult by Pittsburgh's heavy particle pollution and the grime and sweat on her family's clothes, were made more arduous by the city decision to provide decent [municipal] services only to those who could pay for them."[43] In this instance, the labor of working-class women was less efficient because of their living conditions.[44] The South Side did not have access to municipal water supplies until 1914.[45] Any working-class neighborhood near a large water user such as a factory or mill might have had this problem. And as Kleinberg points out, other effects of proximity to factories, such as pollution, affected housework for the worse.

Even such simple amenities as sinks and fixed tubs were not always present. Built-in washtubs, replacing old moveable wooden or metal washtubs, became commonplace in working-class housing by World War I.[46] In Betty Smith's semiautobiographical novel *A Tree Grows in Brooklyn*, around 1910 Francie Nolan's family lives in a tenement apartment in Williamsburg with a pair of built-in soapstone washtubs with a wooden lid. The tubs were designed for laundry and other chores, not for bathing. As Smith wrote, "It didn't make a very good bath tub. Sometimes when Francie sat in it, the cover banged down on her head. The bottom was rubbly and she came out of what should have been a refreshing bath, all sore from sitting on that wet roughness."[47] The family had previously lived in a nicer apartment in another part of Brooklyn with a real bathtub, "an oblong wooden box lined with zinc."[48] As the family's fortunes fell, they found themselves using poorer-quality plumbing fixtures. The tubs in Francie's Williamsburg tenement at least had faucets attached; older tubs simply had drains, requiring the user to pour buckets of water into the tubs to use them.

Women adjusted their patterns of work around the fact that every drop of water used for cooking, cleaning, and bathing had to be carried in and heated on the stove (and sometimes carried back out again). In 1899 the New England Kitchen was established in Boston by dietary reformers who wanted to offer nutritious cooked food and promote plain, healthy recipes. The kitchen's organizers began offering hot water to neighborhood people who could not (or would not) carry and heat water in their own kitchens, especially in hot weather. "The people started it by first asking for what we should never have thought to offer, and now the whole neighborhood draws on our supply of hot water, and this means a great deal for health and cleanliness, especially in the summer months."[49] The kitchen, fitted up with restaurant-style cooking capacity, most likely had running water that was piped directly into the stove to heat, or the building might have had a water heater for hot running water. The large cookstoves of middle-class houses had hot-water reservoirs—large covered metal basins attached to the stove, with a faucet for access—that could produce a constant supply of hot water as long as the stove was kept lit and the reservoir refilled as the water was used. But someone in those houses still had to carry water and the coal to heat it with.

Imagine the logistics of a home kitchen in which producing hot water was so arduous that people would rather walk down the street, or even several blocks, to carry hot water back with them. The people who took advantage of the New England Kitchen's hot water may not have had a reservoir on their stove, may not have wanted to heat the stove in the summer, or may have been boarders or lodgers with no cooking facilities at all. In these kitchens, working-class women avoided cleaning tasks in the summer, and their families bathed less frequently. And if they avoided heating the stove for hot water, they must have avoided cooking on it as well.

It was simply harder to keep one's home clean and to perform other household tasks like cooking in a poor or working-class neighborhood. The Progressive settlement-house workers and home visitors who tried to understand the problems of working people were often taken aback by the difficulty of life under these conditions. One visiting housekeeper wrote in 1917, "With modern equipment, steam heat, electric utensils, and new and sanitary apartments, it is not a difficult task to keep [a home] fresh and clean, but in rickety, shadowy apartment buildings or houses where the floors are worn and rough, with no hot-water service, and too often without even gas for lighting, we can at once recognize the trials and handicaps which confront the housewife in the poorer districts."[50]

Gas was another kitchen utility that was distributed unequally. The wealthiest Americans had experimented with gas fixtures in the 1870s, and by the late nineteenth century many factories, schools, and city streets were lit with utilitarian gaslights. By the early twentieth century working-class homes commonly had gas lighting fixtures, sometimes installed at the renters' own expense.[51] Some urban tenements had coin-operated gas meters to power appliances. In his memoirs of growing up in East Harlem around 1900, writer and educator Leonard Covello recalled that his family had a meter in their apartment that operated the gaslights and the stove. When the money ran out, "in the middle of a meal or at night while I was reading, the gas would lower under a boiling pot of spaghetti or the light would dim" until more coins were inserted. Covello remembered, "My father said it was like having an extra mouth in the family."[52]

Like other fixtures in cheaply built, poorly maintained tenement housing, gas fixtures were often improperly installed. Two women working at the College Settlement in New York City rented a tenement apartment for themselves in the working-class neighborhood surrounding the settlement house. They found that, although new, the house was very poorly built. They reported, "The gas fixtures were poor and ill fitted, so that we had a constant leakage which was both expensive and far from healthful."[53] Some buildings lacked even poorly installed gas or other amenities. On a working-class street in Boston in 1895, all the tenement houses had water and sewage connections, but "not one of them has gas, a hot-water heater, a bath-room, or—trifling but portentous detail—a fly-screen. One badly kept water-closet, located in the cellar, has to answer for all the families of a house."[54] Again, although a landlord might eventually be prevailed upon to improve the toilet facilities or install window screens or (less likely) a water heater, residents might have to count on the city to run gas lines into the neighborhood.

Although kitchen utilities in working-class homes routinely lagged behind those in middle-class homes, American kitchens could still seem very luxurious to European immigrants. A woman who emigrated from Bulgaria in 1929 explained how her new home in America seemed lavish because there was gas: "I drew a picture of the house and sent it to my people and said, 'I'm so lucky to be here. I bet you King Boris doesn't live the way I live.' Because *there was* no gas in Bulgaria, so I knew King Boris couldn't have no gas."[55]

TOOLS

Utilities were a part of the house, the building, or the neighborhood, but kitchen tools were owned by each individual family. The most important tool in the kitchen, the stove remained essentially unchanged from the Civil War until the widespread adoption of gas stoves around 1900. The only major innovation in stoves during that time was the change in fuel, from wood to coal. Most stoves could burn wood or coal interchangeably, so cooks could switch back and forth depending on what was cheaper. In the late nineteenth century, more working-class people probably burned wood, even though coal burned hotter and longer and was less bulky to store. Hard (anthracite) coal was more expensive but burned cleaner and hotter than the cheaper soft coal. The only real advantage to wood over coal was that, in some rural and semirural areas, it was still possible to forage for wood. A woman who emigrated from Austro-Hungary in 1909 at the age of eight recalled that, in her parent's home near Pittsburgh, they used a wood stove since they could not afford coal: "Of course you could have bought coal if you had the money, but if you didn't have the money you had to substitute the wood."[56] Urban dwellers could sometimes pick up coal in the streets that had been dropped by coal haulers or scavenge wood from construction sites and packing boxes.[57] In the early twentieth century, working-class people with coal stoves lagged behind those in the middle class who were acquiring new gas ranges.[58] Cooking on a coal stove of 1900 was more or less the same experience it had been on a wood stove of 1850. Though perhaps slightly more efficient and more convenient to use, the stove still required hauling fuel, tending the fire constantly, and standing uncomfortably close to the source of heat in order to cook. The experience of cooking began to change only with different types of fuels and stoves that could be turned on and off more easily, and that did not emit so much radiant heat.

A stove and fuel of some kind was necessary for any kind of cooking and was therefore an unavoidable expense. When working-class families moved into rental housing, a stove was sometimes provided as part of the furnishings. In other circumstances families had to bring their own stoves. As late as the 1920s, Russian immigrants living in cheap tenements in New York had to bring their own small coal stove.[59] In 1897, the cheapest kitchen stove from the Sears, Roebuck catalog cost $7.20; in that year the average weekly wages of a man working in industry were about $8.48.[60] Used stoves could be purchased for less. In 1911, Mabel Hyde Kittredge, who wrote a book advising tenement dwellers how to furnish their apartment, gave the price of a stove as $9 (for a tenement apartment with five people).[61] Those who wanted a fancy stove "with much nickeling" (shiny metal ornamentation) might pay $20 or more.[62]

Guides for housekeepers regularly acknowledged that cooking stoves were difficult and time-consuming to operate and maintain and warned that they required constant supervision and care to work properly. A wood or coal stove required maintenance every day. If the ashes were not removed each day, the fire would not light; and if the stove were not cleaned regularly, it would not "draw" properly, smoking up the room. Any stove would rust into uselessness if not "blacked" with stove polish as often as every few days. Inexpensive stoves were more or less simple boxes whose heat was hard to control; a complicated system of dampers controlled the heat in more expensive models, requiring time and attention to learn. Wood and coal stoves did not have temperature gauges. To test the heat, cooks used traditional methods that were essentially unchanged from the days of brick hearth ovens, such as holding one's hand near the heat and counting the seconds until it was unbearable.[63] They were dangerous appliances to have in the home. Stoves—even coal-burning ones—could emit noxious gas if used improperly. They could topple over, and hot-water reservoirs might spill and scald.[64]

Finally, stoves had to be fueled constantly in order to maintain the heat while cooking. Susan Strasser makes an important point about these stoves: "Wood and coal stoves were never 'turned on'; they were used only when economical in time, in labor, and in fuel. This made them less flexible than modern gas and electric stoves, which cooks can use one burner at a time."[65] In other words, stoves were either entirely off or on for hours. Wood and coal stoves were very impractical for cooking for one. They were more suited to the full-time housekeeper whose other tasks kept her in the house and who could maintain the fire and cook a variety of dishes at different temperatures as the fire waxed and waned than they were to the wage worker who returned home only to eat. They were also most practical when used for slow-cooking dishes like stews, or when used for several dishes at once to get the most use from the fuel. In this way they were still like the old-fashioned hearth.

Stoves using different kinds of fuel were patented beginning in the 1860s. These new stoves used coal oil, kerosene, or gasoline. They were inexpensive and relatively easy to use, but the burning oil smelled bad and there was great risk of fire and explosion.[66] The 1897 Sears, Roebuck catalogue offered one-burner oil stoves for as little as 85 cents and gasoline stoves for $2.63, adding, "There is positively no danger in using the Acme Gasoline Stove. It cannot explode"—suggesting that consumers were aware of gasoline stoves that *did* explode.[67] Small cooking appliances allowed people to juggle a few different types of fuel to keep costs down. Social reformer and home economist Helen Campbell wrote of the struggles of two formerly genteel women who were reduced to sewing to make a meager living. Campbell was surprised that they only used twelve cents' worth of coal per week, and asked, "How could twelve cents' worth of coal do a week's cooking?" One of the women responded, "It couldn't. It didn't. I've a little oil stove that just boils the kettle, and tea and bread and butter are what we have mostly. A gallon of oil goes a long way, and I can cook small things over it, too."[68] Small families who depended on an oil stove might find themselves limited to cooking "small things" as well: baking bread or cooking a large, economical joint of meat would be more difficult.

Working-class families who had gas lines into their homes and could afford fuel had a variety of appliances from which to choose. Many homes pictured in the photographs taken by journalist and child-labor reformer Lewis Hine had small one- or two-burner gas stoves that connected to the wall or ceiling fixture with hoses. Placed on top of their old coal stoves, the gas stoves were presumably for use in the summertime. These could be used for heating a pot but not for more time-consuming baking. In 1902, a two-hole portable gas stove cost $1.50, or less if secondhand.[69] Early gas stoves could be dangerous as well. Newspapers carried constant mentions of exploding stoves, as in November 1905, when "Gussie Paulkovin, 25 years old, of 244 First Avenue, was preparing Sunday dinner on a gas stove yesterday morning, when the gas blew out violently and enveloped her in a sheet of flame."[70]

Figure 4.3 This family, including all the children, worked together crocheting caps on the Upper East Side of New York City in 1912. On top of their coal stove is a gas hot plate, which could be used without heating the apartment as much as the coal stove would. Photograph by Lewis Hine for the National Child Labor Committee, November 1912. Library of Congress, Prints and Photographs Division, National Child Labor Committee Collection, LOT 7481, no. 3123. Reproduction Number: LC-DIG-nclc-04273.

Well into the twentieth century manufacturers produced hybrid stove models that could burn coal and wood on one side and gas or oil on the other at the same time.[71] A woman who grew up in Pittsburgh recalled that when her family moved into a new house around 1922, they "had big pot belly stoves. When we moved in that house, my dad bought a combination stove, a great big one with four burners of gas and four coal. We used to burn coal."[72] By the 1920s gas was becoming commonplace in working-class homes. In the 1920s about two-thirds of the families in Muncie, Indiana, cooked with gas; most of the remainder used gasoline and coal, and a few cooked with electricity.[73]

Gas burners allowed for much more flexibility in cooking. They could be turned on and off, and so they could reasonably be used for both quick heating and for longer-term cooking. Families who paid for gas by the nickel, like Leonard Covello's, might hesitate to feed the gas meter long enough for a long-simmered sauce, but they could boil the spaghetti quickly and then turn it off when done. Gas burners (sometimes in the form of "hot plates") also made it practical to cook a meal for one and made possible bachelor apartments with kitchenettes where a single person could live alone and prepare his or her own meals.

But what utensils did working-class Americans have in their kitchens? In the late nineteenth century cookware on the American market was made from new, lightweight, and inexpensive materials. Pots, pans, kettles, buckets, and other vessels, previously made of heavy and relatively expensive cast iron, were now made using lighter metals such as aluminum, which appeared after the 1880s. Enameled goods (the lightweight white or blue-speckled pans called enamelware, agateware, or graniteware) were made by a process developed in Germany in the eighteenth century. They were manufactured in large quantities in the United States after the 1870s.[74] Enamel pots and pans sold in the Sears, Roebuck catalog for between fifteen cents and a dollar in 1897.[75] (Sears prices were cheaper than retail but more expensive than those for similar used items.) Formerly expensive items like ceramic dishes and pressed glassware were now mass-produced, and thus sold more cheaply.

There was a general late nineteenth-century enthusiasm for specialized kitchen implements and serving ware. In an era when factory work was increasingly rationalized and mechanized, inventors and manufacturers created kitchen tools for very specialized tasks. Patented gadgets like rotary eggbeaters and apple corers became more common. From the mid-nineteenth century, domestic advisors like Catharine Beecher advocated having the right tool, utensil, or dish for the job. This was related to the ideal of having clearly defined, separate rooms for different household activities; it was simply considered more appropriate to use the correct item. Beecher, writing for a middle-class audience, advised a full complement of at least 144 items for the service of an ordinary middle-class dinner party, counting only cutlery, plates, and bowls.[76] Other items for table service included sauceboats, soup tureens, vegetable and pudding dishes, platters for meat, and specialized dishes for desserts, fruit, and other courses. Wealthy Victorians delighted in even more specialized items, such as cake baskets, caster sets, ice-water pitchers, doilies, asparagus forks, grape scissors, and so on.[77]

Families at all levels of society, though they may not have felt the same need for grape scissors, aspired to a similar profusion of objects. This is one way in which working-class kitchens might have lived up to middle-class ideals. Mabel Hyde Kittredge listed required household goods in her 1911 guide to keeping house in a tenement apartment. Her requirements for the kitchen (including cleaning supplies but not the stove or laundry tools) totaled $22.66. The list included some highly specialized items probably lacking in most working-class kitchens, including a potato masher, an apple corer, a lemon squeezer, and popover cups. Her list is otherwise reasonable and includes dishpans, bread pans (although it seems unlikely that working-class families would also have separate pie tins, layer pans, cake pans, and gem pans), knives, two frying pans, and two saucepans. She noted, "This is a full list, and in case of a very limited income one *can* do without many things."[78] Dishes (including individual butter, sauce, and dessert dishes) totaled $5.74. By the 1920s the list of kitchen items necessary or desirable for working-class families had been pared down somewhat, but it still included a dozen place settings, four sizes of frying pans, three granite (enameled) pans, a boiler, a dishpan, a grater, a bread box, water pitchers, and more.[79]

Though working people might not have had quite as many dishes and utensils as their middle-class counterparts, visual evidence suggests that most seem to have had plenty for ordinary use and for display. The Lewis Hine photographs, taken to demonstrate child labor conditions in the home, show extensive collections of glassware and dishes in some apartments. The working-class families who resorted to low-paying piecework to survive could still afford lots of kitchen goods. One Hine photograph shows Mrs. Palontona and her daughter, Michaeline, making pillow lace in their tenement on East 111th Street in New York in 1911. Although Hine noted that the Palontona's kitchen was "dirty" and both mother and daughter were "very illiterate," the photograph shows several pieces of kitchenware carefully hung on the walls. There were seven different pots and pans, a colander, a funnel, a spatterware coffeepot, four pot lids, a ladle and measuring spoons, a pie plate, and a salt holder.[80] Another 1911 photo was meant to illustrate that in Italian families, the father was often idle while the mother and children worked hard at piecework. In this New York family, in which the father's income was uncertain ("Sometime I make $9.00, sometime $10.00 a week on the railroad; sometime nottin'") and the piecework brought in only $4.00 a week, stacks of dishes are visible on the decorated shelves. A pitcher, large bowl, coffee pot, sugar dish, and at least a dozen each of dinner plates, smaller plates, bowls, cups, and saucers can be seen.[81]

Of course, a household could be operated with a bare minimum of equipment. A woman from Czechoslovakia, who emigrated in 1937 remembered that when she arrived in McKeesport, Pennsylvania, and met her husband, who had emigrated ahead of her, he bought kitchen tools for them: "He went to the store and he buy three cups, three spoons, three forks, three dishes, coffeepot and that—and he buy coffee—then I can make a pot."[82]

By the end of the 1920s, America's food system had irrevocably changed from the form it took in the 1870s. The majority of Americans who lived in cities were buying brand-new food products, as well as more processed versions of familiar foods. Trucks were beginning to surpass railroads as the means to get foods from farm to market (or to factory), and cars were replacing delivery wagons as customers carried home their own groceries. Workers cooked the food in their small kitchens, which were crammed with whatever tools they could afford and surrounded by all the other tasks of living.

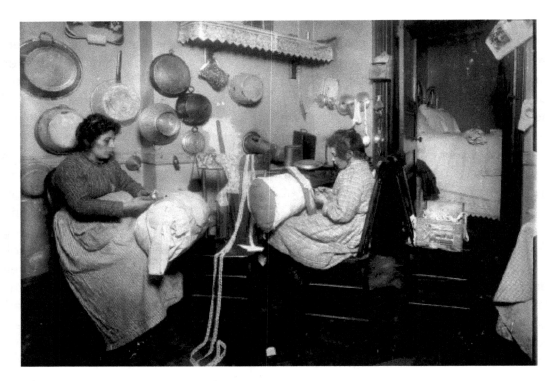

Figure 4.4 Mrs. Palontona and her daughter, Michaeline, making pillow lace in their tenement apartment, New York City, 1911. Notice the wide variety of pots, pans, and tools hung from the walls (probably for convenience and for display), the shelf lambrequin, and the lace trim on the neatly made bed in the second room. Photograph by Lewis Hine for the National Child Labor Committee, December 1911. Library of Congress, Prints and Photographs Division, National Child Labor Committee Collection, LOT 7481, no. 2711. Reproduction Number: LC-DIG-nclc-04111.

Despite the enormous changes, however, food remained at the heart of working-class family life.

Today we have transcended seasonality far beyond the dreams of the people of 1900. In our supermarkets we can easily buy blueberries in November, tomatoes in January, and apples in April. The produce might be grown in hothouses, raised year-round in the Southwest, imported thousands of miles from South America, or just held in cold storage for months after harvest. Critics of the modern food system argue that the industrialization of agriculture has gone too far. They point out that seasonal, local produce tastes better and is more environmentally sustainable. And industrialized foods such as processed American cheese are seen as bland, dishonest, or simply less tasty than "real" cheese. But for Americans of the late nineteenth century, the beginnings of these changes looked like progress. The greater availability of fruits and vegetables rescued consumers from their monotonous diet and the nutritional deficiencies that had been common during the cold months. Processed cheese, although perhaps less tasty than natural cheese, was at least much more consistent, the same every time you bought it. Even relatively simple innovations, like the artificial lighting in henhouses that made eggs more affordable in winter, improved nutrition for everyone. The trade-offs and disadvantages of industrialized agriculture and food processing are undeniable and have become much clearer to us over time, but it's important to remember that in the late nineteenth and early twentieth centuries Americans believed that these changes were making food better for everyone: more widely available, more nutritious, and more reliable.

As they embraced the industrialization of food that brought cheaper meat and produce, working-class Americans were ahead of their time in making the kitchen the heart of the home. Modern American homes—even large, expensive homes designed for the upper classes—are built to showcase the kitchen, with the expectation that families will do most of their living and socializing there. Since 1974, the size of the average American kitchen has grown from 150 to 300 square feet.[83] But in the late nineteenth and early twentieth centuries, the middle class considered the kitchen a hot, odorous, slightly disreputable place where servants or harried housewives did unpleasant work; it was not thought fit for company or public display. In contrast, working-class people truly lived in their kitchens. In part this was because they had no choice: in small, cramped houses and apartments, there were no specialized rooms or much privacy. But the centrality of the kitchen in working-class homes also suggests that the work done there was not limited to women but consisted of a set of tasks that involved the entire family. The work done there might be hot, unpleasant, and monotonous, but the kitchen was where daily life happened.

NOTES

1   Susanne Freidberg's *Fresh: A Perishable History* (Cambridge, MA: Belknap Press of Harvard University Press, 2009) is a fascinating account of the transformation of "freshness" through the nineteenth and twentieth centuries.

2   Harvey Levenstein, *Revolution at the Table: The Transformation of the American Diet* (New York: Oxford University Press, 1988), 30–32; R. Douglas Hurt, *American Agriculture: A Brief History* (Ames: Iowa State University Press, 1994), 184–85; Richard J. Hooker, *Food and Drink in America: A History* (Indianapolis: Bobbs-Merrill, 1981), 229–32.

3   Many of the farmers who moved to the Great Plains had incorrectly believed that there was sufficient rainfall, or that "rain would follow the plow." This did not prove to be the case, and farmers were forced to adapt to the dry environment with different farming technologies. New crops, including drought-resistant strains of wheat and sorghum rather than thirstier corn, were the key.

Gary D. Libecap and Zeynep Kocabiyik Hansen, "'Rain Follows the Plow' and Dryfarming Doctrine: The Climate Information Problem and Homestead Failure in the Upper Great Plains, 1890–1925," *Journal of Economic History* 62, no. 1. (March 2002): 86–120; Hurt, *American Agriculture*, 179.

4   Hurt, *American Agriculture*, 195–200.

5   Ibid., 179.

6   William Cronon, *Nature's Metropolis: Chicago and the Great West* (New York: W. W. Norton, 1991), chapter 3.

7   Roger Horowitz, *Putting Meat on the American Table: Taste, Technology, Transformation* (Baltimore, MD: Johns Hopkins University Press, 2006), 30.

8   Cronon, *Nature's Metropolis*, 243.

9   Hooker, *Food and Drink in America*, 224–26.

10 Freidberg, *Fresh*, 203–18; Harvey Levenstein, *Fear of Food: A History of Why We Worry about What We Eat* (Chicago: University of Chicago Press, 2012), chapter 2.

11 Hooker, *Food and Drink in America*, 229.

12 Ibid., 237.

13 Maria Parloa, *Miss Parloa's New Cook Book and Marketing Guide* (Boston: Estes & Lauriat, 1880), 48.

14 Freidberg, *Fresh*, 94–96.

15 "Food Preservation in New York," *Harper's Weekly*, July 4, 1891, 508. The facilities stored fabrics and tobacco as well as food: "Woolens and fine dress goods keep best at about 50° Fahr., furs and pelts at about 45°, tobacco of the better grades at 42°, eggs at just above the freezing-point, and fish just below that standard. Poultry, game, and meats are best when kept frozen; fine Philadelphia chickens and capons, Boston ducks, New York turkeys, and venison are best when kept at a temperature of between 15° and 20° above zero. Each room is devoted to one class of goods, and is kept at one temperature."

16 Lee A. Craig, Barry Goodwin, and Thomas Grennes, "The Effect of Mechanical Refrigeration on Nutrition in the United States," *Social Science History* 28, no. 2 (Summer 2004): 325–36.

17 William T. Elsing, "Life in New York Tenement-Houses as Seen by a City Missionary," in Robert A. Woods et al., *The Poor in Great Cities: Their Problems and What Is Doing to Solve Them* (New York: Charles Scribner's Sons, 1895), 61. The unsigned foreword to the book states that the articles were written in 1891–93.

18 Mark W. Wilde, "Industrialization of Food Processing in the United States, 1860–1960," PhD diss., University of Delaware, 1988, chapters 3 and 4.

19 On bread, see William G. Panschar, *Baking in America: Economic Development. Volume I* (Evanston, IL: Northwestern University Press, 1956), chapter 3. For ham, see Horowitz, *Putting Meat on the American Table,* chapter 3. For pasta, see Donna Gabaccia, *We Are What We Eat: Ethnic Food and the Making of Americans* (Cambridge, MA: Harvard University Press, 1998), 68.

20 James H. Collins, *The Story of Canned Foods* (New York: E. P. Dutton, 1924), 38.

21 United States Bureau of the Census, *Historical Statistics of the United States: Colonial Times to 1970* (Washington, DC: U.S. Government Printing Office, 1975), 164.

22 Hooker, *Food and Drink in America,* 215; Joseph R. Conlin, *Bacon, Beans, and Galantines* (Reno: University of Nevada Press, 1986), 118–26.

23 In the first half of the nineteenth century, food was "canned" in glass jars or tin cans by a tedious hand process. The tin cans were made by skilled tinsmiths and sealed by hand with solder. Tinsmiths, who had been highly paid, skilled, organized workers, were driven out of the industry with the development of machinery to make and seal the cans in the late nineteenth century. Filling and closing the cans also became mechanized, with the development of the "sanitary can" in 1897, which required no solder but was crimped closed. Collins, *The Story of Canned Foods,* 36. Well into the twentieth century, low-paid women and girls still did the tedious work of preparing food for canning: shucking corn or oysters, shelling peas or peeling tomatoes, and feeding the prepared food into the small fill holes in the tin cans. In the late nineteenth century the canning industry succeeded in developing machinery to perform these tasks, culminating in such triumphs as the mechanical pea-podder and the "iron chink" salmon gutter, so named because it replaced Chinese immigrants in the salmon-packing industry. Levenstein, *Revolution at the Table,* 32.

24 At a time when cookbooks instructed cooks to boil fresh young peas for half an hour (longer for older peas), canned peas were probably not so different in texture from fresh. The Women's Centennial Executive Committee's *The National Cookery Book. Compiled from Original Receipts, for the Women's Centennial Committees of the International Exhibition of 1876* (Philadelphia: Women's Centennial Executive Committee, 1876) suggested that "fresh and young" peas and asparagus should be boiled for an hour (150–51). Fannie Merritt Farmer's *Boston Cooking School Cook Book* (Boston: Little, Brown, 1896) suggested from twenty to sixty minutes of boiling for green peas (34). By contrast, a cookbook published in 1730, *The Frugal Housewife,* advocated cooking vegetables only until crisp-tender: cauliflower must be taken out of the pot "before it loses its crispness, for colliflower is good for nothing that boils till it becomes quite soft ." The taste for very soft vegetables was peculiar to the nineteenth century. Jean McKibin, ed., *The Frugal Colonial Housewife* (reprint, Garden City, NY: Dolphin Books, Doubleday, 1976), 34.

25 Fannie Merritt Farmer, *What to Have for Dinner* (New York: Dodge, 1905).

26 Robert Coit Chapin, *The Standard of Living among Workingmen's Families in New York City* (New York: Charities Publication Committee, 1909), 156.

27 United States Bureau of the Census, *Historical Statistics of the United States*, 329–31.

28 "Italian Housewives' Dishes," *New York Times*, June 7, 1903, 28; Hasia Diner, *Hungering for America: Italian, Irish, and Jewish Foodways in the Age of Migration* (Cambridge, MA: Harvard University Press, 2001), 62.

29 Christine Frederick, *Selling Mrs. Consumer* (New York: Business Bourse, 1929), 162.

30 Scientific management expert Lillian Gilbreth promoted the idea that a middle-class woman could easily do her own housework if her home, especially her kitchen, was well designed and efficient. She used photographs and motion studies to determine the "best way" to do household tasks and published them in *The Quest for the One Best Way* (1925) and *The Homemaker and Her Job* (1927). Sarah A. Leavitt, *From Catharine Beecher to Martha Stewart: A Cultural History of Domestic Advice* (Chapel Hill: University of North Carolina Press, 2002), 54.

31 Lizabeth A. Cohen, "Embellishing a Life of Labor: An Interpretation of the Material Culture of American Working-Class Homes, 1885–1915," *Journal of American Culture* 3, no. 4 (Winter 1980): 752–75.

32 Susan Williams, *Savory Suppers and Fashionable Feasts: Dining in Victorian America* (New York: Pantheon Books, 1985), 56–57.

33 Margaret F. Byington, *Homestead: The Households of a Mill Town* (reprint, Pittsburgh: University Center for International Studies, University of Pittsburgh, 1974), 56.

34 Louise Bolard More, *Wage-Earner's Budgets* (New York: Henry Holt, 1907), 132–34.

35 Katherine Grier discusses the construction and use of lambrequins in *Culture and Comfort: Parlor Making and Middle-Class Identity, 1850–1930* (Washington, DC: Smithsonian Institution Press, 1988), 144–45.

36 Susan Strasser, *Never Done: A History of American Housework* (New York: Pantheon Books, 1982), 100.

37 Byington, *Homestead*, 54.

38 Edith Abbot, *The Tenements of Chicago, 1908–1935* (Chicago: University of Chicago Press, 1936), 59–61.

39 Sophonisba P. Breckenridge, *New Homes for Old* (reprint, Montclair, NJ: Patterson Smith, 1971), 60.

40 Robert S. Lynd and Helen Merrell Lynd, *Middletown: A Study in Modern American Culture* (San Diego: A Harvest Book, Harcourt Brace, 1957), 97.

41 "Tenement Number Six," *Daily People* (New York), August 11, 1911.

42 S. J. Kleinberg, "Technology and Women's Work: The Lives of Working-Class Women in Pittsburgh, 1870–1900," *Labor History* 17, no. 1 (Winter 1976): 62.

43 Ibid., 63.

44 Ibid.

45 S. J. Kleinberg, *The Shadow of the Mills: Working-Class Families in Pittsburgh, 1870–1907* (Pittsburgh: University of Pittsburgh Press, 1989), 92.

46 "Bathtubs are being introduced gradually and set tubs are being included as a matter of course." Mary Kingsbury Simkhovitch, *The City Workers' World in America* (New York: Macmillan, 1917), 37.

47 Betty Smith, *A Tree Grows in Brooklyn* (n.p.: Everybody's Vacation Publishing, 1943), 115.

48 Ibid., 95.

49 Mary Hinman Abel, "A Study in Social Economics: The Story of the New England Kitchen," in Ellen H. Richards, *Plain Words about Food: The Rumford Kitchen Leaflets* (Boston: Home Science Publishing, 1899), 137–38. The account did not describe how, exactly, the people got the hot water back to their homes, but it was probably carried in buckets. Customers of the New England Kitchen had to bring their own containers for food (commonly buckets, basins, and jars), and most working-class families would have had a metal bucket in which to carry water, lunches, or beer.

50 V. G. Kirkpatrick, "War-Time Work of the Visiting Housekeeper," in the *Yearbook of the United Charities of Chicago* (Chicago: United Charities of Chicago, 1917), 18.

51 Strasser, *Never Done*, 71; "Tenement Number Six."

52 Leonard Covello and Guido D'Agostino, *The Heart Is the Teacher* (New York: McGraw-Hill, 1958), 46.

53 Agnes Daley, "Life in a New Tenement House," *Charities: The Official Organ of the Charity Organization Society of the City of New York* 5, no. 28 (December 8, 1900): 3.

54 Alvan Francis Sanborn, *Moody's Lodging House and Other Tenement Sketches* (Boston: Copeland and Day, 1895), 100. From the Immigrant in America microfilm collection, Historical Society of Pennsylvania, reel 69, no. 160.

55 Oral history respondent number S-12-A, pages 48–49 of transcript, in "Women, Ethnicity, and Mental Health: A Comparative Oral History Project, 1975–1977," Archives of Industrial Society, Hillman Library, University of Pittsburgh.

56 Oral history respondent number S-1-A, page 15 of transcript, in "Women, Ethnicity, and Mental Health."

57 Strasser, *Never Done*, 55.

58 See Priscilla J. Brewer, *From Fireplace to Cookstove: Technology and the Domestic Ideal in America* (Syracuse, NY: Syracuse University Press, 2000), for an excellent account of cookstoves.

59 Jerome Davis, *The Russian Immigrant* (New York: MacMillan, 1922), 62.

60 Stove price from *1897 Sears, Roebuck Catalogue* (reprint, Philadelphia: Chelsea House, 1968), 119. Wages from Paul H. Douglas, *Real Wages in the United States, 1890–1926* (Boston: Houghton Mifflin, 1930). Wages calculated from table 73, page 205; hourly earnings for all industry extrapolated to yearly and then to weekly by assuming full employment, 2,080 hours per year.

61 Mabel Hyde Kittredge, *Housekeeping Notes: How to Furnish and Keep House in a Tenement Flat* (Boston: Whitcomb and Barrows, 1911), 1.

62 Maurice Fishberg, *Health and Sanitation of the Immigrant Jewish Population of New York* (New York: Press of Philip Cowen, ca. 1902), 13.

63 At least one domestic advisor and cookbook author, Mary Hinman Abel, acknowledged the difficulty of learning this sort of sense-based traditional technique: "One housekeeper says 'hot enough so that you can hold your hand in until you count twelve,' another 'until you can county thirty,' and the puzzled novice can only inquire 'how fast do you count?' " *Practical Sanitary and Economic Cooking Adapted to Persons of Moderate and Small Means* (Rochester, NY: American Public Health Association, 1890), 95.

64 Brewer, *From Fireplace to Cookstove*, 170.

65 Strasser, *Never Done*, 41.

66 Brewer, *From Fireplace to Cookstove*, 229.

67 *Sears, Roebuck Catalogue*, 115.

68 Helen Campbell, *Prisoners of Poverty: Women Wage-Workers, Their Trades and Their Lives* (reprint, Westport, CT: Greenwood Press, 1970), 119.

69 Abraham Cahan, "A Woman of Valor," in Moses Rischin, ed., *Grandma Never Lived in America: The New Journalism of Abraham Cahan* (Bloomington: Indiana University Press, 1985), 406.

70 "Burned by Gas Explosion," *Daily People* (New York), November 6, 1905. It is possible that this and other mentions of gas stove explosions are actually referring to *gasoline* stoves, which were cheap but notoriously flammable and prone to explosion.

71 Brewer, *From Fireplace to Cookstove*, 238.

72 Oral history respondent number I-5-A, in "Women, Ethnicity, and Mental Health."

73 Lynd and Lynd, *Middletown,* 98.

74 Ellen M. Plante, *The American Kitchen 1700 to the Present* (New York: Facts on File, 1995), 104.

75 *Sears, Roebuck Catalogue, 1897,* 130–32.

76 That is, one dozen forks, one dozen silver spoons, one dozen large knives, one dozen glass tumblers, two dozen wine glasses, one dozen soup plates, and four dozen plates. Williams, *Savory Suppers and Fashionable Feasts,* 81. The list is from Catharine Beecher, *Miss Beecher's Domestic Receipt Book Designed as a Supplement to Her Treatise on Domestic Economy* (New York: Harper & Brothers, 1852), 237.

77 Williams, *Savory Suppers,* 81–87.

78 Kittredge, *Housekeeping Notes,* 7.

79 Angelo Di Domenico's *Graded Lessons in English for Italians: An Aid in Americanization* (Boston: Christopher Publishing House, 1922), an English primer for immigrants, contained a number of sample conversations. In the "conversation at the house furnishing store," the presumed immigrant orders the items mentioned on this list (p. 49). The salesman then suggests a number of other items (an eggbeater, nutcracker, saucepan, funnel, colander, and "a box of tooth picks"), all of which the immigrant gamely agrees to buy as well. Although it is possible that this is simply an exercise in vocabulary, naming all possible kitchen utensils, I have mentioned in my text only the ones the immigrant asked for. Interestingly, the list contains flour and a bread box, but no bread pans or other baking pans.

80 "Mrs. Palontona," December 1911; Call Number: LOT 7481, no. 2711; Reproduction Number: LC-DIG-nclc-04111; National Child Labor Committee Collection, Library of Congress, Prints and Photographs Collection, Library of Congress.

81 "Family of Dometrio Capilluto," December 1911; Call Number: LOT 7481, no. 2689; Reproduction Number: LC-DIG-nclc-04089; National Child Labor Committee Collection, Library of Congress, Prints and Photographs Collection, Library of Congress.

82 Oral history respondent number S-3-A, page 12 of transcript, in "Women, Ethnicity, and Mental Health."

83 "America's Homes Get Bigger and Better," *Good Morning America,* December 27, 2005.

DISCUSSION QUESTIONS

- According to the article, in what ways did industrialization affect the American diet?

- What technological advancements facilitated the changing of how Americans produced and consumed food?

- How did the immigrants, women, and children adapt to the technological developments about food?

- Based on the article, did this new relationship with food reflect this democratic aspect of the American dream? Why or why not?

CHAPTER V

FROM COAST DEFENSE TO EMBALMED BEEF

THE INFLUENCE OF THE PRESS AND PUBLIC OPINION ON MCKINLEY'S POLICYMAKING DURING THE SPANISH-AMERICAN WAR

OBJECTIVES

- Analyze the influence of the American media on the United States during the Spanish–American War.

PREWRITING

- What effect has the media had on events and popular culture in the United States? Has the media traditionally "reported" the news? Or has it "created" the news?

- Why was the United States interested in the conflict between Spain and the revolutionaries in Cuba in the 1890s? Why would it be in the interest of the news media to publish articles about that conflict?

From Coast Defense to Embalmed Beef

The Influence of the Press and Public Opinion on Mckinley's Policymaking During the Spanish–American War

JOSEPH SMITH

The question of the influence that the American press and public opinion exerted on the decision of the United States to go to war against Spain in April 1898 has attracted a considerable historical literature.[1] Less well-known is how policy decisions taken by the McKinley Administration during and after the war were also affected by public attitudes which were largely informed and shaped by the press. The allocation of financial resources to coast defenses and the division of the Atlantic squadron were intended to relieve public anxiety, while the raising of a mass volunteer army and the schemes for an early assault on Havana reflected a response to public expectations. The role of the press was particularly significant in accelerating the evacuation of the army from Cuba and in contributing to the postwar controversy over the treatment of American soldiers by the War Department.

When a major rebellion broke out in Cuba in February 1895 Americans were sympathetic toward what they perceived to be a struggle for freedom from Spanish tyranny. This attitude was stimulated by the American newspaper industry which was engaged in fierce competition for mass circulation.[2] Readers of the so-called "yellow" daily newspapers were bombarded with a steady barrage of sensational and often exaggerated stories reporting not so much on the actual course of the conflict but describing how Spain was turning the island into a wasteland of human misery and carnage. Some articles provoked criticism and even incredulity but they were effective in capturing public attention and thereby ensuring that Cuban affairs were pushed to the forefront of American political debate.

The political ramifications were evident in Congress where numerous resolutions recommending various courses of American action to aid the insurgents were introduced in every session from December 1895 onwards. The impact on the executive was limited because President Grover Cleveland chose to pursue a policy of strict neutrality. In March 1897 the responsibility for conducting American diplomacy passed to William McKinley. As an avid reader of the daily press, the new President kept himself very well-informed on the attitude of the public toward events in Cuba.[3] Nevertheless, in his first year of office he saw his priority as leading America out of economic depression and reluctantly turned his attention to foreign affairs. While he was convinced that the United States should avoid military intervention, he believed that strenuous diplomatic efforts should be made to persuade the Spanish government to bring about an end to hostilities.

The prospect of going to war against Spain, however, was significantly enhanced by the horrific news that the USS Maine had been blown up in Havana harbour on February 15 1898 with the loss of 266 American lives out of a total crew of 354. The conclusion that a treacherous Spanish conspiracy must have been responsible for the explosion dominated the front pages of most of the yellow press. "The Whole Country Thrills With War Fever," stated a typical headline.[4] McKinley resisted political and public pressure for retaliation and appointed a commission of naval officers to investigate and ascertain the cause of the explosion. He did, however, seek to improve the nation's military preparedness by arranging an emergency appropriation from Congress. Known as the "Fifty Million Bill," the measure was promptly passed on March 9. The huge appropriation of $50 million was designed to overawe the Spanish government into making diplomatic concessions. It was also a response to an emerging public concern expressed by residents along the eastern seaboard of the United States that war would expose their homes, property and lives to surprise raids and bombardment by warships that Spain would surely send to operate in the Atlantic. The Spanish navy lacked first-class battleships but was known to possess "overwhelming strength" in modern armoured cruisers.[5]

During March and April the American press attempted to keep track of the whereabouts of the "Spanish War Fleet" which was described as "the most formidable array of vessels that has yet left Spain for the West Indies."[6] The strategic thinking of the day suggested that the Spanish commander, Admiral Pascual Cervera, would form his cruisers into a "fleet in being" whose speed and mobility would outmanoeuvre the slower American battleships and, consequently, disrupt American naval resources and strategy.[7] Should war break out the New York Times warned that the most direct threat to the United States would come from Spanish warships engaging "in guerrilla warfare, swooping down upon coast towns and retreating before they are overtaken."[8] Even the nation's capital at Washington was believed to be virtually defenseless just as it had been in 1814 when invading British troops had burned the White House. In an interview with the press, the Commanding General of the Army, Major General Nelson A. Miles, informed the public: "In the event of war, the problem is to defend our coast cities. The old fortifications were too close to the cities, enabling ships of the enemy to keep out of range and to throw shells into the cities".[9] Secretary of War Russell A. Alger later acknowledged that "the condition of the coast defenses was far from what it should have been."[10]

To strengthen national defenses and allay public anxiety, McKinley made direct use of the emergency $50 million appropriation which had been passed in Congress. A sum of $15 million was allotted for the repair and construction of the army's coastal fortifications especially artillery batteries. The perception of inadequate coast defenses also resulted in the establishment of a Northern Patrol Squadron consisting of five light cruisers to patrol the coastline between the Delaware Capes and Bar Harbor, Maine. In addition, a "Flying Squadron" of several armoured ships was stationed at Hampton Roads, Virginia. By remaining close to shore the squadron offered protection to the east coast from possible Spanish attack. The division of the navy into two sections, however, constrained naval policy options. It prevented the concentration of American naval strength in the waters close to Cuba and was criticized by Captain Alfred Thayer Mahan as a misuse of naval resources and "contrary to sound practice."[11] According to one American naval officer, the Flying Squadron was "the sop to the quaking laymen whose knowledge of strategy derived solely from their terror of a sudden attack by Cervera."[12]

McKinley's resistance to the intense political and public pressure for American military intervention came to an end on Monday April 11 when his "War Message" was read out to Congress. After outlining the evolution of the crisis in Cuba and the diplomatic attempts to reach a peaceful solution, it concluded that American military intervention had now become necessary to bring peace to the island. On April 19, by votes of 42 to 35 in the Senate and 310 to 6 in the House, Congress passed the joint resolution recognizing the independence of the Cuban people and demanding immediate Spanish political and military withdrawal. The President was authorized to use the armed forces of the United States to enforce the resolution. McKinley duly signed the resolution on April 20, and on the next day instructed the navy to enforce a naval blockade of the northern coast of Cuba.

The American press not only favored going to war but also encouraged the public to believe that the American army and navy would strike a quick and victorious blow at Spanish forces in Cuba. Secretary of War Alger had contributed to the expectation of early action by implying in statements to the press that a large force of fighting men could quickly be put into a combat role.[13] In fact, it was generally assumed that war plans were already in place for an immediate attack upon Havana. As early as April 2 the *New York Times* carried a headline stating that "Both The Army And Navy Ready" and "Could Strike A Decisive Blow Within Forty-eight Hours."[14] The first step would be naval bombardment of Havana by the powerful American battleships. "It is likely that little more than a day would elapse after the first shot before the Spanish flag would be down on El Morro or Cabanas," confidently predicted the *New York Times*.[15] The army would act in conjunction with the navy and dispatch a large number of troops to Cuba so that a simultaneous attack on Havana would take place from both land and sea. As Congress debated the War Resolution, the *New York Times* reported: "Both the army and the fleets are ready to act immediately [for] a dash on Havana and a quick sweeping victory that will take the Spanish flag and the Spanish soldier forever out of the island."[16] In Havana, Captain General Ramón Blanco y Erenas was ready and waiting for battle to commence. On learning that war had been declared, he told a large crowd of Spanish loyalists that any approaching American warships would be "hurled back into the sea."[17]

But "a dash on Havana" did not occur. On April 22 the North Atlantic Squadron commanded by Admiral William T. Sampson duly took up its preassigned positions to blockade Havana and the northern coastline of Cuba. American army officers, however, were uncertain as to when, where and how American soldiers would attack Spanish forces in Cuba. "The advance guard of the army of occupation may not move on Cuba this week after all," disappointingly noted the *New York Times* and added, "there is high authority for the statement that the enterprise has been postponed for the present".[18] In reality, public anticipation of an early assault on Havana was overly optimistic because the United States initially lacked an army capable of launching a successful invasion against entrenched defensive forces. Indeed, senior army commanders considered an invasion unnecessary because the decisive battles would surely occur at sea. On April 20 at a special council of war meeting at the White House, General Miles argued against an attack to seize Havana. He pointed out that a land operation was undesirable because it would expose American troops to the many deadly tropical diseases which were known to be endemic in Cuba during the rainy season. "The most powerful influence which has operated to induce President McKinley to decide against sending any United States troops to Cuba at present," remarked the *New York Times*, "is fear of the effects of the climate on the men."[19] At the meeting Miles also disclosed that at least two months were needed to organize a credible American expeditionary force. Moreover, he was particularly concerned that the safe transport of troops could not be guaranteed until the navy secured complete command of the seas by destroying the enemy fleet. In the meantime, army commanders envisaged a limited role for the army consisting mainly of landing small numbers of soldiers to seize isolated beachheads from which supplies could be delivered to the Cuban insurgents.

The pursuit of a strategy emphasizing small-scale overseas operations meant that only a relatively modest increase would be required in the size of the existing regular army. However, the passage of the War Resolution in Congress stimulated patriotic feeling and public pressure for prompt military action. "This became so intense that even the conservative administration [of President McKinley] was over-persuaded," commented General Miles.[20] Consequently, McKinley insisted that the army prepare itself for fighting a major overseas campaign. This was demonstrated on April 23 when he issued the first call for 125,000 volunteers to join the army.[21] Officials at the War Department had wanted less than half this number. They were now compelled to take on the huge challenge of transforming what had been a small peacetime force of regulars into a massive army consisting mostly of volunteer citizen-soldiers. In the process, officials found themselves overwhelmed with the practical problems of recruiting and organizing a new mass volunteer army. Miles reckoned that more than 100,000 of those accepted were neither needed nor could be adequately equipped.[22] Nevertheless, the display of patriotism was sincere and impressive. Sectional differences were forgotten as Alger estimated that at least one million men responded to McKinley's first call for volunteers. From the American heartland in Emporia, Kansas, William Allen White captured the outburst of patriotic feeling:

> In April, everywhere over this good, fair land, flags were flying. Trains carrying soldiers were hurrying from the North, from the East, from the West, to the Southland; and as they sped over the green prairies and the brown mountains, little children on fences greeted the soldiers with flapping scarfs and handkerchiefs and flags; at the stations, crowds gathered to hurrah for the soldiers, and to throw hats into the air, and to unfurl flags. Everywhere it was flags … fluttering everywhere.[23]

The pressure of the press and public opinion for speedy offensive action on Cuban soil remained constant. Its influence on policymakers was evident on May 2, the day after Dewey's glorious naval victory at Manila Bay in the Philippines,[24] when McKinley brought Alger, Miles and Secretary of the Navy John D. Long to the White House to discuss future military strategy. As always, McKinley's preferred option was to make Havana the principal target of a major assault. The plan which emerged involved an amphibious landing of not less than 50,000 men to secure a beachhead at Mariel, about 25 miles west of Havana. This would be followed by an advance on the capital. It soon became evident, however, that the operation could not be executed unless American warships were released to guarantee safe transportation of the army from Florida to Cuba. This was still not possible so long as the reputedly powerful Spanish squadron of armoured warships remained undetected and at large in the Atlantic. Although the *New York Times* reported "the impatience of the country" and that the

"President wants action," it explained that an invasion of Cuba at present "would be suicidal."[25] In the meantime, the force of army regulars assembled in Tampa, Florida, experienced, in the words of Richard Harding Davis, the "rocking-chair period." "The army had no wish to mark time, but it had no choice," summed up the *New York Herald* correspondent.[26]

All war plans were abruptly changed on May 26 when news reached Washington that Cervera's fleet was docked in the harbour of Santiago de Cuba. A council of war was promptly held in the White House and agreed that southeastern Cuba had now become the area of critical strategic significance. It was decided therefore to postpone the projected assault on Havana until later in the year so that the army invasion force could be sent instead to Santiago de Cuba. The Expeditionary Force comprised mainly of regulars of the Fifth [Army] Corps under the command of General William R. Shafter set sail from Tampa on June 8 and landed at Daiquirí and Siboney in eastern Cuba on June 22. Advancing inland from the coast the Fifth Corps defeated a brave Spanish army, attacked Santiago de Cuba and secured the city's formal capitulation on July 17. Alger proudly remarked that "the expedition was successful beyond the most sanguine expectations."[27]

In the weeks following the capitulation of Santiago de Cuba, Shafter's main priority became the preservation of the health of his army. By authorizing American soldiers to fight in Cuba during the disease-ridden rainy season, McKinley had taken a calculated gamble with their health. The most dreaded disease was yellow fever. There was no known cure for this scourge which annually claimed hundreds, if not thousands, of lives in the tropical regions of the Caribbean and Brazil. American surgeons knew very little about the disease. In fact, a combination of anxiety and lack of medical knowledge resulted in their failing to distinguish between yellow fever and the more common and less deadly malarial fever. The first suspected cases of yellow fever among American troops were identified at Siboney on July 6. In accordance with the best medical advice currently available, Alger had instructed Shafter to move his troops from the lowland "fever belt" to higher mountainous ground which was believed to be much healthier.[28] He also stated that cases of yellow fever were to be isolated and not put on troopships for return to the United States. The prohibition included not just the individuals with yellow fever but was also extended to the rest of their regiment. Mindful of political and public concern in the states of the eastern seaboard, Alger was clearly determined not to risk the spread of yellow fever to the United States. The men would eventually be brought home but only when it was judged medically safe for them to leave. Meanwhile, they must remain in Cuba "until the fever has had its run."[29]

Shafter kept his army in place and did not attempt to move troops to higher ground. One reason was the requirement to retain a sufficient force to keep guard over the large number of Spanish prisoners-of-war awaiting repatriation to Spain. Another factor was the poor physical condition of the American soldiers and the impracticability of marching them and transporting their supplies and equipment along virtually impassable trails into the mountains. While Alger's instructions to Shafter were sensible, they did not take into account the reality that an increasing number of American soldiers in Cuba were falling victim everyday to the oppressive tropical climate, lack of medical care, and inadequate rations of food. During the days following the capitulation there was a growing incidence of disease, mainly malaria, typhoid and dysentery. On July 22 the correspondent, George Kennan, estimated that no more than half of the American troops were fit for active duty. He placed the blame not on the rigours of the Cuban climate but on neglect and lack of care caused by "bad management, lack of foresight, and the almost complete breakdown of the army's commissary and medical departments."[30] The American public was made aware of Kennan's damaging revelations when they were first published in *Outlook Magazine* on July 30. They coincided with and endorsed press reports of the poor physical condition of those Americans who were currently returning on troopships from Cuba. A harrowing image was presented in the *New York World*'s description of one of the vessels as "a ship of death and horrors."[31]

General Shafter kept the War Department informed of the increase in cases of sickness among his troops as a matter of routine. There was, however, no warning of the furore which suddenly struck Washington during the early days of August. On August 2 Alger received a telegram from Shafter stating: "I am told that at any time an epidemic of yellow fever is liable to occur. I advise that the troops be moved as rapidly as possible whilst the sickness is of a mild type."[32] After consulting the Surgeon-General, George M. Sternburg, Alger repeated his standing instructions that the army should be moved to high ground as soon as it was feasible to do so. Shafter replied on August 3 saying that this was "practically impossible" given the weakened state of his men, of whom an estimated 75 percent had been or were currently suffering from malaria. But there was evidently no time to spare. "In my opinion," he stated, "there is but one course to take, and that is to immediately transport the 5th Corps and the detached regiments that came with it to the United States. If that is not done, I believe the death-rate will be appalling."[33] Within an hour Alger replied that Shafter should "move to the United States such of the troops under your command as not required for duty at Santiago."[34]

Prior to this exchange of telegrams with Alger, Shafter had convened a meeting on August 3 that was attended by his generals, Colonel Theodore Roosevelt and senior surgeons. They all agreed that the only way to avert an epidemic of yellow fever from breaking out was for the army to return to the United States as quickly as possible. Apprehension was expressed, however, that the War Department would continue to insist upon the bulk of the army remaining in Cuba. To help Shafter in his dealings with Washington, it was decided to compose a written letter of support for immediate evacuation. The resulting document was signed in turn by each general and by Colonel Roosevelt, and became known as the "Round Robin." Its main recommendation took the form of a virtual ultimatum and was bluntly worded: "This army must be moved at once or it will perish. As an army it can be safely moved now. Persons responsible for preventing such a move will be responsible for the unnecessary loss of many thousands of lives."[35]

Shafter sent the Round Robin along with other correspondence to Washington late on August 3 so that it was received the next day by Alger at the War Department. However, the text of the document had been leaked to a correspondent of the Associated Press at the general's headquarters on August 3. The result was the publication of the full text of the Round Robin in the American press on the morning of August 4 at the same time as the note was officially received at the War Department. Already alerted by Kennan's article and the reports of the grim conditions on board the first troopships arriving from Cuba, the public were now presented with sensational headlines in their daily newspapers such as "Shafter Army In Deadly Peril," "Flower Of The American Army Threatened With Death," and "Must Move The Army."[36]

It was by reading the daily press that President McKinley first learnt of the Round Robin. Though circumstantial evidence pointed to Theodore Roosevelt, it proved impossible to discover the source of the leak.[37] Whoever was responsible, the fact was that the signatories were successful in using the press to mobilize the force of public opinion in their favour and thereby effect a dramatic change of policy. At a time when delicate peace negotiations were taking place with Spain, the United States government was admitting publicly that its army in Cuba was in a state of utter collapse. McKinley and Alger, however, could not be seen to be ignoring their duty of care and acceded to Shafter's request for immediate action to save the army. On August 4 the War Department made the public announcement that new instructions were on their way to Shafter to prepare the evacuation of his troops "as fast as transportation can be provided."[38] Even though Alger revealed that he had actually sent virtually the same instructions to Shafter the previous day, the manner of the publication of the Round Robin made it appear that an insensitive administration was being forced to act belatedly and out of shame. Alger bitterly described the publication of the Round Robin as "one of the most unfortunate and regrettable incidents of the war."[39] There was, however, little public sympathy for the Secretary of War.[40] The press reported that Roosevelt had been privately rebuked for his involvement in the leak, but praised the colonel for succeeding "in awakening the War Department."[41] In a similar vein the New York Times remarked, "the commanding officers bullied the department into doing what it should have done two weeks earlier."[42] Shafter and his generals had effectively used the press not only to outmanoeuvre the War Department but also to clear themselves of any imputation of blame for the terrible condition of the army in Cuba. The evacuation of the Fifth Corps proceeded rapidly. It began on August 7 and was completed in less than three weeks. The destination for the evacuees was Montauk Point, New York.

War Department officials had given relatively little thought to preparing a camp in the United States to receive troops returning from Cuba. The matter was not considered to be particularly pressing. Following the capitulation of Santiago de Cuba, the Fifth Corps would be moved to higher ground and was expected to remain in Cuba for some weeks until all signs of tropical disease, especially yellow fever, had been eradicated. Meanwhile, on July 28 Alger approved Montauk Point in the state of New York as the site of the proposed reception camp. Located at the east of Long Island and 125 miles from New York City, it comprised 5,000 acres of virtually uninhabited land owned by the Long Island Railroad Company. The principal attraction of Montauk Point was its geographical remoteness. Troops could be landed and quarantined there until they were judged to be free from yellow fever. The War Department leased the land, and on August 2 signed contracts with local private companies to construct temporary housing and provide a supply of water. It was envisaged that a camp and medical facilities would be established for around 5,000 men.

Hardly had these arrangements been made when the Round Robin was published on August 4 and was followed by the decision to commence at once the evacuation of the whole Fifth Corps to Montauk Point. The generals had secured their objective, but it was the officials of the War Department who faced the consequences. Quite clearly, Montauk Point was not ready. The drilling of wells and laying down of wooden floorboards only started on August 5. Ironically, Montauk Point's very remoteness became a disadvantage because it meant a lack of an existing network of roads and available local supplies. The single-track railway linking Montauk Point with New York City was soon congested. Nevertheless, a "camp" consisting mainly of thousands of tents speedily came into existence. It was named Camp Wikoff, in honour of Colonel Charles Wikoff of the 22nd US Infantry who had been killed in the battle for the San Juan Heights.

Evacuees from Cuba began arriving at Montauk Point as early as August 8. Every day new units arrived, consisting of weak, emaciated men many of whom were visibly suffering from malarial fever or its after-effects. The impression was given of the return of a defeated rather than an all-conquering army. Many of the first arrivals were described as "in shabby condition" with "well worn uniforms" and some were "nearly barefoot."[43] Despite the best efforts of War Department officials, medical staffs and local contractors, the correspondent of the New York Times considered the camp to be "in a more or less chaotic state."[44] The image of sick and emaciated men returning from Cuba only to endure further suffering at Camp Wikoff was underlined by emotive headlines in the press such as "Some Of Our Heroes Forced To Drink From A Polluted Pond," "Not Enough Tents At Montauk," and "Sick Soldiers Sleeping On Ground."[45] The commander in charge of the camp, General Joseph Wheeler, privately complained that the press was "addicted to misrepresentation" and gave too negative a picture.[46] There was, however, little that he could do to assuage the pain and shock of the public as trains arrived each day at the camp bringing "hordes of mothers, wives, sisters, and sweethearts, in search of warriors bold, crippled, scarred, or worn."[47]

Conditions steadily improved in September, however, as shortages were remedied and the camp's affairs were energetically administered by General Wheeler. As men recovered their health, they were allowed to leave for their homes. The last batch of soldiers left Camp Wikoff on October 28. In a period of almost eleven weeks the camp received more than 20,000 evacuees. Of these 257 died while at the camp.[48] Cases of yellow fever were minimal and no epidemic occurred. Alger contended that the camp's record of achievement was "creditable," and cited the comment of Shafter that "it was the best camp I ever saw."[49] The seal of official approval was also given by President McKinley's visit to the camp on September 3. Nonetheless, the controversy surrounding the Round Robin and the reports of suffering at Camp Wikoff [50] were severely damaging to the reputation of the McKinley Administration. Blame was increasingly personalized and fastened, not upon President McKinley or senior military officers, but directly upon Secretary of War, Alger. In popular speech the word "Algerism" was used as a pejorative term to denote maladministration and callous insensitivity. "The War Department is the scandal of President McKinley's Administration," declared the *New York Times* and described Alger as "a public nuisance and a public danger."[51] "We are sick and tired of Secretary Alger," summed up an editorial.[52]

To appease public opinion McKinley appointed a special presidential commission to investigate the War Department's conduct of the war. It was also an astute political move designed to forestall the appointment of a Congressional inquiry whose remit would be broader and politically partisan. The *New York Times* suspected that an official whitewash was intended and that "it is the business of the commission to make a nice, pleasant, ladylike report that the President can read with pleasure and Alger with pride."[53] Under the chairmanship of General Grenville M. Dodge, the "Dodge Commission" commenced its formal proceedings on September 26 1898 and continued until February 9 1899. No doubt to the satisfaction of McKinley and Alger, the first witnesses who appeared before the Commission revealed little that was particularly controversial or newsworthy. This changed abruptly on December 21 1898 when General Miles gave evidence. The general rekindled his longstanding personal feud with Alger[54] by accusing the War Department of including stocks of canned roast beef treated with chemicals in the food supplied to the army. Miles declared that soldiers in Cuba had suffered considerable sickness after eating what he graphically described as "embalmed beef." The press welcomed the opportunity to expose the "Great Beef Scandal" and to run sensational headlines such as "Alger's Embalmed Beef Smelt Like A Cadaver."[55] The New York Herald drew an analogy with the Round Robin in noting that Miles was technically in breach of discipline by speaking out in public, but that this was eminently justified "for the sake of the ill-fed, not to say poisoned, private soldier."[56]

The final report of the Commission dismissed Miles's allegation that beef had been treated chemically. While the canned beef was generally deemed of good quality, it was acknowledged that it had proved to be an unsuitable product for use in the tropics. The final report also found no incriminating evidence of corruption or mal-administration by the War Department[57]. While the New York Times condemned the report as "shameful" and "cowardly," the generally muted response of the public to the findings showed that McKinley had successfully achieved his aim of using the commission to deflect political criticism.[58] Moreover, the heightened emotions arising from the war with Spain had not only been moderated by the passage of time but also overshadowed by other issues such as the conclusion of the Treaty of Paris, the occupation of Cuba, and the great debate over the annexation of the Philippines.

While the exact influence of the press and public opinion on McKinley and his policymaking can never be known, there is no doubt that he was an assiduous reader of the daily press and was sensitive to developments in public opinion. The perception of public anxiety over the inadequacies of coast defense resulted in improvements in coastal fortifications and in the decision to split the Atlantic fleet into two separate squadrons. The weight of public expectation for an early engagement with the enemy in a land battle strengthened McKinley's desire that his military commanders should formulate and execute plans for a "dash on Havana." After the end of the fighting in Cuba, the assumption of a gradual and orderly withdrawal of the American army from the island was upset by the publication of the Round Robin. By deliberately leaking their letter to the press, American generals in Cuba brought the issue directly to the attention of the public and thereby compelled the War Department to agree to the immediate and precipitate evacuation of the army from Cuba. Subsequent negative press coverage of conditions at Camp Wikoff stimulated growing public criticism of the shortcomings and insensitivity of the War Department and led McKinley to set up a presidential commission of investigation. Although the work and findings of the Dodge Commission were favourable to McKinley, the controversy over "embalmed beef" showed the capacity of the press to inform and influence public opinion. By highlighting the sensational allegations made by General Miles, the press challenged the idea of "a splendid little war"[59] and endorsed instead the growing post-war public perception that Washington's management of the war effort had been characterized by bureaucratic incompetence and insensitivity.

NOTES

1   The classic accounts are M. Wilkerson, *Public Opinion and the Spanish-American War: A Study in War Propaganda*, New York: Russell & Russell, 1932, and J. Wisan, *The Cuban Crisis as Reflected in the New York Press*, New York: Columbia University Press, 1934. See also the influential article by G. Auxier, "Middle Western Newspapers and the Spanish-American War, 1895–98," *Mississippi Valley Historical Review* 26, 1940, pp. 523–34. A readable overview of American journalists and their activities is C. Brown, *The Correspondents' War: Journalists in the Spanish-American War*, New York: Charles Scribner's Sons, 1967.

2   The most prominent battle was being fought out in New York between Joseph Pulitzer's *New York World* and William Randolph Hearst's *New York Journal*.

3   The celebrated journalist, Ida Tarbell, visited McKinley in the White House and noted his close and friendly relations with reporters. Each day he read five or six New York dailies, the Washington papers, one or two from Chicago, and up to a half dozen from other large cities. In addition, Tarbell remarked that "articles of special value and suggestiveness are frequently read and discussed" in conversations with friends and in cabinet meetings. See "President McKinley in War Times," *McClure's Magazine* 11, 1898, 213–14. For the importance that McKinley attached to his relationship with the press, see R. Hilderbrand, *Power and the People: Executive Management of Public Opinion in Foreign Affairs, 1897–1921*, Chapel Hill: University of North Carolina Press, 1981, pp. 30–3. For a brief period in early 1898 McKinley evidently stopped reading daily newspapers. See G. Linderman, *The Mirror of War: American Society and the Spanish-American War*, Ann Arbor: University of Michigan Press, 1974, p. 28.

4   *New York Journal*, February 18 1898.

5   *New York Times*, April 2 1898.

6   Ibid., March 31 1898.

7   Admiral William T. Sampson, the commander of the North Atlantic Squadron, believed that the Spanish squadron was "the fastest in the world." See W. Sampson, "The Atlantic Fleet in the Spanish War," *The Century Magazine* 57, 1899, 889.

8   *New York Times*, April 15 1898.

9   *New York Times*, March 31 1898.

10 R. Alger, *The Spanish-American War*, New York: Harper & Brothers, 1901, p. 10.

11 A. Mahan, *Lessons of the War with Spain, and Other Articles*, Boston: Little Brown, 1899, p. 56.

12 Captain Robley D. Evans of the *USS Iowa*, quoted in D. Trask, *The War with Spain in 1898*, New York: Macmillan, 1981, p. 84.

13 Alger evidently indicated that an army of 40,000 could be put in the field at ten days' notice. See M. Leech, *In the Days of McKinley*, New York: Harper & Brothers, 1959, p. 198. The *New York Times* claimed that Alger had said in August 1897 that "within thirty days after war broke out he could put into the field 'millions of fighting men'." See *New York Times*, August 9, 1898.

14 Ibid., April 2 1898.

15 Ibid., April 12 1898.

16 Ibid., April 19 1898.

17 *The Times* (London), April 23 1898.

18 *New York Times*, May 2 1898. On April 24 McKinley had approved the order given to the Asiatic Squadron under Commodore George Dewey to proceed with an attack on the Philippines.

19 Ibid.

20 N. Miles, *Serving the Republic*, New York: Harper & Brothers, 1911, p. 272.

21 For the political debate over organizing the army, see G. Cosmas, *An Army for Empire: The United States Army in the Spanish-American War*, Columbia: University of Missouri Press, 1971, pp. 80–101.

22 Miles, *Serving the Republic*, p. 270. More than 200,000 volunteers were eventually called out. Around 35,000 saw service overseas. See Cosmas, *An Army for Empire*, p.266.

23 W. White, "When Johnny Went Marching Out," *McClure's Magazine* 11, 1898, quoted in Brown, *The Correspondents' War*, p. 158.

24 Problems with communications from Manila meant that Dewey's victory was not fully confirmed until a few days later on May 7.

25 *New York Times*, 19 and May 20 1898. The Pacific Ocean held no such danger from the Spanish navy so that a force of 2,500 troops was prepared and set sail from San Francisco for the Philippines on May 25.

26 R. Davis, *The Cuban and Porto Rican Campaigns*, New York: Scribner's, 1898, p. 42.

27 Alger, *The Spanish-American War*, p. 296. For an outline of the military campaign see J. Smith, *The Spanish-American War: Conflict in the Caribbean and the Pacific, 1895–1902*, London: Longman, 1994, pp. 119–59.

28 Alger to Shafter, July 13 1898, quoted in Alger, *The Spanish-American War*, p. 256.

29 See Cosmas, *An Army for Empire*, p. 258.

30 George Kennan, *Campaigning In Cuba*, Port Washington: Kennikat Press, 1899, pp. 215–16.

31 *New York World*, August 1 1898, quoted in Brown, *The Correspondents' War*, p. 435. The troopship in question was the *Concho*.

32 Shafter to Alger, August 2 1898, quoted in Alger, *The Spanish-American War*, p. 262.

33 Shafter to Alger, August 3, 1898, quoted in ibid., p. 263.

34 Alger to Shafter, August 3 1898, quoted in ibid., p. 265.

35 The text of the Round Robin is printed in ibid., p. 266.

36 See *Salt Lake Herald* and *St Paul Globe*, August 5 1898.

37 Roosevelt claimed that he had shown a draft of the document to assembled pressmen. See R. Paine, *Roads of Adventure*, Cambridge, Mass.: Houghton Mifflin, 1922, pp. 269–71. Colonel Leonard Wood believed that the leak had come from Shafter. On this see H. Hagedorn, *Leonard Wood: A Biography*, 2 vols, New York: Harper & Brothers, 1931, vol. I, p. 201.

38 Adjutant General Henry C. Corbin to Shafter, August 4 1898, quoted in Alger, *The Spanish-American War*, pp. 271–2.

39 Ibid., p. 269.

40 The publication of the leaked document not only embarrassed the War Department but also threatened to disrupt diplomatic negotiations which were currently taking place in Washington to bring a formal end to the war.

41 *Salt Lake Herald*, August 5 1898.

42 *New York Times*, August 25 1898.

43 *New York Times*, 9 and August 10 1898.

44 Ibid., August 10 1898.

45 Quoted in J. Dyer, *'Fightin' Joe' Wheeler*, University, La.: Louisiana State University Press, 1941, pp. 369–70.

46 Wheeler to Mark Hanna, September 5 1898 quoted in ibid., p. 372.

47 *New York Tribune*, September 11 1898, quoted in ibid., p. 372.

48 More American soldiers died at Camp Wikoff than had been killed in combat in Cuba.

49 Alger, *The Spanish-American War*, pp. 438, 448.

50 The press was also highly critical of the primitive living conditions experienced by volunteers at the training camps in Chickamauga Park, Georgia, and Camp Alger, Virginia.

51 *New York Times*, 9 and August 25 1898.

52 Ibid., 27 August 1898.

53 *New York Times*, November 28 1898.

54 Miles had clashed with Alger over the plan for an assault on Havana and had argued that the Expeditionary Force should be directed to Puerto Rico rather than Cuba. See E. Ranson, "Nelson A. Miles as Commanding General, 1895–1903," *Military Affairs* 29, 1965–6, 183–90.

55 *Salt Lake Herald*, April 5 99.

56 *New York Herald*, March 21 1899.

57 The commissioners adopted an ambivalent attitude toward Alger, and ended their report with the critical statement that "there was lacking in the general administration of the War Department during the continuance of the war with Spain that complete grasp of the situation which was essential to the high efficiency and discipline of the Army." See "Report of the Commission Appointed by the President to Investigate the Conduct of the War Department in the War With Spain," 56th Congress 1st Session, Senate Document No. 221, 8 vols, Washington DC: General Printing Office, 1900. vol. 1, p. 116. After a short interval Alger resigned his office in August 1899.

58 *New York Times*, May 8 1898, quoted in E. Ranson, "The Investigation of the War Department, 1898–99," *The Historian* 34, 1971, 98.

59 John Hay's famous phrase was included in a letter written to Theodore Roosevelt and dated July 27. It was therefore coined before the Round Robin, Camp Wikoff, and the Beef Scandal. Hay's letter is quoted in W. Millis, *The Martial Spirit: A Study of Our War with Spain*, Boston: Houghton Mifflin, 1931, p. 340.

DISCUSSION QUESTIONS

- According to the article, why did many Americans want to go to war with Spain? Were these reasons emotional or rational?

- Based on the article, what affect did "yellow journalism" have on United States policy during the Spanish–American War era? Did these journalists base their reporting in fact?

CHAPTER VI

THEODORE ROOSEVELT AND THE PROGRESSIVE ERA

OBJECTIVES

- Analyze the leadership of Theodore Roosevelt during the Progressive Era in the United States.

PREWRITING

- Consider the "American Dream." Was it in danger of getting snuffed out due to the excesses of the Gilded Age?

- Consider what socialist and communist revolutionaries had prophesized would happen to a society like that of the United States during the Gilded Age: a revolution. Was the Progressive Era an effort to avert such a revolution? Was Theodore Roosevelt's style of leadership needed for such change?

Theodore Roosevelt and the Progressive Era

RONALD K. HUCH

Like the Reconstruction Era in American History, the Progressive Era was largely a failure. The failure was not as complete as Reconstruction was, for there were some improvements in social and economic policy, though the extent of these improvements is open to question. The Progressives in American society and politics recognized that the United States government paid precious little attention to the well-being of its citizens. Those who exposed the worst aspects of American society were predictably reviled by the old Republican guard, which believed that misery resulted from either laziness or lack of character.

In the political realm, the Progressive Era focused upon cleaning up some of the most egregious corruption in city and state government. There were not, alas, enough progressive politicians to make a significant dent in the peculation that shortchanged American citizens from coast to coast, but at least some of the reformers were able to make an impact. The two most celebrated in this regard were Robert La Follett and Hazen Pingree. La Follett, from Dane County, Wisconsin, made his mark as a reforming governor in that state. He claimed that he was awakened to corruption when, as a young member of Congress, he was offered a bribe. Elected governor in 1900, La Follett quickly brought reform to Wisconsin government that he hoped would become a model for the country. He put railway and utility companies under public control, created a state income tax, and did all he could to improve circumstances for workers in the state. The impact of populist ideas can be seen in his reforms. What La Follett did for Wisconsin, Pingree did for Detroit and later, as governor, for the state of

Michigan. Like La Follett, Pingree was determined to bring corrupt utility companies under public control and provide improved living conditions for his constituents. The successes of La Follett and Pingree, as well as those of Samuel Johnson in Toledo and Henry Truelsen in Duluth, were impressive, but there were not enough progressive reformers to dramatically change the face of urban politics.

By far Theodore Roosevelt was the most charismatic progressive. Although born into a prominent Republican family, Roosevelt never felt comfortable with the politics of the Gilded Age. He had associated with the Mugwumps, a reform element in the Republican Party, in the 1880s, but the real turning point for him appears to have resulted from his time as police commissioner in New York City. There, he walked the streets with Jacob Riis, journalist and author of *How the Other Half Lives*, and saw for himself the misery of life in the city. It caused him to recognize that all levels of government showed very little interest in the well-being of the vast majority of those who lived in the United States. It was a realization that was going to play a large role in how he conducted his presidency.

There were so many aspects to the life of Theodore Roosevelt that a historian finds it difficult to highlight them all. At the same time he became aware of the enormous disparity between those who were well-off and those who were in despair, Roosevelt was convinced that the country needed to make its presence felt on the world scene. By the 1890s, he had become a major advocate for naval power. He had himself studied and written about the War of 1812 while a student at Harvard, and when he read Alfred Mahan's *The Influence of Sea Power upon History, 1660–1783*, he was convinced that path to U.S. influence was the sea. His insistence on this point is what led to President William McKinley's appointing him as an assistant naval secretary in 1897. Seeing that England and Germany were locked in an all-out challenge for naval supremacy by spending huge portions of their national budgets on building ever-bigger ships of the line, Roosevelt believed that the U.S. needed to continue to expand its naval fleet. This conviction followed him to the White House in much the same way as did his determination to undermine the worst aspects of the Gilded Age.

Between 1897 and 1900 Roosevelt became an American celebrity. The Spanish–American War was the primary reason. This Splendid Little War, as it became known, resulted in the United States gaining the world presence that Roosevelt envisioned. Reports of his exploits as leader of the Rough Riders were in newspapers across the country. Roosevelt was keenly aware of the importance of a "good press." He made himself accessible to reporters throughout his career and was not above embellishing a story. Reporters adored Roosevelt because he made their work so much easier. By the time the war with Spain ended, Roosevelt was the most popular Republican in the United States. The Gilded Age Republicans found this alarming. They did not want the reform tendencies of Roosevelt to flourish. But what to do with him? In the 1900 election, it was clear that McKinley would be re-elected and party leaders pressured McKinley to put Roosevelt on the ticket as the candidate for vice president. They reasoned that Roosevelt would, like every other vice president, "disappear" in that office. It was a good way to make him ineffective. McKinley had no objections and the two were easily elected in 1900.

It turned out to be a fateful election. Not long after the March, 1901 inauguration, McKinley was shot dead and Theodore Roosevelt, who was mountain climbing in New England at the time of McKinley's death, was now president. That office, and the country, would never be quite the same again.

The most important thing to remember about Theodore Roosevelt's presidency is that he pushed that office to the limits of the Constitution. After a series of weak to mediocre presidents after Lincoln, Roosevelt showed the American people what could be achieved when a president was not completely beholden to the rich and powerful. During the time he held the office, 1901–1909, Roosevelt injected himself into nearly all corners of social, economic, and international issues, not excepting college football.

By the time he became president, Roosevelt's back story was well known to most Americans. He had triumphed over childhood asthma, the deaths of his first wife and mother on Valentine's Day in 1884, and a self-banishment to the Badlands of North Dakota. He was known for his physical strength and his abiding interest in a number of intellectual pursuits, of which the study of history was the most profound. He had instant credibility with the public who expected him to show concern for the things that mattered in their lives. He was a dynamo on domestic issues from the time he entered the White House. The scope of his interests and concerns defies adequate recounting. We must, however, identify those that, at the time at least, reflected a change in attitude from the federal government's heretofore lack of attention to all but the upper level of American society.

The Northeastern Pennsylvania anthracite dispute in 1902 is often cited as an example of how Roosevelt departed from past practices. From the time industrial capitalism developed in the United States after the Civil War, no government, at any level, gave support to workers in any dispute with business owners. The response to any industrial action by labor never changed: call out the police, call out the National Guard, call out the Pinkerton thugs. The Homestead Steel Strike in 1892 is representative of actions taken by business, local, state, and federal governments against those who produced the steel for Andrew Carnegie and Henry Clay Frick. Similar reactions occurred throughout the 1890s when workers and their organizations challenged railway companies in Illinois, Michigan, Missouri, and New York. Roosevelt's position in the anthracite stand-off was a surprise to many, especially those in his own party. That the president became involved at all in this dispute between miners and mine owners was the first major shock. But the fact that he did not show the usual deference toward big business confounded those who saw labor unions as a threat to free enterprise and the market economy.

Roosevelt's support for the miners is sometimes overstated. His main objective was to prevent a strike that would leave many in the cold, literally, during the winter months. He was never anti-big business, but he did seek to achieve a fair settlement between the miners' union and owners. When it appeared that his efforts to achieve a compromise were not likely to succeed (mostly because the mine owners refused to accept wage increases and fewer hours), Roosevelt threatened to take over the mines and have the army mine the coal. It was an unimaginable threat, and to do so would have left owners without profit and miners without jobs. It was clear that the president intended to follow through, and a resolution favoring the miners was achieved. Roosevelt had thus established new dimensions for the influence of Washington.

Although Roosevelt did not articulate his most progressive views on big business and universal health care until he ran for president on the Progressive Party (Bull Moose) ticket in 1912, his domestic efforts while he was president reveal his determination to move away from the Gilded Age. While his attitude toward the journalists (principally Lincoln Steffens, Upton Sinclair, and Ida Tarbell) appears to have been ambivalent (he called them "muckrakers"), Roosevelt nonetheless agreed with their condemnation of so much in American politics and business. Sinclair's novel *The Jungle*, in which he exposed the horrors in the meat-packing industry, clearly pushed Roosevelt to support the Pure Food and Drug Act in 1906. This attempt to regulate the food and pharmaceutical industries did not achieve all that was promised, but it did show that the federal government saw the need to provide some protection for American consumers. The Food and Drug Administration, created by the legislation, continues to exist with varying degrees of success.

Roosevelt had long railed against the rampant and widely accepted corruption that was part and parcel of all local and state governments. Thus, Steffens' *The Shame of Our Cities*, which exposed the unrelenting peculation in city governments, was something of which the president was well aware. He looked with considerable favor on the efforts of Robert La Follett and Hazen Pingree and encouraged local politicians to break the pattern of awarding contracts to private water companies on the basis of how much the companies would kick back to urban politicians.

The publication in 1902 of Ida Tarbell's investigative *The History of the Standard Oil Company* was, for Roosevelt, further evidence of the existence of good monopolies and disreputable monopolies. Surely, Standard Oil was in every regard disreputable. Tarbell, with the help of a Standard Oil executive who furnished her with internal company communications, detailed how Standard Oil used intimidation, price-fixing, bribery, and thugs to drive smaller oil producers out of business. That her own father was one of those driven out of his Western Pennsylvania business by Standard Oil provided motivation for her study. At the time, most of the country's oil came from Western Pennsylvania. It was not until 1912 that interest developed in the Texas oil fields. The railroad companies were another example of how companies created monopolies that worked against the public interest. Once again, echoes of the populist movement were heard in Roosevelt's administration. In 1903, Roosevelt strongly endorsed the Elkins Act, which forbade railroads to give rebates to selected shipping customers. The practice of rebates worked against those who were small shippers or who lived in the back country. This was followed by the Hepburn Act of 1906, which aimed at establishing consistency in rates charged by the railways. It also provided for the conservation of millions of acres of public land. Roosevelt's interest in preservation and conservation is well known. During his time as president he initiated the creation of National Parks, especially in areas of timberland. He also supported the building of dams and canals intended to protect land in the West. Over fifty million dollars was devoted to these projects from the federal budget.

Roosevelt's interest in the circumstances for black people in America reveals uncertainty and inconsistency. By inviting Booker T. Washington to dinner at the White House, he signaled his support for the moderate position taken by Washington on race relations in the South. Roosevelt thought this was a safe invitation, as Washington's view that blacks should "cast down their bucket" where they were was well received by whites in the South. He was therefore not prepared for the virulent reaction of the Southern press that excoriated him for entertaining a black man in the White House. This might indicate that blacks were equal to whites. The reaction of white Southerners no doubt explains, in part, why Roosevelt backed away from pushing for greater equity between blacks and whites. There was also his strong support for eugenics, which promoted the notion of distinct racial characteristics, characteristics that always proved white superiority. Roosevelt lamented on one occasion that white Western European women were not breeding enough. People of Western European ancestry were clearly better than those from South and East Europe, Asia, or Africa. He did appoint some blacks to minor government positions, something his predecessors did not do, and he disapproved of violent acts against blacks he had appointed. On the other hand, Ida Wells' accounts of white terrorism against blacks throughout the South appeared to make little impression on the president.

Roosevelt's opinion that the United States should make its presence known as a great power formed the basis of his international policies. In 1904, during his State of the Union Address, Roosevelt added a new dimension to the Monroe Doctrine known as the Roosevelt Corollary. It held that in any dispute between a European country and a country in Central or South America, the United States was the arbiter. In other words, a European country could pursue its interests in the Western Hemisphere only through Washington. Further, the Corollary stipulated that the United States could use military force against a Central or South American country. Thereafter, the United States sent such forces on a fairly regular basis.

Roosevelt's crowning achievement in the minds of many, and in his own, was the building of the Panama Canal. For centuries there had been discussion of the need for a waterway that would link the Pacific and the Atlantic without going around the Cape of Good Hope at the tip of South America. The successful completion of the Suez Canal in the 1860s stimulated greater interest in building a canal through Central America. A French company was created to undertake the project, but the exposure of corrupt behavior by company executives and government politicians scuttled the effort. Members of the United States Congress then began to look at whether or not the U.S. could build the canal. It was widely agreed that such a canal would have enormous economic benefit for the shipping trade. Engineers argued whether such a canal should be attempted through Nicaragua or Panama, but eventually it became clear that the topography of Nicaragua was too difficult. It was acknowledged that tropical diseases would be a problem, but the benefits of the canal outweighed concern for those who would build it. Once the Panama route had acceptance, Roosevelt sprang into action. He convinced England to surrender any claims to a joint control of the canal, bought out what claims the failed French company had, and proceeded with negotiations for permission to construct the canal through the Isthmus of Panama. Those negotiations would prove to be a problem; a problem that Roosevelt cut through in a Machiavellian manner.

Panama was a province of Colombia and any attempt to build the canal required Roosevelt to negotiate with the Colombian government in Bogota. A deal was arrangement whereby the United States would pay a substantial sum to Colombia for the right to construct the canal, but the Colombian Senate refused to ratify the agreement, insisting the U.S. should pay more. It was then that Roosevelt decided to proceed in a different way. When it became apparent that Panamanian politicians were unhappy with the failure of Colombia to work out a deal with the United States, Roosevelt jumped in. As there was already a sense among Panamanians that the country should be independent from Colombia, Roosevelt decided to inspire, plan, and pay for an "uprising" by Panamanians demanding independence. He even sent a gunboat to protect against the possibility of Colombian interference. As soon as the phony independence demands were made, Roosevelt immediately recognized Panama as an independent country. He then negotiated with Panamanian politicians to build a canal through the isthmus. It took over ten years, and over 5,000 deaths from tropical disease and accidents, to complete the project, but Roosevelt believed that it was one of his most important achievements. Roosevelt was no longer in office when the first ship traveled the canal in 1914, his efforts were quickly justified. The Panama Canal was an immediate boon to the world economy and clearly strengthened America's position as a world power. After a few decades had passed, Panamanians began to resent the arrangements they had agreed to in 1903. They were particularly disturbed by the Canal Zone, which gave the United States sovereignty over the five miles on each side of the canal. By the second half of the twentieth century, objections from Panama grew more intense and President Jimmy Carter negotiated a new arrangement with Panama that stipulated that on December 31, 1999, the canal would come under the control of Panama. The United States, however, retained considerable influence over matters relating to the canal, including assistance for necessary widening to accommodate ever-larger vessels on the high seas.

Roosevelt's handling of the circumstances leading to the canal's construction has been compared to the disreputable way in which the United States acquired Hawaii. That criticism is certainly justified, but it made perfect sense to the president. Roosevelt believed, as his corollary to the Monroe Doctrine clearly indicates, that the United States needed to dominate the Western Hemisphere. It was not possible to allow unreliable governments in Central and South America to stand in the way of the interests of the United States. It was an extension of his domestic policies that were directed toward showing that the interests of all the citizens of the United States had to be foremost in the plans of whoever was president. It was the same philosophy that led him to challenge Standard Oil and the food and pharmaceutical industries.

There is no question that Theodore Roosevelt raised the prestige of the American presidency at home and abroad. When the Russo–Japanese War came to an end in 1905, Roosevelt was asked to negotiate the treaty between the two countries. He met with Russian and Japanese representatives in Portsmouth, New Hampshire, where an agreement was reached. No other president before Roosevelt would have been asked to undertake such a task involving two distant countries. The Japanese, who had crushed Russia in this war, were not entirely happy with the agreement Roosevelt accepted, but his efforts made him the first United States president to receive the Nobel Peace Prize. Roosevelt was more than pleased to receive this award, as it was further proof of the enhanced standing of the United States.

Near the end of his time as president, Roosevelt sought to show the world the strength of the United States navy. In 1907 he sent the "Great White Fleet" around the world. The name came from the fact that the ships were all painted white above the water line and it proved to be a point of pride for Roosevelt as the fleet sailed into ports from South America to Australia to the Philippines. The White Fleet was proof, in Roosevelt's mind, that the United States had reached a level of parity with any European country as a great power.

In 1907, Roosevelt let it be known that he did not wish to be a candidate for president in 1908. Instead, he intended to endorse someone he trusted to carry on the progressive philosophy: William Howard Taft. Taft seemed to be in concert with

Roosevelt on most issues. Roosevelt's popularity was such that the Republican Party could scarcely go against his wishes and Taft was duly nominated. The Democrats offered a familiar name, William Jennings Bryan, to run against Taft, but Bryan's populist allure had waned significantly since 1896. Taft won a solid victory and, for the most part, followed the path established by Roosevelt. He attacked the monopolistic trusts with much greater zeal than had Roosevelt, and he expanded the National Park system. Yet, for reasons that are not altogether clear, Roosevelt began to turn on his friend. He may have thought Taft's devotion to conservation was insufficient; he may have believed Taft's legendary weight problem was unbecoming a president; or, he may simply have thought that Taft was not the progressive he had imaged. Whatever lay behind Roosevelt's growing distaste for Taft, it became more entrenched as time passed.

It was assumed that Taft would be re-nominated by the Republicans in 1912, but Roosevelt had other ideas. Having convinced a large number of his supporters that Taft was inadequate, he determined to put himself forward as a candidate in 1912. The Republican Party did not respond as Roosevelt had expected. To many in the party, Taft was more in line with their economic and social views. They were happy when Roosevelt decided not to run again. Besides, Roosevelt had stepped up his attacks on American big business earlier in 1912. He had also talked about providing every U.S. citizen with universal health care. These were not things conservative Republicans wanted to hear.

When it became apparent that the convention had no interest in denying Taft a second term, Roosevelt and his supporters stormed out. Many declared their intention to support the Democratic candidate, Woodrow Wilson, but Roosevelt decided to form a third party instead. Officially, it bore the title Progressive Party, but it became better known as the "Bull Moose Party," as it seemed to reflect Roosevelt's charging personality. As the candidate of the Progressive Party, Roosevelt threw the 1912 presidential election into a three-way race. The result was that the Republican vote was split between those who endorsed Roosevelt's progressive views and those who were far more conservative. This allowed Woodrow Wilson to win an unexpected victory. Roosevelt had thought his popularity with the American people might carry him to the presidency again and he was disappointed when that did not happen. On the other hand, he had succeeded in defeating the man he had come to detest. Taft's political career essentially ended with the election loss. He did not appear to be especially disappointed that he was no longer president. Unlike Roosevelt, he had never been comfortable in that office. In 1921, President Warren Harding appointed Taft to the Supreme Court as chief justice. Taft thus became the only person in United States history to be president and chief justice.

The 1912 election marks the end of the Progressive Era. While Wilson was perceived as a progressive, he was reticent to push progressive philosophy with enthusiasm. Roosevelt continued to make public appearances where he encouraged a greater attention to the evils of big corporations and the disparity between rich and poor. In 1918, he seemed to be preparing for another run at the presidency in 1920, but illness struck him down and he died in 1919.

There is no question that Theodore Roosevelt changed the office of president in dramatic fashion. He pushed the office to the limits of the Constitution (his adversaries thought he exceeded those limits) and he made it clear that a president is the president of all the people, not just the wealthy and influential. It was a remarkable and much-needed turnaround from the presidents of the Gilded Age. In Roosevelt's mind there was really nothing beyond the purview of the president if it affected the well-being of a significant number of Americans. Unfortunately, this rarely included the well-being of black Americans. He never quite believed that black people were equal to whites. His attitude in this regard, along with his enthusiastic support for eugenics, must temper the praise heaped upon him by historians. At the same time, it is beyond doubt that he established the foundation upon which President Franklin Roosevelt could expand the role of the federal government to the benefit of most Americans.

DISCUSSION QUESTIONS

- According to the article, how did Roosevelt's leadership differ from his predecessors? Compared to the leadership shown by the Gilded Age presidents, was this an improvement? Or was it instead an abuse of power? Regardless, was someone like Roosevelt necessary to initiate such change?
- How did Theodore Roosevelt's leadership increase the power and prestige of the United States abroad?
- Why was Theodore Roosevelt interested in Progressive reform? Were his efforts successful in reforming the social and economic problems from the Gilded Age? Why or why not?

CHAPTER VII

FRANCE, 1918

OBJECTIVES

- Analyze the causes of American entry into World War I and the experiences of Americans during that war.

PREWRITING

- What were the reasons that Woodrow Wilson gave Americans for entry into World War I?

France, 1918

SHERMAN L. FLEEK

Private Neibaur wrote, "On the 10th of February[1918] I was transferred to the Forty-second, or Rainbow Division. Continued with them until I was wounded and disabled."[1] The 42nd Division arrived in France in segments beginning in November 1917 and was one of the first of four American divisions to arrive in France to form the first major combat units of the AEF, or the American Expeditionary Force. World War I was America's first major conflict abroad deploying millions of men, billions of dollars of resources, and huge army formations. To lead such a major and complex campaign, the United States needed an exceptional army officer to command this force. That leader was one of several major generals in the Regular Army, and one of the older ones for that matter, who had a nickname gained from his early years with a black cavalry regiment on the frontier that stuck: "Black Jack."

A Missourian and West Point graduate of 1886, John J. Pershing was one of the most promising officers in the army at the turn of the century.[2] When President Theodore Roosevelt decided to promote him from captain to brigadier general, skipping three ranks and hundreds of other more senior officers, Pershing was a marked man. "Teddie" Roosevelt, the old Rough Rider, fought with "Black Jack" in Cuba in 1898, forming a friendship and mutual regard that paid off, at least for the former cavalryman of the 10th Cavalry.[3] When another crisis came along on the Mexican border in 1916, Pershing led more than 130,000 soldiers and guardsmen to find and punish the Mexican revolutionaries.[4]

When President Wilson contemplated the requirements for a commander for the American Expeditionary Forces, he wanted an experienced and determined officer. Even before the war he had first considered the battle-hardened veteran of the Philippine Insurrection (1899–1902) and Medal of Honor recipient Major General Frederick Funston. But Funston suddenly died during the winter of 1917 of a massive heart attack just weeks before the declaration of war. Pershing was Wilson's second choice and proved to be an outstanding and perhaps better choice.[5]

General Pershing had the tremendous task of organizing, deploying, training, and leading an expeditionary force that later grew into an army group of nearly two million soldiers. Pershing and the AEF had several bloody campaigns with the Germans before them. He also had a few battles with the Allies. By any standard his was an incredible feat. Pershing had a lot of help, and he especially was blessed with a crop of mostly decent, God-fearing, and dedicated American soldiers. The greatest challenge that Pershing faced was probably not the Germans or training and leading a vast army, but the Allies themselves. Great Britain and France, as we will see, constantly wanted to "amalgamate" the AEF and distribute individual soldiers and smaller units, no larger than regiments, to their own divisions and corps, assigning them permanently, for the duration of the war. Perhaps Pershing's greatest service was to keep the AEF intact.[6]

However, Pershing and his staff realized some adjustments had to take place. Not all the divisions arriving were needed on the front immediately. Officers, NCOs, and soldiers were also needed as replacements to those divisions in the sectors. The reason Neibaur was transferred to the 42nd was because the 41st Division no longer served as a combat unit but became a training depot division, a pool for replacements assisting other divisions as they arrived. The AEF recommended that the shortage of officers in other divisions should be taken from the 42nd Division. It seemed likely that the 42nd would face the same fate as the 41st Division. Fortunately for the 42nd Division, its chief of staff was Colonel Douglas MacArthur, who would not accept the stripping of the Rainbow Division that he helped create and name. He quarreled with the AEF staff over this and many other issues, several exchanges becoming altercations, and then he made a visit to Chaumont, the AEF headquarters. There he convinced Brigadier General James Harbord, the AEF chief of staff, to keep the 42nd Division intact. Harbord in turn convinced Pershing. It worked. The Rainbow Division remained an active combat division but MacArthur paid a heavy price by alienating the AEF staff.[7]

A difficult challenge that Private Neibaur now faced was his new company and regiment. He was among strangers from a region very different from Idaho. The 167th Infantry Regiment consisted of soldiers mostly from Alabama. Assigned to M Company, Neibaur served as an automatic rifleman in a typical infantry squad of ten to twelve soldiers, led by a sergeant with a corporal next in the chain of command. "I am having a pretty good time now," Neibaur wrote home, "but not as good as I would if I had been left in my old company," meaning M Company of the 2nd Idaho Infantry. "The boys I am with now are from the south. Of course they are good fellows and all that but still they have different ways that seem a bit funny to me."[8]

Colonel William Screws, commanding officer of the 167th Infantry Regiment, was a regular army major when the United States entered the war in 1917. He served in an Alabama National Guard regiment during the Spanish-American War. Guy F. Jennings, *Illustrated Review, Fourth Alabama Infantry, United States Army, Montgomery, Alabama, 1917.*

The 167th Infantry Regiment, its new designation from the War Department, was once a famed volunteer regiment in the Confederate States Army, the 4th Alabama. The 4th Alabama served during the Civil War in many campaigns and battles, especially in Virginia, thus having a strong record and lineage, as did the "Fighting" 69th New York, now the 165th Regiment, both serving in the 42nd Division. These two regiments of the Civil War had not faced each other in combat directly, though they both fought in some of the same battles: Fredericksburg (December 1862) and Gettysburg (July 1863) just to name two.[9]

The commanders and key leaders of the 167th Infantry were mostly Alabama guardsmen or Regular Army officers hailing from Alabama. Of course, as in all the regiments by the time, when it went to the trenches, the regiment retained many of their original soldiers, but replacements were from all three components: a few regular soldiers but mostly guardsmen and draftees. This occurred in all three categories of regiments and divisions. None were completely of one component, though they often kept enough men to retain their original character. The commanding officer of the 167th Infantry was Colonel William Screws, a Regular Army officer from Montgomery, Alabama, who served in the 3rd Alabama during the Spanish-American War but later gained a commission in the Regular Army while serving in the Philippines, rising to the rank of major by 1917. The commander of Private Neibaur's 3rd Battalion of the 167th Infantry was Major Dallas B. Smith.[10]

The guardsmen from Alabama were mostly rural boys from the hills of lower Appalachia, and many entered the army with special concerns. Wisconsin national guardsman and physician Major James W. Frew, while screening new soldiers, wrote of the Alabamans of the 167th Infantry: "from a medical standpoint the Alabama regiment caused us a great deal of worry and trouble. They were nearly all boys from the mountains and rural districts and as soon as they hit camp they began to have their baby diseases. Measles, diphtheria, and scarlet fever were soon raging and the whole regiment was put under strict quarantine. After we arrived in France over 600 of them came down with mumps inside of two weeks."[11] These soldiers were just a snapshot of the health issues that the AEF and Pershing faced. Neibaur and his comrades had to endure these common but incapacitating diseases.

* * * * *

Private Thomas Neibaur's official personnel file recorded that he participated in five campaigns or battles during World War I. Most battles and engagements in American history are grouped into campaigns with inclusive dates. One can often see "Campaign Streamers" hanging from unit colors (regimental flags) in parades and military ceremonies. They represent the campaigns in which that unit fought. Of course, the official dates, or inclusive dates, as determined later by army officials and historians, may not always coincide with what soldiers experienced or with the campaign dates on certain earlier records, but they generally are similar. Sometimes, larger campaigns include battles and other campaigns previously not recognized. In Thomas Neibaur's case, his records note: Lunéville Sector, February 18 to March 20, and Baccarat Sector, March 25 to June 12. His service in these two sectors on the western front fall under three separate campaign groupings. His service in various campaigns will be identified according to both his personal records and the official campaigns that show his participation in some of the battles in the Great War.

SOMME DEFENSIVE, MARCH 21–APRIL 6, 1918

THE 42ND DIVISION IN THE LUNÉVILLE SECTOR, FEBRUARY 18–MARCH 20

Thomas recorded his first experiences in trench warfare in this way: "On the 21st of February we were sent into the trenches in the Sector of Lorraine. It was our first time in the trenches, and, although it was very quiet, we thought it was terrible." He added that, as new soldiers inexperienced in combat, "there may have been a dozen shots [bullets] during the night but we, at that time, thought it was a heavy bombardment."[12]

According to the official army records, Private Neibaur served in his first tactical or combat operation beginning February 21, 1918, when he entered the Lunéville Sector in Lorraine in the northeastern part of France on the German border. Neibaur and the 42nd deployed in a sector of the western front in Alsace-Lorraine, perhaps one of the most historical areas in Europe. This beautiful part of France and Germany had been fought over and occupied as a point of bitter animosity between the Germans and the French for centuries. There were few locations in Europe which war has visited more often and with more intensity.

All wars create or spawn incorrect images or legends. One concerning World War I was that, once in the front lines units stayed in combat in the trenches, constantly, without breaks, while attacks across "no-man's-land" occurred every day. Soldiers and leaders are not machines, and they require rest, refitting, and diversions at times, or soon the mental and physical strain and anguish can destroy the morale and fitness of a soldier and a unit. Neibaur and his fellow Americans were in allied France; however, the Yanks were still in a strange land with a different culture and strange language. These factors, too, add anxiety for a soldier, though the overriding situation of stress was combat and service on the front lines.

"The sight that greeted us brought an immediate and positive reaction," wrote a soldier of the 168th Infantry from Iowa upon arriving at the front with the other 42nd units. He continued:

> "Desolate" was the only name for it. A mass of rusty barbed wire was strung on crisscrosses of posts that seemed to grow from the ground. Ghost-like trees to the right were splattered with shell scars. Some had fallen into the mass of twisted wire and upturned earth. Others were broken off at various heights, like so many match sticks.

The expanse of desolation sloped up a gentle rise. The German trenches were hidden behind the crest some 200 yards away.[13]

Thomas narrated how the rotation system in the trenches worked at this time. "The First Battalion of my regiment [167th Infantry] would be in the front line trenches eight days, then would be relieved to do reserve duty"—that is, manual or logistic work, such as improving roads and communication trenches and manning the ubiquitous command posts (called "PC" in World War I for "post of command). These were necessary manual tasks that relieved the soldier from the tension of tactical duty. He continued, "The Second Battalion would take its place, and so likewise the other eight days at a time."[14]

The men of the 167th Infantry entered the trenches for the first time where they experienced and endured some anxious, dangerous, and strange circumstances. In order to keep "cooties" out of their hair, many of them shaved their heads. They were the first Rainbow soldiers to withstand attacks by German aircraft. In fact on February 18 a German bomb from an airplane nearly demolished Colonel Screw's regimental headquarters near Glonville.[15]

Another favorite myth of the war was the austere, terribly primitive, and always mud-filled trenches depicted in some war films and photographs. This picture was partially true, but not always, because some trench systems were highly developed, with several stories tunneled into the earth, mazes of passages and tunnels, underground kitchens, dormitories that could house several dozen men, and offices with electric lights, toilets, wooden floors, stairs, ceilings, and ventilation ducts. In order to make such improvements, the lines would have to be static for months. In a few locations, such as the forts surrounding Verdun, the French army built fortifications with concrete structures for gun emplacements and fighting positions. Trench warfare was more than just a new tactic devised to counter the new instruments of death—rapid-fire artillery and the machine gun.[16] There were many privations and problems from the wet and cold of European winters, the rain, and also "critters." Thomas mentioned in one letter that rats were everywhere, in the trenches and in the camps—"the rats are so thick one can hardly sleep for them." He also said, "We have another little animal over here it is very small and is a great pest . . . we call them lice."[17] Life in the army, in war and especially in the trenches, was not fun.

Actually, in modern warfare the most deadly weapon has been artillery, now equaled by aerial bombardment and close air attacks. Trenches and fortifications provided distinct advantages to massed forces, which have been summarized as "principles of defense" by military historians. British military historian Paddy Griffith wrote, "The principles of defence are of course as old as warfare itself, and they include such aspirations as the maximum early warning, the maximum protection and the maximum firepower." The trench lines were designed like a long, continuous "W" where fighting positions provided interlocking fields of fire, hopefully at maximum effective ranges of the weapon systems. Besides protection, firepower, and early warning, trench systems had to be habitable, where soldiers could derive a modicum of shelter, comfort, dry and warm conditions, and access to food and water. Early warning came from barbed wire, concertina wire, flares, trip wires, and new terms born in the trenches: "listening posts" and "observation posts." These latter were small detachments, sometimes of only two soldiers positioned a few hundred yards in advance, listening and watching for night patrols or the signs of general assaults. Tin cans, whistles, flares, and bells provided extra early warning devices. Officers and lookouts employed crafty little periscopes so they could see but not be seen over the trench lines.[18]

Perhaps one of the most ingenious and revolutionary developments in trench warfare was the "defense in depth." Again, it was not a new idea, since ancient and medieval fortresses had outer, middle, and inner walls or citadels, yet the World War I version was an elaborate system of interconnecting, intrasupporting, and mutually designed systems. Communication trenches normally ran perpendicular to and connected the defensive trenches. Thus, soldiers could enter the trench system hundreds of yards in the rear and negotiate a labyrinth-like maze, marked by sign posts and other indicators, to finally reach the most forward trench line. It was a difficult and dreadful proposition to assault, overwhelm, and defeat a series of trenches manned by thousands of soldiers with machine guns, mortars, rifles, grenades, and also poisonous gas, arranged for defense in depth. By 1917, the huge frontal assault was used only when operation planners and leaders felt they had an overwhelming advantage or what is called today, a "combat multiplier," as in the great offensives of 1918. A combat multiplier is a distinct tactical advantage in battle. One simple problem was that, once a breach was made and penetration occurred through the enemy lines, the nature of this warfare prevented such successes from being exploited quickly as in the past with cavalry or maneuver forces. Thus, the no-man's-land of wire, trenches, shell craters, and obstacles inhibited tactical successes. The intervention of air forces and armored warfare were previews of how to eliminate the problem in later wars.[19]

* * * * *

On April 18, 1918, Thomas Neibaur wrote his parents that "you cannot guess how pleased it makes me feel to get good cherry [sic] letters from home." Thomas had been in France three months and also in the 42nd Division for two months without yet being in direct combat, though he had been on the front lines. Like any soldier he was homesick, lonely, and probably apprehensive about fighting. Yet like most soldiers, he also looked forward to finally doing something—in fulfilling the mission and doing what soldiers are trained to do: fight. "Well dear folks," he wrote, "I have been to the

The five German "Ludendorff Offensives." From Eisenhower, *Yanks*.

trenches [can't] tell you much about it except that I had a few pretty exciting times but came through without a scratch and am feeling fine now."[20]

AISNE, MAY 27–JUNE 5, 1918

THE 42ND DIVISION IN BACCARAT SECTOR, MARCH 25–JUNE 12

The Americans had the unusual situation during this training phase of the war to serve with or under French units and commanders. In this first instance, the 42nd was attached to the French VII Corps. The division remained in the Lunéville Sector until March 23, and then concentrated near Gerbéviller in the Baccarat area. On March 27, the Rainbow Division was relieved and prepared to move to the 7th Training Area for "rehabilitation," meaning reconstitution and recovery, but on March 28 the orders were cancelled and the division remained in the trenches at Baccarat.[21]

There is little doubt for the reason Neibaur and his comrades did not move to the rehabilitation camp. At 0716 in the morning of March 21, 1918, the Germans launched Operation Michael, with mammoth artillery pieces mounted on railcars throwing shells weighing hundreds of pounds, which took several airborne minutes to travel seventy-four miles before falling in Paris. Twenty such rounds killed 256 Parisians that day. This attack began the Ludendorff Offensives, five in total, which were Germany's last hope for victory.[22]

In the fall of 1917, revolution overtook Russia and that swaggering giant fell. This relieved a million German soldiers and tens of thousands of guns to be transferred to the western front. In a vain hope to defeat Great Britain and France before the United States could effectively intervene, Quartermaster General Eric Ludendorff, the German version of a chief of staff, planned and conducted Operation Michael under the watchful eyes of Field Marshal Paul von Hindenburg. The offensive actually began at 0450 with 6,100 German artillery pieces commencing a five-hour barrage while tens of thousands of men along a thirty-mile front prepared to go "over the top."[23]

The German offensive was a tidal wave and the numbers were staggering: some 3,575,000 men deployed in 192 combat divisions of some 12,000 men each. A full third of the German forces—some sixty-nine divisions—would attack in successive waves along a sixty-mile front; also 3,670 aircraft conducted close air support missions for ground operations. The main objective was to defeat the British Expeditionary Force (BEF) in a general assault against the British 1st and 3rd Armies near the Belgian frontier at Arras, while a smaller or secondary effort was to split the "seam" (or the tactical boundary) between the 5th Army of the BEF, and the French 6th Army near Compiegne. The Allies held one distinct but still relatively nascent advantage: the Germans had ten tanks and the Allies had eight hundred tanks in this sector.[24]

Operation Michael, the first Ludendorff offensive, lasted until April 5 and pushed the British back some twenty miles to final defensive positions. The onslaught did not break the BEF nor the French line in the south. The British suffered 163,000 casualties, the French 77,000, and the attacking Germans 250,000.[25] A week later, the second offensive, Operation Georgette, began a little north of the first offensive. In May came the third offensive, and then the fourth, until the fifth and final offensive hit a brick wall in July near Reims. By mid-July 1918 much of the defensive wall in the south consisted of American divisions. Though not exactly proportional, from the first offensive in March to the last in July, the German front was smaller and the gains fewer. The final German success in July gained only a narrow sliver of territory against the French. The Germans forever lost their gamble for victory.[26]

But in March German morale and optimism remained high. Hindenburg and the high command were employing a new tactic for the western front, something developed and executed with great success against the Russians by German General Oskar von Hutier. It was the roving barrage or "barrage box." The tactic called for artillery to create a deadly and protective wall immediately in front of and on the flanks of assaulting troops, creeping forward as the troops advanced. Highly trained companies and battalions of "storm troopers" would advance swiftly to surprise and overwhelm defenders by penetrating defensive positions and bypassing enemy strongpoints. The storm troopers carried only light machine guns, rifles, flame throwers, and light mortars, thus having tremendous firepower for light infantry tactics. General Hutier came west and assumed command of the German 18th Army—the spearhead and center army of two army groups in the offensive.[27]

The new German tactics were impressive and sometimes decisive in a localized sector, but they were not powerful enough to overwhelm the entire Allied front in 1918. The Ludendorff offensives were like the last rounds that two exhausted and bleeding boxers experienced as they gasped for air and strength while swinging and delivering pitiful punches, enduring blows in return, and pacing themselves for the final knockout blow. The analogy is not perfect, because how does one factor in the surge of American forces? As a second wind, there was a sense of renewed confidence perhaps. Thus, the German boxer was wasted and the Allied boxer, exhausted, bloodied, and wavering, suddenly felt a new strength and vigor.

* * * * *

Thomas Neibaur saw and experienced some of these last actions. They must have brought a sense of history as they unfolded before him. Yet, as a young doughboy, his thoughts, hopes, and prayers often turned to home. He said that he finally received nine letters from Tressa, his girlfriend of sorts from his Sandpoint days, in March and April 1918. It had been two months since he had received any news from his family, though other letters seemed to find him. It was always a difficult proposition when soldiers were deployed overseas or transferred to new units, because the mail had a hard time finding them. Thomas faced both situations. Letters from home are a soldier's salvation. A strange situation occurred in reference to girls other than Tressa.[28] In a letter written in June 1918, Thomas mentioned a girl named Lenora Simmons from Liberty, Idaho, who had written to him. Thomas wrote, "I cannot figure out who she is. I have no recollection of a girl by that name." He also received letters from another girl or young woman, Nellie, as he named her. He provided no other information in any of his letters and there is no other information regarding these girls.[29] In the same letter he mentioned receiving a letter from Libbie, his older sister born in 1893 and who died in 1943. It may seem to be an interesting circumstance that Thomas received a letter from a girl he could not remember, but it is a simple part of life.

In April after experiencing some time in the trenches and limited fighting, Thomas wrote home to his parents, "Well, dear folks, you don't know how it makes me feel when I think how far away I am from every one I love." As he expressed these sentiments of loneliness, he also was "willing to sacrifice most anything for my country for I know that the cause we are fighting for is a good cause and I know God will help us win in the end." One of the curious and perplexing qualities of war is that each side thinks it is fulfilling God's will. Soldiers, citizens, and leaders prayed to the same God for victory, safety, and success. Each side was convinced that God would bless their effort. So was Thomas Neibaur.[30]

Thomas also addressed an interesting part of a soldier's life during war that is often overlooked: the service and benefits of such organizations as the International Red Cross and the Young Men's Christian Association. "The Y. M. C. A. is very active in this part of the country [France]. I am writing now in their building," he wrote on April 18 but did not mention the city. The 42nd Division was still operating in the Baccarat Sector in Lorraine. He said that the YMCA provided writing stationery, cakes, confections, and "tobacco sometimes." One would gather that he was using tobacco again; smoking was such a common practice among American soldiers. The tension and stress of combat encourages use of chemical substances, including alcohol, for relief or escape. There is no evidence at this time though that Thomas consumed alcohol as he would later in life. Yet it is probable that he joined fellow soldiers in occasional drinking when alcohol could be obtained.[31]

Another interesting aspect of Thomas's letters in a war theater was the army's requirement to censor letters. All letters going home were read by company officers to ensure that no sensitive or operational information went to unauthorized sources. On one of Thomas's letters there is the inscription in ink, "OK, CP 7," probably meaning, "command post" or "check point" number seven. This process dealt with operational security, safeguarding tactical operations, besides such innocuous information as unit strength, commanding officers' names, locations, types of weapons, training problems, or any information that could be seen, used, or delivered to enemy sources. It seems rather silly perhaps, but such information, especially verbalized in bars or public gatherings, became an easy source for informants and one of the oldest and sometimes most reliable forms of espionage. Of Neibaur's two dozen extant letters, only one, dated April 18, 1918, has the markings of a censor.[32]

* * * * *

"This sure is a green country over here but still it is as good as can be expected of a country that has been in war for four years," Thomas wrote home on May 28. He remarked how farmers plowed their fields while cattle and sheep roamed about in pastures just a few miles from the front with little regard to the war raging, the noise, and the rumblings of artillery. Since some of the lines of battle had hardly changed or moved in a year or two, life in rural France seemed to return to normal to a degree. Thomas also mentioned that he was staying in a French family's farmhouse. This was a common practice during the war. He said that there were six U.S. Army mules in the barn and nine other American soldiers quartered in the house with him. Thomas was astonished that French farmhouses had a barn and stalls on the ground floor while the upper floors were the living area for the family.[33]

Quartering Thomas Neibaur and other American soldiers in French homes was a normal practice of war. From ancient times, whether friend of foe, forced or invited, soldiers have been quartered, often with families. The first units of the AEF arrived in France in the late summer of 1917. Quarters, whether in tents, camps, or permanent structures was one of the many challenges that General Pershing and his staff faced. Logistics, the art of war of supplying, feeding, transporting, quartering, and providing health care, is one of the most challenging and difficult tasks of war. Some will argue that logistics during war is more important than combat itself. Napoleon Bonaparte is believed to have said that an "army marches on its stomach."

By the end of the war, some two million American soldiers had arrived in France. The immensity and complexity of supporting such a large number of troops are almost unfathomable to imagine. The AEF had to bring much of its materiel and provisions from the United States because France and England were strained to the point of exhaustion in resources to feed and support their own armies and citizens, let alone Americans. Imagine how many loaves of bread it took to feed a thousand men for one day, for a week, or for a month; how many blankets, pairs of socks, kerosene lamps, and bullets it took to supply an army as large as the AEF. Imagine also the network needed to receive, account for, transport, store, and then distribute all this material in a combat zone.

Initially, there were severe problems in establishing a logistical organization, and the frontline units and troops suffered accordingly. As with any large and quick mobilization, the growing pains of assets and resources and also the supply demands and requirements overwhelmed the bureaucracy. In the summer of 1918, the crisis was no longer unavoidable and General Pershing appointed some of his best officers and men in the army to lead and manage this incredibly difficult task. A very capable officer, Major General James G. Harbord, had commanded the 2nd Division (Regular Army with a U.S. Marine brigade) for only a few weeks when Pershing ordered him to manage the supply system and establish order out of chaos. Soon his organization was performing amazing feats to support the AEF. Harbord gathered a team of effective and efficient officers from the old army and developed a smooth, if not perfect, functioning supply and transportation service.[34] Harbord's replacement as commander of the 2nd Division was a U.S. Marine Corps officer, Major General John Lejeune, a rather unique situation in American military history where an officer of one service commanded a large unit of another service.

Pershing and Harbord established an entirely separate logistical entity designated the Services of Supply, or SOS, to manage this mammoth operation. In order to not impair France's logistical system, the Americans developed and, in some cases, built their own independent railroad system and network from St. Nazaire, La Pallice near Rochefort, and Pauillac, an inland port near Bordeaux, on the western coast of France four hundred miles from the front. Warehouses, locomotives, train cars, derricks, and hundreds of ships lined the skyline of these three previously small French ports. Hundreds of train cars transported hundreds of tons of goods east to staging areas near the center of the AEF sector at Chaumont, with momentum gaining in 1918 as more and more troops arrived. Of course, the French government and its citizens helped in many ways, but the vast system was an American production using Yankee ingenuity and resolution.[35] The man Pershing appointed to supervise the transportation network was a Utahan and a Mormon, Brigadier General Frank T. Hines.[36]

* * * * *

General Pershing was determined that the AEF would remain intact, with its own organizations and leaders. Corps and armies formed when more men arrived. He wanted American officers commanding American units of American soldiers. There were several attempts, as already mentioned, when the most senior British and French politicians and commanders were determined to use American soldiers as replacements for their diminishing ranks. Yet, Pershing was a realist and knew initially his army needed combat experience. He did not have the men, nor the resources, and especially not the equipment to face the hardened German veterans in the late fall of 1917 and early 1918. Therefore, most units, such as the 42nd Division, were attached to the French and British corps for training. The Allies also supported and trained the Americans with equipment. The AEF had no aircraft, no tanks, and few artillery pieces. It used French machine guns and the famous French "75" field gun of 75mm caliber.

A major operational and political change caused by the crisis of the Ludendorff offensives was the desperate need for the Allies—finally, after four years of combat—to establish a "supreme council of war" and also appoint a supreme commander. This step raised enormous political and diplomatic issues among the Allied powers of France, Great Britain, Italy, and the several other smaller nations. The Americans, so new to the game, were an afterthought; they could not sit at the table and serve on the council, but could order from the menu. There was no possibility that an American general, Pershing, would become supreme commander, nor would the Americans

An American soldier firing the French Chauchat automatic rifle and assisted by a loader (right). The 8mm Chauchat was one of the most commonly used weapons during the war, but Americans called it the "no shot" because it was notorious for jamming. Courtesy of the U.S. Army Signal Corps Collection.

have much voice in the decisions.[37] When asked his opinion concerning a supreme war council and commander, American President Woodrow Wilson replied, "We not only accede to the plan for unified conduct of the war but we insist on it." The contest that finally arose ended on March 25, when Britain conceded to France and Field Marshal Ferdinand Foch was appointed Allied Supreme Commander. Though unified in name and concept, the Allies still operated and clung to their own nationalistic goals.[38]

One of the first measures that the Supreme Council of War attempted was to wrestle control of six inbound divisions from the United States. The British wanted the infantry regiments and the machine gun battalions as reinforcements, but not the support and artillery units, thus decreasing the size of the divisions significantly and destroying unit cohesiveness. Pershing vigorously fought this, for he knew that if he gave ground on stripping these six American divisions of their core infantry regiments and firepower and transferring them to British control, the AEF would soon unravel. However, he accepted that, with all the equipment and other resources the Allies provided to the AEF, he had to relent and allow some of the divisions in France to serve under Allied armies and corps in an emergency. The 42nd Division was attached to the French VII Corps under the command of General Georges de Bazelaire serving in the Lunéville and Baccarrat sectors. At least Pershing was able to keep tactical integrity at the division level until he could organize larger American formations. And time was Pershing's ace. He knew that eventually, with hundreds of thousands of new doughboys arriving, he would soon have the sheer numbers and weight to force his operational and tactical plans forward. For now he had to wait, support the effort, and allow his divisions to gain valuable combat experience while chafing under Allied operational control.

★ ★ ★ ★ ★

Ludendorff's next offensive, Operation George commenced April 9 and lasted nearly three weeks until the twenty-ninth. A month later was the next offensive, Operation Blücher, named for the Prussian commander at Waterloo in 1815. It is also known merely as the Aisne offensive, based on the Aisne River. This offensive began May 27 and ended June 5. It was after this offensive that Neibaur's Rainbow Division was relieved and pulled out of the line. The 42nd Division did not face all of these offensives, for they were spread out over half of the western front in France. Only the portions of the Aisne attacks in May through June involved direct fighting for the 42nd. Yet the Rainbow Division and its 27,000 men experienced more cruel menace of war.

In a letter dated May 28, Thomas wrote, "I am still well and happy . . . have been to the trenches three times now have had some pretty exciting times but came through without a scratch each time." The exciting times he mentioned could refer to any number of combat incidents and dangers, or perhaps to one the most abominable inventions of war: poison gas.[39]

In the same letter he wrote, "Now dear mother do not worry because I tell you I have been to the trenches as there is not much danger the worst thing is the gas." The employment of poison gas was a new horrifying aspect of a new war for a new century. The horror and dread it produced has been amply depicted in war films, popular literature, and more serious accounts. Its tactical and combat employment is little understood. Briefly, poison gas was not used directly as a means to inflict great numbers of casualties, it was a means to cause panic and alarm. The French were the first to use gas in the war, dispensing tear gas in 1914. The Germans in 1915 at the second battle of Ypres employed chlorine gas against French colonial troops. Soon both sides were employing it as a way to disrupt, discourage, and limit the foe's planning and tactics.[40] Using poison gas successfully required skill based on many conditions, such as wind direction, ambient temperature, terrain elevations, dissipation rates, sunlight intensity, proximity of enemy and friendly lines, the type of gas (persistent or nonpersistent), and dispersing systems; these were all huge planning factors in gas warfare. It was not a matter of just dropping gas bombs on the enemy and watching them convulse and die like ants.[41]

The delivery means was also extremely critical and potentially lethal for the employing force. Artillery was perhaps the safest for friendly forces, but it was limited in area and density, which effective gas attacks required. Dispensing gas had a challenging set of problems; Wind changes could be disastrous to one's own forces. Especially difficult was carrying the heavy gas cylinders forward far enough that the gas effects did not incapacitate one's own force. It was a careless commander who allowed his own forces to suffer through a poison cloud drifting and also settling across his own lines as it moved in the variables of wind toward the enemy. There were many technical imperatives, the most serious being how it would affect one's own troops if the conditions were not ideal. So poison gas was not a favorite choice of either side during the war; it produced only 2 percent of overall casualties. Commanders had to consider that if used in supporting an attack, then friendly troops had to advance, pass through, and survive it, a sometimes daunting imperative that convinced commanders there was a better way.

"We have good gas masks to protect us," Thomas wrote, "the only thing is getting them on in time."[42] The gas mask employed by American soldiers was a primitive but effective device considering the era and gases used. It was a facial mask or respirator that had a large, uncomfortable clip that attached to the soldier's nose like a clothespin. The mask was connected by a hose to an air filtration canister in a small canvas bag, which was carried by straps and positioned directly on the man's chest. If gas attacks were likely, then soldiers often slept with them on and wore them during their duties in the trenches. It was a crude, awkward, uncomfortable but effective system.[43]

The most common types of chemical gas were the incapacitating mustard (persistent) and the lethal phosgene (non-persistent, first used by the French). Chlorine, the first widely used agent, had many limitations, hence the development of other agents. Basically, the nonpersistent agents were very powerful gases when first released but dissipated quickly from weather and terrain conditions and were more suited for offensive operations rather than defensive. Persistent gases could last for many hours, even a day or so under optimum conditions; thus, they were more favorable for defensive operations, ideal for stopping or impeding an attack. Whatever the type, tactics, terrain, and locations, gas warfare was a frightening monster, but compared to high-explosive artillery or infantry attacks, it was not nearly as lethal.[44]

Some of the finest art and literature is created as a result of war relative to gas warfare. Lieutenant Wilfred Owen in the British Army wrote one of the most famous poems of the war:

DULCE ET DECORUM EST

Bent double, like old beggars under sacks,
Knock-kneed, coughing like hags, we cursed through sludge,
Till on the haunting flares we turned our backs
And towards our distant rest began to trudge.

Men marched asleep. Many had lost their boots
But limped on, blood-shod. All went lame; all blind;
Drunk with fatigue; deaf even to the hoots
Of gas shells dropping softly behind.
Gas! GAS! Quick boys!—An ecstasy of fumbling,
Fitting the clumsy helmets just in time,
But someone still was yelling out and stumbling
And flound'ring like a man in fire or lime . . .
Dim, through the misty panes and thick green light,
As under a green sea, I saw him drowning.
In all dreams, before my helpless sight,
He plunges at me, guttering, choking, drowning.
If in some smothering dreams, you too could pace
Behind the wagon that we flung him in,
And watch the white eyes writhing in his face,
His hanging face, like a devil's sick of sin;
If you could hear, at every jolt, the blood
Come gargling from the froth-corrupted lungs,
Obscene as cancer, bitter as the cud
Of vile, incurable sores on innocent tongues,
My friend, you would not tell with such high zest
The old Lie: Dulce et decorum est
Pro patria mori.*

Lieutenant Wilfred Owen was killed in action on November 4, 1918, a week before the armistice.

★ ★ ★ ★ ★

The 42nd Division and Neibaur's 167th Infantry Regiment endured several gas attacks in April and May 1918. Hundreds of soldiers were "wounded" or incapacitated, many of them dying from what is called "dry-land drowning" when their lungs filled with fluids. The throat, ears, eyes, and nostrils are affected to such a degree that there occurs blindness, hearing loss, and severe inflammation of the skin. It was a dreadful sight to see men choke, writhe, gasp, collapse, vomit, and die with involuntary spasms of inhuman contortions from extreme suffering. One observer of the 42nd Division wrote, "Below us in the valley hung low clouds of gas. They settled right there, and those of us on higher ground were safe. But we wore our masks for three hours." Wrote

---

* Latin for "To die for the fatherland is a sweet thing and becoming."

medical orderly Lawrence Stewart of the Iowa 168th Infantry, "A large percentage of officers and men of the sanitary detachment died or suffered severely from the gas. . . . Little help could be given the gas victims. We placed them on stretchers, kept them quiet as possible and hurried them to the hospital." As mentioned, there was little medical science could do to assuage the pain and suffering, especially those most severely poisoned. Mustard gas, a type of blistering agent, was terrible for its assault on exposed skin, burning and inflaming, producing grotesque boils, sores, and blisters and the same inside the lungs.[45]

On May 1 and 2, the Germans delivered hundreds of artillery rounds of both phosgene and mustard on two complete trench lines of the 42nd Division, whose effects persisted to various degrees for nearly two days. It must have been like hell.[46] In some later sources, Thomas Neibaur said that he was gassed during the war. This affliction, along with his smoking for most of his life, possibly led to his early death by tuberculosis. Being gassed was eventually recognized as a "wound" by the Army, as much as being hit by enemy bullets or shrapnel, though some soldiers deplored this official recognition.[47]

* * * * *

According to historian James Cooke in his *The Rainbow Division in the Great War*, a unit history of the 42nd Rainbow Division, "the 167th Infantry Regiment was quickly developing into the most aggressive and combat-proficient unit in the Rainbow Division." The process or analysis Cooke used to establish this claim, other than the fact that they were "rural boys," he did not mention. The 167th conducted one of the 42nd Division's first raids across no-man's-land on March 4, when the division had just arrived in the Lunéville Sector. Sergeant Varner Hall from Birmingham captured prisoners from the 77th Bavarian Infantry Regiment.[48] Capturing prisoners, for both sides, was a huge source of intelligence and demonstrated a prime necessity of war: vigilance. Frontline soldiers had to keep alert and not be lulled into apathy. Apparently, the Alabama troops were very good at patrolling and aggressive action. Sergeant Hall's exploits were just the first of literally hundreds of such patrols and reconnaissances into no-man's-land.[49]

After the war, Neibaur commented about the roughness and aggressiveness of his fellow soldiers in the 167th Infantry: "They were a bit rough and a bit rowdy. But there were no boys who'd stand by closer. . . . They were full of life and pep they had to be doing something all the time. If there was nothing doing, then they'd have to do *something*. They'd raise hell."[50] Cooke continued, "The 167th manifested a desire to fight unmatched by any other regiment" in the 42nd Division.[51] The regiments of the two brigades, the 83rd and 84th, continued tactical operations for limited objectives.

Sometimes they served as diversionary forces for larger, coordinated operations. During this entire time, the Allies were on the defensive from the huge German spring offensives.

* * * * *

War has a lasting effect on any soldier who sees and lives it. War's cruelty, horror, and privation usually cause negative outcomes and hardly benefit the individual. Yet it can also sometimes change people in a good way. War is associated with military service; and for Thomas Neibaur, his military experience changed him, even without considering the Medal of Honor, which of course changed his life. On July 10, Thomas wrote to his parents in Idaho perhaps the most remarkable letter of his time in France. Below is the major portion of his thoughts about what the army and the war was doing to him and about his longing for home.

> I am enjoying the best of health have never been sick but about two days since I have been in France. We have been having lovely weather for the last month until a few days ago. We were sleeping in the open air and when the storm came up we had to pitch our shelter tents and all our blankets got wet before we could get them set.

> You know this war game is making a man of me you remember how I used to be always leaving things around well I have got over that now. I have more stuff to look after now than I ever had at home my equipment consists of my rifle, cartrige [sic] belt, bayonet, canteen, cup, mess kit, helmet, gas mask, clothing, bed and reserve rations and I have them all to look after. You know when a fellow gets to thinking that his rifle, bayonet and gas mask is the only thing that will save his life he will take good care of them. And as for being a man physically why I am as hard as nails and as tough as leather I can carry a heavy pack twenty miles a day without tiring and can stand most any thing. I have slept night after night wet to the skin and never thought of a cold.

> Besides making us men physically I am more a man both mentaly and moraly [sic]. When a man is lying in a trench with the boche [Germans] only a few yards away and is expecting an attack at any moment. I'll tell you it sure makes him do some hard thinking and by thinking he learns what God is.

And we are taking more of an interest in government affairs. A few months ago we only thought of [President Woodrow] Wilson as a man who had lots of money and influence who sat in the white house amid luxuries while we paid taxes to keep his expenses. Now we see him as a great man at the head of the great nation in the war whose name is on the tongue of nearly every nation in the world be it allied or enemy or neutral I tell you dad the Kaiser sure is helping to make ours a wonderful nation and the future whenever we the young men of today are the leading men of the nation.

Well dear folks I know it will not be long before this awful war is over and we can all be together again. I think the enemy is gathering together all his forces for one big effort which will be his last and I don't think the time is very far off.[52]

At midnight on July 14, four days later, the French anniversary of Bastille Day, the Germans attacked for the last time during the war.

NOTES

1 Neibaur, "How Private Neibaur Won the Congressional Medal of Honor," 783.

2 See Vandiver, *Black Jack,* for a detailed biography.

3 Eisenhower, *Yanks,* 28.

4 Millet and Maslowski, *For the Common Defense,* 337.

5 Eisenhower, *Yanks,* 27.

6 Ibid., 16–17.

7 Ibid., 86–87; see also MacArthur, *Reminiscences,* 53. On one occasion MacArthur was recommended for the Medal of Honor, but the awards board of the AEF at Chaumont disapproved the recommendation and instead awarded him the second highest decoration for bravery, the Distinguished Service Cross, his second during World War I. MacArthur would always claim that his quarrelling with the AEF staff cost him America's highest award, the same decoration that his father, Arthur MacArthur, received during the Civil War.

8 Thomas Neibaur to Neibaur Family, April 18, 1918, France, Marian Neibaur Hunkerford Collection.

9 Patricia L. Faust, ed., *Historical Times Illustrated Encyclopedia of the Civil War.*

10 Reilly, *Americans All*, 42.

11 Cooke, *The Rainbow Division in the Great War*, 14.

12 Neibaur, "How Private Neibaur Won the Congressional Medal of Honor," 784.

13 Cooke, *The Rainbow Division in the Great War*, 60.

14 Neibaur, "How Private Neibaur Won the Congressional Medal of Honor," 784.

15 Ibid.

16 See Griffith, *Fortifications of the Western Front, 1914–1918*, 21–22.

17 Thomas Neibaur to Neibaur Family, June 28, 1918, France.

18 Griffith, *Fortifications of the Western Front*, 21–34.

19 Ibid., 49–50; Millet and Maslowski, *For the Common Defense*, 400–401.

20 Thomas Neibaur to Neibaur Family, April 18, 1918, France.

21 *United States Army in the World War, 1917–1919*, 277.

22 Eisenhower, *Yanks*, 101, 107–8.

23 Gilbert, *The First World War*, 406–7; Marshall, *World War I*, 352–53.

24 Eisenhower, *Yanks*, 107.

25 The term "casualties" has the ambiguous meaning of the number of dead, killed in action (KIA), and also wounded and missing in action (WIA and MIA). Not all reports during that time broke down the numbers exactly into these columns, thus the general term of casualties.

26 Livesey, *The Historical Atlas of World War I*, 150.

27 Eisenhower, *Yanks*, 104.

28 Thomas Neibaur to Neibaur Family, April 18, 1918, France.

29 Thomas Neibaur to Neibaur Family, May 28, 1918, France.

30 Thomas Neibaur to Neibaur Family, April 18, 1918, France.

31 Ibid.

32 Ibid.

33 Thomas Neibaur to Neibaur Family, May 28, 1918, France. This letter has the pencil notation, "Leslie Neibaur nice letter from brother in France," though it was addressed to his mother. Who wrote this comment is unknown but Leslie Neibaur was Thomas's older brother, born in 1886 and died in 1923.

34 Whitehorne, *The Inspectors General of the United States Army: 1903–1939*, 177–80.

35 Eisenhower, *Yanks*, 48–50; Millet and Maslowski. *For the Common Defense*, 368–70.

36 Roberts, *Legacy*, 80.

37 Eisenhower, *Yanks*, 119.

38 Marshall, *World War I*, 307.

39 Thomas Neibaur to Neibaur Family, May 28, 1918, France.

40 Keegan, *The First World War*, 197–99.

41 Eisenhower, *Yanks*, 212–13.

42 Thomas Neibaur to Elizabeth Neibaur, May 28, 1918, France.

43 Cooke, *The Rainbow Division in the Great War*, 86.

44 Eisenhower, *Yanks*, 212–13.

45 Cooke, *The Rainbow Division in the Great War*, 89.

46 Ibid., 88.

47 Ibid., 86.

48 The Imperial German Army had units from the kingdoms that had joined with Prussia to create the German Empire in 1871. Adolf Hitler, the future Nazi dictator, served in the 16th Bavarian Infantry during the war on the western front.

49 Cooke, *The Rainbow Division in the Great War*, 61.

50 Hopper, *Medals of Honor*, 211.

51 Cooke, *The Rainbow Division in the Great War*, 61.

52 Thomas Neibaur to Neibaur Family, July 10, 1918, France.

BIBLIOGRAPHY

UNPUBLISHED SOURCES

Boone, Joseph F. "The Roles of the Church of Jesus Christ of Latter-day Saints in Relation to the United States Military, 1900–1975." PhD diss., Brigham Young University, 1975.

Kirby, George Gill. *My Life and Times*, L. Tom Perry Special Collections, Brigham Young University Library.

Neibaur Family Genealogical Record, The Church of Jesus Christ of Latter-Day Saints Family History Library, Salt Lake City, Utah.

Neibaur, Alexander, Journal, L. Tom Perry Special Collections, Brigham Young University Library.

Neibaur, Thomas C. Letters and other Documents, courtesy of Marian Neibaur Hunkerford Collection, Lancaster, Ohio; copies on file.

Summers, Norman L. Diary, Military History Institute. Carlisle Barracks, Pennsylvania.

GOVERNMENT AND MILITARY RECORDS

1880 U.S. Census Index, Bear Lake County, (Idaho Territory) Idgen Web Project Archives

Neibaur, Thomas C. Military Records. Idaho State Historical Society.

AEF General Headquarters. *United States Army in the World War 1917– 1919: Military Operations of the American Expeditionary Forces*. Collection on CD, 17 vols. Washington, D.C.: Historical Division, Department of the Army, 1948.

———. General Orders, No. 26, dated February 11, 1918, Headquarters, AEF, France.

———. Bulletin, No. 25, dated May 9, 1918, Headquarters, AEF, France.

The Medical Department of the United States Army in the World War, Washington D.C.: GPO 1925

Report of the First Army, American Expeditionary Forces: Organization and Operations; Fort Leavenworth, Kans.: General Service Schools Press, 1923.

BOOKS AND PAMPHLETS

Alberts, Donald E. *From Brandy Station to Manila Bay: A Biography of General Wesley Merritt*. Austin, Tex.: Presidial, 1980.

Allen, James B., and Glen M. Leonard. *The Story of the Latter-day Saints*. Salt Lake City: Deseret Book, 1972.

Arrington, Leonard J. *Great Basin Kingdom: An Economic History of the Latter-day Saints, 1830–1900*. Urbana and Chicago: University of Illinois Press, 1958.

———. *Brigham Young: American Moses*. Urbana and Chicago: University of Illinois Press, 1986.

Beal, Samuel M. *The Snake River Fork Country*. Rexburg, Idaho, 1935.

Bennett, Richard E. *Mormons at the Missouri: Winter Quarters, 1846–1852*. Norman: University of Oklahoma Press, 1987.

Bigler, David. *Fort Limhi: The Mormons Adventure in Oregon Territory*. Vol. 6, *Kingdom in the West: The Mormons and the American Frontier*. Spokane: Arthur H. Clark, 2003.

———. *The Forgotten Kingdom: The Mormon Theocracy in the American West, 1847–1896*. Vol. 2, *Kingdom in the West: The Mormons and the American Frontier*. Spokane: Arthur H. Clark, 1998.

Bushman, Richard L. *Joseph Smith: Rough Stone Rolling.* New York: Alfred A Knopf, 2005.

Campbell, Alexander E. *Establishing Zion: The Mormon Church in the American West, 1847–1869.* Salt Lake City: Signature, 1988.

Churchill, Winston. *The Birth of Britain; A History of the English Speaking Peoples,* Vol. 1. New York: Dodd, Meade and Company, 1956.

Clarke, John D. *Gallantry Medals and Decorations of the World.* Barmsely, South Yorkshire, England: Leo Cooper, 2001.

Cooke, James J. *The Rainbow Division in the Great War: 1917–1919.* London, Conn.: Praeger, 1994.

Davies, Norman. *Europe: A History.* NY: Oxford University Press, 1996.

Dickson, Paul, and Thomas B. Allen. *The Bonus Army: An American Epic.* New York: Walker, 2004.

Doubler, Michael. *I Am the Guard: The Army National Guard, 1636–2000.* Washington, D.C.: Government Printing Office, 2001.

Dunlop, Richard. *Donovan: America's Master Spy.* New York: Rand McNally, 1982.

Eisenhower, John S. D. *Yanks: The Epic Story of the American Army in World War I.* New York: Free Press, 2001.

Faust, Patricia L., ed. *Historical Times Illustrated Encyclopedia of the Civil War.* New York: Harper and Row, 1986.

Fleek, Sherman L. *History Maybe Searched in Vain: A Military History of The Mormon Batalion.* Spokane, Wash.: Arthur H. Clark, 2006.

Fromkin, David. *Europe's Last Summer: Who Started the Great War in 1914?* New York: Alfred A. Knopf, 2004.

Furniss, Norman. *The Mormon Conflict, 1850–1859.* New Haven: Yale University Press, 1960.

Gilbert, Martin. *The First World War: A Complete History.* New York: Henry Holt, 1994.

Godfrey, Matthew C. "Charles W. Nibley, 1907–1925." In *Presiding Bishops,* compiled by Michael W. Winder. Salt Lake City: Eborn, 2003.

Gregory J. W. Urwin, *The Unites States Infantry: An Illustrated History, 1775–1918.* New York: Sterling, 1991.

Griffith, Paddy. *Fortifications of the Western Front, 1914–1918.* Oxford and New York: Osprey, 2004.

Heitman, Francis B. *Historical Register and Dictionary of the United States Army from Its Organization, September 29, 1789, to March 2, 1903.* 2 vols. Washington, D.C.: Government Printing Office, 1903; reprinted, Urbana: University of Illinois Press, 1965.

Hickman, William A. *Brigham's Destroying Angel, Being the Life, Confession, and Startling Disclosures of the Notorious Bill Hickman, the Danite Chief of Utah.* Edited by J. H. Beadle. New York, Shepard, 1872.

Hill, Jim Dan. *The Minute Man at War and Peace: A History of the National Guard.* Harrisburg, Pa.: Stackpole, 1964.

Holzapfel, Richard N., and T. Jeffrey Cottle. *Old Mormon Nauvoo: Historic Photographs and Guide.* Provo, Utah: Grandin, 1990.

Hopper, James. *Medals of Honor.* New York: John Day, 1929. Keegan, John. *The First World War.* New York: Alfred A. Knopf, 1999.

Kimball, Stanley B. *Heber C. Kimball: Mormon Patriarch and Pioneer.* Chicago and Urbana: University of Illinois Press, 1986.

Jenson, Andrew. *Latter-day Saint Biographical Encyclopedia.* 4 vols. Salt Lake City: Andrew Jenson Historical, 1901–1936.

Lee, David D. *Sergeant York: An American Hero.* Lexington: University Press of Kentucky, 1985.

Livesey, Anthony. *The Historical Atlas of World War I.* New York: Henry Holt, 1994.

MacArthur, Douglas. *Reminiscences; General of the Army Douglas MacArthur.* New York: McGraw-Hill, 1964.

Manchester, William. *American Caesar: Douglas MacArthur, 1880–1864.* New York: Dell, 1983.

Manning, Robert. *Above and Beyond: A History of the Medal of Honor from the Civil War to Vietnam.* Boston: Boston Publishing, 1985.

Marshall, S. L. A. *World War I.* Boston: Houghton Mifflin, 1964.

Maslowki, Peter, and Don Winslow. *Looking for a Hero: Staff Sergeant Joe Ronnie Hooper and the Vietnam War*. Lincoln and London: University of Nebraska Press, 2004.

Mason, Francis K. *Ribbons and Medals: The World's Military and Civil Awards*. New York: Doubleday, 1974.

Millet, Allan R. and Peter Maslowski. *For the Common Defense: A Military History of the United States of America*. New York: Free Press, 1984.

Nibley, Charles W. *Reminiscences, 1849–1931*. Salt Lake City: Charles W. Nibley Family, 1934.

Nofi, Albert A. *The Gettysburg Campaign: June and July 1863*. New York: Gallery Books, 1986.

Pope, Stephen. *Dictionary of the Napoleonic Wars*. New York: Facts on File, 1999.

Reilly, Henry J. *Americans All: The Rainbow at War. Official History of the 42nd Rainbow Division in the World War*, 2nd ed. Columbus, Ohio: F. J. Heer, 1936.

Roberts, B. H. *A Comprehensive History of The Church of Jesus Christ of Latter-day Saints*. 6 vols. Salt Lake City: Deseret News Press, 1930.

Roberts, Richard C. *Legacy: History of the Utah National Guard from the Nauvoo Legion Era to Enduring Freedom*. Salt Lake City: Utah Guard Association, 2003.

Scharffs, Gilbert W. *Mormonism in Germany: A History of the Church of Jesus Christ of Latter-day Saints in Germany between 1840 and 1970*. Salt Lake City: Deseret Book, 1970.

Schindler, Harold. *Orrin Porter Rockwell: Man of God/Son of Thunder*. Salt Lake City: University of Utah Press, 1966.

Scholem, G. *Sabbataai Sevi: The Mystical Messiah*. Princeton: Princeton University Press, 1973.

Smith, Joseph Jr. *History of the Church of Jesus Christ of Latter-day Saints*. 7 vols. Salt Lake City: Deseret Book, 1978.

Smythe, Donald. *Pershing: General of the Armies*. Bloomington: Indiana University Press, 1986.

Sonne, Conway B. *Saints on the Seas: A Maritime History of Mormon Migration 1830–1890*. Salt Lake City: University of Utah Press, 1983.

Tuchman, Barbara W. *The Guns of August*. New York: Ballantine, 1994.

Truss, Ruth Smith, "The Alabama National Guard's 167th Infantry Regiment in World War I," Alabama Review Vol 56. No. 1, January 2003.

Urwin, Gregory J.W. *The United States Infantry: An Illustrated History, 1775–1918*. New York: Sterling, 1991

Utley, Robert M. *Frontier Regulars: The United States Army and the Indian, 1866–1891*. Lincoln and London: University of Nebraska Press, 1973.

Vandiver, Frank E. *Blackjack: The Life and Times of John J. Pershing*. 2 Volumes. College Station: Texas A&M University, 1977.

Whitehorne, Joseph W. A. *The Inspectors General of the Unites States Army: 1903–1939*. Washington, D.C.: U.S. Army Center of Military History, 1999.

Winter, Denis. *Death's Men: Soldiers of the Great War*. New York: Penguin, 1979.

PERIODICALS

Arrington, Leonard. "Launching Idaho's Sugar Beet Industry." *Idaho's Yesterdays* (Fall 1965): 17–28.

Bennett, Richard E. '"How Long, Oh Lord, How Long?' James E. Talmage and the Great War." *The Religious Educator* 3, no. 1 (2002). 89–102

Church of Jesus Christ of Latter-day Saints. Conference Reports. October 1914 and June 1919.

Gates, Susa Young. "Alexander Neibaur." *Utah Genealogical and Historical Magazine* 91 (April 1914). 52–62

Hartley, William. "From Boys to Men: LDS Aaronic Priesthood Offices, 1879–1996." *Journal of Mormon History* (Spring 1996): 80–136.

Kuhl, Raymond. "Home Sweet Home." *Michigan History* (May/June 2002).

Lyon, Glade, comp. and ed. *Idaho's Medal of Honor Recipients*. 1990.

Neibaur, Thomas C. "How Private Neibaur Won the Congressional Medal of Honor." *Improvement Era* (July 1919): 782–90.

Time magazine, January 4, 1943.

Truss, Ruth Smith, "The Alabama National Guard's 167th Infantry Regiment in World War I." *Alabama Review* 56, no. 1 (January 2003): 3–34.

Woods, Fred E. "The Life of Alexander Neibaur." *Mormon Historical Studies* 7, nos. 1 and 2 (Spring/Fall 2006): 23–36.

NEWSPAPERS

Deseret News [Salt Lake City, Utah]

Rexburg Journal

Idaho Falls Daily Post

Idaho Journal [Pocatello]

Idaho Statesman

Salt Lake Tribune

ELECTRONIC SOURCES

www://neibaur.org/journals/alexnotes.htm

Bergen County Historical Society "Camp Merritt, New Jersey: September 1917–January 1920" www.bergencountyhistory.org

DISCUSSION QUESTIONS

- According to the article, how did the experiences of war affect American soldiers?

- What kind of hardships did American soldiers endure during World War I? Was this something for which they were prepared?

- Explore the morale of the American soldier during World War I. What was the state of mind when soldiers first joined the fighting? Was that the same when the war ended? Why or why not?

CHAPTER VIII

THE XENOPHOBIC 1920S

OBJECTIVES

- Analyze the change in focus in the United States after World War I from progressive reforms and international wars to a return inward and "business as usual".

PREWRITING

- Examine the immediate consequences of World War I. Did President Wilson oversell the war by making impossible promises to Americans? What events happened abroad during the war that would cause Americans to want to restrict immigration into the United States?

The Xenophobic 1920s

BILL ONG HING

M anifested in the Red Scare of 1919–20, the reactionary, isolationist political climate that followed World War I led to even greater exclusionist demands. To many Americans, the ghost of Bolshevism seemed to haunt the land in the specter of immigrant radicals, especially after the 1919 wave of industrial unrest in immigrantdominated workforces of the coal, steel, meatpacking, and transportation industries. In 1919, an anarchist placed a bomb on the doorstep of Attorney General A. Mitchell Palmer, and while the blast's only victim was the would-be terrorist, it sparked Palmer and his young assistant, J. Edgar Hoover, to launch a crusade to deport all alien "Reds." (See Chapter 11.) In reaction to the isolationist political climate, Congress passed a variety of laws placing numerical restrictions on immigration.

The reactionary, exclusionist sentiment of the time was combined with the ethnic. The 1917 literacy law (see Chapter 3) was inadequate for restrictionists, who remained concerned about the continuing entry of southern and eastern Europeans. Southern and eastern European immigrants numbered 4.5 million in 1910; by 1920 the figure surged to 5 .67 million. The 100 percent American campaign was alarmed that one-fifth of the California population was Italian American by then.

Shortly after the 1917 act, the Anarchist Act of 1918 expanded the provisions for exclusion and deportation of subversive aliens and authorized their expulsion without time limitations. Until that time, the law had dealt only with the quality of the aliens who sought to enter from Europe through the literacy requirement. The number of Chinese, Japanese, and most other Asians was under control by then. No attempt had been made to limit the number of eastern and southern European entrants. At the conclusion of World War I, immigration again began to increase. Widespread fear of inundation by a flood of immigrants from the war-devastated countries of Europe developed. The isolationist mood of the period and a severe postwar depression augmented the already strong sentiment for further restrictions.[1]

In addition to the menace of leftist political influence emanating from parts of Europe, public and congressional arguments in support of more restrictive legislation stressed recurring themes: the racial superiority of Anglo-Saxons, the fact that immigrants would cause the lowering of wages, the unassimilability of foreigners, and the usual threats to the nation's social unity and order posed by immigration. Popular biological theories of the period alleging the superiority of certain races were influential. The theories of Dr. Harry N. Laughlin, a eugenics consultant to the House Judiciary Committee on Immigration and Naturalization in the 1920s, were influential:

> We in this country have been so imbued with the idea of democracy, or the equality of all men, that we have left out of consideration the matter of blood or natural born hereditary mental and moral differences. No man who breeds pedigreed plants and animals can afford to neglect this thing....
>
> The National Origins provisions of the immigration control law of 1924 marked the actual turning point from immigration control based on the asylum idea ... definitely in favor of the biological basis.[2]

The immigration laws of the 1920s were the culmination of strong political and social arguments that eastern and southern Europeans were not the right stock from which true Americans were bred.

UNDERSTANDING THE SACCO AND VANZETTI CASE IN THE CONTEXT OF AMERICA IN THE 1920S

The confluence of negative social and political images of certain unwanted immigrants in the 1920s is epitomized by the Sacco and Vanzetti case. Negative sentiment toward Italian immigrants was exacerbated by the arrest of two immigrants, Nicola Sacco and Bartolomeo Vanzetti, for armed robbery and murder. Sacco and Vanzetti were

THE XENOPHOBIC 1920S | 143

poor, atheists, and draft dodgers. They were exactly the kind of people Americans felt might be guilty of anything. In addition, they were anarchists who believed, as many anarchists did, that violence could remedy the injustices of society.[3]

At 3:00 P.M. on April 15, 1920, a paymaster and his guard were carrying a factory payroll of $15,776 through the main street of South Braintree, Massachusetts, a small industrial town south of Boston. Two men standing by a fence suddenly pulled out guns and fired on them. The gunmen snatched up the cash boxes dropped by the mortally wounded pair and jumped into a waiting automobile. The bandit gang, numbering four or five in all, sped away, eluding their pursuers. At first this brutal murder and robbery, not uncommon in post–World War I America, aroused only local interest.

Three weeks later, on the evening of May 5, 1920, Sacco and Vanzetti fell into a police trap that had been set for a suspect in the Braintree crime. Both men were carrying guns at the time of their arrest and their behavior aroused suspicion. As a result they were held and eventually indicted for the Braintree crimes. Vanzetti was also charged with an earlier holdup attempt that had taken place on December 24, 1919, in the nearby town of Bridgewater. This marked the beginning of one of twentieth- century America's most notorious political trials.

Contrary to the usual practice of Massachusetts's courts, Vanzetti was tried first in the summer of 1920 on the lesser of the two charges, the failed Bridgewater robbery. Despite a strong alibi supported by many witnesses, Vanzetti was found guilty. Most of Vanzetti's witnesses were Italians who spoke English poorly, and their trial testimony, given largely in translation, failed to convince the jury. Vanzetti's case had also been seriously damaged when he, for fear of revealing his radical activities, did not take the stand in his own defense.

For a first criminal offense in which no one was harmed, Vanzetti received a prison sentence that was much harsher than usual—ten to fifteen years. This signaled to the two men and their supporters a hostile bias on the part of the authorities that was political in nature and pointed to the need for a new defense strategy in the Braintree trial. The arrest of Sacco and Vanzetti coincided with the intensive, politically repressive Red Scare era of 1919 to 1920. The police trap they had fallen into had been set for a comrade of theirs, suspected primarily because he was a foreign-born radical.

While neither Sacco nor Vanzetti had any previous criminal record, they were long recognized by the authorities and by their communities as anarchist militants who had been extensively involved in labor strikes, political agitation, and antiwar propaganda. They were also known to be dedicated supporters of Luigi Galleani's Italian-language journal *Cronaca Sovversiva*, the most influential anarchist journal in America, feared by the authorities for its militancy and its acceptance of revolutionary violence.

Cronaca, because of its uncompromising antiwar stance, had been forced to halt publication immediately upon the entry of the U.S. government into World War I in 1917. Several of its editors were arrested and at war's end deported to Italy in 1919.

The repression of the journal involved a bitter social struggle between the U.S. government and the journal's supporters. It was a former editor of *Cronaca* who was suspected of blowing himself up during a bombing attempt at Attorney General Palmer's home in Washington, D.C., on June 2, 1919; that act led Congress to vote funds for antiradical investigations and launched the career of J. Edgar Hoover as the director of the General Intelligence Division in the Department of Justice. The Sacco–Vanzetti case would become one of Hoover's first major responsibilities.

In 1920, as the Italian anarchist movement was trying to regroup, Andrea Salsedo, a comrade of Sacco and Vanzetti, was detained and, while in custody of the Department of Justice, hurled to his death. On the night of Sacco's and Vanzetti's arrests, authorities found in Sacco's pocket a draft of a handbill for an anarchist meeting that featured Vanzetti as the main speaker. In this treacherous atmosphere, when initial questioning by the police focused on their radical activities and not on the specifics of the Braintree crime, the two men lied about their political views.

THE TRIAL AND ITS AFTERMATH

These falsehoods created a "consciousness of guilt" in the minds of the authorities, but the implications of that phrase soon became a central issue in the Sacco-Vanzetti case. Did the lies of the two men signify criminal involvement in the Braintree murder and robbery, as the authorities claimed, or an understandable attempt to conceal their radicalism and protect their friends during a time of national hysteria concerning foreign-born radicals, as their supporters were to claim? On the advice of the anarchist militant and editor Carlo Tresca, a new legal counsel was brought in—Fred H. Moore, a well- known socialist lawyer from the West. He had collaborated in many labor and IWW trials and was especially noted for his important role in the celebrated Ettor–Giovannitti case, which came out of a 1912 textile strike in Lawrence, Massachusetts.

Moore completely changed the nature of the legal strategy. He decided it was no longer possible to defend Sacco and Vanzetti solely against the criminal charges of murder and robbery. Instead, he would have them frankly acknowledge their anarchism in court, try to establish that their arrest and prosecution stemmed from their radical activities, and dispute the prosecution's insistence that only hard, nonpolitical evidence had implicated the two men in common crimes. Moore would try to expose the prosecution's hidden motive: its desire to aid the federal and military authorities in suppressing the Italian anarchist movement to which Sacco and Vanzetti belonged.

Moore's defense of the two men soon became so openly and energetically political that its scope quickly transcended its local roots. He organized public meetings, solicited the support of labor unions, contacted international organizations, initiated new investigations, and distributed tens of thousands of defense pamphlets throughout the United States and the world. Much to the chagrin of some anarchist comrades, Moore would even enlist the aid of the Italian government in the defense of Sacco and Vanzetti, who were still, nominally at least, Italian citizens. Moore's aggressive strategy transformed a little known case into an international cause célèbre.

On July 14, 1921, after a hard-fought, six-week trial, during which the themes of patriotism and radicalism were often sharply debated by the prosecution and the defense, the jury found Sacco and Vanzetti guilty of robbery and murder. However, the verdict marked only the beginning of a lengthy legal struggle to save the two men. It extended until 1927, during which time the defense made many separate motions, appeals, and petitions to both state and federal courts in an attempt to gain a new trial.

The petitions and motions contained evidence of perjury by prosecution witnesses, indications of illegal activities by the police and the federal authorities, a confession to the Braintree crimes by convicted bank robber Celestino Madeiros, and powerful evidence that identified the actual gang involved in the Braintree affair as the notorious Morelli Gang. All of the requests were rejected by Judge Webster Thayer, the same judge who earlier had so severely sentenced Vanzetti. Judge Thayer even ruled on a motion accusing him of judicial prejudice. His conduct—or misconduct—during the trials and the appeals was another of the controversial issues surrounding the case, but it too would prove insufficient to bring about a new trial.

From the beginning, Moore's strategy of politicizing the trial in tradition-bound Massachusetts had been controversial and confrontational. His manner of utilizing the mass media was quite modern and effective in terms of publicizing the case, but it required enormous sums of money, which he spent too freely in the eyes of many of the anarchist comrades of Sacco and Vanzetti, who had to raise most of it painstakingly from workingpeople, twenty-five and fifty cents at a time. Moore's efforts were called into question even by the defendants, when he, contrary to anarchist ideals, offered a large reward to find the real criminals. As a result, in 1924 a respected Boston lawyer, William Thompson, replaced Moore and assumed control of the legal defense. Thompson, a Brahmin who wanted to defend the reputation of Massachusetts law as well as the two men, had no particular sympathy for the ideas of the two men, but he later came to admire them deeply as individuals.

Thompson's defense focus no longer emphasized the political, but these aspects of the case, once they had been set in motion, could not be stopped and continued to gain momentum. Throughout America, liberals and well-meaning people of every sort, troubled and outraged by the injustice of the legal process, joined the more politically radical anarchists, Socialists, and Communists in protesting the verdict against Sacco and Vanzetti. Harvard law professor Felix Frankfurter, the future Supreme Court justice, who did more than any individual to rally "respectable" opinion behind the two men, saw the case as a test of the rule of law itself. His own research revealed that members of the "Joe Morelli gang" and "Celestino Madeiros" were the culprits at South Braintree, not Sacco and Vanzetti. Standing against the defenders of Sacco and Vanzetti were conservatives and patriots who wanted to defend the honor of American justice and to uphold law and order. The defendants' detractors came to see these protests as an attack upon the "American way of life" on behalf of two common criminals.

On April 9, 1927, after all recourse in the Massachusetts courts had failed, Sacco and Vanzetti were sentenced to death. By then the dignity and the words of the two men had turned them into powerful symbols of social justice for many throughout the world. Public agitation on their behalf by radicals, workers, immigrants, and Italians had become international in scope, and many demonstrations in the world's great cities—Paris, London, Mexico City, and Buenos Aires—protested the unfairness of their trial. Prominent individuals like Albert Einstein, Anatole France, Dorothy Parker, Thomas Mann, John Dos Passos, and Edna St. Vincent Millay spoke in favor of the defendants. Letters of protest flooded American consulates and embassies in Europe and South America. Judge Webster Thayer's house was placed under protection. The *Communist International* urged all Communists, Socialists, anarchists, and trade unionists to organize efforts to rescue Sacco and Vanzetti.

This great public pressure, combined with influential behind-the-scenes interventions, finally persuaded the governor of Massachusetts, Alvan T. Fuller, to consider the question of executive clemency for the two men. It was at this penultimate moment that Fuller asked Harvard President Lawrence Lowell to head a special commission—one of the century's notorious "blue-ribbon panels" designed to legitimate state authority—to review the Sacco and Vanzetti case. The Lowell Commission began with an assumption of guilt and, while it criticized certain aspects of Judge Thayer's conduct, the panel upheld the verdict and sentence. An appeal to President Calvin Coolidge was refused. Sacco and Vanzetti were electrocuted on August 21, 1927.[4]

After their execution, the fight to clear Sacco's and Vanzetti's names continued for the next fifty years. In 1977, then-Massachusetts Governor Michael Dukakis issued a proclamation declaring August 2 3 a memorial day for Sacco and Vanzetti, as well as all the Italian immigrants who had been denied a fair trial. This proclamation, which was based on the review of the case by Dukakis's legal counsel, recognized for the first time that the prosecutors and Judge Webster Thayer had committed a variety of abuses during the trial. It sought to vindicate the names of Sacco and Vanzetti and their families, and called for vigilance "against our susceptibility to prejudice, our intolerance of unorthodox ideas and our failure to defend the rights of persons who are looked upon as strangers in our midst."

Massachusetts's attempts to clear Sacco and Vanzetti—and its own reputation—continued as recently as 1997. On the seventieth anniversary of their execution, Thomas Menino, the first Italian American mayor of Boston, formally accepted and dedicated a memorial to Sacco and Vanzetti that had been previously rejected three times. The bronze sculpture, made in 1927 by Gutzon Borglum, who is best known for carving the presidential faces in Mt. Rushmore, shows Sacco and Vanzetti facing tilted scales of justices. Borglum carved it when President Calvin Coolidge refused to grant them a stay of execution. Merino said that accepting the memorial was Boston's acknowledgment that Sacco and Vanzetti did not receive a fair trial.[5]

The 1927 outcome of the Sacco and Vanzetti case effectively killed the anarchist movement in the Italian American community. Italian anarchists created a sort of "alternative society" within American capitalism. They formed in their communities small enclaves, close networks of family and friends. Their strong ethical imperative was part of their culture as much as the belief in the necessity of violence in political activity. It informed not only the urge to political action as a means to obtain freedom and justice, but their social norms and personal code of behavior as well. Their networks were bound by deeply felt solidarity, by a sense of belonging to a community with a mission, and by a commitment to the betterment of humanity. The vivid vignettes of militant anarchists support, albeit with romantic overtones, such a contention.[6]

The revolutionary anarchists believed that social revolution was not just a remote possibility. They may have been mistaken, but their view was far from irrational. Before 1914 the world—at least the world of Europe and the cultures derived from it— was still full of hope.[7]

When the United States entered the war in 1917, a great wave of repression was mobilized against all radical movements in the country. The war meant the triumph of American finance-capitalism and the American state, and it brought down the curtain on the radical movements of the time. [8]

By the time that Sacco and Vanzetti were arrested, the work of repression had been done. The Italian-immigrant anarchist movement did not disappear but it gradually ceased to be a significant force, and with the cut off of immigration its years were numbered.[9]

Italian immigrants did, of course, come from a country where traditions of antiauthoritarianism—antistate, anticlerical, antipadrone—were strong and the same kind of battles as in the United States were in fact fought out in Italy during the same era. More than immigrants from some other countries, Italian immigrants may have brought with them a certain intolerance toward authoritarian systems. But only a few came with radical ideas; they sought a better life and found a world that was not very different from the old. If in Italy they had been despised as peasants, here they were despised as Italians. Their life-situations and job-situations in the United States, and the political and economic developments here, were the reasons why many Italian immigrants, like immigrants from other cultures, were responsive to radical ideas, including anarchism. The Italian immigrants heard these anarchist ideas mainly from intellectuals who escaped persecution at home by going off to the New World, where they helped create new circles of anarchism. Unintentionally, the Italian government contributed to the dissemination of anarchism around the world: the anarchist ideas of the exiles found resonance in the lives immigrants were living.[10]

NATIONAL ORIGINS QUOTAS

On the immigration policy front, the result of the continued assault on southern and eastern European immigrants was the Quota Law of 1921, enacted as a temporary measure. This legislation introduced for the first time numerical limitations on immigration. With certain exceptions, the law allocated quotas to each nationality totaling 3 percent of the foreign-born persons of that nationality residing in the United States in 1910, for an annual total of approximately 350,000. Since most of those living in the United States in 1910 were northern or western European, the quota for southern and eastern Europeans was smaller (about 45,000 less). The latter groups filled their quotas easily, but northern and western European countries did not fill their quotas under this law,[11] This law was scheduled to expire in 1922, but was extended to June 30, 1924.

In. the meantime, a permanent policy of numerical restrictions was under consideration and was enacted in 1924. One problem with the 1910 model for the 1921 law was that that was the end of the decade that had witnessed a large influx of southern and eastern Europeans. So a 1910 population model would include a higher proportion of southern and eastern Europeans than earlier years. Thus, the landmark Immigration Act of 1924, opposed by only six senators, took an even greater malicious aim at southern and eastern Europeans, whom the Protestant majority in the United States viewed with dogmatic disapproval.

The 1924 legislation adopted a national origins formula that eventually based the quota for each nationality on the number of foreign-born persons of that national origin in the United States in 1890—prior to the major wave of southern and eastern Europeans. The law provided that immigrants of any particular country be reduced from 3 percent under the 1921 law to 2 percent of the group's population under the new law. And instead of 1910 as the population model year for determining how many could enter, the 2 percent was based on a particular nationality's population in 1890, when even fewer immigrants from southern and eastern Europe lived in the United States. The message could not have been clearer: the racial and ethnic makeup of the country in 1890 should be perpetuated, prior to the influx of southern and eastern

Europeans (and, for that matter, Asians). The quota formula was hailed as the "most far reaching change that occurred in America during the course of this quarter century," enabling a halt to "the tendency toward a change in the fundamental composition of the American stock." The *fundamental American stock* was western European, and the quota laws were designed to keep it that way.

This formula resulted in a sharp curtailment of immigrants from southern and eastern Europe, and struck most deeply at Jews, Italians, Slavs, and Greeks, who had immigrated in great numbers after, and who would be most disfavored by such a quota system. Quota immigrants were limited to approximately 165,000 per year, with the proportion and number even smaller for southern and eastern Europeans than before. However, natives of the Western Hemisphere countries could enter without numerical restriction. Other nonquota groups included wives and children of U.S. citizens and returning lawful residents. Those who entered in violation of visa and quota requirements were deportable without time limitation. Another provision, aimed at Asians, barred all aliens ineligible to citizenship, thus completely barring Japanese (as well as all other Asians), some of whom had continued to enter under the 1907 Gentlemen's Agreement. (See Chapter 2.)

The 1924 law provided that in 1929 a new quota would take effect. The national origins formula used the ethnic background of the entire U.S. population, rather than the first-generation immigration population, as its base for calculating national quotas. Because the U.S. population was still predominantly Anglo-Saxon, the national origins quota restricted the newer immigrant groups more severely than the foreign-born formula of the previous quota laws. The national origins quota allotted 8 5 percent of the total 150,000 to countries from northern and western Europe, while southern and eastern countries received only 15 percent of the total.

The national origins formula was complicated by economic times. Soon after it took effect, the U.S. economy collapsed. The Great Depression limited immigration; only about half a million immigrants arrived during the 1930s. (See Appendix.) In 1932, at the height of the Great Depression, emigration far exceeded immigration, as *35,576* entered while over 100,000 departed. The potential for immigration increased during those years, however, with the growth of highways and increased airplane traffic. By 1938, there were 186 ports of entry into the country. On June 14, 1940, the INS was transferred from the Department of Labor to the Department of Justice.[12]

The impact of the national origins quota system on the southern and eastern European population in the United States is evident from census information on the foreign-born population of the country. They numbered about 1.67 million in 1900. After the big immigrant wave of the first decade of the twentieth century, the figure almost tripled to 4.5 million in 1910. The population surged again in the next decade to 5.67 million in 1920. However, after the quota systems of 1921 and 1924 took effect, the number of immigrants from those regions of Europe declined. (See charts in the Introduction.) The population increased to only 5.92 million by 1930. The figures for immigrants from specific countries are also telling. The population of Italian immigrants increased only 11.18 percent between 1920 and 1930, after experiencing a 176 percent jump in the first decade of the century. The number of Polish immigrants in the United States increased only 11.4 percent during the 1920s, and the number of Hungarians in the country actually declined from 397,283 to 274,450.

CONCLUSION

The national origins quota laws of the 1920s resulted from the continued sense of ethnic and racial superiority of Anglo or western European stock for the foundation of who could become a true American. The 1917 literacy law alone was insufficient to stem the flow of Jews, Catholics, and Italians seeking to immigrate. By reverting to the 1890 population as the model from which to gauge the "right" proportion of immigrants to enter, southern and eastern Europeans were blatantly targeted, since their U.S. populations were relatively small in that census. The 1920s also witnessed increasing hysteria aimed at Socialists and anarchists, many of whom were believed to be developing in southern and eastern Europe. Sacco and Vanzetti and their supporters came to epitomize all that was potentially wrong with Italian immigrants: they were poor, not particularly educated, non-English-speaking, Catholic, and filled with radical anarchist ideals on behalf of the working class.

The Immigration Acts of 1917 and 1924 thus became the twin elements of immigration policy, one proclaiming qualitative restrictions and the other numerical limitations. These provisions remained pillars of immigration policy for decades.

NOTES

1 Charles Gordon and Harry Rosenfield, *Immigration Law and Procedure* 1–11 to 1–12 (New York: Matthew Bender, 1981).

2 Arnold H. Leibowitz, *Immigration Law and Refugee Policy* 1–10 to 1–11 (New York: Matthew Bender, 1983).

3 Interview with Arthur Schlesinger, Jr. accessed at <http://www.courttv.com/greatesttrials/sacco.vanzetti/schlesinger.html on October 18, 2001>.

4 "The Sacco-Vanzetti Project 2002: 75 Years Since the Execution" accessed at <http://www.saccovanzettiproject.org/pages/hstrcl.htmbon October 8, 2001.

5 Drawn from *The Case of Sacco and Vanzetti*, an article running in March 1927, in *The Atlantic* by Feliz Frankfurter. Accessed at <wysiwyg://104/http://www.theatlantic.com/unbound/flashbks/oj/frankff.html> on September 22, 2001.

For more information on this topic see also *Men, Mobs and the Law: Defense Campaigns and United States Radical History* by Rebecca Nell Hill, Ph.D. diss., University of Minnesota, 2000.

6 Another example of the influence the two men played in social culture was the Official Bulletin of the Sacco-Vanzetti Defense Committee of Boston, Massachusetts. The committee was concerned with efforts to obtain a new trial for Sacco and Vanzetti after their conviction for the murder of F. A. Pamenter and A. Bardelli in Massachusetts.

7 David Wieck, *What Need Be Said*, Sacco Vanzetii Project 2002: 75 Years Since The Execution, at <http://www.saccovanzettiproject.org/pages/context/wiecke.html>.

8 Id.

9 Id.

10 Id.

11 There was a nonquota exception of which some southern and eastern Europeans took advantage. The law permitted a person to be admitted to the United States as an immigrant if the individual had resided in the Western Hemisphere for one year (later changed to five years). So by temporarily living in a Western Hemisphere country, the quota could be avoided.

12 David Weissbrodt, *Immigration Law and Procedure* 13 (St. Paul, Minn.: West Group, 1998).

DISCUSSION QUESTIONS

- After examining the article, why were Sacco and Vanzetti on trial? Was it because they were foreign? Or that their politics were unacceptable and seen as dangerous by the standards of the time?

- In what ways didMoore attempt to defend Sacco and Vanzetti? Did he appeal to logic or emotion? Given the attitudes in the United States in the 1920s, was this an effective strategy?

CHAPTER IX

DEPRESSION

DEPRIVATION AND DESPAIR

OBJECTIVES

- Analyze the effects of the Great Depression on Americans.

PREWRITING

- What were the causes of the Great Depression? Were average Americans prepared for it? How did they endure the hardships of the Depression?

Depression
Deprivation and Despair

JANET POPPENDIECK

The stock market crash in the autumn of 1929 did not immediately cause grave apprehension among farm leaders. Some segments of the agricultural press, in fact, believed that the collapse of paper values might help to restore balance between the farm and nonfarm sectors. "The farmers of America are milking their cows and slopping their pigs as usual, while mother gets the breakfast and dresses the children for school," commented the *Prairie Farmer* in November. "Farm conditions are steadily improving, and the deflation of stock speculation will help to give farmers more adequate and cheaper credit, and to teach the nation that the stockyards are more important than the stock market."[1]

Like so many other optimistic predictions in the aftermath of the Crash, hope that the farmer was somehow immune to the impact of rapid deflation proved to be ill founded. The onset of the Depression intensified farm problems. When employment fell off, so did the nation's ability to buy farm products. As millions of unemployed workers and their families cut meat, milk, and fresh produce from their diets in an attempt to get by on savings or scanty relief, the food they could not afford piled up in warehouses or rotted in the fields, signaling deeper ruin in the countryside.

As the Depression deepened, industrialists were able to protect their price structure to some degree by curtailing output. In agriculture, price rather than output bore the brunt of adjustment to the Depression-induced decline in demand. Between 1929 and 1934, while industrial production declined 42 percent in volume and 15 percent in price, agricultural production declined only 15 percent in volume but 40 percent in price. The disparity between industrial and agricultural prices that had angered and mobilized farmers throughout the twenties grew worse. In comparison with the prewar years of 1910–1914, the ratio of the prices farmers received to the prices they paid for industrial goods fell from 109 in 1919 and 89 in 1929 to 64 in 1931. The proceeds from sixteen bushels of wheat, more than the average yield of an entire acre, were required to purchase a four dollar pair of shoes. In Iowa, some found it more economical to burn corn as fuel than to feed it to hogs that brought less than three dollars per hundredweight. [2]

The intensification of farm problems altered the focus of Federal Farm Board activities from the organization of cooperatives to price-supporting purchases. In the face of rapid accumulation of huge wheat and cotton surpluses and disastrous breaks in the prices of these two commodities, the Farm Board financed purchases of millions of bushels of wheat and bales of cotton through the Grain and Cotton Stabilization Corporations. The stabilization operations originally had been intended as a means of holding minor, temporary surpluses off the market for brief periods of time, not as a method for dealing with major overproduction, and they were not accompanied by any measures to reduce the quantities of wheat and cotton produced. As a result, the Farm Board's stocks of wheat and cotton grew steadily, and although the price declines were apparently slowed by the board's actions, prices remained so low that the organization could not sell its holdings without defeating its own purposes and adding to the difficulties of farmers. In fact, when the board announced its withdrawal from the wheat market in June 1931, stating that it could not justify further wheat purchases, the Kansas City price of wheat plunged approximately twenty-seven cents a bushel, undoing much of the price supporting effect of the board's purchases. As in any situation of sharp price fluctuation, those growers, cooperatives, and handlers who sold while the price was supported benefited from Farm Board operations while those who sold too early or too late did not, and the Farm Board made many enemies. [3]

Farmers might have withstood the sharp price declines brought about by the Depression had they not been so severely burdened by taxes and debts. Both had been calculated when prices were significantly higher, and much farm debt had been contracted at inflated wartime interest rates. New Deal historian Arthur Schlesinger has provided a cogent summary of the farmers' plight: "A cotton farmer who borrowed $800 when cotton was 16 cents a pound borrowed the equivalent of 5000 pounds of cotton; now, with cotton moving towards 5 cents, he must pay back the debt with over 15,000 pounds of cotton." [4]

The result of the overwhelming debt burden was, in many cases, forced sale: mortgage foreclosure, bankruptcy, or delinquent tax sale—the heartbreaking loss of home, land, and years of investment. Agricultural economists estimate that in the years 1930–1935 as many as one-sixth of all farms in the nation were subject to forced sale of some type. The percentage would be even higher for farms producing significant commercial crops since many small subsistence farms lacked commercial value and thus were not mortgaged. Furthermore, the figure masks the additional thousands of supposedly voluntary sales that were actually debt-induced transfers to mortgagees.[5]

The figure also masks the human realities of debt-financed farming. The contemporary reader may have difficulty in appreciating the personal tragedies behind the statistics. One farmer, writing to the Rockefeller Foundation in search of help, articulated the poignant mixture of fears, hopes, and frustrations that told the story of thousands:

> we are going to have to give up our place the first Monday in January to the People's State Bank of Abbeville for $3500 mortgage. During normal times this property was worth from ten to fifteen thousand dollars. Work is very scarce in this county at the present time and we are very much in need of some assistance at this time. I am fifty years old, married and have two daughters fourteen and twelve years respectively. They are unusually bright and attractive children and I am so anxious to have them get as good an education as possible.[6]

Even the loss of a farm, and with it the hope for a comfortable old age or the plan for a child's education, did not necessarily free the farm family from the mesh of indebtedness. "The struggles people had to go through are almost unbelievable," recalls a farmer interviewed by Studs Terkel. "A man lived all his life on a given farm, it was taken away from him. One after the other. After the foreclosure, they got a deficiency judgment. Not only did he lose his farm, but it was impossible for him to get out of debt."[7] A farmer's wife remembers the bitterness of forced sale:

> This neighbor woman lost her husband, and of course he was owing in the bank. So the auctioneers come out there, and she served lunch, and she stood weeping in the windows. "There goes our last cow…." And the horses. She called 'em by names. It just pretty near broke our hearts. They didn't give her a chance to take care of her bills. They never gave her an offer. They just came and cleared it out. She just stood there crying.[8]

Some of the dispossessed became tenant farmers on the farms they had once owned. Some found work as hired hands or joined the swelling ranks of migrant laborers. Some remained near the land they had farmed, subsisting on charity and hoping for better days, a human reminder to their more fortunate neighbors of the consequences of the Depression. "To see these neighbors wiped out completely," another Iowa survivor recalls, "and they would just drift into towns and they would have to be fed."[9]

Dispossessed farmers constituted only a fraction of those who had to be fed. Unemployment had already begun to rise in 1928. In the months following the Crash, it spread across the nation like a killing frost, reaching at least 4 million wage earners, or nearly one out of every ten, by the spring of 1930. No one knew exactly how many people were out of work because the nation had no system for collecting such information, but most estimates agreed that the number of jobless workers had climbed to nearly 8 million by the spring of 1931 and grew steadily until the spring of 1933 when the most widely accepted figures indicated that approximately 15 million persons, or a third of the work force, were out of work.[10] There was no public unemployment insurance to cushioned the blow. Despite years of effort by Progressives, no state had an unemployment insurance law on the books when the Depression began. A few employers had experimented with plans voluntarily, and a few labor unions maintained unemployment funds or negotiated contracts including employer payments, but the proportion of the unemployed covered by such arrangements never reached even one percent of the labor force.[11] Being fired or laid off during the Depression meant the abrupt and complete termination of income, often without warning.

For the individual worker, the path from layoff to relief line was a bitter one. At first, the family lived on savings and the hope of finding another job. Occasionally, a wife or child was able to find part-time work. Then, as unemployment grew and factories posted permanent "no help wanted" signs, both the hopes and the savings ran out. Borrowing came next—against insurance policies until they lapsed, from more fortunate friends and relatives, and finally as credit from the grocer and sometimes the landlord. An extensive study of the impact of unemployment undertaken by the National Federation of Settlements under the leadership of Helen Hall found that after savings and insurance policies lapsed, most families sold their furniture or lost it through failure to meet payments, then failed to meet mortgage payments and lost their homes, and finally sold or pawned wedding rings and other personal effects. Many doubled up with other families in already crowded apartments to save on rent. Almost all cut back substantially on food. They did not apply for relief until they had piled up mountains of unpaid bills and all forms of credit had been exhausted.[12] "The human consequences of prolonged unemployment," social welfare historian Clarke Chambers tells us, "were unhappily easy to summarize: malnutrition, sickness, comfortless homes, crowded housing, family discord, desertion, lowered morale and loss of self respect, humiliation and pervading anxiety, hopes abandoned for talented young children, bitterness and resentment for the parents."[13]

In his intensive case studies of families of unemployed workers, E. Wight Bakke documented the impact of job loss on family consumption patterns. "Economy," he reported, "was chiefly exercised through the curtailing of expenditures involved in the normal pattern of food supply." The families in his sample spent an average of eight cents per person per meal and an average of 39 percent of their total expenditure on food. Guests were no longer invited to dinner; some families cut the number of meals per day from three to two. Fresh fruit disappeared, and eggs replaced meat; margarine or "drippings" replaced butter. "Dependence on one staple almost exclusively under the impact of severe reduction in income was not uncommon," according to Bakke. "The staple tended to vary with the national or racial group: macaroni for the Italians, corn bread for the negroes [sic], beans supplemented by pancakes for the native White Americans…. Monotony is not the only vice of such limited diets," he concluded. "In the words of one man whose family lived for nearly a month on soup, beans and spaghetti, 'You know that stuff fills you up, but you don't feel right; no pep or fight. You just want to sleep all the time." For many families, Bakke found, giving up milk was the most difficult adjustment. He reports the reaction of a former clock company employee: "When you give up milk, as you finally do if you ain't on relief—they make an allowance for it—why then maybe for the first time you think you might be better off on relief."[14] Eventually, millions of families swallowed their pride and applied for aid from local governments or voluntary (private) social agencies. And as they did so in increasing numbers, the inadequacy of pre-Depression relief arrangements became steadily more obvious.

The English Poor Law tradition of local responsibility for relief of destitution with heavy reliance on private charity had taken firm root in American soil. The isolation of the frontier settlements and plantations, the fierce independence of the incorporated towns, the religious and ethnic diversity that fostered mutual aid arrangements among successive waves of immigrants all contributed to the notion that the American way of relief was exemplified by self-reliant communities of neighbors taking care of their own. As industrialization and urbanization eroded the social and economic basis for this approach and the poor became strangers rather than neighbors, their incarceration in almshouses or county poor farms where they could be carefully supervised became the preferred method of assistance. The almshouses, however, were not able to keep up with the volume of misery produced in a largely unregulated industrializing economy, and each succeeding depression left more people receiving outdoor relief, that is, relief in their own or a relative's home rather than "indoors" in an institution. In the late nineteenth century, the Charity Organization Movement, strongly influenced by Social Darwinist ideology, attacked public relief, both as an inducement to indolence among the poor and as a hotbed of graft and corruption among urban political bosses. Although the Charity Organization societies that developed in most of the nation's large cities generally fell short of their goal of eliminating tax-funded outdoor relief altogether, they did succeed in imposing their own approach of careful investigation and supervision—the emerging methods of social casework—on many public and most voluntary relief agencies. The Progressive movement of the early twentieth century that emphasized the prevention of poverty by protecting workers from illness, industrial hazards, and exploitation gave some attention to relief and secured "mother's aid" or "widow's pension" legislation in some states, but only a few states actually contributed any state funds, and all made participation a local option. The development of professional social work in the postwar era and the growing fascination with psychological explanations for behavior increased the emphasis placed by both municipal and voluntary relief agencies on individual factors leading to poverty and dependency and thus on supervision and treatment of relief clients.[15]

Both ideologically and organizationally then, the nation was unprepared for the relief task imposed by massive unemployment. Many small towns or rural areas had no relief agencies at all or none except a county poorhouse that served as a dumping ground for the destitute aged, the retarded, the severely handicapped, and the mildly insane. Large cities generally had some form of "home relief" or public outdoor relief geared to helping a few thousand families; in addition, urban areas often had a haphazard patchwork of voluntary agencies, each with its own special focus, one serving a particular neighborhood, another serving a single religious or ethnic group, another devoted to a specific problem or task. Only in a few communities were these agencies organized into a local community chest or united fund. For disaster relief in case of flood, fire, or other acts of God, a chapter of the American National Red Cross provided aid, and rescue missions or shelters furnished bed and board for the homeless and transient. Inadequate even in good years, such relief arrangements were rapidly overwhelmed by the avalanche of need unleashed by the Depression.[16]

Despite the obvious inadequacies of this hodgepodge of voluntary and municipal relief efforts, belief in the superiority of the American way of neighborly concern was widely shared at the outset of the Depression. Mayors and social welfare leaders joined governors and members of Congress in pointing with dismay to the British dole, and asserting the value and capability of local institutions. No one was a more ardent champion of the American way than the president himself. Hoover believed strongly that "personal feeling and personal responsibility of men to their neighbors [were] the soul of genuine good will ... the essential foundation of modern society," and he continued to assert the superiority of individual generosity throughout his term of office. "A cold and distant charity which puts out its sympathy only through the tax collector," he told a 1932 audience, "yields only a very meager dole of unloving and perfunctory relief."[11] Where voluntary giving was unable to meet the need and public funds were necessary, Hoover believed that responsibility rested firmly at the local level of government where he saw "the very basis of self government"[18] and "the bedrock principle of our liberties."[19]

Given these beliefs and his conviction that stressing unemployment would shake business confidence and retard recovery, it is not surprising that the president was slow to organize unemployment relief efforts nor that he adopted a policy of "official optimism" concerning the depth and duration of the nation's economic problems. Not until the fall of 1930 did the president appoint a presidential body to assist local communities in coping with unemployment, and even then, the President's Emergency Committee for Employment (PECE) was to provide only coordination, information exchange, and encouragement to local bodies.[20] Despite the appointment of the PECE, the flow of optimistic predictions by those in power continued. The president, echoed by many of the nation's governors and the heads of major corporations and financial institutions, maintained a steady barrage of hopeful pronouncements: the "business downturn" would be short lived, it represented a healthy purge of inflated paper values, and prosperity awaited a strengthened nation "just around the corner." Hardly anyone talked about a depression, and no one knew how many people were in need of assistance.[21]

Such official optimism retarded the development of sound relief measures, and initial efforts to respond to the growing unemployment problem were pitifully inadequate. Local governments and community chests sponsored spruce-up and odd-job campaigns to persuade homeowners to create jobs for the unemployed; garden plots were allocated so that those out of work could grow their own vegetables; and the jobless were exhorted to use their initiative to devise such small enterprises as selling fruit or pencils. Even New York Congressman Fiorello La Guardia, soon to emerge as a champion of federal relief, proposed a scheme whereby every man with a job would buy a suit for an unemployed man, thus stimulating employment in the garment industry. Upon finding a job, presumably because he was so well dressed, the beneficiary would in turn purchase a suit for another jobless worker.[22] Very few voices were heard predicting a long depression or calling for major changes in the distribution of relief.

Nevertheless, the actual relief-giving agencies soon encountered a steady increase in applications for assistance. In major cities studied by social work administrator and historian Josephine Brown, for example, the number of families receiving assistance quadrupled between the first quarter of 1929 and early 1931. At first both private and municipal agencies, recognizing that the new poor were accustomed to working for a living, established work relief programs and attempted to create jobs that would not compete with private industry nor give hard-pressed local governments an excuse to cut payrolls. But local work relief, whether privately or publicly funded, could not keep up with the rising tide of unemployment. As the volume of need expanded, both municipal and private agencies modified their programs and sought ways of making the relief dollar go further. Community chest–supported agencies curtailed recreational and counseling activities to free funds for more tangible assistance. At first, the private family agencies continued the provision of cash grants for relief, a practice valued because it allowed some freedom of choice to recipients. As caseloads grew to staggering proportions, however, the time once available for supervising clients disappeared, and the portion of the family budget that the agency could supply dwindled. Many agencies adopted an emergency or disaster relief approach, replacing cash with grocery orders or direct provision of goods "in kind," that is, groceries, secondhand clothing, or household items.[23]

As the pressure on the relief dollar mounted relentlessly, many local agencies, both public and voluntary, attempted to take advantage of wholesale food prices by establishing commissaries where relief clients could receive food. As this system spread, it drew substantial criticism, because it caused embarrassment and discomfort for recipients and because it reduced the business of local food retailers. One social worker writing in *The Family* in the autumn of 1932 summarized the negative evaluation of the commissary approach: "At their worst, commissaries draw together crowds of disheartened people, who, in unattractive surroundings, have doled out to them a monotonous and inadequate diet, under circumstances that are bitterly humiliating."[24] By the end of 1932, studies of the commissary system had been conducted in New York, New Jersey, and other cities, and small, decentralized food outlets or direct arrangements between relief agencies and local merchants were recommended as alternatives to the large central commissary.[25]

Experience with the commissary system intensified the antipathy of social workers and relief administrators for relief in kind. Many saw such adaptations as a regression to an earlier and even more inadequate stage of relief provision. Writing in the early 1970s, Helen Hall, who spent the Depression years as director of New York's famous Henry Street Settlement, recalled, "Our depression had really brought us back to the breadbasket, the grocery order, the commissary, welfare cafeterias, and the script commissaries that had multiplied over the country, all humiliating forms of warding off starvation. One community after another grasped at something that seemed to offer economies to the community but not security to the unemployed."[26]

Cash grants, food orders, and commissary privileges, however inadequate, were generally given only to those who had homes and families. In many cities, unattached individuals and even couples with no children living at home were ineligible for all forms of relief in their own homes. Soup kitchens, breadlines, and flop houses were the only relief available to them. Many large cities established shelters or municipal lodging houses, but as the number of homeless people and transient job seekers grew, so did "Hoovervilles" of makeshift shacks erected in vacant lots or on the edges of cities from junk and salvage. Some cities created public kitchens to supplement the traditional rescue missions, but most free meal programs were funded by private charitable donations. In the early years of the Depression, especially in the winter of 1930-1931, breadlines proliferated; some eighty-two separate breadlines were operating in New York City alone. Like the commissaries, the breadlines drew the criticism of established social welfare leaders and agencies. Some were rackets, collecting more money in donations than they spent on providing food. Some, those run by the Hearst newspaper chain, for example, were viewed as publicity stunts for their sponsors. Even those that were altruistic and relatively well run were perceived as problems by organized charities; not only did they compete for charitable contributions, but their visibility gave the impression that a great deal of relief activity was in progress, and they were conducive to abuses that gave the unemployed a bad name and deterred much-needed giving.[27]

The relief arrangements of local governments and traditional social agencies were supplemented by the efforts of individuals and groups not normally philanthropic in purpose. Eating clubs at Princeton University began sending the leftovers from their tables to the unemployed, and a reporter for the *Brooklyn Eagle* suggested a central warehouse where families could send leftovers for distribution to those in need. A man calling himself "Mr. Glad" gave out coffee, sandwiches, gloves, and nickels in Times Square. Gangster Al Capone opened a breadline in Chicago. St. Louis society women distributed unsold food from restaurants. Someone placed baskets in New York City railway stations to enable commuters to donate vegetables from their gardens. Harlem radio personality Willie Jackson opened a penny restaurant where meals were sold for one cent per dish.[28]

In the long run, neither the economies reluctantly implemented by established relief agencies nor the spontaneous activities of the well-intentioned were able to squeeze enough out of available dollars to meet the need, and severe distress became evident. Numbers tell part of the story. When the major voluntary relief organizations began raising money for work relief in New York City in the fall of 1930, the standard wage rate for common labor in the city was approximately $5.50 per day. Thus, a fully-employed, low-wage worker could anticipate a wage of about $27.50 a week or $121.00 per month. In comparison, the emergency Work Bureau, established by the city's private charities, paid an average of $15.00 weekly to the jobless on work relief. In Philadelphia where the cost of living was similar, a work relief program initiated late in 1930 began by paying $4.00 per day. By the end of 1931, however, the average relief grant per family in that city had fallen to $4.39 *per week*.[29] In May 1932, the grant was cut again, reducing the weekly average to $4.23 per family. Of that amount, testified the executive secretary of the Community Council of Philadelphia, "about $3.9 3 is an allowance for food, … about two thirds the amount needed to provide a health maintaining diet."[30] At one time in New York, the average weekly grant fell to $2.39 with less than half of the unemployed heads of families receiving any relief at all.[31] Some cities made no pretense of supplying a reasonable budget. Baltimore gave its needy families an average of eighty cents worth of commodities each week, and Atlanta provided sixty cents per week for white recipients and less for blacks. Dallas excluded both blacks and Mexicans from relief. Some cities ran out of funds; Cincinnati paid each family the weekly grant every other week in hopes that some other means of support might be found during an off week. Most simply dropped families from the rolls and waited for them to reapply.[32]

What did people do in such circumstances? One study of four hundred families dropped from the rolls in Philadelphia found that they stayed alive principally by begging and foraging in garbage cans. Another Philadelphia study of an eleven-day hiatus in relief detailed the strategies employed by families to tide themselves over until help arrived in the form of an appropriation of dubious constitutionality by the state legislature. The study, summarized in *Fortune*, found that necessity provoked considerable ingenuity:

> One woman borrowed fifty cents, bought stale bread at three and one half cents a loaf, and the family lived on it for eleven days. Another put the last food order into soup stock and vegetables and made a soup. When a member of the family was hungry, he ate as little as he could. Another picked up spoiled vegetables along the docks, and except for three foodless days, the family ate them. Another made a stew with her last food order, which she cooked over and over daily to keep it from spoiling. Another family lived on dandelions. Another on potatoes. Another had no food for two and one half days. And one in ten of the women were pregnant and one in three of the children of nursing age. And they "got along."[33]

Scavenging in dumps and in the refuse piles of markets was a common strategy, not without its hazards. A committee of prominent Chicagoans visited one of that city's incinerators in 1932 to investigate reports of widespread scavenging. "A new truckload of 'soft' restaurant garbage, which consisted very largely of such food as watermelon, was dumped when the committee was present," noted the *Social Service Review*. "It was a warm day, the odors were bad, and there were clouds of flies everywhere. About a dozen people were waiting for this truckload and picked up vegetables and scraps of various kinds which they took away, some of them eating pieces of food they picked up."[34] On cooler days, the crowds were considerably larger; a Cicero man was arrested at one Chicago dump for striking a man who tried to cut in front of him in the line waiting for the truck. "Lines form every day at the garbage dump from eight in the morning to five in the afternoon," reported the Cicero *Herald*. "Men and women come there to see if they can't find food to carry back home with them. They get some, if they come early enough."[35]

Garbage dumps were not the only places from which people carried food home; jobs were another source. Not only household employees, but also those who worked for restaurants, hospitals, prisons, and other institutions serving meals supplemented their meager earnings by taking food home. A waitress interviewed by Studs Terkel remembered that her father, a railroad man laid off when the Depression struck, "always could get something to feed us kids." He got a part-time job in a Chinese restaurant. "We lived on those fried noodles. I can't stand 'em today." Next he got work delivering samples of breakfast cereals. "We lived on Corn Flake balls, Rice Krispies, they used to come out of our ears. Can't eat 'em today either."[36] School children hid tidbits from school lunches in pockets or book sacks to carry home to younger brothers and sisters. Another woman interviewed by Terkel recalled that she and other girls living in an orphanage routinely gave their brown bag lunches, packed by the dietitian at the home, to down-and-out men in the park. "We'd go through the park when we walked to school…. The men there waited for us to go through and hand them our lunches…. These were guys who didn't have work….They weren't bums. These were hard luck guys."[37] Some of these hard luck guys probably turned around and took the lunches home to wives and children. "Father sleeping at Municipal Lodging House because he could get more to eat there than at home and frequently brought food home from there in pockets for children and wife," reads the report of an investigator for the Welfare Council of New York City who followed up on a neighbor's report that a woman and five children were starving in Brownsville. "Only other food they had for weeks came from under pushcarts."[38]

Sometimes, in desperation, mothers would send their children out to ring the doorbells of strangers. "Excuse me, Mister, but we have no eats in our house and my mother she said I should take my brother before we go to school and ring a doorbell in some house and ask you to give us something to eat," a little girl told writer Louis Adamic when he answered his mother-in-law's doorbell one winter morning. Adamic chatted with the children while his mother-in-law fed them breakfast and packed a lunch for them. The girl was polite and talkative while the boy was angrily silent. "He's always like this when he's hungry and we gotta ring doorbells," his sister explained. Adamic followed up by visiting the children's school where he was told that the number of children seeking meals on the way to school or from the school itself was on the rise.[39]

Not all of the strategies of the unemployed were as demeaning. Along the West Coast, mutual aid organizations formed by jobless workers arranged to exchange the services of members for the right to pick and distribute local farmers' unmarketable crops.[40] Relief gardens and canneries were popular. In some communities, relief recipients and others in need marched on welfare offices demanding expanded benefits, a tactic that was frequently successful.[41] Sometimes action to secure food was even more direct. Groups of men would enter a grocery store, gather up supplies, and ask for credit. When told that business was conducted on a cash basis only, the men would simply pack up the goods and leave. The stores generally refrained from calling the police, one observer reported, for fear that news coverage might lead to the spread of the practice.[42] "Such radicalism as existed," wrote historian Dixon Wecter from the vantage point of the early fifties, "was mainly the plain man's instinctive resentment of poverty surrounded by shops bursting with food and farms smothered under their own productive surplus."[43] In a less-organized fashion, people accosted customers leaving grocery stores and relieved them not of their money but of their food purchases, and families sent their children out to steal from wholesale markets and pushcarts and to snatch milk from the front stoops in affluent neighborhoods. As the Depression wore on, Baltimore and Ohio Railroad President Daniel Willard's famous comment, "I'd steal before I would starve," became a reality for many.[44]

Conditions in rural areas were worse than those in the cities. Many rural areas had no relief apparatus other than a county Red Cross chapter more oriented toward rescuing families trapped by floods or tornadoes than those stranded by economic upheavals.[45] The national Red Cross declined to undertake any unemployment relief until 1932, but many local chapters tried to respond to immediate need. "The situation locally is so overwhelming that no agency is standing on ceremony these days, but all are endeavoring to give relief as speedily as possible," reported one chapter to the national headquarters.[46] Nevertheless, Red Cross work at the local level suffered from the hazards of voluntarism. As critic and essayist Edmund Wilson observed of the organization's work in the hills of Kentucky: "The people in the local chapters ... get no pay for their work of raising money, investigating cases and distributing relief, and as they also have their own businesses and household duties to attend to, it is sometimes hard for them to get around to their work for the Red Cross."[47] Even where other agencies existed to supplement the Red Cross, fundraising was difficult. The farm families who formed the backbone of the rural economy had exhausted any savings they might once have had in the long agricultural slump of the twenties, and rural banks, also weakened by a decade of low farm prices, failed earlier than the big city banks, further depleting rural resources.

Then, in the summer of 1930, a severe drought prostrated virtually all of the South and extended as far to the Northwest as Montana and as far to the Northeast as Pennsylvania. Although the Great Drought of 1930–31 has been historically eclipsed by the Dust Bowl drought of mid decade, for those directly affected, the first drought of the 1930s was catastrophic. Agricultural production in the drought area was sharply reduced to half of normal levels in some of the hardest-hit states. As harvest season approached, many small farmers had no crops at all. The crisis in animal feed was especially acute since normal pasturage and forage had dried up. In the debt-financed farm economy of much of the drought region, the prospect of no crops meant the inability of settling the year's indebtedness and thus, in most cases, no prospect of borrowing the seed and furnish that would get the farmer's family through the winter and permit them to plant a new crop in the spring. Bank failures were epidemic in the drought area, further reducing the availability of credit. The alternate sources of livelihood that farm families could turn to in good times—jobs in construction or in factories—were largely eliminated by the Depression, and the drought made the Depression worse by destroying what little purchasing power remained to farm families after years of low farm prices.[48]

Southern Illinois, many areas in Pennsylvania, southern Appalachian coal mining locales, and other regions were hit by both drought and the virtual collapse of the coal industry. When, in keeping with American relief ideology, desperate farm families turned to their coal mining neighbors for help, they found them equally desperate, wiped out by unemployment. Conditions in such areas became so severe as the winter of 1930-1931 wore on that the President's Emergency Committee for Employment (PECE) made an investigation. "The facts are," wrote Colonel Woods to Judge John Payne, the chairman of the American National Red Cross, upon the former's return from a trip to West Virginia, "that in many of the country districts in the state, and particularly in the coal mining camps, there exists at the present time desperate suffering." Woods attested to the fact that the local authorities had tried to alleviate the situation, but "their funds now … are very thin, and they have little prospect of raising more, since the whole district has been hit so hard for several years by the plight of the bituminous coal industry. This leaves many families," Woods continued, "in a condition where immediate help is needed if almost incredibly hard conditions, lack of food, lack of clothing, are to be mitigated." Woods concluded that it was already too late for prevention. "The need now is for the promptest sort of relief to alleviate acute suffering."[49]

Such privation in the countryside seemed incredible to some urbanites. How could a farmer be without food? "I am in the fullest sympathy with the farmer," declared New York Senator Royal Copeland early in 1932. "I was born on a farm. My relatives are farmers…. But there is never a day on the farm when they can not go out and kill an old rooster and parboil him long enough to make him edible … But in New York, or in Boston, or in any other of the cities, when hunger comes they have nothing to eat but sidewalks." Senator Norbeck of South Dakota replied, "the Senator has been talking about that rooster for a year. Has it not occurred to him that the rooster may be gone by this time?" "Yes," replied Copeland, "but my experience with farming farmers indicates that roosters are born every day"—the record notes laughter—"or every year; so I think perhaps there is a rooster still on the farm."[50]

However, there had been no rooster in many of the most depressed rural areas for quite a while. In the cotton and tobacco regions of the South, the single cash crop system had gradually undermined the production of food for home use. The dual hardships of drought and depression found ' many sharecroppers and tenant farmers without livestock, poultry, or gardens to sustain them. In the areas where the drought hit hardest, many were forced to sacrifice livestock when pasturage and forage dried up because they could not obtain credit to bring in feed from outside the region.[51] In the mining camps that had been spared by the drought, different factors hampered self-provisioning. Since many of the miners had been born on farms, PECE urged the mine operators to permit farming on company land, and the Red Cross distributed packets of seed. Even where the skills needed for farming were still intact, however, the tools and livestock were long gone, as were jars and other equipment needed for large-scale canning.[52] The resources for a return to subsistence agriculture were simply not available to those who needed them most.

Rural families, like their urban counterparts, had strategies for surviving. "Just how did you manage?" Helen Hall asked a group of West Virginia coal miners' wives on a visit to the stricken region. In her autobiography, she recalls this response: "It 'pears like it 'ud be easy to say, honey, but our ways 'ud be hard fur you to understand. You see it was gravy soup lot o' th' time—just gravy soup…. You puts flour in a pan an' browns it, an' then you stirs water inta it." "Is that what you gave your baby? … I must have sounded accusing," Ms. Hall recalls, "for the mother said apologetically, 'Oh, no, honey, not when I cud help it. A neighbor up th' way has a cow, an' she wuz mighty good to me. She sent up half a pint o' milk when she had it over. Sometimes it wuz ev'ry other day, an' sometimes none fur a week. But it helped a powerful sight.'"[53]

The miner's diet, Irving Bernstein asserts, "was a national disgrace," sometimes consisting of "'miner's strawberries' (beans—for variety white beans one day and red the next), 'bulldog gravy' (flour, water, and a little grease), a 'water sandwich' for the miner's lunch pail (stale bread soaked in lard and water)."[54] Some subsisted on what they could gather in the woods. "We have been eating wild greens since January this year, such as Polk salad. Violet tops, wild onions. forget me not wild lettuce and such weeds as cows eat as a cow wont eat a poison weeds," wrote a Harlan County, Kentucky resident to the editor of *The Nation*.[55]

And like their fellow sufferers in the cities, rural citizens used direct action to obtain necessities. In England, Arkansas early in 1931, a group of about forty persons, denied aid by the local Red Cross agent because he had run out of application forms, headed for town determined to get food even if they had to take it by force. Shouting, "we are not going to let our children starve," a growing crowd persuaded local leaders to distribute provisions to several hundred people without charge.[56] Exaggerated by the press, the "food riot" at England became a symbol of the destitution of the drought sufferers, of the inadequacy of the Red Cross, and of the limits to the patience of the hungry. But it was by no means the only example of rural direct action. At Henryetta, Oklahoma, a crowd of several hundred marched on shops to obtain food. In the Ozarks, a crowd of backwoods people forcibly unloaded a carload of grain donated by Iowa farmers and shipped at the expense of editor and future Secretary of Agriculture

Henry Wallace, rather than wait for the Red Cross agent who was supposed to oversee the distribution. Striking miners in Harlan County, Kentucky looted stores and raided gardens.[57]

Despite such actions, deprivation began to take its toll in both city and countryside. A study conducted in New York City found that 95 persons diagnosed as suffering from starvation were admitted to the city's four largest hospitals in 1931, 20 of whom died. Another 143 admissions were diagnosed as malnutrition, and 24 of these died. A survey of Pennsylvania's rural areas in 1931 found a rise of 25 percent in malnutrition among children and reported that the number of new patients at tuberculosis clinics had nearly doubled since 1929, a figure that the state's secretary of health attributed to growing malnutrition. A doctor reporting on the health of West Virginia miners' children in the fall of 1931 found their average weight 12 percent below standard and their diet conducive to infection and disease. A Columbia University professor of public health told a congressional committee that the records of the New York City Association for Improving the Condition of the Poor showed a deterioration in weight and growth among the children of the unemployed. And the Milbank Memorial Fund studied the health of seventy-five hundred families in eight cities, finding the rate of illness much higher among the poor and highest among those whose incomes had dropped sharply since 1929.[58]

The deprivation, even the malnutrition, might have been more acceptable if the food to relieve the need had not been so obviously available. As the breadlines lengthened, the huge surpluses of food and fiber that had troubled farmers for a decade took on new meaning. In the eyes of many, they became at once the means by which hunger might be relieved and the decisive element in the moral argument for its alleviation. "Starvation in a country which has been blessed with foodstuffs over and above the supply needed for itself and other countries where it finds markets is unthinkable," wrote a Tennessee judge who urged President Hoover to arrange for distribution of surplus grains.[59] "One of the tragedies of the present depression has been the fact that thousands of persons have been suffering acutely from hunger, or at least have been forced to do without nourishing food, during a year when the farms of the country were producing some of the largest crops ever grown upon them," declared an Ohio newspaper. "Elevators are bursting with grain for which there is no market, yet thousands have been suffering for want of bread," the editorial continued. "These two sides of the picture don't jibe. If Americans are hungry and there is food, they should be fed."[60] Commerce Secretary Lamont expressed the Hoover administration's concern in similar if more guarded terms: "In a country one of whose difficulties is to dispose of a surplus of many commodities, no person, seeking work in order to provide for himself and his dependents, should be permitted to suffer from lack of food or fuel."[61] Other conservatives used stronger language. "It is a disgrace and an outrage," declared Representative Hamilton Fish of New York, "that this country of ours, with an overabundance of food stuffs, should permit millions of our own people to continue to be undernourished and hungry."[62]

For some observers, the juxtaposition of hunger and abundance symbolized the irrationality of the entire economic structure. It is "a sad indictment of our economic system that great masses of people can be hungry in a nation that is burdened with surplus food crops," wrote a California fruit grower who devised a plan to preserve ripe fruit and distribute it to charitable agencies on a nonprofit basis. [63] A system that permitted citizens to go hungry while storehouses were bursting with food "must be radically wrong in some particulars," Senator Robert Wagner told a Senate committee investigating unemployment.[64] Recalling what seemed to him the paralysis of the Hoover years, one New Dealer reflected: "If on an island the natives had piled all the food up on one side and drawn a line across it and then they'd all got back on the other side and said it was taboo and they couldn't get across to get the food, why we would have laughed at them, but somewhat the same damn thing was happening in this instance."[65] "We are able to produce so much," commented The Nation, "that a good share of us live in perpetual fear of having nothing, and all of us periodically, as at present, stop producing because we can find nobody who is able to buy the things everybody wants. Surely there was never a more insane situation outside of a madhouse."[66]

"Americans of the Hoover years of the Great Depression," historian Albert Romasco has written, "were a people perplexed by plenty…. America's poverty was not cut in the familiar pattern of the past; it was … the poverty of abundance."[67] Intellectual observers and social critics were fascinated by the novelty of the situation. "The writers of Ecclesiastes were wrong. There was some new thing under the sun, something the world had never seen before; want in the midst of plenty. Even stranger still, want begot by plenty," wrote radical editor Oscar Ameringer of what he called the "dying days of the Old Deal."[68] In past depressions, hopes would have centered on good crops, observed historian James Truslow Adams in an essay marking the advent of 1933. "Today, so far from there being any dread of famine or lack of commodities of any sort, we actually fear nature's bounty as exploited by our own too efficient methods."[69] Comparing these economic conditions to the depressions of 1837 and 1873, political commentator Walter Lippmann told the National Conference of Social Work that "in the mentality of the people there is a profound difference between this crisis and all its predecessors. This is the first time when it is altogether evident that man's power to produce wealth has reached a point where it is clearly unnecessary that millions in a country like the United States should be in want."[70]

The new era of abundance presented humanity, or Western civilization at least, with a new challenge to its ingenuity. "We have brought mass production to the highest level. We can produce goods for everybody. However, not one of us has given consideration to mass consumption," chided H. G. Wells in a radio broadcast in the fall of 1930.[71] Some observers were pessimistic: "What we dread," asserted James Truslow Adams, is "the ending of what I have elsewhere called 'the American Dream' from failure of mind and character to control and organize the vast forces at our disposal."[72] Others were more optimistic: "It is not a shortage of the good things of life that bothers us; it is a surplus," declared Henry Wallace. "Our fields and our factories produce more than the present economic system permits our people to consume. Human greed and human dumbness got us into this mess; it is up to human brains to get us out,"[73] But in all the hopes and fears, a conviction prevailed that the juxtaposition of want and abundance was a new situation calling for new actions and new ideas. "We cannot regard … poverty as incurable," Congressman James Mead of Buffalo told the House of Representatives as it headed for adjournment in the summer of 1930, "in a land where the warehouses are bursting with a surplus of supplies."[74]

NOTES

1   *Prairie Farmer,* November 9, 1929, p. 21, quoted in James F. Evans, *Prairie Farmer and WLS* (Urbana: University of Illinois Press, 1964), p. 141.

2   Schlesinger, *Old Order,* pp. 174, 175; Benedict, *Farm Problem,* pp. 10, 11; Dean Albertson, *Roosevelt's Farmer: Claude R. Wickard and the New Deal* (New York: Columbia University Press, 1961), p. 65.

3   Benedict, *Farm Problem,* pp. 92, 101–132.

4   Schlesinger, *Old Order,* p. 185.

5   Benedict, *Farm Problem,* pp. 49, 138-139.

6   John Stokes to the Rockefeller Foundation, December 20, 1930, *Records of the President's Emergency Committee on Employment* (hereafter PECE), Record Group 73, National Archives.

7   Oscar Heline in Studs Terkel, *Hard Times: An Oral History of the Great Depression* (New York: Avon Books Discus, 1970), p. 252.

8   Ruth Loriks in *ibid.* , p. 266.

9   Harry Terrell in *ibid.,* p. 250.

10 Paul Webbink, "Unemployment in the United States, 1930–1940," *Papers and Proceedings* of the American Economic Association, vol. 30, 53rd annual meeting, 1940 (American Economic Review, 1941), pp. 250-251.

11 Irving Bernstein, *The Lean Years* (Boston: Houghton Mifflin, 1972), pp. 489-491.

12 Marion Elderton, ed., *Case Studies of Unemployment* (Philadelphia: University of Pennsylvania Press, 1931), pp. xxx-xxxi, xli-xlvii; Schlesinger, *Old Order,* pp. 167-168; see also Louis Adamic, *My America, 1928-1938* (New York: Harper, 1938), pp. 283-293.

13 Clarke A. Chambers, *Seedtime of Reform: American Social Services and Social Action 1918-1933* (Minneapolis: University of Minnesota Press), p. 146.

14 E. Wight Bakke, *The Unemployed Worker: A Study of the Task of Making a Living Without a Job* (New Haven: Yale University Press, 1940), pp. 266-268.

15 Josephine Brown, *Public Relief, 1929-1939* (New York: Holt, 1940); Blanche D. Coll, *Perspectives in Public Welfare: A History* (Washington: U.S. Government Printing Office, 1970); Walter Trattner, *From Poor Law to Welfare State* (New York: Free Press, 1979).

16 Brown, *Public Relief,* p. 10.

17 Herbert Hoover, "Address to the Welfare and Relief Mobilization Conference," *Public Papers of the Presidents, Herbert Hoover, 1932-1933* (Washington: U.S. Government Printing Office, 1976), p. 294.

18 Herbert Hoover, "Lincoln's Birthday Address," text of radio address as printed in the *New York Times,* February 13, 1931.

19 Herbert Hoover, "Address to the Welfare and Relief Mobilization Conference," *Public Papers,* p. 294.

20 Bernstein, *The Lean Years,* pp. 302-304; E. P. Hayes, *Activities of the President's Emergency Committee for Employment* (Concord, New Hampshire: Rumford, 1936).

21 Frances Piven and Richard Cloward, *Regulating the Poor: The Functions of Public Welfare* (New York: Pantheon, 1971), pp. 48-49; Schlesinger, *Old Order,* pp. 164-165; Gilbert Seldes, *The Years of the Locust: America, 1929-1932* (Boston: Little, Brown, 1933), pp.9-11, 54-56, 161, 162; Harris G. Warren, *Herbert Hoover and the Great Depression* (New York: Oxford University Press, 1959).

22 Arthur Mann, *LaGuardia: A Fighter Against His Times, 1882-1933,* vol. 1 (Philadelphia: J. B. Lippencott, 1959), p. 290.

23 Brown, *Public Relief,* pp. 73-74; Margaret Wead, "Drifts in Unemployment Relief," *The Family,* November 1932, pp. 225-226.

24 Wead, "Drifts," p. 226.

25 Joanna C. Colcord, "The Commissary System," *The Family,* November 1932, pp. 235-240.

26 Helen Hall, *Unfinished Business* (New York: Macmillan, 1971), p. 51.

27 Dixon Weeter, *The Age of the Great Depression, 1929-1941* (New York: Macmillan, 1952), p. 16; Caroline Bird, *The Invisible. Scar* (New York: David McKay, 1966), p. 26; H. L. Lurie, testimony in Congress, subcommittee of the Senate Committee on Manufactures, *Federal Aid for Unemployment Relief,* 72d Cong., 2d sess., 1933, pp. 64-67; Adamic, *My America,* pp. 296, 297.

28 These are but a few of the many examples of informal assistance measures undertaken by individuals and groups. Many anecdotal accounts of the Great Depression contain descriptions of such efforts. The samples cited here come from: Bird, *The Invisible Scar,* pp. 24- 25; Robert Bendiner, *Just Around the Corner: A Highly Selective History of the Thirties* (New York: Harper & Row, 1967); Edward Robb Ellis, *A Nation in Torment: The Great American Depression, 1929-1939* (New York: Capricorn Books, 1971), pp. 125-131; *Amsterdam News,* September 14, 1932.

29 Bernstein, *The Lean Years,* pp. 292-302; "No One Has Starved," *Fortune,* September 1932, pp. 19-28.

30 Karl de Schweinitz, testimony in Congress, subcommittee of the Senate Committee on Manufactures, *Federal Cooperation in Unemployment Relief,* 72d Cong., 1st sess., 1932, pp. 20, 21.

31 "No One Has Starved," pp. 22, 23.

32 Frances Piven and Richard Cloward, *Poor People's Movements: Why They Succeed, How They Fail* (New York: Vintage Books, 1979), pp. 60, 61.

33 "No One Has Starved," pp. 27, 28.

34 "Notes and Comment," *The Social Service Review* 6 (December 1932), pp.637-639.

35 Quoted in Mauritz Hallgren, *Seeds of Revolt: A Study of American Life and the Temper of the American People During the Depression* (New York: Knopf, 1933).

36 Dynamite Garland in Studs Terkel, *Hard Times,* p. 115.

37 Dorothe Bernstein in *ibid.,* p. 123.

38 Quoted in Hallgren, *Seeds of Revolt.*

39 Adamic, *My America.*

40 Bernstein, *The Lean Years,* pp. 416-420.

41 Piven and Cloward, *Poor People's Movements,* pp. 49-60.

42 Adamic, *My America,* p. 309.

43 Dixon Wecter, *The Age of the Great Depression*, p. 36.

44 Daniel Willard, "The Challenge to Capitalism," *Review of Reviews* 83 (May 1931), p. 61.

45 Bernstein, *The Lean Years*, pp. 362-363; James L. Fieser to Herbert Hoover, June 1, 1931, PECE; Edmund Wilson, "Red Cross and County Agent," in *The American Earthquake* (Garden City: Doubleday, 1958), pp. 249-266.

46 Charles Hurd, *The Compact History of the American Red Cross* (New York: Hawthorne Books, 1959), p. 209.

47 Wilson, "Red Cross and County Agent," p. 252.

48 David E. Hamilton, "Herbert Hoover and the Great Drought of 1930," *Journal of American History* 68 (March 1982), pp. 850-875; Robert Cowley, "The Drought and the Dole," *American Heritage* 23 (February 1972), pp. 16-19, 92-99.

49 Woods to Payne, February 14, 1931, PECE.

50 *Congressional Record*, 72d Cong., 1st sess., 1932, p. 1186.

51 Hamilton, *Hoover and the Drought*, pp. 852-853; "Arkansas's Fight for Life," *Literary Digest*, February 28, 1931; Charles Morrow Wilson, *The Fight Against Hunger* (New York: Funk and Wagnalls, 1969), pp. 92, 93.

52 See Braverman, *Labor and Monopoly Capital*, for a discussion of the destruction of self-provisioning skills and resources that accompanied the commodification of food.

53 Hall, *Unfinished Business*, p. 48.

54 Bernstein, *The Lean Years*, p. 363.

55 Quoted in Hallgren, *Seeds of Revolt*.

56 Cowley, "The Drought and the Dole"; Hamilton, "Hoover and the Drought," pp. 869-870.

57 Bernstein, *The Lean Years*, pp. 378, 422; Wilson, *The Fight Against Hunger*, pp. 100-105.

58 Eleanor Flexnor, "Yes, There Is Starvation in New York City," *Better Times*, April 11, 1932, p. 4; Bernstein, *The Lean Years*, pp. 329-332; Harry Hopkins, *Spending to Save: The Complete Story of Relief* (New York: W. W. Norton, 1936), pp. 79-82.

59 Judge Will Cummings, statement quoted in the Chattanooga, Tennessee *Times* and the *Congressional Record*, 72d Cong., 1 sess., 1932, p. 1406.

60 "Using Surplus Grains," editorial in the Mount Vernon, Ohio *Republican News* and reprinted in the *Congressional Record*, 72d Cong., 1st sess., 1932, p. 1407.

61 Herbert Hoover, "Statement on the Purposes and Methods of the Cabinet Committee on Unemployment," October 21, 1930, *Public Papers*, p. 438.

62 *Congressional Record*, 72d Cong., 1st sess., 1932, p. 5191.

63 J. R. McCleskey to William G. McAdoo, October 25, 1930, PECE.

64 Quoted in Schlesinger, *Old Order*, p. 225.

65 Samuel Bledsoe Memoir, COHC, p. 47.

66 "Less Work—More Pay," *The Nation*, October 15, 1930, p. 393.

67 Romasco, *Poverty of Abundance*, p. 3.

68 Oscar Ameringer, *If You Don't Weaken: The Autobiography of Oscar Ameringer* (New York: Henry Holt, 1940), p. 449.

69 James Truslow Adams, "America Faces 1933's Realities," *New York Times Sunday Magazine*, January 1, 1933.

70 Walter Lippmann, "Poverty and Plenty," pp. 234-235.

71 H. G. Wells, excerpted in the *New York Times*, November 9, 1930.

72 Adams, "American Faces 1933's Realities."

73 "To Bring Back Prosperity," *Wallace's Farmer and Iowa Homestead*, December 20, 1930, p. 1954.

74 *Congressional Record*, 71st Cong., 2d sess., 1930, quoted in Jordan A. Schwarz, *The Interregnum of Despair: Hoover, Congress and the Depression* (Urbana: University of Illinois Press, 1970), p. 30.

DISCUSSION QUESTIONS

- What aspects does the article emphasize about the Depression? What does it overlook?
- Does the article rely on emotion or hard data to convey its argument? Is such an approach useful in informing people about the Great Depression?
- Based on the article, what was the response of the United States government to the Great Depression? Was this approach consistent with the "welfare capitalism" ideology of the 1920s?

CHAPTER X

THE WORKING CLASS GOES TO WAR

OBJECTIVES

- Analyze the experience of World War II on the American working class.

PREWRITING

- Consider the hardships that Americans endured during the Great Depression. Why were Americans willing to accept wartime conditions when the fighting was far away? What opportunities existed for Americans at the home front that did not exist before the war?

The Working Class Goes to War

GARY GERSTLE

M ost Americans still regard World War II as "the good war". We see
ourselves as having fought hard in a noble cause, contributing our
manufacturing might, manpower, and dollars to an international crusade
to defeat fascism and resuscitate democracy. A spirit of cooperation, unity,
and generosity impelled us to work long hours, purchase large numbers of
war bonds, and good-naturedly endure sharp restrictions on our freedom
to consume and spend. We emerged from the war with a renewed faith
in ourselves as a people, convinced that American wizardry in production,
combined with the American commitment to fair play, would bring prosperity to our nation and set a shining example for the world.

In quiet and piecemeal ways historians in the 1970s and 1980s were busy
prying the "true history" of the war out of the grip of this powerful collective
memory. Though John Morton Blum did not intend his 1976 book *V Was
for Victory* to be more than mildly revisionist, it did hold up for scholarly
reflection a series of unpleasant truths about the war: that in this war for democracy and against racism, the government refused to desegregate the
armed forces; that it imprisoned more than 100,000 Japanese Americans;
that it awarded the vast majority of military contracts to the largest American
corporations, accelerating the monopolization of American industry; and
that it promised Americans a cornucopia of consumer goods—everything
from nylon stockings to suburban homes—to sustain their slumping patriotism. Other scholars picked up where Blum had left off, and in the space
of a decade they published a rash of indictments of 1940s American society
and of the government's conduct of the war. These revisionist accounts

focused on the racism, anti-Semitism, and sexism that permeated the home front; on the government policies that weakened labor and small business and strengthened corporate control of American life; on the many Americans who, far from committing themselves to a worldwide crusade, quickly grew cynical about the war and "did their part" for the most pragmatic and selfish of reasons.[1]

This assault on the idea of "the good war" was particularly strong in regard to the experience of labor. Many Americans today would not dare think or say that national goodness might somehow be associated with strengthening labor's economic and political power. But this sense of opposition between labor and national well-being is fairly recent. Those of us who can still remember a time when liberalism and the Democratic Party were strong know how integral organized labor was to liberalism's popularity and success. The two were seen as having arisen together in the 1930s, nurtured by a warm, caring president whose affection for ordinary Americans knew few bounds. Their places in American politics were secured in the 1940s when the nation, under the liberal Roosevelt's leadership, gained a great military triumph abroad and economic prosperity at home. The labor movement was thought to have contributed vitally to this double achievement: its full cooperation with industry made possible the manufacturing feats on which Americas military victory and economic vigor so clearly rested. The government, in turn, rewarded labor's cooperation by encouraging union growth: union membership nearly doubled (from 8 to 15 million between 1939 and 1945) until it encompassed 35 percent of the nation's workforce. By 1945–46, the American labor movement enjoyed the kind of economic and political power it had never known, power it used to provide unionized workers with job security, high wages, health insurance, pensions, college educations, and homeownership. World War II, in this view, had been more than good; it had been the best of wars for American workers.

The attack on this memory was triggered by Nelson Lichtenstein's influential 1982 book *Labor's War at Home*. Lichtenstein portrayed labor's experience in World War II in far more ambivalent terms: there were pluses, to be sure—full employment, increasing incomes, improved benefits, government support of unionization—but there were also substantial negatives. The government had trumpeted an "equality of sacrifice" policy, by which it meant that no one group would be asked to give more to the war effort than any other; but workers discovered that their wages were often held down while employers' profits were permitted to rise. Workers had given up the right to strike in exchange for the right to bring all workplace grievances to a government agency—the War Labor Board—that would expeditiously process and fairly judge all claims. But grievances accumulated so quickly amid the stresses of war production (around-the-clock-schedules; constant infusion of new workers, often different in race, ethnicity, or religion from those already employed; a shortage of experienced foremen to staff rapidly expanding supervisory ranks) that the War Labor Board could not handle them quickly or judiciously enough. Anger in the ranks of American workers mounted until it exploded in wave after wave of wildcat strikes in 1944 and 1945. More American workers participated in strikes in those two years than in any similar period since 1919—more than in any two consecutive depression years.

Union leaders, according to Lichtenstein, might have sided with this rank-and-file surge, using it to renegotiate the rules of the wartime labor system in a way that increased labor's power and ensured equality of sacrifice in fact as well as in theory. This is what John L. Lewis had accomplished by endorsing the walkout of his United Mine Worker coal miners in 1943. But most labor leaders, in Lichtenstein's view, were too scared of the growing strength of conservatives, too fearful of antagonizing their liberal friends, and too alarmed by rank-and-file rambunctiousness. Rather than side with the wildcat strike movement, they joined hands with government administrators to clamp down on strikers, to refuse their demands, to threaten prosecution if they persisted with their unauthorized protests. In so doing, labor leaders tamed the most vigorously democratic and independent portions of their unions, deepened labor's dependence on the government, and accelerated the flow of union power away from the rank and file (the workers themselves) and toward the encrusted upper echelons of union bureaucracies. In other words, the labor movement (Lichtenstein had in mind the progressive Congress of Industrial Organizations) disarmed itself, made itself weaker than it might have been, and thus found itself with a far more limited role in national life than it might have had. These developments would haunt organized labor during the postwar period and keep it from achieving the national economic and political power it thought it deserved. In short, "the good war" was a lot less good for American labor, Lichtenstein argued, than most people thought.[2]

Lichtenstein's powerful revisionism entailed more than a reassessment of the labor movement. It also raised questions about the engagement of American working people with the war. In Lichtenstein's book the working class did not go to war—if by "going to war" we mean enthusiastically supporting the war effort by volunteering for military service, or working especially hard to support the "boys" overseas, or vocally endorsing the nation's war aims and ideals. Instead, the working class went to work Support for the war there was, but not in the sense of overriding or supplanting economic concerns or class loyalties. The working class remained apart from the American nation. The war was not really their war, not really a people's war.

Lichtenstein did not offer a sustained argument or marshal evidence for this point of view; rather, it was a perspective threaded through his work, one that seemed to correspond to the high number of wildcat strikes—strikes that interrupted the war effort and could be interpreted as a protest against it—and one informed as well by Lichtenstein's own deep-rooted suspicion that patriotism and nationalism were inimical to working-class solidarity.[3]

In the decade and a half since the publication of his book, Lichtenstein's argument for the 1940s as a critical decade in labor's history has become widely accepted among labor and political historians, whose own research has confirmed Lichtenstein's once provocative findings. But his argument for the separateness of class from nation has fared less well, for the accumulating evidence points to workers' deep patriotic engagement with their identity as Americans and with the welfare of their nation.[4] I shall review some of this evidence and then assess its implications for understanding labor politics in the 1940s.

Some of the strongest evidence for working-class patriotism is also the oldest and most obvious: popular reactions to the Japanese attack on Pearl Harbor. Everyone who was older than ten in 1941 seems to remember exactly when and where they heard the news of the Japanese attack. The powerful antiwar sentiment present in American society in the 1920s and 1930s vanished overnight and did not resurface, though the war carried on for four long years and claimed hundreds of thousands of American lives. No other major war America has fought in this century generated such enthusiastic support and so little public protest.[5] The Korean War never enlisted more than lukewarm support. World War I and the Vietnam War both sparked large, angry, and determined antiwar movements that powerfully influenced domestic and foreign policy for years after the conflagrations had ended.[6]

Recent social history has confirmed, moreover, some standard myths concerning the war's popularity. In the textile city of Lowell, Massachusetts, for example, Marc Scott Miller has uncovered evidence of young working-class men clamoring to join the military. The few who tried to evade the draft or who took advantage of legal deferments were often treated as "wimps." "Girls" whose "boys" had gone overseas were expected to remain romantically faithful for the wars duration. War spirit found its way into schools, comic strips, and children's games. A sudden fascination with warplanes and the romance of flying gripped high-school boys. Among young adults, war bond rallies and dances were wildly popular. War bond administrators, in turn, had little difficulty raising the money required for the war, even as they embarked on their fourth, fifth, and sixth bond drives. Similarly, Red Cross officials easily found enough blood donors to keep an adequate supply of plasma flowing to the war zones.[7] Such evidence seems to corroborate the claim made by another scholar, Mark Leff, that during World War II Americans "gloried in the feeling that they were participating in a noble and successful cause."[8]

The significance of labor unions or of "class-conscious" workers in this war effort is not clear from Miller's study. But in my own work on another New England textile city—Woonsocket, Rhode Island—I found that unions and labor militants contributed essential bonds, blood, and moral support to the war.[9] No single union activity in the years 1941 to 1945 occupied more time or involved more members than war bond drives and servicemen support committees. Many union locals regularly oversubscribed the war bond quotas assigned them. In February 1944 the city's labor movement made Woonsocket the nation's first city to surpass its bond quota in the government's Fourth War Loan Campaign. The next month union members received the news that Woonsocket was the American city with the second highest per capita contribution to the Russian War Relief Society. Servicemen committees in virtually every local raised money through dances or through the profits of plant vending machines and cooperative cafeterias to send checks, gift packages, and letters to their members in the armed forces.

Participation in the war effort was common to all union locals, regardless of their particular ethnic or political orientation.[10] Within Woonsocket, it was as strong among conservative French Canadians—who formed a majority of the workforce—as among radical Belgians; it was equally evident among the Irish, Italian, and Polish workers who belonged to union locals outside the city. Anecdotal testimony adds to the evidence suggesting a profound rank-and-file commitment to the war. Pat Murphy, an Irish lathe operator, impressed his union steward one day by turning out five pieces rather than the assigned four, saying it was a birthday gift to his son in the armed forces. Phillipe Plante, a French Canadian watchman at a spinning mill, achieved union recognition for solemnly saluting the mills American flag every day before lowering it. A score of French and Belgian union members, many of whom had fought the Germans in World War I, began broadcasting morale-boosting radio messages to the forces of resistance in their native land. Emily Hart, a French Canadian textile worker with a husband in the navy and a brother in the army, donated five pints of blood to the Red Cross plasma drive. And Mary Bednarchuk, an aging Polish textile worker eager to retire from mill work, was determined to "keep going until the war is over" to demonstrate support for her son, a much decorated aerial gunner, and his fellow soldiers.[11]

It is likely that many working-class blood donors, bond purchasers, and care package senders cared less about the nation's official war aims than about getting a loved one home alive. Some grew perturbed at the endless appeals to patriotism that always concluded with a request for more money. Still, the average worker's personal investment in the war, measured in terms of family members or kin serving in the military and risking death, made a skeptical, detached attitude toward the country's war aims difficult to maintain. Mary Bednarchuk, whose stated loyalty was *to* her son, not her nation, nevertheless lavished great attention on her son's many medals and diligently collected newspaper and magazine clippings describing his heroic acts. In such ways did loyalty to kin merge imperceptibly with patriotic feeling. Similarly, a Lowell, Massachusetts, mother with five sons in the service, her daughter later re-called, followed the war "every which way she could, because of [her] ... boys being here and there." "She had put a big map in the dining room and, oh, she just followed everything that was going on during the war.[12] In such circumstances, distinctions between personal involvement with the war and ideological commitment to it proved difficult to maintain.

The government, meanwhile, ran sophisticated propaganda campaigns to further mesh national war aims with individual concerns. We still know far too little about these campaigns; those historians (like John Morton Blum) who have studied them have generally not understood the advertising techniques many were based on.[13] Unlike the ham-fisted, overbearing propaganda campaigns of World War I, those of World War II benefited from shrewd advertising innovations in the 1920s and 1930s. The principle of market segmentation, in particular, increased the sophistication and effectiveness of government propaganda. This principle, first adopted by advertising agencies in the 1930s, flowed from the recognition that 130 million Americans did not constitute a single consuming public. Tastes differed, depending on whether those in question were black or white, Yankee or immigrant, male or female, old or young, working class or middle class. Advertisers had to take such differences into account. In some cases this meant identifying the public most interested in a product and constructing an advertising campaign calculated to appeal to its particular tastes. In other cases, especially when a product—such as toothpaste or war bonds—was to be sold to all Americans, advertisers began fashioning several campaigns, each directed at one market segment.[14]

The Treasury Department, under the direction of Secretary Henry Morgenthau, assembled a sophisticated team of advertisers, many "drafted" from Madison Avenue's most successful agencies, to convince Americans to buy war bonds. Morgenthau also hired as consultants individuals with extensive knowledge of European ethnic groups, blacks, and other minority populations to help the advertisers determine how best to tap the patriotic ardor of these particular groups.[15] The Treasury Department, as a consequence of this effort, sent out different appeals to different market segments. Consider two war bond advertisements appearing in Woonsocket in 1944, one in the city's daily newspaper, the *Woonsocket Call*, the other in the city's labor paper, the *ITU News*. The *Call*'s success (in terms of subscriptions and advertising) depended on middle-class readers. The *ITU News*, by contrast, was intended for the city's heavily ethnic working class. The war bond advertisements appearing in these two newspapers had strikingly different themes. The *Woonsocket Call* ad, which had been paid for by local Woonsocket industrialists and merchants, stressed that war bonds were a good business investment. "Bonds are safe, they pay a good return, they're easy to buy. When they mature, they mean new machinery and equipment, new conveniences for the house, money for the childrens schooling, funds for retirement." These were words intended for businessmen, small and large, whose attention never wavered far from profit and loss, not even (apparently) in a world war.[16] No appeal to financial self-interest appeared in the *ITU News* ad, however; no effort was made to tell workers how war bond purchases would someday bring them savings for a home or desired consumer goods. The labor appeal was couched instead in terms of religious tolerance, racial equality, and cultural pluralism. The advertisement exalted America's time-honored commitment to the inherent equality of all people, of whatever race, creed, or religion. It emphasized how Hitler's doctrines of racial superiority challenged that principle, how Hitler mocked America, depicting it as a weak nation because its blood was "tainted by many strains." Americans had to fight to prove Hitler wrong, to show him that ethnic and racial diversity was a source of strength, not weakness, and to preserve America's historic role as a land of freedom and opportunity for all.[17]

The point of comparing the *Woonsocket Call* and *ITU News* advertisements is not to contrast the self-interestedness of businessmen with the idealism of workers; it is to point out how much the representation of an America made strong by the contribution of different ethnic groups appealed to the personal desires of ethnic workers for inclusion and acceptance in their adopted home. From the start, ethnic workers' attraction to unionism in Woonsocket and elsewhere had been in part a manifestation of their desire to overcome the second-class treatment conferred on them because of their ethnic identity. In the 1930s, unionism was a vehicle not only for gaining economic power but also for overcoming cultural discrimination. Within their own unions, workers attempted to show that individuals from different ethnic groups could work together in an atmosphere of unity, free of bigotry. They imagined reconstructing America along similar lines. They believed that Franklin Roosevelt shared this culturally egalitarian vision and was eager to see it realized.[18]

Building a pro-labor, culturally tolerant America, however, was more easily imagined than accomplished. Millions of workers remained unorganized throughout the 1930s. Those who did belong to unions stayed poor, the continuation of the depression making substantial income gains rare. Meanwhile, opposition to labor and to the New Deal's young welfare state was mounting in corporate boardrooms and in the homes of middle-class Americans who had been scared by labor's militancy and by its association with communism. Father Charles Coughlin, Gerald L. K. Smith, and other hatemongers were reinvigorating the forces of prejudice. For a time Roosevelt's determination to fight these trends wavered. But with the war, and with the need to mobilize for a total fight against Nazi aggression, the prospects of renewing the fight for economic and cultural equality brightened.[19]

The outspoken celebration of America's ethnic diversity that occurred during the war had no precedent in American history. Countless Hollywood war movies built their plots around a multiethnic (and in some cases multiracial) platoon or boat crew whose members' devotion to each other gave them the strength to fight and the will to triumph.[20] A similar theme began appearing in juvenile fiction. John Tunis's *All-American*

(1942), for example, tells how a WASP, a Jew, an Irish youth, and a black, who first meet on a ball field, join hands to combat prejudice in their high school and their town.[21] A new liberal journal, *Comnwn Ground,* founded with much fanfare in 1940, conceived of its mission as telling a story "not now being covered by any other magazine": that "of the coming and meeting on this continent of peoples belonging to ...60 different national, racial, and religious backgrounds."[22] A 1944 pamphlet of the Congress of Industrial Organizations' Political Action Committee told it this way: "They came from England and from Ireland . . . . They came from Russia and from Germany. They came from Italy and from Poland. They came from Yugoslavia. Africa. . . . They came from all the corners of the earth to share in our way of life.'[23] A sense of urgency gripped those intent on telling this story: "Never has it been more important,' noted the editors of *Common Ground,* "that we become intelligently aware of the ground Americans of various strains have in common; that we sink our tap roots deep into its rich and varied cultural past and attain rational stability in place of emotional hysteria; that we reawaken the old American Dream, a dream which, in its powerful emphasis on the fundamental worth and dignity of every human being, can be a bond of unity no totalitarian attack can break."[24]

The outpouring of such sentiments cannot be understood simply as war propaganda. The rise of Hitler had genuinely appalled many Americans. It particularly unnerved the nation's liberals and radicals, who had been certain that vicious racial bigotry was characteristic of primitive societies, not advanced ones like Germany. Articles and books, popular and scholarly, on the roots of religious prejudice and on improving intergroup relations began rolling off the presses. The contradiction between America's professed commitment to equality and its discriminatory treatment of its black citizens—"the American dilemma" to use Gunnar Myrdal's 1944 phrase—received the sort of attention it had not been given since the early days of Reconstruction. Social scientists who had been quietly fighting intellectual racism in the United States (such as the anthropologist Franz Boas and his disciples Margaret Mead and Ruth Benedict) suddenly found themselves with large audiences hungry for sociological and psychological explanations of bigotry. Benedict and Mead, among others, were brought into the nation's service to contribute their knowledge and opinions to government war efforts.[25]

The rise of Hitler and America's war against him, in other words, had prompted a serious rethinking of the American liberal agenda.[26] Government propagandists certainly made use of this new liberal focus, but they did not create it. Their job was to work the genuine yearning for racial and religious equality into advertising messages and to transmit them to groups where the effects were likely to be substantial. Little is known about the procedures actually used by government bond sellers and other propagandists to match advertising messages with particular audiences. But there can be no doubt that the message of America as a land of diversity reached and profoundly touched ethnic workers; so too did the idea that the nation—as represent-ed by the federal government—was leading the fight against prejudice. For ethnic workers the war was the historic moment when they felt fully accepted as Americans. They were fighting for America and America was fighting for them. As a group of ethnic unionists in Woonsocket declared in 1944: "We shall protect and amplify ... de-mocracy in America and in every peace-loving nation of the world, so that the soldiers of every race, creed and color—the Colin Kellys and the Meyer Levins and the Dorie Millers, the black men and the white and the yellow, the Catholic, the Protestant and the Jew, 'SHALL NOT HAVE DIED IN VAIN.'"[27] Here was another instance of the personal—in this case the desire of Catholic unionists to overcome discrimination they had long endured—merging with the political task of delivering to Hitler's Germany (and to its racist propaganda) a knockout blow.

Further evidence of ethnic workers' desire for integration into American society can be found in sharply rising naturalization rates. Though there had been no mass immi-gration since 1921, the nation still harbored 11.6 million foreign-born, about a third of whom (approximately 4 million) had yet to become citizens.[28] The proportion of aliens was highest among those who had come from eastern and southern Europe in the late nineteenth and early twentieth centuries and from Canada and Mexico. More than 1.5 million of these aliens became citizens in the war years alone (1941-45)—from 35 to 40 percent of the alien population—by far the highest rate of naturalization recorded for any five-year period since the Census Bureau began tracking these statistics in 1907.[29] Contrary to some popular and scholarly impressions, only a small part of these wartime naturalizations—10 percent—occurred as a result of military induction; the rest were voluntary acts by civilians.[30] By 1950 the proportion of naturalized citizens within each of the major European immigrant groups exceeded 70 percent and some-times reached 80 percent. Moreover, the substantial differential in percentages that had long distinguished "old immigrants" from "new immigrants" had disappeared: by 1950, for example, the percentages of naturalized Poles and naturalized Britons were virtually identical—72 for the former, 75 for the latter.[31]

Because the census did not break down naturalization by occupation, the number of working-class immigrants who became citizens during these years cannot be determined with precision, but it was probably high. The eastern and southern European groups most often seeking citizenship during the war years were those heavily concentrated in working-class occupations. Thus it seems fair to interpret these naturalization patterns as evidence of Euro-American workers' deepening connection to America, reflecting the growing perception that the nation was prepared to welcome those it had long shunned.

The growing enthusiasm for America manifested in rising naturalization rates was propelled by an additional factor, a fully mobilized economy. Unemployment—still 14 percent in 1940—vanished by 1943 as war production triggered an insatiable demand for labor. A tight labor market pushed wages up. In manufacturing, the average weekly earnings grew 65 percent between 1941 and 1944; adjusting for inflation and higher income taxes still leaves a net gain of 27 percent. Fifteen million workers—a full third of the prewar workforce—moved up the occupational ladder during the war's course. Largely as a result of government policies, the poorest paid enjoyed the greatest wage increases. The government added additional value to jobs by requiring employers to offer their workers nonwage benefit packages that included paid vacations and hospitalization insurance.[32]

These gains did not mean that inequities, injustices, and inconveniences in the workplace went unnoticed. On the contrary, the classification of factory work and the wages assigned particular jobs caused conflict between workers and bosses and among different groups of workers who were constantly jockeying for labor market advantage. The influx of new workers to war production centers, meanwhile, everywhere overwhelmed local transportation systems and housing, adding further frustrations to daily life. The resentments and discomforts of wartime living, however, must be set alongside the growing remuneration and security of wartime employment. By itself this economic experience would not have been enough to bring about inclusion of workers who had keenly felt their marginality, but in conjunction with the wartime celebration of the nation's multicultural character it allowed European ethnics to believe that the American dream was finally within their grasp. In this way one very substantial portion of the American working class, its European ethnic component, became deeply engaged with the war. This working-class segment did not just go to work. It went to war. Its commitment to the war may explain why the furious labor strife anticipated by many observers of the time never materialized. "While we have had quite a few strikes," observed Edwin Witte, chair of the Michigan region of the War Labor Board, in July 1943, "the big explosion we have been looking for has never come." 33

African American workers were far more ambivalent about the war. The ideological assault on Hitler's racism, so prominent in government propaganda, found as receptive an audience among blacks as among European ethnics. The Treasury Department cultivated blacks as assiduously as it hawked its wares to ethnics, and blacks responded by purchasing large numbers of war bonds. Moreover, African Americans found new economic opportunities in war work. Because of labor shortages, industrial jobs from which blacks had long been excluded were now accessible. More than a million responded by leaving southern rural areas, where most of the black population was still concentrated, for factory work in the industrial centers of the South and North. Those who made this journey often experienced a dramatic rise in income, magnified by the poverty-level wages characteristic of the agricultural economy they emerged from.[34]

But few African Americans could embrace the war effort or America with the same enthusiasm evident among Euro-Americans. The government compromised its campaign against racism by refusing to desegregate the military. Throughout the war, black soldiers were trained and fought (when they were allowed to fight) in all-black units.[35] Moreover, white America was plainly nervous about—and often cruelly hostile to—the participation of blacks in the celebration of national diversity. More often than not, they were excluded from cinematic and literary representations of the multicultural platoon. When blacks were included they were often given a subordinate status: they could be seen but not heard, or they could be heard as long as their comments and actions supported, but did not supplant, those of the (white) leading men. Thus in *Guadalcanal Diary*, a 1943 war movie stressing the role of ethnic marines—Irish, "Brooklynese," and Hispanic—in the early assaults on the island, only one black enlisted man (a sailor) is allowed to appear. Materializing on-screen while the marines are still on their troopships, he is asked to identify the battleships and destroyers that have just joined the invasion force. The scene conveys a kind of interracial affection as the black sailor is surrounded, even nuzzled, by a chummy group of whites. But the scene lasts all of ten seconds, during which the black seaman utters a mere half dozen words (all proper nouns). He appears in no other scene; he is permitted no role in the film's main action—the landing on the island and the assault on the Japanese. He thus can take no part in the ordeal by fire that forges the motley marine crew into true Americans.[36]

In their evaluations of the Congress of Industrial Organizations (CIO), African American workers confronted a similar dilemma: whether to celebrate the CIO for the new kind of racial inclusion it seemed to offer or to condemn it for the racist habits it condoned. Specifically, they had to balance their high regard for the antiracist campaigns of the CIO's top brass and communist activists with the racism rampant in the ranks of white workers, South and North. A significant number of the wartime wildcats were "hate strikes," initiated by whites to protest the introduction of blacks to their workplaces. These strikes occurred not only in cities such as Mobile, Alabama, where industrial unionism was new, but also in urban centers such as Detroit where the CIO and progressive politics were thought to be entrenched. In early June 1943, the promotion of three black workers to positions hitherto occupied by whites triggered a vicious strike at a Packard engine factory in Detroit. The rising racial tension prompted an editor of a Catholic labor paper to warn that "there is a growing, subterranean race war going on in the City of Detroit which can have no other ultimate result than an explosion of violence."[37] The explosion came on 20 June in a full-fledged race riot that rocked the city and shocked the nation. In two days of massive violence, 34 people (25 of them black) were killed and 675 were wounded. Property losses totaled $2 million, and a million man-hours of war production were lost. The *Detroit Times* pronounced it "the worst disaster which has befallen Detroit since Pearl Harbor."[38]

It would be tempting to blame Detroit's hostile racial climate on the hundreds of thousands of white, racist southerners who had streamed into the city in the preceding two years, attracted by the promise of good wages in the war plants.[39] But racism was equally apparent among the city's European ethnic populations.[40] These ethnics' embrace of America may well have intensified their prejudice against blacks, for many conceived of Americanization in racial terms: becoming American meant becoming white. Becoming white, of course, acquired meaning and conferred status only in a society that still denigrated blackness. Thus the ethnic workers who freed themselves from racial discrimination during the war years often were anxious to reinforce the racist boundary separating white from black. Only by insisting on that division, it seems, could they enjoy the full fruits of their assimilation. Many refused to work alongside blacks or share neighborhoods with them. Some were eager to participate in rituals that white Americans had long used to intimidate blacks. An Italian American interviewed by Studs Terkel understood this desire all too well: "There were riots in Harlem in '45. I remember standing on a corner, a guy would throw the door open and say, 'Come on down.' They were goin' to Harlem to get in the riot. They'd say, 'Let's beat up some niggers.' It was wonderful. It was new. The Italo-Americans stopped being Italo and started becoming Americans. We joined the group. Now were like you guys, right?"[41]

Because blacks had to balance their wartime experience of harassment and discrimination against their hopes that the war might erode racism, they approached the war effort with more circumspection and skepticism than did white ethnics. Some could not deny the satisfaction they took in the stunning success of the Japanese attack on Pearl Harbor, a strike that in their eyes dealt a serious blow to the prestige of the white race. "I don't want them [the Japanese] to quite win," admitted one black to another, "but to dish out to these white people all they can dish out to them."[42]

Others had to struggle hard to convince themselves and fellow African Americans that the nation—in spite of its history of slavery and racism—deserved their loyalty and, if necessary, their lives. William Pickens, director of the Inter-racial Section of the Treasury Department's Savings Bond Division, experienced this struggle acutely as he encountered audience after audience of blacks who wanted to be told what and why they should sacrifice for America. The significant volume of war bonds African Americans purchased and the large number of young men they sent to fight suggests that they found a satisfactory rationale, but the struggle to do so was not easy. When Pickens's (white) boss congratulated him in 1945 for his fine work in selling savings bonds, he acknowledged that the job had required "superb patience and Christian fortitude," not just to convince blacks of America's virtues but to help Pickens turn the other cheek to whites—including some in his own agency—who racially insulted him in large and small ways.[43] Bartow Tipper, a steelworker, trade unionist, and civil rights activist in 1940s Aliquippa, Pennsylvania, remembered the red-hot anger that spread among Jones and Laughlin's black steel workers in the summer of 1943 because of their continued exclusion from the most desired jobs—jobs monopolized by Italian and eastern European unionists: "We'd tell everybody: 'Were tired of being pushed in the corner.' We'd done give our lives for this war, we done work hard for this war—and we can't get no jobs. Can't move up. And so we said, therefore: 'We'll tear this place up. We can't take it no more.'"[44]

Tipper and his fellow black workers, in fact, didn't tear the place up. Federal negotiators, chastened by the racial violence in Detroit, rushed in to mediate the dispute and arranged a compromise settlement that eased African American anger. Black workers could be placated. They understood that the war had offered their people rare economic opportunities, not to be lightly tossed away. In the years immediately following the war, Tipper used to upset his white bosses by declaring: "Goddamit, I wouldn't care if there was a war every week! The only time we ever made a lot money, the only time we'd ever get anything done, was when the war come."[45] In Tipper's double recollection of rage at racial injustice and appreciation for the new opportunities the war offered blacks, we can discern the ambivalence that characterized the attitudes of so many African Americans to the war.

Because of their mixed wartime experience, cultural incorporation into the nation was slower among African Americans than among European ethnics. Their patriotism was more subdued, and the nation's claims on them were fewer. Indeed, one can discern in black workers' attitudes evidence to bolster the revisionist argument that American workers remained "apart" from the nation during World War II. But black workers were not sufficiently numerous or well enough accepted by white workers for their wariness to spread throughout the working class.[46] The African American experience does provide, however, a useful comparative perspective from which to evaluate the effects of war patriotism on the white working class, and especially its European ethnic majority.

The white ethnic workers who became so devoted to America during the war did not lose their class consciousness. They continued to skirmish with their bosses. The massive strike wave in 1946 testifies to their continuing ability to understand their class interest and act aggressively in its behalf.[47]

Still, it became harder to act on these class instincts now that they provoked the wrath—and police power—of a nation that ethnic unionists much admired. This dilemma had not existed for unionists in the 1930s, when the state—or large portions of it, the president included—endorsed the labor movement's vision of what the country should become and countenanced its militant posture.[48] "The average man once more confronts the problem that faced the Minute Man," noted Franklin D. Roosevelt during his 1936 nomination acceptance speech, a moment when the New Deal was at its most ambitious and the labor movement was near the zenith of its political power. The average man, Roosevelt continued, must fight a war against the economic royalists, "take away their power," and thereby "save a great and precious form of government for ourselves and for the world."[49] Roosevelt's invocation of the American Revolution offered powerful sanction to a mass movement that had insistently called attention to the conflict between America's rich and poor.

But the war prompted Roosevelt to jettison his "economic royalist" harangues, especially once he decided to rely on corporate America to direct the economy's war mobilization. Government propagandists, meanwhile, sought to popularize a notion of nationhood that was inclusive and a language of patriotism steeped in metaphors of harmony and mutual respect rather than of antagonism and struggle. If this stress on respect encouraged campaigns for cultural and racial equality, it robbed labor of the leverage needed to increase its power at capital's expense. Patriotism in the 1940s required a different sort of behavior from workers than in the 1930s. Militant protests could not be so easily wrapped in "red, white, and blue"; those packaged this way no longer attracted much sympathy or support beyond the factory gates and union halls. Workers pursuing their economic grievances at all costs risked being stigmatized as un-American—not something that many working-class Americans, especially those ethnics whose allegiance to their nation was quickening, wanted to endure.[50] It may be that many of the wildcat strikes, which tended to involve few workers and to be short, were intended by the wildcatters themselves as a kind of limited protest: here was a way to bring a perceived injustice to light without unduly damaging the nation's military or economic welfare. One piece of evidence to support this view is their timing. As Alan Clive has shrewdly pointed out, the incidence of wildcats rose in months when the news from the war was good, and declined when the outcome of crucial battles was in doubt.[51]

My emphasis on the extent of white working-class patriotism does not negate the central point of Lichtenstein's revisionism, that the 1940s were a time when labor failed to achieve its larger political ambitions. It does suggest, however, that the roots of this failure lie not only in the timidity of union leaders but in the rank and file's affection for "America," in the desire of ordinary ethnic workers for recognition and acceptance as Americans, and in their willingness to believe in the essential goodness of the war and of their nation. Patriotism was a doubleedged sword, one that could both help and injure the workers who espoused it. In the 1940s it did both—helping European ethnics feel fully at home in America while simultaneously frustrating the ambition of those who sought to extend popular control over the nation's economic institutions.

If this analysis is correct, it seems that black workers—whose patriotism was more circumspect—preserved in the postwar era a greater freedom of action, a greater readiness to define Americanism in terms that made sense to them rather than in terms set forth by the government. Black workers, in fact, did seem to defy the cold war consensus more easily than white workers. They were more willing than their white counterparts, for instance, to associate with communists. Those who became civil rights activists in the 1950s were more prepared than white unionists to disrupt the narrow political confines that protest movements had been channeled into and to challenge both the moral authority and the police powers of their nation.[52] For African Americans in the 1950s and early 1960s, American patriotism remained a spur to social action rather than to complacency. Their war had yet to be won.

NOTES

1 John Morton Blum, *V Was for Victory: Politics and American Culture during World War II* (New York, 1976). A list of revisionist scholarship would include (but would certainly not be limited to) Peter Irons, *Justice at Home* (New York, 1983); John W. Dower, *War without Mercy: Race and Power in the Pacific War* (New York, 1986); Karen Anderson, *Wartime Women: Sex Roles, Family Relations, and the Status of Women during World War II* (Westport, Conn., 1983); Thomas Cripps, "Racial Ambiguities in American Propaganda Movies," in *Film and Radio Propaganda in World War II,* ed. K. R. M. Short (Knoxville, Tenn., 1983), 125–45; Robert B. Westbrook, "'I Want a Girl, Just Like the Girl That Married Harry James': American Women and the Problem of Political Obligation in World War II," *American Quarterly* 42 (1990): 587-614; David Wyman, *The Abandonment of the Jews: America and the Holocaust* (New York, 1984); Paul Fussell, *Wartime: Understanding and Behavior in the Second World War* (New York, 1989).

2 Nelson Lichtenstein, *Labor's War at Home: The CIO in World War II* (New York, 1982). Lichtenstein and others had begun to sketch out this interpretation in the 1970s. See *Radical America* 9 (July-October 1975), an issue devoted to labor and the home front, and Martin Glaberman, *Wartime Strikes: The Struggle against the No-Strike Pledge in the UAW during World War II* (Detroit, 1980). See also George Lipsitz, *Class and Culture in Cold War America: "A Rainbow at Midnight"* (South Hadley, Mass., 1982), an important revisionist account that received less attention than Lichtenstein's work.

3 On historians' suspicions of patriotism and nationalism, see Joshua Freeman, "Delivering the Goods: Industrial Unionism during World War II," *Labor History* 19 (1978): 581-83, 590-93.

4 Lichtenstein, in fact, has revised his own views on the subject and now attributes far more significance to the role of patriotism in shaping working-class consciousness. See, for example, his "The Making of the Postwar Working Class: Cultural Pluralism and Social Structure in World War II," *History Today* 51 (1988): 42-63, and the volume he coedited with Howell John Harris, *Industrial Democracy in America: The Ambiguous Promise* (New York, 1993), the introduction in particular.

5 I am not including such military actions as the Persian Gulf War in the category "major wars."

6   On the history of antiwar movements, see Charles Chatfield, *The American Peace Movement: Ideals and Activism* (New York, 1992).

7   Marc Scott Miller, *The Irony of Victory: World War II and Lowell, Massachusetts* (Urbana, Ill., 1988).

8   Mark H. Leff, "The Politics of Sacrifice on the American Home Front in World War II," *Journal of American History* 77 (1991): 1296.

9   Gary Gerstle, *Working-Class Americanism: The Politics of Labor in a Textile City, 1914-1960* (New York, 1989), chap. 9.

10 There were virtually no blacks in Woonsocket.

11 Gerstle, *Working-Class Americanism*, 298-301.

12 Miller, *Irony of Victory*, 81.

13 This is also true of Alan Winkler, *The Politics of Propaganda: The Office of War Information, 1942-1945* (New Haven, 1978), and Frank W. Fox, *Madison Avenue Goes to War: The Strange Military Career of American Advertising* (Provo, Utah, 1975). Mark Leff does not address the issue of market segmentation in his article "The Politics of Sacrifice on the Homefront," but his piece is nevertheless a most interesting analysis of how Americans were "sold" on the war. See also Robert Griffith, "The Selling of America: The Advertising Council and American Politics, 1942-1960," *Business History Review* 57 (1983): 388-412.

14 Lizabeth Cohen discusses the introduction of market segmentation principles in her *Making a New Deal: Industrial Workers in Chicago, 1919-1939* (New York, 1990), 329.

15 Thus, for example, William Pickens, NAACP field secretary, was hired by the Treasury Department in 1942 to advise the advertising experts on selling war bonds in black communities. William Pickens Record Group (hereafter Pickens papers), microfilm, Schomburg Collection of *Negro Literature and History*, New York Public Library.

16 "I Died Today.... What Did You Do?" *Woonsocket Call*, 30 June 1944.

17 *ITU News*, "Whose Blood Killed Private Parkins?" 13 October 1944. For the discussion of other advertisements emphasizing this theme, *see* Gerstle, *Working-Class Americanism*, 295-301.

18 Gerstle, *Working-Class Americanism*, chaps. 4-6; Cohen, *Making a New Deal*, chap. 8.

19 On the excitement that war mobilization initially unleashed in labor's ranks, see Nelson Lichtenstein, "From Corporatism to Collective Bargaining: Organized Labor and the Eclipse of Social Democracy in the Postwar Era," in *The Rise and Fall of the New Deal Order, 1930-1980*, ed. Steve Fraser and Gary Gerstle (Princeton, 1989), 122-52.

20 See, for example, *Sahara* (1943), with Humphrey Bogart.

21 I am indebted to Russell Kazal for bringing this book to my attention; Kazal, "'There Aren't Any Peasants in This Nation': Class, Pluralism, Nationalism, and Football in John R. Tunis's *All-American,*" unpublished manuscript, University of Pennsylvania, 1993, in author's possession.

22 *Comnwn Ground* 1 (autumn 1940): 2.

23 CIO-PAC, *This Is Your America* (New York, 1944), published in Joseph Gaer, *The First Round: The Story of the CIO Political Action Committee* (New York, 1944), 20.

24 *Common Ground* 1 (autumn 1940): 103.

25 Gunnar Myrdal, *An American Dilemma: The Negro Problem and Modem Democracy* (New York, 1944), 2 vols.; Walter A. Jackson, *Gunnar Myrdal and America's Conscience: Social Engineering and Racial Liberalism, 1938-1987* (Chapel Hill, N.C., 1990); Robin M. Williams Jr., *The Reduction of Intergroup Tensions: A Survey of Research on Problems of Ethnic, Racial, and Religious Group Relations* (New York, 1947); Carey McWilliams, *Brothers under the Skin* (Boston, 1951); Ruth Benedict, *The Races of Mankind* (New York, 1943); John Dower, *War without Mercy: Race and Power in the Pacific War* (New York, 1986), chap. 6.

26 See Gary Gerstle, "The Protean Character of American Liberalism," *American Historical Review* 99 (October 1994): 1043-73; Philip Gleason, "Americans All: World War II and the Shaping of American Identity," *Review of Politics* 43 (1981): 483-518; and Richard W. Steele, "The War on Intolerance: The Reformulation of American Nationalism, 1939-1941," *Journal of American Ethnic History* 9 (1989): 11-33.

27 *ITU News*, 26 May 1944.

28 U.S. Department of Commerce, Bureau of the Census, *Historical Statistics of the United States, Colonial Times to 1970* (White Plains, N.Y., 1989), 114-16.

29 The second-highest naturalization rate during an equivalent five-year period, achieved in the years 1936 to 1940, was only 16.8 percent, less than half the wartime total. Ibid.

30 That more women than men were naturalized in these years underscores the civilian character of this process. Ibid.

31 Proportions of naturalized Poles in 1920 and 1930 stood at 28 and 50 percent, respectively, far less than for naturalized English people (63 and 67 percent). By 1950 French Canadians had reached the 70 percent naturalization threshold, but Mexicans, in a strikingly divergent pattern (only 26 percent), had not. Reed Ueda, "Naturalization and Citizenship," in *The Harvard Encyclopedia of American Ethnic Groups*, ed. Stephan Themstrom (Cambridge, Mass., 1980), 747.

32 Lichtenstein, "Making of the Postwar Working Class"; Geoffrey Perrett, *Days of Sadness, Years of Triumph: The American People, 19391945* (Madison, Wisc., 1985), 325-56; Howell John Harris, *The Right to Manage: Industrial Relations Policies of American Business in the 1940s* (Madison, Wisc., 1982), 41-89.

33 Alan Clive, *State of War: Michigan in World War II* (Ann Arbor, Mich., 1979), 77.

34 Richard M. Dalfiume, "The 'Forgotten Years' of the Negro Revolution," *Journal of American History* 56 (1968): 90-106; Joe William Trotter Jr., *Black Milwaukee: The Making of an Industrial Proletariat, 1915-1945* (Urbana, Ill., 1985); William H. Harris, *The Harder We Run: Black Workers since the Civil War* (New York, 1982); "Summary: Activities of William Pickens for 1943," and letter from Pickens to Charles W. Adams, 6 March 1944, reel 3, Pickens papers; Lichtenstein, "Making of the Postwar Working Class."

35 Richard M. Dalfiume, *Desegregation of the U.S. Armed Forces: Fighting on Two Fronts, 1939-1953* (Columbia, Mo., 1969). The government also dragged its heels in desegregating industry, a reluctance that prompted A. Philip Randolph to threaten a march on Washington in 1941. Randolph called off the march when a worried government established the Fair Employment Practices Commission. See Louis Rucharmes, *Race, Jobs, and Politics: The Story of the FEPC* (New York, 1953), and Herbert Garfinkel, *When Negroes March: The March on Washington Movement in the Organizational Politics of FEPC* (New York, 1959).

36 Richard Slotkin offers some perceptive comments on the multiethnic platoon in his *Gunfighter Nation: The Myth of the Frontier in Twentieth-Century America* (New York, 1992), 318-26.

37 Quoted in August Meier and Elliott Rudwick, *Black Detroit and the Rise of the UAW* (New York, 1979), 192.

38 Robert Shogan and Tom Craig, *Detroit Race Riot: A Study in Violence* (Philadelphia, 1964), 89; Harvard Sitkoff, "The Detroit Race Riot of 1943," *Michigan History* 53 (1969): 183-206; Sitkoff, "Racial Militancy and Interracial Violence in the Second World War," *Journal of American History* 58 (1971): 661-81; Joshua Freeman, "Delivering the Goods."

39 On the white southerners' migration to Detroit, see Clive, *State of War*, 170-85.

40 Blum, *V Was for Victory*, 199-204.

41 Studs Terkel, *"The Good War": An Oral History of World War II* (New York, 1984), 141-42. On Americanizing ethnics' hostility to blacks, see also Arnold R. Hirsch, *Making the Second Ghetto: Race and Housing in Chicago, 1940-1960* (New York, 1983), 171-211, and David R. Roediger, "Whiteness and Ethnicity in the History of 'White Ethnics' in the United States," in his Toward the Abolition of Whiteness: Essays on Race, Politics, and Working Class History (London, 1994), 181-98.

42 William Pickens quotes these words of a fellow African American in his essay "The American Negro and His Country in World War," n.d., reel 3, box 6, Pickens papers.

43 Letter from James Houghtelling to William Pickens, 29 October 1945, reel 3, box 6, Pickens papers.

44 Interview with Bartow Tipper, conducted by Charles Lane, 1982; transcript in author's possession. See also Charles Lane, "Honoring Our Commitments: The Role of the United Steel Workers of America in Controlling Rank-and-File Militancy under the World War II No-Strike Pledge" (senior thesis, Harvard University, 1983).

45 Ibid.

46 For a markedly different interpretation, see George Lipsitz's *Class and Culture in Cold War America*, chap. 1, which posits that black- initiated wildcats and public protests in World War II impelled all workers—white and black—to challenge the authority of their employers and their nation and thus intensified working-class militancy. Given the racial and ethnic divisions within the American working class, I find this view too optimistic.

47 See ibid. for a comprehensive account of the postwar strike wave (though one that pays little attention to ethnicity and Americanization).

48 On the close relation between the 1930s labor movement and portions of the New Deal state, see Steve Fraser, "The 'Labor Question,'" in Fraser and Gerstle, *Rise and Fall of the New Deal Order*, 55-84.

49 *The Public Papers and Addresses of Franklin D. Roosevelt* (New York, 1976), 5:230-36.

50 For a more extended discussion of this issue, see Gerstle, *Working-Class Americanism*, chap. 9.

51 Thus Clive writes, "Michigan strikes dropped sharply in the invasion month of June, 1944, and fell again at the turn of 1945 in the wake of the near-disaster at Bastogne." *State of War*, 76.

52 See Michael K. Honey, *Southern Labor and Black Civil Rights: Organizing Memphis Workers* (Urbana, Ill., 1993), 242-44, 288-89.

DISCUSSION QUESTIONS

- What reasons did Americans have to support the war effort? Did these reasons coincide with the government's official war aims?

- What evidence does the author provide to support his argument that the support for the war was pragmatic? What statements in the article undercut that argument? Was the author correct? Why or why not?

- Did World War II create a sense of unity for Americans? What evidence does the article show to prove or disprove that?

CHAPTER XI

THE COMMODITY GAP

CONSUMERISM AND THE MODERN HOME

OBJECTIVES

- Analyze the sense of political and domestic consensus during the 1950s in the United States.

PREWRITING

- What similarities exist between the 1920s and the 1950s? Are they both a period of conservative reaction? Consider the events that affected the United States at home and abroad that in turn influenced the 1920s and the 1950s.

The Commodity Gap: Consumerism and the Modern Home

ELAINE TYLER MAY

> As a normal part of life, thrift now is un-American.
>
> —WILLIAM H. WHYTE, JR., 1956

> No man who owns his own house and lot can be a Communist. He has too much to do.
>
> —WILLIAM J. LEVITT, DEVELOPER OF LEVITTOWN, 1948[1]

The sexually charged, child-centered family took its place as the embodiment of the postwar American dream. The most tangible symbol of that dream was the suburban home—the locale of the good life, the evidence of democratic abundance. It did not take long for this consumer-laden dream house to land squarely in the middle of cold war politics. One remarkable example demonstrates the direct link between the suburban American dream and the international dynamics of the cold war. In 1948, when Europe was still recovering from World War II, American officials worried that political instability might lead some nations to embrace communism. Leaders in the United States were particularly worried that Italy might go communist. A critical election was approaching, and there were several "hot spots" in the country where impoverished Italians appeared to be leaning toward voting for the Communist Party. At that time, Richard Moore, an aide to California congressman Richard Nixon, was trying to figure out a way to influence the Italian election. Prior to joining Nixon's congressional staff in Washington, Moore had worked in the television industry in California. So he contacted John Guedel, creator of several early television shows, and asked for help.

Guedel came up with an idea: the "Win a Future" contest. Anyone who entered the contest had a chance to "win a future," which included a house in the newly completed suburban development of Panorama City, in the San Fernando Valley. The house would contain the finest new appliances and furnishings, and the lucky winner would also receive a new car and a job. According to Guedel, anyone could enter the contest by writing a letter stating in 100 words or less why it is better to live under capitalism than communism, enclosing ten cents, and sending it to the television station. Each week, one contestant was selected to appear on the television show *People Are Funny* and have an opportunity to solve a riddle in order to "win a future." Six hundred and forty thousand Americans entered the contest. The letters were collected and sent to Italy, along with CARE packages of food. The United States Army translated the letters and distributed them with the CARE packages to Italian voters in key areas at risk of electing communists. Apparently, the effort worked: The communists were defeated in the 1948 election in Italy. Meanwhile, contestant Vivienne George finally solved the riddle and "won a future." As it turned out, the future she won was not so bright. She and her husband, a disabled World War II veteran, only lived in the house for a few months. They were the first residents to move into Panorama City, and they were too isolated, especially considering his medical needs. The promised job never materialized, and the national notoriety left the Georges vulnerable to the demands of many people who believed that the couple were now fabulously wealthy.[2]

Although Vivienne George was the only one to "win a future," like many other Americans she discovered that the American dream did not fully live up to its promise. But the suburban home, complete with modern appliances and furnishings, continued to serve as a tangible symbol of the American way of life, and as a powerful weapon in the cold war propaganda arsenal. A decade after the "Win a Future" contest, Richard Nixon was no longer a congressman. He was now vice president under Dwight D. Eisenhower. In 1959, Eisenhower sent Nixon to represent the United States at the American Exhibition in Moscow, where a "model home," similar to the one in Panorama City won by Vivienne George, was on display. Let us now return briefly to the site of the famous "kitchen debate," where Vice President Richard M. Nixon articulated the essence of American superiority by pointing to the consumer-laden suburban home. The ideal home Nixon described was one that obliterated class distinctions and accentuated gender distinctions. The "model home" he extolled was not a mansion but a modest ranch-style structure, "within the price range of the average U.S. worker," complete with modern appliances that would "make easier the life of our housewives." Although Vivienne George had to solve a riddle to win her house in the suburbs because she couldn't otherwise afford it, for Nixon, the most important feature of the suburban home was its availability to Americans of all classes.

"Let us start with some of the things in this exhibit," Nixon began. "You will see a house, a car, a television set—each the newest and most modern of its type we produce. But can only the rich in the United States afford such things? If this were the case, we would have to include in our definition of rich the millions of America's wage earners." Nixon felt certain that the possibility of homeowner-ship would defuse the most dangerous potential of class conflict. As he explained to Soviet premier Nikita Khrushchev, "Our steel workers, as you know, are on strike. But any steel worker could buy this house. They earn $3 an hour. This house costs about $100 a month to buy on a contract running twenty-five to thirty years." Khrushchev countered, "We have steel workers and we have peasants who also can afford to spend $14,000 for a house." But for Nixon, homeownership represented even more than a comfortable way of life; it was the validation of the free enterprise system.[3]

Nixon's frame of reference was the family: "There are 44 million families in the United States. Twenty-five million of [them] live in houses or apartments that have as much or more floor space than the one you see in this exhibit. Thirty-one million families own their own homes and the land on which they are built. America's 44 million families own a total of 56 million cars, 50 million television sets and 143 million radio sets. And they buy an average of nine dresses and suits and 14 pairs of shoes per family per year."

Nixon then described other miracles of domestic technology. Pointing to a television screen, he said, "We can see here what is happening in other parts of the home." Khrushchev, scorning the American obsession with gadgets, chided, "This is probably always out of order. … Don't you have a machine that puts food into the mouth and pushes it down? Many things you've shown us are interesting but they are not needed in life. … They are merely gadgets." Yet both leaders took the commodity gap seriously. The Soviet premier continued, "Newly built Russian houses have all this equipment right now. Moreover, all you have to do to get a house is to be born in the Soviet Union. So I have a right to a house. In America if you don't have a dollar, you have the right to sleep on the pavement. Yet you say that we are slaves of communism."

Khrushchev further accused Americans of building houses to last only twenty years, so builders could continually sell new ones. "We build firmly," said the Soviet leader. "We build for our children and grandchildren." But Nixon argued that after twenty years, the older home or kitchen would be obsolete. Linking consumer aspirations to scientific expertise, he explained that the American system was designed to take advantage of new inventions and new techniques. Unimpressed, Khrushchev replied, "This theory does not hold water." But for Nixon the theory did hold water, for it reflected his belief in the potential for individualism and upward mobility.

The metaphor that prevailed throughout the debate was that of a race. But it was not the arms race or the space race; it was the consumer race—centered on the home. Khrushchev estimated that it would take only seven years before the USSR would reach the American standard of living. Already in eight years, grain and milk output had nearly doubled, and television sets were up from sixty-seven thousand to a million. The terms of the cold war were set in these figures. Nixon was willing to concede Russian successes in the space race, but he argued that domestic consumer goods were the most meaningful measure of American superiority over the Soviet Union: "There are some instances where you may be ahead of us, for example in the development of the thrust of your rockets for the investigation of outer space; there may be some instances in which we are ahead of you—in color television, for instance." Not to be outdone, Khrushchev claimed, "No, we are up with you on this, too." Nixon remarked, "We welcome this kind of competition because when we engage in it, no one loses, everyone wins." Thus, the commodity gap took precedence over the missile gap.

In Nixon's vision, the suburban ideal of homeownership would tame two potentially disruptive forces: women and workers. In appliance-laden houses across the country, working-class as well as business-class breadwinners could fulfill the new American work-to-consume ethic. Homeownership would lessen class consciousness among workers, who would set their sights toward the middle-class ideal. The family home would be the place where a man could display his success through the accumulation of consumer goods. Women would reap rewards for domesticity by surrounding themselves with commodities; they would remain content as housewives because appliances would ease their burdens. For both men and women, homeownership would reinforce aspirations for upward mobility and diminish the potential for social unrest.

Nixon was not the only one who believed that the American preoccupation with procurement would be a safeguard against the threat of class warfare and communism. Mayor Joseph Darst of St. Louis, expressing the views of liberal anticommunists, wrote to the city's board of aldermen in 1951 that if everyone had good housing, "no one in the United States would need to worry today about the threat of communism in this country. Communists love American slums. Our clearance of these slums and erection of adequate housing is one of the most effective answers we can give communism locally."[4]

For those who agreed that economic optimism was essential to keep the free enterprise system alive and well, there were reasons to rejoice. The postwar years witnessed a huge increase in discretionary spending power, an increase that surpassed gains in income or prices. Between 1947 and 1961, the number of families rose 28 percent, national income increased over 60 percent, and the group with discretionary income (those with money for nonnecessities) doubled. Rather than putting this money aside for a rainy day, Americans were inclined to spend it. A 1946 Gallup poll indicated that in spite of persistent pockets of poverty and fears of another depression, the desire to spend was much stronger than the desire to save. This is not to say that the concern for future security was tossed to the wind; on the contrary, security remained a high priority. Americans were only slightly more hopeful about the economic future in 1945 than they had been in 1937 at the depth of the depression. Fears of another depression were widespread, and one-third of the population was still in poverty.[5] But the increase in income for the middle and working classes, combined with new governmental supports, encouraged Americans to invest their money in purchases. Social Security no doubt eased their fears of poverty in old age, and veterans' mortgages facilitated expenditures for homeownership. Americans responded with guarded optimism by making purchases that would strengthen their sense of security. In the postwar years, investing in one's own home, along with the trappings that would enhance family life, seemed the best way to plan for the future.

Instead of rampant spending for personal luxury items, Americans were likely to spend their money at home. In the five years after World War II, consumer spending increased 60 percent, but the amount spent on household furnishings and appliances rose 240 percent. In the same five years, purchases for food rose only 33 percent, and for clothing a mere 20 percent. From the depression onward, the trend in spending was striking. Between 1935 and 1950, the money income of Americans increased 50 percent. But this increase was not divided evenly among purchasing categories. Expenditures for food and drink increased only 30 percent; for clothing, 53 percent; for personal care, 69 percent; and for education, 73 percent. These increases were modest compared to the increases in expenditures for household operation (108 percent), recreation (185 percent), and automobiles (205 percent). In the four years following the end of the war, Americans purchased 21.4 million cars, 20 million refrigerators, 5.5 million stoves, and 11.6 million televisions and moved into over 1 million new housing units each year. The same patterns extended into the 1950s, a decade in which prosperity continued to spread.[6]

The locale for this consumer-oriented family life was suburbia. The suburban home caught the imagination as well as the purse strings of postwar Americans. A study of the psychology of spending noted, "The impact of suburbia on consumer behavior can hardly be overstated…. Young people chose to marry early, to have several children in the early years of marriage, to live in … nice neighborhoods, and to have cars, washing machines, refrigerators, television sets, and several other appliances at the same time." Americans channeled their spending accordingly. With the exception of the very poor, those of ample as well as modest means exhibited a great deal of conformity in their consumption attitudes and behavior. Spending patterns reflected widely shared beliefs about the good life, which seemed within reach of many, even those of the lower-middle and working classes.[7]

Consumer patterns, then, reflected one more aspect of containment behavior as the nation's affluent majority poured their income into homes and family pursuits. The old version of the virtuous home was a much more ascetic one. Still, the values associated with domestic spending upheld traditional American concerns with pragmatism and morality, rather than opulence and luxury. Purchasing for the home helped alleviate traditional American uneasiness with consumption: the fear that spending would lead to decadence. Family-centered spending reassured Americans that affluence would strengthen the American way of life. The goods purchased by middle-class consumers, like a modern refrigerator or a house in the suburbs, were intended to foster traditional values.[8]

Pragmatism and family enrichment were the keys to virtuous consumerism. The commodities that people bought promised to reinforce home life and uphold traditional gender roles. After all, American women were housewives; their lives were functional, not merely ornamental. In general, male breadwinners provided the income for household goods, and their wives purchased them. Public opinion polls taken after the war indicate that both men and women were generally opposed to employment for women and believed that a woman who ran a home had a "more interesting time" than did a woman with a full-time job. There were, however, circumstances in which employment for women was approved—especially if the income it generated fostered family life. For example, one poll showed that postwar women and men believed that if a young couple could not marry because the man was not earning enough to support them both, "the girl should take a job so they can get married right away."[9] By and large, however, employment for married women was discouraged. Given these prevailing attitudes, it is no wonder that Nixon continually interchanged the words *woman* and *housewife* as he extolled the American way of life at the Moscow exhibition.

Yet that equation should be examined closely, since not all married women were full-time homemakers during the 1950s. In fact, the postwar years brought more wives into the paid labor force than ever before. Americans felt a great deal of ambivalence toward women's employment—a legacy of the depression and the war. On the one hand, it was unfortunate if a wife had to hold a job; on the other hand, it was considered far worse if the family was unable to purchase what were believed to be necessities for the home.

During these years, the very definition of household needs changed to include many more consumer items. Since it was the homemaker's responsibility to purchase these items, women sought employment, ironically, to promote their role as consumers. The economic importance of women's role as consumers cannot be overstated, for it kept American industry rolling and sustained jobs for the nation's male providers. Nearly the entire increase in the gross national product in the mid-1950s was due to increased spending on consumer durables and residential construction.[10] Many employed wives considered their jobs secondary to their role as consumers and in tune with the ethic of togetherness and subordination that characterized their marital relationships. This was one legacy that depression-bred daughters inherited: Women sought employment to bolster the family budget but not to disrupt domestic power relationships. As long as their employment provided a secondary source of income and did not undermine the authority of the male breadwinner, it was acceptable to the family.[11]

The house and commodity boom also had tremendous propaganda value, for it was those affluent homes, complete with breadwinner and homemaker, that provided evidence of the superiority of the American way of life. Since much of the cold war was waged in propaganda battles, this vision of domesticity was a powerful weapon. Although they may have been unwitting soldiers, women who marched off to the nation's shopping centers to equip their new homes joined the ranks of American cold warriors. As newscaster and noted cold warrior George Putnam said in 1947, shopping centers were "concrete expressions of the practical idealism that built America … plenty of free parking for all those cars that we capitalists seem to acquire. Who can help but contrast [them] with what you'd find under communism?"[12]

Consumers no doubt had fewer global concerns in mind. They had saved their money for specific purposes. During the war, a survey of bank depositors indicated that 43 percent were eager to spend their money on "future needs," and half of those specified purchases for the home. Leading architects helped give tangible form to these desires by publishing plans for "dream houses" in leading magazines like the *Ladies Home Journal*. Construction companies also fed consumer longings by selling scrapbooks for saving ideas for future houses, with sections divided into the various rooms of the home. The Andersen Window Company, for example, which was well aware of the potential market, distributed three hundred and fifty thousand embossed scrapbooks before the end of the war. By June 1944, appliances topped the list of the most desired consumer items. When asked what they hoped to purchase in the postwar years, Americans listed washing machines first, then electric irons, refrigerators, stoves, toasters, radios, vacuum cleaners, electric fans, and hot water heaters. Advertisers claimed that these items constituted the American way of life that the soldiers were fighting for.[13]

The pent-up desires for homes and appliances represented something more than mere fantasies of luxurious living. The need for wartime housing was great. Dislocated war workers needed $100 million worth of new housing, which prompted a construction boom during the war. By 1943, residential real estate buying reached levels unknown since the 1920s. But wartime building was inadequate to meet the increasing need. The housing shortage reached crisis proportions after the war. In 1945, 98 percent of American cities reported shortages of houses, and more than 90 percent reported shortages of apartments. By 1947, 6 million families were doubling up with relatives or friends. The housing industry gained tremendous momentum after the war in the face of these immediate needs, and it took advantage of the conversion of production technology for peacetime use.[14] Supply and demand came together to foster an explosion in residential housing after the war. But the expansion did not take place equally in all types of housing; nor were the new dwellings available to all Americans. Largely as a result of governmental policies, massive suburban developments of single-family houses took precedence over apartments and inner-city dwellings. The Servicemen's Readjustment Act of 1944 (the GI Bill of Rights) created a Veterans Administration (VA) program of guaranteed mortgage insurance, expanding the Federal Housing Authority (FHA) program dating back to 1934. The new programs, which provided federal insurance for loans to white veterans, encouraged private investors to enter the housing mortgage market. In addition, the tax benefits for homeowners became substantial in the 1940s. The government also financed large suburban tracts, such as those built by William Levitt. With all these incentives for building and purchasing suburban residences, it soon became cheaper to buy than to rent. Provided they were white, veterans could buy homes in Levittown, with a thirty-year mortgage and no down payment, by spending only $56 per month. At the same time, the average apartment rental in many cities was $93. These overpriced, often substandard apartments were left to Americans of color, who were excluded from the suburbs. When asked why black families were not allowed to purchase homes in Levittown, William Levitt claimed that he was in the business of building houses, not solving social problems. As a result of such racist attitudes and the policies they generated, social problems that did not exist at the time emerged in the years to come.[15]

Postwar governmental policies fostered the construction of the vast majority of new housing in the suburbs. Housing starts went from 114,000 in 1944 to an all-time high of 1,692,000 in 1950. The cold war made a profound contribution to suburban sprawl. In 1951, the *Bulletin of Atomic Scientists* devoted an issue to "defense through decentralization" that argued in favor of depopulating the urban core to avoid a concentration of residences or industries in a potential target area for a nuclear attack. Joining this effort was the American Road Builders Association, a lobbying group second only to the munitions industry. As a result of these pressures, Congress passed the Interstate Highway Act in 1956, which provided $100 billion to cover 90 percent of the cost for forty-one thousand miles of national highways. When President Dwight D. Eisenhower signed the bill into law, he stated one of the major reasons for the new highway system: "[In] case of atomic attack on our key cities, the road net must permit quick evacuation of target areas."[16]

Many people believed that the suburbs also provided protection against labor unrest, which might lead to class warfare and its presumed inevitable result, communism. The report of a 1948 meeting of a San Francisco businessmen's association, chaired by the ex-president of the National Association of Home Builders, argued for the dispersion of industry outside central cities: "Conditions under which employees live, as well as work, vitally influence management-labor relations. Generally, large aggregations of labor in one big [central-city] plant are more subject to outside disrupting influences, and have less happy relations with management, than in smaller [suburban] plants."[17]

The suburban growth that resulted from these policies was neither universal nor inevitable; in Europe, centralization rather than decentralization predominated. In the United States, the FHA and VA mortgage policies, the highway system, the financing of sewers, the government subsidies for suburban developments such as Levittown, and the placing of public housing in the center of urban ghettos facilitated the dispersal of the white middle class into the suburbs and contributed to the decay of the inner cities. Furthermore, blacks were excluded from the suburbs by de facto segregation and the FHA's redlining policies that denied mortgages to black families, more than by poverty. Although there were a small number of black as well as racially integrated suburbs, the vast majority of suburban neighborhoods were restricted to whites.[18]

In 1946, as a result of all these supports for homeownership, for the first time a majority of the nation's white families lived in homes they owned. Over the next fifteen years, 12 million more families became homeowners. By the 1950s, most of those who purchased homes did so to buy a better house or move into a better neighborhood. Loans available to homeowners favored purchase over repair, which further spurred the movement of the white population into newly constructed suburban developments. Between 1950 and 1970, the suburban population doubled, from 36 million to 74 million; 83 percent of the nation's growth during those years took place in the suburbs.[19]

Although the suburbs were clearly designated for whites only, they offered a picture of domestic comfort available to those with modest incomes. These homes represented the American way of life, democratic and affordable, that Nixon would extoll in Moscow. Confirming Nixon's assertion of the American desire for change and newness, upgrading was a widespread motive for spending. The nation's consumers continually replaced, improved, or expanded their homes, appliances, and cars, long before those items had worn out. Federal policies, combined with increased affluence, made it possible for white Americans of moderate means to indulge their desires for newness and mobility.[20] In these ways, the cold war goal of defusing class conflict succeeded in the suburbs, where families of white-collar and blue-collar workers lived side by side.

Federal programs did more than simply blur class lines and spur a trend toward homeownership in the expanding suburbs. Policies that reflected and encouraged the American domestic ideology fostered and reinforced a particular kind of family life. In effect, these federal programs provided subsidies and incentives for couples to marry and have several children. Houses were designed to accommodate families with small children. Builders and architects assumed that men would be away at work during the day and houses would be occupied by full-time homemaker-mothers. In the first Levittown, a standardized suburban development built by William Levitt, 17,400 houses accommodated 82,000 residents. The structures were mass-produced and inexpensive, with a flexible interior design that was easily expandable if the family increased in size. Kitchens were near the front entrance, so mothers could keep an eye on their children as they cooked. Living rooms featured picture windows facing the backyard, also to facilitate the supervision of children. Appliances were included in the purchase price. The one-story design gave the home an informal look and was practical for families with young children, since there were no stairs, which could be dangerous. As young parents of the baby boom moved into these homes, it is no wonder that the first Levittown quickly earned the nicknames "Fertility Valley" and "The Rabbit Hutch."[21]

By stimulating these particular kinds of suburban housing developments and providing subsidies to homeowners, the federal government effectively underwrote the baby boom, along with the lifestyle and community arrangements that fostered traditional gender roles in the home. The government, along with the National Association of Home Builders, provided plans in the 1950s for smaller, inexpensive ranch-style homes that would allow for openness, adequate room for appliances and other consumer goods, and the easy supervision of children. Appliances were intended not to enable housewives to have more free time to pursue their own interests, but to help them achieve higher standards of cleanliness and efficiency, while allowing more time for child care. The suburban home was planned as a self-contained universe. Technological advances made housework efficient and professional; lawn mowers and cake mixes guaranteed a perfect result. In addition, homes were designed for enjoyment, fun, and togetherness. Family members would not need to go out for recreation or amusements, since they had swing sets, playrooms, and backyards with barbecues at home.[22]

Leisure pursuits encouraged a further infatuation with commodities. One of the most powerful of all postwar entertainments—the television set—sat squarely in people's living rooms. By the 1950s, televisions were selling at a rate of over 5 million a year. Television also fostered the classless ideal. Commercials extended the reach of advertising into people's homes, as did the abundant lifestyles portrayed on the screen. As historian George Lipsitz noted, situation comedies in the postwar years, especially those aimed at ethnic or working-class audiences, eased the transition from a depression-bred psychology of scarcity to an acceptance of spending. In shows like *I Remember Mama* or *The Honeymooners*, dramas of daily life often revolved around

Figure 11.1 Ranch-style suburban home, built circa 1950. The style exudes a sheltered look of protection and privacy, surrounded by a tamed and controlled natural world. *(Courtesy of Judy Tyler.)*

the purchase of consumer goods for the home. Characters in these programs urged each other to buy on installment, "live above our means—the American way," and spend rather than save. Commodities would solve the problem of the discontented housewife, foster pride in the provider whose job offered few intrinsic rewards, and allow children to "fit in" with their peers. Consumerism provided a means for assimilation into the American way of life: classless, homogeneous, and family-centered.[23]

The desire for the single-family home as a refuge against a chaotic world was not a postwar creation. Indeed, it dates back to housing reformers of the nineteenth century who first articulated the suburban family ideal. But it achieved new vigor in the postwar years, largely because the ideal was now within reach of most middle-class and many working-class Americans. In its modern manifestation, the suburban ranch-style home was to blend in with nature. As historian Clifford Edward Clark, Jr., observed, "The ranch house ... was ... seen as creating a unity with nature, but it was a unity that pictured nature as a tamed and open environment. ... The 1950s design standards conceived of the natural world in a simplified and controlled way that eliminated anything that was wild or irregular."[24] (See Figure 11.1.)

The contained, natural style, enhanced by modern technology and design, offered a sense of security as well as privatized abundance. The natural look was more personal and even sensual than the formalized structures of public life and business. And although most ranch-style tract homes were relatively small, standardized one-story structures, the flexible interior space allowed for individuality—something increasingly lacking in the highly organized and bureaucratic world of work.[25]

Who purchased these homes, and did they satisfy their owners' needs and desires? According to surveys at the time, about half those who purchased houses in 1949 and 1950 were white World War II veterans in their mid-thirties with young children. The second half were about ten years older; their housing needs or financial resources had changed, prompting them to buy larger homes in the suburbs. Both groups were parents of the baby-boom generation. The second group included Americans of the age and circumstances of the respondents to the Kelly Longitudinal Study (KLS). The residents of Levittown, however, were more likely to belong to the first group: younger, less affluent, and largely working class. In his study of Levittown, Herbert Gans found that most of the residents claimed to be satisfied with their living arrangements.[26]

Nevertheless, there were frustrations. Like expectations for exciting sexuality or fulfilling child rearing, the suburban ideal often promised more than it delivered. Many homeowners wished for more space but had to make do with smaller houses because of financial constraints. If spaciousness was an elusive goal for many suburbanites, so was the life of the happy housewife. Women in Levittown often complained about feeling trapped and isolated, facing endless chores of housekeeping and tending to children. For them, suburban life was not a life of fun and leisure but of exhausting work and isolation. In addition, since houses and neighborhoods were created with young children in mind, adolescents often chafed against the small rooms, lack of privacy, constant supervision, and absence of stores, restaurants, and other public gathering places where they could socialize in their neighborhoods. And although parents frequently mentioned the benefits of togetherness and the ability to spend more time with their families, the time-consuming commute for the men, and for the 25 percent of suburban women who were employed, actually reduced the amount of time available for families to share. Nevertheless, most homeowners expressed contentment with their residences, largely because they were significantly more spacious and comfortable than their previous dwellings, even if they did not measure up to one's "dream house."[27] Once again, postwar Americans lowered their expectations and expressed satisfaction with their suburban lot.

Although these suburban tracts have borne the brunt of scorn for their lack of individuality and mass-produced sameness, they did offer a modicum of comfort and convenience to growing families of modest means. Most of the contract-built houses, like those in Levittown, had central heating, indoor plumbing, telephones, automatic stoves, refrigerators, and washing machines—conveniences that most middle-class Americans would not like to sacrifice. Yet these isolated enclaves also weakened extended-family ties, promoted homogeneity in neighborhoods, intensified racial segregation, encouraged conformity, and fostered a style of life based on traditional gender roles in the home.[28]

With the exception of avant-garde intellectuals and a small number of politically active feminists, few Americans articulated viable alternatives to the suburban lifestyle. Those who complained that life did not fit the ideal, like overworked housewives in Levittown, generally tried to alleviate their miseries with more money or goods. The ideal itself was rarely called into question, at least not publicly. Nevertheless, it was difficult to achieve, even for those who could afford it. These were by and large affluent middle-class Americans, well educated and ambitious, who believed in the American dream and belonged to the postwar consensus. The men worked in a highly organized and bureaucratized economy, struggling to earn enough to afford the trappings of the good life. Fully one-fourth of their wives entered the paid labor force, often in part-time jobs when the children were at school, to help pay for the appliances and furnishings they desired. Whether or not they were employed, the women focused their energies on the home, and together both husbands and wives sought personal fulfillment in their families, surrounded by children and consumer goods. They entered marriage with a utopian vision that included happiness as well as security. Did the "good life" in consumer-laden houses fulfill their expectations? The responses of the couples in the KLS provide some answers.

These men and women were among the comfortable group of white middle-class Americans able to take advantage of the fruits of prosperity. Eighty-five percent had a family income of over $5,000 a year, although only thirteen percent earned over $15,000. Most had never been heavily in debt; 98 percent had never received any kind of public assistance and only 30 percent had received aid from relatives or friends. Their purchasing habits reflected a national pattern: Personal extravagance was rare, but consumption for family enrichment was a high priority. They exhibited a desire for consumer goods combined with a concern for future financial security. About 70 percent of the sample spent between $1,000 and $3,000 in housing expenses per year; 63 percent had one car and 33 percent had two cars. Slightly more than half had purchased their cars new.[29]

Reflecting the values of the time, which linked status to consumer purchases as well as to occupational level, Kelly rated the "prestige value" of the cars each family owned. He determined that 45 percent fell into the "low prestige" category; 30 percent, the middle; and 22 percent, the high. Only 3 percent owned cars in the "super-high prestige" range, such as a Cadillac. Most said they had one or two thousand dollars to spend per year above basic needs and rarely, if ever, purchased anything on the installment plan. These, then, were well-to-do but conservative people, not extravagant consumers.[30]

Like the rest of the middle class, the KLS respondents sought an expansive, affluent life within the security of their suburban homes. They spent their money in ways that would achieve that goal. The most important spending priority for 60 percent of the respondents was future financial security; for 23 percent, it was "increasing day-to-day living for family members"; and for 15 percent, it was "providing special opportunities for children." Clearly, security and family-oriented pursuits, not personal luxuries, were their major concerns.[31]

These women and men reveal how deeply domestic aspirations were rooted in the postwar success ethic. The increasing emphasis on familial rewards as validation for work found expression in the popular literature as well. Elizabeth Long's study of best-selling novels in the decade after World War II reveals a dramatic shift. In 1945, popular novels celebrated a vision of entrepreneurial success. But by 1955, themes had shifted toward more personal rewards. Heroes now made choices between work and leisure, family and the public world. They were more likely to accommodate themselves to the job and accept a secure place in the organizational hierarchy. According to Long, in these later novels the individual depends on others for happiness, and on the organization merely for a job. She called this theme the "corporate suburban" model, in contrast to the entrepreneurial model that prevailed a decade earlier. A typical mid-fifties best seller was Sloan Wilson's *The Man in the Grey Flannel Suit,* in which the protagonist is the new type of corporate hero who accommodates himself to bureaucratic constraints and wants to get ahead without sacrificing his family. Success is defined not by being at the top, but by having a secure, balanced life. In all these novels, successful career women are portrayed as "selfish"; female ambition is associated with sexual promiscuity. Suffering is the final lot for most such women in these stories.[32]

Husbands in the KLS sample reflected the values expressed in these novels. The family, rather than the workplace, was the arena in which men demonstrated their achievement. Work appeared relatively meaningless without the family to give purpose to men's efforts. When the men responded to an open-ended question asking what marriage had brought them that they could not have gained if they had remained single, many referred to the motivation it provided them to work hard and succeed. One husband wrote that his marriage gave him "the incentive to succeed and save for the future of my family." Others mentioned "greater incentive to succeed in business career," "feeling of accomplishment," "a family to work for," and "greater financial security." Echoing Nixon's remarks, many of these husbands wanted to make life better for their wives. In return, they expected to be appreciated. One husband complained that the "chief weakness of our marriage seems to be her failure to feel any … accomplishment from mutual efforts—particularly the family increases in net worth—house and car, furniture, insurance and bank accounts."[33]

What is interesting about all these responses, particularly their frequency of occurrence, is that these husbands claimed that they would have had neither the motivation nor the success without marriage. Clearly, the provider role itself—and an economically dependent wife's recognition and appreciation of it—often offered a greater source of satisfaction than the actual work a man performed. Men were likely to place this aspect of their role in the center of their feelings of marital satisfaction. Ten husbands mentioned a better financial position as a benefit of marriage, another thirteen listed security and stability, and eleven others included social position; forty-three said marriage gave them a sense of purpose and responsibility. Together, these responses made up the third largest category of answers to the question of what marriage gave them that they would not have had without it, following closely after love and children.

The potential tragedy in this situation was that in spite of widespread prosperity, the provider role was a heavy burden, and not all men could be successful at it. Nor was the status of family breadwinner always adequate compensation for an otherwise monotonous or dissatisfying job. Just as material goods could contribute to marital harmony or even compensate for unhappiness to some extent, the failure to achieve or appreciate the fruits of prosperity could cause tension. One case illustrates how this could happen. Charlotte Oster complained that her aspirations for the good life were continually thwarted by her husband Brad's failure to achieve what she thought was an appropriate standard of living. "Having been forced to buy, after three wartime evictions, in a section which was not quite up to the social standards we were used to, we found it hard to accept the choice of friends of our oldest daughter…. It has been very hard to keep her within the boundaries of what we consider the proper social standards."

Charlotte's dissatisfaction was not lost on Brad, who was acutely aware of his inability to provide adequately for a wholesome family environment. Charlotte noted that he "is often upset because he thinks he hasn't provided for us as well as he would like to, and considers himself rather a failure." Nevertheless, she said that marriage brought her "four wonderful children, a home of our own, and always something better to look forward to and strive for." In the last section of the survey, in which respondents were asked to add anything that had not already been covered, Charlotte wrote the saga of her and Brad's marriage:

> We were married during the depression years on a shoestring; my husband lost his job soon after, and went into business for himself, also with no capital. Though he was excellent in his field (photography), he didn't have the drive necessary to sell himself, and we had very meager living for several years, till he got a factory job during the war. Though he did well, he liked having his own independence, and after

quitting at several factory jobs because he didn't like the unfairness or domination, he started another business with a partner, in aerial photography. Then a series of unfortunate setbacks began … eviction … hurricane damage to his place … injuries…. Now my husband is back working for another aerial concern, but he dislikes the work, feels he is too old to start at the bottom in another line, and therefore is inwardly upset a good deal of the time…. I have always felt that he shouldn't cater to his feeling of having to be independent, and that he should take any kind of a good job with a steady pay … which would give us all a much stronger feeling of security.

Charlotte's words demonstrate the centrality of the provider role and the difficulties it could create when it conflicted with a man's effort to achieve independence and personal fulfillment through work. The Osters' marriage lasted until 1961, when the couple divorced.[34]

Although some husbands in the sample were content to be "organization men" as long as they could bring home the fruits of material success, others shared with Brad Oster a need for autonomy at work. But like him, they were likely to find that this need placed in jeopardy their ability to be good providers and, in turn, created marital friction. In a similar case, Maureen Gilford complained, "My husband is a tireless worker but insists on working *in his own business* and has made so many changes, it has been a constant struggle for 18 1/2 years with just one short period of success. I don't feel my standards are the cause of his hard work. So he is always tired and has little time for enjoyment. I feel badly about this, preferring that he get a modest *but steady salary* and work for someone else. It has made me pinch pennies for years. Also, I have to work *hard* to increase our income and have little time for my own use. Too much housework, *too much work* altogether."

Maureen longed for more leisure, more planned activities together, and more regular hours for her husband: "He is always tired and overworked." She said he had some emotional disturbances from worry about business and too many job changes: "I wish he had *more time* for the children and for himself." George Gilford wrote little in his report. He said marriage brought him "a good way of life." He sacrificed "nothing material" and rated his marriage as generally satisfying, although he, too, worried about providing for his family's needs, particularly a college education for both his children. Nevertheless, the fulfillment of the provider role would not necessarily satisfy George's need for meaningful work.[35]

The men in these cases faced the double anguish of failure to earn an adequate living in work they enjoyed and failure to be successful providers. For others, the breadwinner role, if performed successfully, might offer compensation for dissatisfaction at work. For women, marriage offered the possibility of material comforts and social standing—something a single woman earning a meager wage was not likely to achieve. Women also might gain some measure of autonomy in their domestic responsibilities—something that neither they nor their husbands were likely to find easily in the paid labor force. In addition, as wives of productive breadwinners, women might be able to gain the trappings of success unavailable to them in the work and public arenas. Suburban houses, after all, were not built with single working women in mind.

Some women focused their personal ambitions vicariously on their husband's careers. One husband noted that this focus contributed to his own drive. "Being somewhat lazy to begin with," he wrote, "the family and my wife's ambition have made me more eager to succeed businesswise and financially." Other wives were explicit about the centrality of material possessions to their marital and family satisfaction. One equated marriage with keeping up with the Joneses while at the same time expressing individuality: "We feel that our possessions are as good as if not better than our neighbors as they are different, antique as to modern, and we hold that thought to us dearly."[36]

Another woman, Lucille Windam, elaborated on this theme more fully, offering a shopping list of name-brand consumer items as evidence of a successful marriage. Yet her testimony also provides a glimpse of the difficulties that might arise even if—or perhaps because—one lived fully in accord with the domestic consumer ethic. She wrote:

> One fortunate thing which is important in our marriage is our fortunate change in income bracket. When we were married my husband earned $30 a week. We rented a five room flat, … had a baby, etc. Now we have five children and an income of over $25,000 a year. We own our 8 room house—also a nice house on a lake. We have a sailboat, a Cris Craft, several small boats. We own our own riding horse which we keep at home. Our oldest child goes to a prep school. We have a Hammond organ in our home…. Our two sons at home own expensive instruments. We have and carry a lot of life insurance. Unless some disaster hits us, we see our way clear to educate all our children thru prep school and college.

It is important to note the kind of consumerism Lucille mentioned: All the goods were geared toward home, family leisure, education, and recreation. She did not mention diamonds, mink coats, or other personal luxuries. Yet here again is the potential hazard of domestic consumerism becoming the center of personal identity, for this woman's pride in her shopping-list definition of marital success was tempered by the complaint she added, almost as an afterthought: "My reaction to all this is that my husband doesn't seem content to save. He continually seeks something new to own; he doesn't keep his interest in any one thing very long." Her final remark is most telling, since it reflects the connection between success, consumerism, and domestic power relations: "He has terrific drive and aggressiveness, and I feel he tries to own all of us in the family too much." It is clear from Lucille's bitter words that the domestic consumer ethic, even at its most opulent, might be rife with tension. For her, family-oriented consumerism was the measure of successful married life and provided some compensation for her obvious disappointment in her relationship with her husband. For her husband, ambition and drive for power were expressed through his acquisition of goods and his total domination at home. Together they created an imperfect domestic relationship; nevertheless, that relationship clearly offered them both enough reasons for staying married.

Consumerism and children were the rewards that made the marriage worthwhile for Lucille Windam. In dedicating herself to the task of raising her children, she gained a sense of achievement that she believed she would not have found elsewhere. Her husband's ample income made her homemaking career possible. Even though she felt he was "overbearing, expects too much of me, and is inconsiderate of me," she appreciated his "ability to do almost anything he tries, his popularity, and his generosity to me financially." That financial generosity meant that she could devote herself to her children and provide them with all the finest things that money could buy: "I've worked hard at making my marriage work—for my own and for my children's sake…. Certainly—materially—I never could attain the things I have now. Of course, the children are a great satisfaction. My job seems to swamp me sometimes but I am really very fond of my family and I do try to treat each as a special individual so each personality is important and each child can have every advantage we can possibly give. I can't imagine my life without children. I have no special talents so as a career person I'm sure I would not be a great success. As a mother and homemaker, I feel I am quite successful." Although she blamed her lack of "talent," rather than the lack of viable opportunities, she turned her creative efforts toward homemaking with the dedication and high standards of a professional.

Yet this domestic success was gained at a price: "Because of the size of our family, we have very little personal fun—I mean no clubs or activities. I used to be very active in PTA, church (taught Sunday school), and garden club, but my last two children now 4 and 2 years old changed all this. I just stay home with them and taxi my oldest boys around. Our oldest boy, almost 15, is away at prep school, but in our rural community I have to drive someone somewhere every day. I expect to get back into community life when my younger children are in school all day. I feel quite stale as though I don't use my mind enough." Still, she claimed to be satisfied with her marriage, in spite of a "stale" mind and an "overbearing, inconsiderate" husband. The children, apparently, made it all worthwhile; the affluence made it all possible.

Ronald Windam also claimed to be satisfied with their life together. He took pride in his role as provider. He wrote that marriage had brought him "stability, a family which I very much admire and enjoy doing my best to provide for." As for sacrifices, he wrote, "There is nothing other than Utopia, and a little give and take in sexual relationship. Other than that, there has been no sacrifice." Like so many of their peers, Ronald and Lucille Windam resigned themselves to their disappointments and looked on the bright side. Although their affluent suburban lifestyle fell short of their dreams, they were determined to make the best of it.[37]

Consumerism in the postwar years went far beyond the mere purchase of goods and services. It included important cultural values, demonstrated success and social mobility, and defined lifestyles. It also provided the most vivid symbol of the American way of life: the affluent suburban home. There can be no doubt that the gender roles associated with domestic consumerism—homemaker and breadwinner—were central to the identity of many women and men at the time. It is also evident, however, that along with the ideology of sexual containment, postwar domestic consumerism required conformity to strict gender assumptions that were fraught with potential tensions and frustrations. Suburban homes filled with material possessions could not always compensate for the dissatisfactions inherent in the domestic arrangements consumerism was intended to enhance and reinforce. In fact, those very domestic arrangements, although idealized and coveted at the time, were the source of countless miseries. As one looks through the "window of vulnerability" in the cold war era, one sees families inside their suburban homes struggling to achieve the postwar dream of abundance and security. Many men and women made heroic efforts to live according to the ideal of domestic containment. Some were able to carve out meaningful and rewarding lives within its limits. For others, the rewards remained elusive.

NOTES

1   William H. Whyte, Jr., "Budgetism: Opiate of the Middle Class," *Fortune,* May 1956, p. 133; Levitt quoted in Kenneth Jackson, *Crabgrass Frontier: The Suburbanization of the United States* (New York: Oxford University Press, 1985), p. 231.

2   See David Colker, "Building a 'Future' in 1948," *Los Angeles Times,* September 4, 1999, p. 1A. I am grateful to David Colker of the *Los Angeles Times,* who told me about this context and put me in touch with John Guedel. In a phone interview on July 13, 1999, John Guedel told me his version

of the story. Guiliana Muscio, of the University of Padua, confirmed that the story of the Italian election is true. For other studies of American popular culture in the international context of the cold war, see Reinhold Wagnleitner and Elaine Tyler May, eds., *"Here, There, and Everywhere": The Foreign Politics of American Popular Culture* (Hanover, N.H.: University Press of New England, 2000).

3 Quotes from the debate in Moscow are from "The Two Worlds: A Day-Long Debate," *New York Times,* 25 July 1959, pp. 1, 3; "When Nixon Took on Khrushchev," a report on the meeting and the text of Nixon's address at the opening of the American National Exhibition in Moscow on 24 July 1959, printed in "Setting Russia Straight on Facts about the U.S.," *U.S. News and World Report,* 3 August 1959, pp. 36–39, 70–72; and "Encounter," *Newsweek,* 3 August 1959, pp. 15–19.

4 Letter to board of aldermen from Mayor Joseph Darst, 13 December 1951, Raymond Tucker Papers, Box 104, Special Collections, Olin Library, Washington University, St. Louis, Mo.

5 George H. Gallup, *The Gallup Poll, Public Opinion 1935–1971,* vol. 1: *1935–1948* (New York: Random House, 1972), p. 594; Hadley Cantril, ed., *Public Opinion, 1935– 1946* (Princeton, N.J.: Princeton University Press, 1951), pp. 829, 831; and Susan Hartmann, *The Home Front and Beyond: American Women in the 1940s* (Boston: Twayne, 1982), p. 8.

6 George Katona, *The Mass Consumption Society* (New York: McGraw-Hill, 1964), pp. 14–15, and *The Powerful Consumer: Psychological Studies of the American Economy* (New York: McGraw-Hill, 1960), pp. 9–32; U.S. Bureau of the Census, *Historical Statistics of the United States, Colonial Times to 1970,* part 1 (Washington, D.C.: U.S. Government Printing Office, 1975), pp. 49, and 316–320; and Hartmann, *The Home Front and Beyond,* p. 8.

7 Katona, *The Powerful Consumer,* p. 27.

8 See Daniel Horowitz, *The Morality of Spending* (Baltimore: Johns Hopkins University Press, 1985), especially Chapter 8, for shifting ideas on spending in the 1930s.

9 Cantril, *Public Opinion,* pp. 1047–1048.

10 Katona, *The Powerful Consumer,* pp. 46, 156.

11 See Winifred D. Wandersee, *Women's Work and Family Values, 1920–1940* (Cambridge, Mass.: Harvard University Press, 1981), for a discussion of changing material expectations and the role of women's employment in family support. On the depression's legacy of employment for women, see S. Bennett and Glen Elder, Jr., "Women's Work in the Family Economy," *Journal of Family History* 4 (Summer 1979), pp. 153–176.

12 George Putnam, newscast in the documentary film by the Archives Project, *The Atomic Cafe,* 1982, Thorn Emi Video.

13 National Association of Savings Banks survey and Office of Civilian Requirements survey, cited in John Morton Blum, *V Was for Victory: Politics and American Culture during World War II* (New York: Harcourt Brace Jovanovich, 1976), pp. 100–101; Clifford Edward Clark, *The American Family Home, 1800–1960* (Chapel Hill: University of North Carolina Press, 1986), p. 195.

14 Clark, *American Family Home*, pp. 102–103.

15 Jackson, *Crabgrass Frontier*, pp. 231–232.

16 Clark, *The American Family Home*, p. 213; Jackson, *Crabgrass Frontier*, pp. 231–232, 249.

17 "Should-Must Cities Decentralize?" *Commonwealth*, 31 May 1948, quoted in John H. Mollenkopf, "The Postwar Politics of Urban Development," William K. Tabb and Larry Sawyers, eds., *Marxism and the Metropolis* (New York: Oxford University Press, 1978), p. 131.

18 Jackson, *Crabgrass Frontier*, pp. 11, 190–193, 203–218, and 283–295. On racial segregation and redlining in the postwar suburbs, see also Thomas Sugrue, *The Origins of the Urban Crisis: Race and Inequality in Postwar Detroit* (Princeton, N.J.: Princeton University Press, 2005); Robert O. Self, *American Babylon: Race and the Struggle for Postwar Oakland* (Princeton, N.J.: Princeton University Press, 2005); and Cynthia Mills Richter, "Integrating the Suburban Dream: Shaker Heights, Ohio," Ph.D. Dissertation, University of Minnesota, 1999.

19 Clark, *The American Family Home*, pp. 221–233; Jackson, *Crabgrass Frontier*, Chapters 11, 12.

20 Katona *The Mass Consumption Society*, pp. 14–18, 265–273.

21 Jackson, *Crabgrass Frontier*, p. 235.

22 Clark, *The American Family Home*, p. 219.

23 Stuart Ewen, *Captains of Consciousness: Advertising and the Social Roots of the Consumer Culture* (New York: McGraw-Hill, 1976); George Lipsitz, "The Meaning of Memory: Family, Class and Ethnicity in Early Network Television Programs," *Cultural Anthropology* 1 (November 1986), pp. 355–387.

24 Clark, *The American Family Home*, pp. 198, 210–213, 236.

25 Ibid., pp. 210–213.

26 Herbert Gans, *The Levittowners: The Ways of Life and Politics in a New Suburban Community* (New York: Pantheon, 1967), pp. 163–165.

27 Ibid., pp. 153–155, 206–212, and Clark, *The American Family Home*, pp. 224–243.

28 Jackson, *Crabgrass Frontier*, pp. 235–243.

29 Calculated from KLS items D43C61, D45C34, D45C36, and D45C35, pertaining to income and debts.

30 Calculated from KLS items D43C62, D43C57, D43C56, D43C55, and D43C53, pertaining to expenditures for housing, cars, and installment buying.

31 Calculated from KLS items D43C63–D43C67, pertaining to factors most important in determining the way extra money was spent.

32 Elizabeth Long, *The American Dream and the Popular Novel* (Boston: Routledge & Kegan Paul, 1985), pp. 52–76. See also Sloan Wilson, *The Man in the Grey Flannel Suit* (New York: Simon & Schuster, 1955).

33 Cases 224, 250, 24, 237, 244, 72, KLS.

34 Case 153, KLS. The reader is again reminded that the names of the KLS respondents used in this chapter are the author's invention and that the KLS identified respondents only by case number. For a provocative discussion of the tensions in the male provider role that illuminates issues raised in this case, see Barbara Ehrenreich, *The Hearts of Men* (Garden City, N.Y.: Doubleday, 1983).

35 Case 109, KLS.

36 Cases 244 and 75, KLS.

37 Case 62, KLS.

DISCUSSION QUESTIONS

- According to the article, what arguments did Americans make in the 1950s to prove that free-market capitalism and representative democracy were superior systems to communism? Why did Americans embrace these arguments?

- What was the experience of women in the 1950s? How was that different from previous periods in American history?

- Why did American families accept the routine of consumer life in the 1950s? Was this similar to that of the 1920s?

CHAPTER XII

BRINGING THE VIETNAM WAR INTO THE AMERICAN LIVING ROOM

OBJECTIVES

- Analyze the effects of the media's role on American opinion about the Vietnam War.

PREWRITING

- Examine the role of the media in previous American wars. What is the balance between an uncensored media that may undermine the nation's war effort with that of living up to the highest ideals in the Constitution? What is the reaction among the American populace when they learn of war atrocities?

Bringing the Vietnam War Into the American Living Room

RODGER STREITMATTER

TV news becoming a major force coincided not only with the Civil Rights Movement but also with the US military buildup in Vietnam. Network evening news programs expanded from fifteen minutes to half an hour in 1963; the first ground troops were sent to Indo-china in 1965. The Vietnam War, therefore, became the first televised war. It also eventually became the least successful foreign war in American history.

Many media and political experts have argued that by bringing grisly images of battle into the American living room, TV news played a key role in turning the public against the Vietnam War and, ultimately, in hastening the end of that conflict. Although those observers are divided on whether ending the war was the right or wrong decision, they agree that TV showed the raw horror of war in ways that print journalism couldn't. Violence, carnage, and human suffering were depicted in withering reality, while topics such as politics and strategy, which weren't easily translated onto film, were downplayed. So TV viewers were left to conclude that the Vietnam War was costing American lives but wasn't justified.

Numerous scholars and journalists have made this point. In the book *The Vietnam Legacy*, Edward Shils wrote, "Television gave the American people vivid images of certain aspects of the war in Vietnam which they could never have gotten from reading newspapers and periodicals. It made them see the war as a meaningless destruction of lives." And veteran NBC commentator Edwin Newman concluded, "Television brought the Vietnam War into our living rooms on a nightly basis. They produced close-up, sensational images of war. American viewers saw the real experience of war transformed into theatrics on the twenty-one-inch screen. And they recoiled."[1]

AMERICA'S LONGEST WAR

President Truman initiated US involvement in Vietnam in the early 1950s by sending military aid to the French colony. Truman and the men who entered the White House after him hoped to stop Vietnam from following China, its neighbor to the north, into communism. In 1954, Vietnam was divided in half—Ho Chi Minh's communist government in the north was headquartered in Hanoi, and the prodemocracy government in the south was centered in Saigon. American involvement continued under both Republican and Democratic administrations, with President Eisenhower dispatching military advisers to South Vietnam and President Kennedy increasing the number of those advisers. President Johnson took an even stronger hand against the communists, committing the first troops to Indochina.

Vietnam moved onto most Americans' radar in 1964. US military personnel announced that North Vietnamese patrol boats had fired on American destroyers in the Gulf of Tonkin, prompting Johnson to order a retaliatory strike that destroyed twenty-five boats and an oil depot. At LBJ's request, Congress passed the Gulf of Tonkin resolution, assuring its support for "all necessary action" to defend US forces in Southeast Asia.

In 1965, Johnson ordered offensive bombing raids and sent ground troops, with the number of GIs in Vietnam reaching 175,000 by year's end. Although the Americans were better equipped than the North Vietnamese, they weren't familiar with the style of warfare practiced by the rebel Viet Cong guerrilla fighters. Time after time, the enemy evaded the Americans by *melting* into the jungle. Determined to defeat the communists, Johnson continued to escalate the war effort. By 1967, the number of US troops exceeded 500,000.

Ultimately, the United States paid a high price for fighting in Vietnam, with more than 58,000 Americans dying in the war. The number of Southeast Asians who died isn't known, with estimates generally ranging from 1 million to 3 million.

THE MOST POWERFUL MEDIUM IN HISTORY

Although television existed during the Korean War, it hadn't yet evolved into a major news medium. By the mid-1960s, however, more people were receiving their news from TV than from newspapers. And as the Vietnam War continued, that balance increasingly shifted toward television. By 1972, two out of three persons surveyed named television as their major news source.[2]

At the height of the war, the evening news programs were drawing huge numbers of viewers. ABC, CBS, and NBC attracted a combined audience of 35 million per night. One of the most committed of those viewers was President Johnson, who was so obsessed with television news that he had three TV sets in the Oval Office, one for each network.

Television correspondents in Vietnam, as well as their print counterparts, were free to go wherever they wanted and report whatever they found, for this was the first—and last—American war without military censorship. During the early years of fighting, journalists were such committed cheerleaders for the government that officials felt voluntary guidelines were fully adequate. Those rules identified fifteen categories of information, such as troop movements, that were off-limits. Violation of the rules meant a reporter would lose his or her accreditation, but that happened only four times during the entire war.

Through 1967, television coverage was overwhelmingly favorable to US policy. After the Tet Offensive in early 1968, however, TV's portrayal of the war became much more critical.

Technological advances boosted the capabilities of TV news. New, lightweight cameras combined with jet air transportation and communication satellites meant that, for the first time, film from the front became a regular part of daily news coverage. Further advances meant that black-and-white images were transformed into color ones—blood could be seen in all its horrific brilliance.

EXPOSING THE HORRORS OF WAR

From the moment ground troops arrived in Vietnam in 1965, television presented viewers with the most realistic battlefront images possible. TV defined the reality of war as, in a word, *blood*.

Television coverage brought the reality of the battlefield—such as this image of First Cavalry Division medic Thomas Cole enduring his own suffering while trying to care for his wounded buddies—into the American living room. © *Associated Press/Henri Huet.*

Typical was a 1967 piece in which NBC's Greg Harris joined a platoon of GIs. "In the first twenty-six days of the present operation," Harris reported on air, "this particular unit killed 270 VC while suffering only three wounded Americans." Film then showed US soldiers charging into a village, bayonets drawn. Harris continued, "Today the Viet Cong lost the use of Cong Phu. Tomorrow they will lose the use of another village, then another." As Harris wrapped up his report, the film showed the huts in the village burning.[3]

Dozens of such reports aired day after day, week after week. Each told of a unit burning a village, with film often showing dead bodies—many of them charred. NBC correspondent Jack Perkins said matter-of-factly during one report about a village being burned, "There was no discriminating one house from another. There did not need to be. The whole village was destroyed."[4]

Although lurid images of dead and wounded Vietnamese soldiers and civilians often filled the screen, the most sought-after film was of blood flowing from the veins of American GIs. An NBC News vice president said at the time, "It's not a Vietnamese war; it's an *American* war in Asia. And that's the only story the American audience is interested in." He told his correspondents to concentrate on providing graphic images of US soldiers engaged in combat.[5]

The bloody scenes were often featured as dramatic close-ups, with flames engulfing thatched roofs and black smoke billowing into the sky serving as backdrops. Typical was a heart-wrenching NBC sequence that showed a young GI screaming in anguish, "It hurts! It hurts!" as medics rushed him past the eye of the camera, his right leg reduced to a bloody stump.[6]

A ZIPPO CIGARETTE LIGHTER IGNITES A FIRESTORM

The most controversial story of the early years of the war was by Morley Safer of CBS. One day in 1965, Safer was having coffee with some Marines when one of them asked if he'd like to join them on a field operation the next day. Safer jumped at the chance. After an amphibious carrier took them to Cam Ne, the men marched single file into the village and, in orderly fashion, burned every hut to the ground. The film was riveting. As the huts burst into flames, the Marines could be seen warning the Vietnamese peasants to run. But the film also showed that the warnings were useless because they were in English, while the confused looks on the women's and children's faces communicated that they understood only Vietnamese. The most poignant detail on the film, however, evolved from what the Marines used to ignite the thatched roofs: Zippo cigarette lighters.

When the film arrived in New York, network executives recognized the explosive nature of a report that depicted American soldiers cavalierly destroying a Vietnamese village by pulling lighters out of their pockets. Fred Friendly, the producer who'd piloted Edward R. Murrow through his battles with Joseph McCarthy ten years earlier, was awakened in the middle of the night. Friendly agreed to run the footage.

Safer's narrative for the story began with a recitation of facts—"The day's operation burned down 150 houses, wounded three women, killed one baby, and netted these four prisoners"—as Safer pointed to four elderly men. The correspondent, clearly shocked by the horror he'd witnessed, then added his own highly critical comments, "Today's operation is the frustration of Vietnam in miniature."[7]

Friendly didn't go home after the "Zippo segment" aired. Instead, he went to his office and began answering the phone calls from hundreds of angry Americans who cursed CBS for portraying GIs as heartless killers.

Among those callers was President Johnson. The leader of the free world called Frank Stanton, president of CBS News. Johnson's first question was as vivid as the film itself—"Frank, are you trying to *fuck* me?" Letting loose with the full fury of his monumental temper, Johnson continued, "Your boys just shat on the American flag."[8]

TET STUNS A NATION

The single most significant military action in the war erupted in late January 1968 when the North Vietnamese orchestrated the Tet Offensive. Named for the Lunar New Year holiday that coincided with it, this ambitious attack included simultaneous assaults on more than 100 sites—virtually every city, town, and military base in South Vietnam. The most dramatic action was by a Viet Cong suicide squad on the US Embassy in Saigon, killing five American soldiers. That action ended after a few hours, but heavy fighting continued throughout the south for another ten days.

Tet's repercussions were enormous. On the communist side, following an initial advantage gained from the surprise factor, the ground taken was lost again. The offensive was, in short, a military failure. Because of the reaction in the United States, however, the Viet Cong could claim a major psychological victory. Tet shocked the American public, which had believed that success in Vietnam was imminent. The offensive seriously damaged the credibility of the Johnson administration, as the American people were suddenly impatient with this prolonged war. And in a presidential election year, the public had a direct means of expressing its dissatisfaction.

The role television news played in the Tet Offensive was momentous. Just as Vietnam was America's first TV war, Tet was America's first TV superbattle. The story had drama, suspense, and enormous public interest. With the communists acting offensively and taking the US military by surprise, the very future of democracy seemed to be on the line. Television news pulled out all the stops to cover the story.

The US Embassy was the focal point of coverage for three days, as an ongoing gun battle on the grounds provided a live-action bonanza for TV crews. Barrages of automatic weapon fire, scenes of men running for cover behind trees, and the lifeless bodies of two fallen GIs made for some of the most eye-popping news images in American military history—as exciting as a Hollywood blockbuster.

CBS and NBC quickly produced news specials on Tet. Alarmist in tone, the programs portrayed the offensive as a brutal bloodbath, with lengthy footage that was unmatched in its sheer volume of gore and carnage. The prime-time spectacles strongly reinforced the message that Tet was a devastating defeat for the United States.

At the same time that the networks filled their TV screens with portraits of havoc and an American military run amok, they also filled the ears of the public with words of pessimism. Jeff Gralnick of CBS told his audience, "The Viet Cong proved they could take and hold almost any area they chose." ABC's Joseph Harsch expressed a similar skepticism toward US forces when he reported, "Best estimates here are that the enemy has not yet, and probably never will, run out of the manpower to keep his effort going. It is the exact opposite of what American leaders have, for months, been leading us to expect."[9]

In the midst of the crisis, it was understandable that the networks had initially reported incomplete or inaccurate information. Impossible to excuse, however, was the fact that ABC, CBS, and NBC all continued to portray Tet as a Viet Cong victory even after American officials provided indisputable evidence that the offensive had failed. Despite those facts, the networks neglected to set the record straight, allowing their hasty judgments to stand.

Later in 1968, field producer Jack Fern proposed that NBC undertake a three-part series showing that Tet had, in fact, been a military failure for the Viet Cong. Network executives rejected the proposal, saying such a series would only confuse viewers. The executives told Fern, "Tet was already established in the public's mind as a defeat, and, therefore, it *was* an American defeat."[10]

THE SHOT FELT AROUND THE WORLD

The TV image that, more than any other, burnt the brutalities of war into the consciousness of the American people was the filmed execution of a Vietnamese man on a Saigon street a few days after the Tet Offensive began.

NBC correspondent Howard Tuckner and his cameramen were standing on a street near the An Quang Pagoda, a center of government opposition, on the fateful morning. At the far end of the block, they saw several South Vietnamese soldiers with a prisoner wearing casual civilian clothes—plaid shirt, black shorts, no shoes. The soldiers walked toward the newsmen to present the prisoner to General Nguyen Ngoc Loan. The cameramen began filming the prisoner, showing that his hands were tied behind his back and that he'd been beaten.

The prisoner was marched down the street toward Loan, who then drew his snub-nosed .38 revolver. The prisoner stood three feet from the general, his eyes downcast. Without speaking to the man, Loan lifted his right arm and stretched it out straight as his index finger squeezed the trigger. There was the crack of a shot and a grimace on

The American public was shocked by the image of a South Vietnamese general—a man supported by the United States—assassinating a Viet Cong officer on a Saigon street.
© *Associated Press/Eddie Adams.*

the prisoner's face as the bullet slammed into his brain. The dead man's legs folded under him. As he fell to the ground, blood spurt from his head.[11]

Tuckner cabled NBC in New York: "THIS STORY IS COMPETITIVE. CBS AND ABC WERE THERE BUT WE ARE THE ONLY ONES WHO HAVE FILM OF THE EXECUTION." Tuckner ended the cable by flagging the fact that there could be "BLOOD SPRAYING OUT" of the prisoner's head and then referring to the cameraman: "IF HE HAS IT ALL, IT'S STARTLING STUFF."[12]

He had it all. He also had a huge audience. Because of the excitement that the Tet Offensive had created, the NBC audience watching that night's program had jumped from 15 million to a staggering 20 million. And the color images of the execution made history: a televised death.

Robert Northshield, executive producer of the *NBC Huntley-Brinkley Report*, aired the film, cutting it immediately after the gunshot to spare viewers from the spurting blood. Northshield "went to black" as soon as the man hit the ground and then kept the screen empty for three seconds to provide a buffer between the stomach-wrenching image and the commercial that followed. Even so, the producer later acknowledged, "It was the strongest stuff American viewers had ever seen."[13]

Tuckner's narration was terse. He merely said who the men in the images were—although the victim wasn't identified by name—and let the film roll. "Government troops had captured the commander of the Viet Cong commando unit. He was roughed up badly but refused to talk," Tuckner said. "A South Vietnamese officer held the pistol taken from the enemy officer. The Chief of South Vietnam's National Police Force, Brigadier General Nguyen Ngoc Loan, was waiting for him."[14]

Viewers were horrified. More than a thousand of them called NBC to complain that the film was in bad taste, particularly because it was aired during the early evening when children might be watching. Tuckner defended airing the chilling scene, saying, "The film showed, at a time when all eyes were on Saigon, that although the United States went over there ostensibly to keep South Vietnam free from communism and the communists were accused of atrocities, that a leading figure of the Saigon government killed a man in the street without a trial."[15]

The film had a huge impact on the American public. *Time* magazine said, "That picture lodged in people's memories" because it showed a South Vietnamese government official "cold-bloodedly executing" a thin, frightened man by "blowing the suspect's brains out." In his study of the impact of television on American society, NBC's Edwin Newman said, "This film revolted the nation. 'What was this war turning us into? What kind of people allowed such things to happen?' Television pictures were disturbing. Public opinion was moving. Television caused the change."[16]

EXPOSING THE WAR AS UNWINNABLE

The man who set the tone for TV coverage after the Tet Offensive was Walter Cronkite. The avuncular CBS anchor, with his kind and gentle manner, had shepherded the nation through many momentous events, including the 1963 Kennedy assassination. The anchor of the country's most-watched news program, Cronkite had supported the American military's effort in Vietnam during the early and mid-1960s. President Johnson, aware of Cronkite's prestige and power, called him to the White House three times during 1966 and 1967 for private meetings.

But all of that was before Tet. Like other Americans, Cronkite was shocked by the first news reports of the communist offensive. On that fateful night, he was in the CBS newsroom in New York. As the news flashes from Saigon came clattering across the teletype, Cronkite ripped a page from the machine and screamed incredulously, "What the hell is going on?" Reading on to discover that communist forces had penetrated the US Embassy compound, he cried out the same refrain that people all across America would soon echo, "I thought we were *winning* this war!"[17]

Cronkite decided to find out what, indeed, was going on in Vietnam. It was a risky step, as it meant shedding his mantle of impartiality and sharing his personal impressions about the most important story of the era. But at this moment when the public was utterly confused, Cronkite decided it was his duty as the signature figure in the country's largest network news operation to clarify the situation for his viewers.

So Cronkite went to Southeast Asia to interview soldiers and visit battle sites. Then the anchorman—the person that polls identified as the most trusted man in America—broadcast the most influential program of his life. Footage on *Report from Vietnam by Walter Cronkite* showed him wearing a steel helmet and flak jacket as he walked through the rubble of warfare.

Cronkite began, "Who won and who lost in the great Tet Offensive against the cities? I'm not sure. The Viet Cong did not win by a knockout, but neither did we." Cronkite went on to predict other standoffs in the fighting, "It seems now more certain than ever that the bloody experience of Vietnam is to end in a stalemate."[18]

He then told America exactly where he, personally, stood on the future of the war. "It is increasingly clear to this reporter that the only rational way out, then, will be to negotiate—not as victors, but as an honorable people who lived up to their pledge to defend democracy, and did the best they could." His final expression that lingered on the screen combined pained acceptance with solid resolve.[19]

The country's most influential newscaster had determined that, for the first time in two centuries, the United States wasn't able to win a foreign war. Rather than continue to sacrifice human lives, he said, American officials should negotiate a peace settlement and leave Vietnam.

Cronkite's assessment had unprecedented impact. For among the millions of Americans who put great stock in what the anchorman said was Lyndon Johnson. And when the program ended, the commander in chief said sadly, "If I've lost Cronkite, I've lost the war." Opinion polls confirmed Johnson's fear. In one of the most dramatic shifts of public opinion in history, within six weeks after the Tet Offensive began, one American in five switched from supporting the Vietnam War to *not* supporting it. This meant that for the first time since the war began, a majority of Americans opposed the war.[20]

A month after Cronkite's special, Johnson shocked the nation with a double-barreled announcement. He wouldn't run for reelection, and he would begin reducing US participation in the war.

Observers have pointed to Cronkite's program and Johnson's subsequent decision to downsize the war as a clear example of the news media's mighty power in shaping history. David Halberstam of the *New York Times* wrote, "Cronkite's reporting changed the balance; it was the first time in American history a war had been declared over by an anchorman."[21]

Because Cronkite's assessment coincided with the news media's portrayal of the Tet Offensive as a Viet Cong victory, the impact of the two events can't be separated. What is clear, though, is that coverage changed radically. Before January 1968, editorial comments by TV journalists had run four to one *in favor of* US policy. But after that point, comments ran two to one *against* US policy.[22]

Contributing to the negative tone of the coverage were two high-profile revelations related to Vietnam. In November 1969, freelance journalist Seymour Hersh reported the My Lai massacre. During that event, which had occurred a year and a half earlier, American soldiers had destroyed an entire Vietnamese village, killing between 200 and 500 civilians. My Lai dealt a devastating blow to the US military, with Lieutenant William Calley being convicted of mass murder. The second revelation exposed the shocking realities of what forces had driven US policy toward Vietnam. In June 1971, the *New York Times* and *Washing-ton Post* began reporting on secret government documents, known as the Pentagon Papers, that showed American military action often hadn't been guided by humanitarian concern but by the political benefit of an administration fighting a war. Although the government attempted to block publication of the material, the US Supreme Court sided with the newspapers, saying the material didn't endanger national security—it merely embarrassed the government.

TELEVISION NEWS HELPS END A WAR

The many journalists and scholars who argue that TV images were a major force in turning the American people against the war in Vietnam are on solid ground. The process began in the mid-1960s, when the blood of dead and wounded American GIs, as well as that of Vietnamese soldiers and civilians, first began to flow across the television screen.

Then came Tet. Television images of the Viet Cong penetrating the US Embassy compound, with bodies of GIs lying in camera range, showed the American people that—regardless of what the politicians and military brass were saying—the United States wasn't winning the war. And then viewers witnessed a South Vietnamese officer—a man fighting on *our* side—shooting an untried prisoner in cold blood. After those images and Walter Cronkite's bleak assessment, American public opinion shifted. People were finally willing to say that they'd been supporting a hideous and inhuman war. And they refused to continue.

For a book with the goal of documenting the impact that the news media have had on American history, it's sufficient to establish that TV coverage of the Vietnam War played a key role in bringing the fighting to an end. When the discussion includes not only a divisive war but also how the news media should cover future conflicts, however, that discussion seems incomplete without taking the final precarious step of questioning whether TV news hastening the end of the Vietnam War was a positive or a negative contribution to history.

Both journalists and government officials have identified the central issue. Nationally syndicated columnist Bob Greene wrote, "The argument can be made that any war—even World War II—shown in the gory, close-up way in which television showed Vietnam, is destined to lose the public's support; that once they have seen the videotape, all they will want is out." Dean Rusk, who served as secretary of state in the 1960s, made the same point, saying that the impact of Vietnam battle scenes on the ordinary citizen every day was powerful. "One can reflect upon what might have happened in World War II if Dunkirk had been on television," Rusk said. "So I think we need to do a good deal of thinking about whether or not an armed conflict can be sustained for very long if the worst aspects of it are going to be reflected on television every day. There may have to be certain kinds of censorship."[23]

When television news brought the "worst aspects" of the Vietnam War into the American living room, it was doing its job. As long as a free press remains fundamental to the democratic form of government, the news media's accurate depiction of reality—no matter how vivid or horrifying that reality may be—is a positive contribution to that country. TV news showed the American people exactly what their military was doing halfway around the world, and, knowing that information, the people chose not to continue.

At some point, the men and women elected to positions of national leadership in this country may succeed—as Rusk suggested—in limiting what freedom of the press means. But until that loathsome day, there's no question that reporting the realities of war is both the duty and the responsibility of the American news media. If the people of the United States are willing to send men and women into battle, they also must be willing to acknowledge that death, destruction, and human suffering are byproducts of that decision.

NOTES

1 See, for example, Edward Jay Epstein, *News from Nowhere: Television and the News* (New York: Random House, 1973), 9; George N. Gordon, *The Communications Revolution: A History of Mass Media in the United States* (New York: Hastings House, 1977), 226, 315–316; David Halberstam, *The Powers That Be* (New York: Knopf, 1979), 429; Daniel C. Hallin, *The "Uncensored War": The Media and Vietnam* (New York: Oxford University Press, 1986), 147; Guenter Lewy, *America in Vietnam*

(New York: Oxford University Press, 1978), 433; Timothy P. Meyer, "Some Effects of Real Newsfilm Violence on the Behavior of Viewers," *Journal of Broadcasting* 15 (Summer 1971), 275–285; Don Oberdorfer, *Tet!* (Garden City, NY: Doubleday, 1971), 239, 241; Austin Ranney, *Channels of Power: The Impact of Television on American Politics* (New York: Basic, 1983), 4–5, 133–134; Edward Shils, "American Society and the War in Indochina," in *The Vietnam Legacy: The War, American Society and the Future of American Foreign Policy*, ed. Anthony Lake (New York: New York University Press, 1976), 49; William Small, *To Kill a Messenger: Television News and the Real World* (New York: Hastings House, 1970), 3; *Television*, PBS, aired on Washington, DC, station WETA, 15 February 1988; Kathleen J. Turner, *Lyndon Johnson's Dual War: Vietnam and the Press* (Chicago: University of Chicago Press, 1985), 4. For specific quotations, see Shils, "American Society," 49; *Television*, PBS.

2 Ranney, *Channels of Power*, 13–14; US Senate, Committee on Governmental Operations, *Confidence and Concern: Citizens View American Government* (Washington, DC: Government Printing Office, 1973), 79. In the Roper survey, which allowed multiple responses, 58 percent of the respondents said television was their major news source, 56 percent said newspapers were, 26 percent radio, and 8 percent magazines. According to the Louis Harris poll commissioned by the US Senate, 64 percent of respondents said they relied on television as their major news source.

3 *NBC Huntley-Brinkley Report*, 27 October 1967.

4 Ibid., 11 January 1966.

5 Epstein, *News from Nowhere*, 250.

6 *NBC Huntley-Brinkley Report*, 11 August 1967.

7 *CBS Evening News with Walter Cronkite*, 5 August 1965.

8 Halberstam, *Powers That Be*, 490.

9 *CBS Evening News with Walter Cronkite*, 2 February 1968; *ABC Evening News*, 1 February 1968.

10 Edward Jay Epstein, *Between Fact and Fiction* (New York: Vintage, 1975), 225.

11 George A. Bailey and Lawrence W. Lichty, "Rough Justice on a Saigon Street: A Gatekeeper Study of NBC's Tet Execution Film," *Journalism Quarterly* 49, no. 2 (Summer 1972), 222–223.

12 Ibid., 224.

13 Epstein, *Between Fact*, 221.

14 Bailey and Lichty, "Rough Justice," 227.

15 Ibid., 229, 238.

16 "By Book and Bullet," *Time*, 23 February 1968, 32; *Television*, PBS.

17 Oberdorfer, *Tet!* 158.

18 *Report from Vietnam by Walter Cronkite*, 27 February 1968.

19 Ibid.

20 For the Johnson quotation, see presidential aide Tom Johnson on *Cronkite Remembered*, CBS, 23 May 1996; Hallin, *Uncensored War*, 170; Ranney, *Channels of Power*, 5; Small, *To Kill*, 123; Turner, *Johnson's Dual War*, 232. On the shift in public opinion, see John E. Mueller, *War, Presidents, and Public Opinion* (New York: Wiley, 1973), 201.

21 Halberstam, *Powers That Be*, 514.

22 Hallin, *Uncensored War*, 161.

23 Bob Greene, "How Do You Fight a War with TV Looking On?" *Los Angeles Times*, 13 April 1982, B-5; *Television*, PBS.

REFERENCES

Braestrup, Peter. *Big Story: How the American Press and Television Reported and Interpreted the Crisis of Tet 1968 in Vietnam and Washington.* Boulder, CO: Westview, 1977.

Hallin, Daniel C. *The "Uncensored War": The Media and Vietnam.* New York: Oxford University Press, 1986.

Oberdorfer, Don. *Tet!* Garden City, NY: Doubleday, 1971.

DISCUSSION QUESTIONS

- According to the article, how did television play a key role in turning the American public against the Vietnam War?

- How was the relationship between the media and the military different during the Vietnam War than in previous American wars?

- After examining the article, how did the American people balance freedom of the press with military expediency during the Vietnam War? Is this a balance still being adjusted today?

CHAPTER XIII

VIOLENCE IN THE STREETS

WATTS AND THE UNDERMINING OF LIBERALISM

OBJECTIVES

- Analyze the effects of Civil Rights radicalism during the 1960s, using the case study of Watts, California.

PREWRITING

- Given the turmoil of the 1960s and the slow progress toward civil rights since Reconstruction, was Watts a "powder keg?" What socioeconomic factors contributed to the simmering unrest in the community?

Violence in the Streets

Watts and the Undermining of Liberalism

JAMES T. PATTERSON

Americans who tuned in to CBS on the evening of August 5 had no reason to think they would see gripping footage of the Vietnam War. By then, the TV networks were devoting a fair amount of air time to coverage of the conflict. But most of the coverage had been brief, and it had hardly been hostile to the administration. The anchor for *CBS Evening News*, Walter Cronkite, maintaining a pose of impartiality on the air, was at that time privately sympathetic to the US effort. But viewers were in for a shock that evening. CBS correspondent Morley Safer and his camera crew featured footage in which a calm and collected American marine took out his Zippo cigarette lighter and, ignoring the pleas of an elderly and anguished peasant woman, set fire to thatched huts in the South Vietnamese village of Cam Ne. Fire from lighters and flamethrowers soon burned down some 150 dwellings, destroying the village. Safer, who was standing in front of the burning huts, stated, "This is what the war in Vietnam is all about."

The CBS correspondent explained that the marines, believing that the villagers had been aiding the Vietcong, had retaliated by wounding three women, killing one baby, and taking four old men as prisoners. "There is little doubt," Safer reported, "that American firepower can win a battle here. But to a Vietnamese peasant whose house has meant a life of back-breaking labor, it will take more than presidential promises to convince him that we are on his side."[1]

CBS received a barrage of calls from disbelieving viewers, some of whom, accusing CBS of lying, insisted that what they had seen could not possibly have taken place. But many others who saw the footage came to understand that it was a shockingly succinct visual depiction of why the United States would never "win" in Vietnam. As a Pentagon colonel explained, "The trouble is that in this kind of war you don't know the VC from the civilians. … You've got to drop grenades into caves or tunnels and you can't always know there are some babies in them."[2]

When Johnson heard about the footage, he was incensed. Privately he accused Safer, a Canadian, of being a communist. That night he woke up Frank Stanton, the president of CBS, to vent. "Frank," he roared, "are you trying to fuck me?… Your boys shat on the American flag." He demanded to know how CBS could "employ a Communist like Safer, how could they be so unpatriotic as to put on an enemy film like this?"[3]

This was classic Johnson—lightning quick to learn of media reports, to question the patriotism of people (like Safer) who annoyed him, and to think nothing of rousing a corporate executive from his sleep and berating him. His reaction showed how tense he continued to be following his announcement of escalation on July 28. Though the networks did not run reportage anywhere near as critical as Safer's later that year, LBJ's relations with the media, long since testy, continued to deteriorate.

Insofar as Vietnam was concerned, however, Johnson need not have worried too much in early August. Having announced his decision to escalate, he was pleased to note that the Dow Industrial Index, which had lagged a bit in recent weeks, did not fall. On the contrary, it gained thereafter. LBJ was especially gratified to learn from polls that some two-thirds of the American people were still behind him.[4]

The president also had defenders in the media. When Lippmann, still hammering away at him, criticized him for "pretending to profess that we can be the policeman of the world," a *New York Herald Tribune* editorial immediately rebutted him. "For better or worse," it said, "the U.S. is the 'policeman' on which the threatened people in China's expansionist path depend for whatever hope they have of independence and freedom."[5]

Johnson also knew that Congress, unwilling to "desert the boys," would support his requests for money to back the troops and that it would respond negatively to vehement antiwar protests. When antiwar protestors here and there began burning their draft cards that August (few had done so before then), he asked for a law to deter the practice. Congress responded immediately, approving a bill that made burning draft cards a federal offense punishable by fines of up to $10,000 and five years in prison. LBJ signed it on August 31.[6]

Congress also continued to support LBJ's domestic agenda. Having recently enacted Medicare and the Voting Rights Act, it pressed onward without protest. On August 3, the House Judiciary Committee approved LBJ's bill to liberalize the immigration system, 27–4. On August 10, the Senate confirmed his nomination of Thurgood

Marshall as solicitor general. All indications were that Congress, providing butter as well as guns, would support Great Society bills still under consideration.

On August 11, the day after Marshall was confirmed, however, an especially damaging blow to liberal dreams occurred: a huge racial disturbance in Watts, a large black neighborhood in south central Los Angeles, broke out only five days after LBJ had signed the Voting Rights Act and lasted six days and nights. The destruction and its political aftershocks demoralized Johnson and left the once proud and luminously effective civil rights movement in a state of disarray from which it never recovered.

———————————————

The trouble in watts started, as it often did in urban racial disturbances during the 1960s, with a confrontation between white police and black residents. At seven PM on August 11, a hot and humid evening, a twenty-one-year-old black man, Marquette Frye, was pulled over for drunk driving. His detainment was routine (he later pleaded guilty and paid a fine), but he resisted arrest. His brother, a passenger, and his mother, who lived nearby, rushed to help him. Additional police officers, having been called as backup, used batons to subdue and arrest all three.

Soon a rapidly growing crowd of Watts-area black people was surrounding the scene. As they watched the struggle, someone grumbled, "It's just like Selma." One of the policemen then felt someone spit on him; a seemingly pregnant black woman was identified as the culprit and dragged into a squad car. Infuriated, the crowd erupted by pelting the police with bricks, stones, and bottles.[7]

To avoid provoking more unrest, the Los Angeles police withdrew from the area. But that night and into the early morning angry blacks—mostly young men—set about looting and setting fires to buildings. Some chanted, "Burn, baby, burn!" The next day, violence escalated. Some blacks stoned white firefighters who were trying to douse fires. Others threw stones at white motorists, dragged them from their cars and beat them, or struggled physically with police.

Late on the morning of the thirteenth, Glenn Anderson, California's lieutenant governor (the governor, Pat Brown, was out of the country) authorized the dispatch of national guardsmen to reinforce the police. By early the next morning, more than three thousand were on hand, but by then the business district of Watts had become so devastated that onlookers called it "Charcoal Alley." It was not until August 16, by which time there were more than thirteen thousand guardsmen in Watts—an astonishingly high number—that the worst of the disturbances abated.

But the destruction that had occurred between August 11 and 16 was staggering. Thirty-four people were killed; some 1,000 were reported injured. A total of 3,438 adults and 524 youths were arrested. The damage, which affected nearly 1,000 buildings, was estimated at $40 million. On August 16, the *Los Angeles Times* described Watts as a "holocaust of rubble and ruins not unlike the aftermath in London when the Nazis struck, or Berlin after Allies forces finished their demolition."[8]

As many commentators noted at the time, watts seemed an unlikely place for a massive urban disturbance. *Newsweek* wrote, "To a Harlem Negro oppressed by moldering tenements, Watts might look like the promised land with its wide boulevards, grassy back yards, and single- and two-story houses."[9] Palm trees lined some of the streets; there were nine public swimming pools in the area. Black officeholders in Los Angeles included a congressman, two assemblymen, and three city councilors. African Americans held a quarter of the jobs in county government.[10]

And yet Watts was hardly a promised land. It was a black ghetto where some 250,000 people were forced to reside because whites would not tolerate them in their own neighborhoods. Four times as many people per square block lived in Watts as in the rest of the city. More than 30 percent of its black male adults were unemployed. Rising numbers of unmarried young women and their children were trying to make do on welfare. Because the mayor of Los Angeles, Sam Yorty, was feuding with the OEO over administration of antipoverty money, $20 million in federal funding had not reached the city. Los Angeles officials, ignoring complaints by black residents about the brutality of police, had admitted few blacks to the city's force of 8,000 officers. No black cop had a rank above sergeant. Of the 205 policemen assigned to Watts, 200 were white.[11]

All these problems fed the rage that gripped many residents of the area. Indeed, the rebelliousness of black city-dwellers, as the rising appeal of Malcolm X had shown, ran wide as well as deep throughout the United States. It stemmed not only from poverty, overcrowding, and racial discrimination but also from the higher expectations that the civil rights movement had helped to excite by 1965. As Johnson himself had pointed out in his address at Howard University in June, black Americans in the cities had become painfully aware of the ease of life that whites all around them were enjoying and therefore of their own relative deprivation. As LBJ had added, they were yearning for equality not just "as a right and a theory but equality as a fact and a result."[12]

So profound was the anger of blacks in Watts that peacemakers who tried to reason with the activists had little success. One was Martin Luther King, who interrupted a holiday to fly to Los Angeles. Arriving when the troubles had subsided, he addressed a neighbor-hood association meeting, only to be greeted in part with derision. "Sending King down here ain't nuthin', man," an onlooker muttered. "But goddammit they better do something down here, brother, or next time it won't be a riot. It'll be a war." Another black man agreed, "Aw, they're just sending another nigger down here to tell us what we need." A third man mocked King, chanting, "'I had a dream, I had a dream'—hell, we don't need no dreams. We want jobs."[13]

Reactions such as these made it obvious to King that the rage of black Americans in the cities had reached a boiling point while he had been fighting against racism, Southern-style, in Selma. As he put the matter, "'I worked to get these people the right to eat hamburgers, and now I've got to do something… to help them get the money to buy [them].'"[14] James Farmer, national director of CORE, agreed with King. He conceded, "Civil rights organizations have failed. No one had any roots in the ghetto." Bayard Rustin added, "We must hold ourselves responsible for not reaching them. … We've done plenty to get votes in the South and seats in the lunchrooms, but we've had no programs for these youngsters."[15]

Johnson at first responded to the troubles in Watts with a mixture of disbelief, rage, and self-pity. On the second day of the disturbances, he had flown to his ranch in Texas for rest and relaxation. As the burning and looting escalated, Joseph Califano, a top aide for the coordination of domestic policies, called him from Washington for instructions. For more than two days, however, Johnson did not answer the phone. "He just wouldn't accept it," Califano recalled. "He refused to look at… the situation."[16] When LBJ at last answered one of Califano's calls, he showed that the disturbances had hurt him personally. "How is it possible? After all we've accomplished? How can it be?" Repeating an ugly rumor that had circulated among Southern whites during the Reconstruction era, he predicted that blacks were going to "end up pissing in the aisles of the Senate." Betraying his crisis-driven suspiciousness that communist elements were at work, he ordered an investigation into whether a "Communist conspiracy" was behind the rioting. He also told Califano to be sure that Governor Brown did not allow Ronald Reagan, then preparing to run against Brown for governor in 1966, to "make political hay out of the riots."[17]

A little later, Johnson calmed down enough to authorize $29 million in emergency aid for Watts residents.[18] But he recognized, as did civil rights leaders, that such a modest amount of money would do little to assuage the anger—or significantly improve the situation—of blacks in the area. And he remained furious. On August 19, he stated publicly, "A rioter with a Molotov cocktail in his hands is not fighting for civil rights any more than a Klansman with a sheet on his back and a mask on his face. They are both… lawbreakers, destroyers of constitutional rights and liberties, and ultimately destroyers of a free America."[19]

The next day, he engaged in a lengthy phone conversation with King, who—still shaken by what he had seen—spoke of the "risk of full-scale war." "So now what should we *do* about it?" LBJ demanded. King spoke of the need to "get this poverty program going in Los Angeles." "We'll get at it," Johnson promised. Conveying an understanding of ghetto life, he also told King, "There's no use giving lectures on the law as long as you've got rats eating on people's children, and unemployed, and no roof over their head, no job to go to, and maybe with a dope needle in one side and a cancer in the other."[20]

LBJ's anguish was understandable: after all, no twentieth-century American president had done more for civil rights. But his anger was visceral and, as in his reference to the KKK, extreme. As careful observers were to point out, neither outside agitators nor communists had caused the disturbances. Moreover, few of those who participated in the uprising were out of control. Even the burners and looters were for the most part selective, zeroing in on certain kinds of white-owned businesses and stores. Many structures—private homes, service stations, schools, libraries, and other public buildings—were left alone. And the blacks involved were not killers: of the thirty-four people who lost their lives, only five were white.[21]

Nevertheless, millions of white Americans shared Johnson's fury at the rebels. Thanks to nearly round-the-clock television coverage of the action, some of it filmed by helicopters, they had been mesmerized by the "orgies," as many commentators called them, of looting and burning. They had heard the cry "Burn, baby, burn!" Many whites wondered whether conspirators with a revolutionary political agenda were staging an insurrection. Others denounced the burners and looters as lowlifes. Governor Brown blamed the troubles on "a hoodlum gang element that took advantage of a situation." Oscar Handlin, a Pulitzer Prize–winning social historian at Harvard, echoed Brown, branding the rioters as "disorderly elements taking advantage of an occasion for looting."[22]

Many other white Americans, including liberals who had vigorously supported civil rights, rejected the idea that Watts was a left-wing conspiracy or that lowlifes had spearheaded the violence. They understood that blacks in ghettos such as Watts had legitimate grievances. But they also sensed that a pivotal change was taking place. As Charles Silberman, a perceptive observer of racial trends, was soon to observe, a "taboo" that had long restrained the rage of African Americans was disappearing. Silberman reminded his readers of a five-line poem penned twenty-three years earlier by the black writer Langston Hughes. Negroes, Hughes had written, were mostly docile and un-threatening. But Americans must beware the day when they change their minds and begin to fight for their rights.[23]

Silberman was correct. As Hughes had predicted, many black Americans were changing their minds, and they would no longer be docile. Outraged by the persistence of racism, they were also tiring of what they had come to identify as the patronizing stance of white liberals. They were losing faith in the nonviolent, interracial strategies that had dominated civil rights activism during the early 1960s. Some, as in Watts, were reacting violently. Others were determined to oust whites from major roles in civil rights organizations and to take control of fights for equality and justice.

Many of the rebels in Watts recognized that acts of violence would deprive them of the moral high ground that the nonviolent movement had so richly earned. But with their expectations whetted, they were eager, as Malcolm X had demanded, to be heard. One man boasted, "We won, because we made the whole world listen to us." Like many others in the freedom struggle, he believed that black people should take command of their own destinies. Moynihan later put the matter in a slightly different way, noting that long-suffering black people had ceased to act as "victims." He added, however, that after Watts, "the black urban population became, in effect, an aggressor."[24]

Subsequent surveys concerning watts managed to convey the depth of urban black rebelliousness. Ramsey Clark, a liberal who was then LBJ's deputy attorney general, headed one of the investigations, a task force that reported back to LBJ. After talking at length to black people in Watts, Clark and others in his group told the president that poverty, unemployment, racial discrimination, and excesses by white police had caused the troubles. The government, Clark urged, should seek a massive public jobs program.[25] LBJ, however, rejected suggestions that whites were primarily to blame for what had happened; as during the formation of the War on Poverty in 1964, he rejected the idea of a large-scale federal employment effort. Instead, he looked forward to the report of a commission he had encouraged Governor Brown to set up in the immediate aftermath of the disturbances. Its head, as Johnson had urged, was John McCone, who had been director of the CIA until Raborn replaced him before the late-April rebellion in the Dominican Republic.

The 101-page McCone Commission report, issued in December, paid considerable attention to the disorienting results of mass migrations of blacks to the Los Angeles area over the previous several decades. Many Negroes who had arrived, it argued, had not adjusted satisfactorily to the difficult challenges of urban life. The commission also cited a number of socioeconomic woes: high unemployment, overcrowded housing, failing schools, and the like. It called for creation of a City Human Relations Commission that would fight against "prejudice and discrimination in employment, housing, education, and public accommodations." The report was prescient, warning that the troubles in Watts "may seem by comparison to be only a curtain raiser for what could blow up in the future."[26]

But the McCone Commission report also noted the destructive role of "riffraff," and it reprimanded black leaders who shouldered no personal responsibility for the outbreak. Critics complained that it paid more attention to poverty than to racism. Worst of all, many critics observed, the report avoided focusing on the LAPD, whose tough-minded chief, William Parker, had rejected charges of police brutality and had been outspoken in his denunciation of black participants in the disturbances.[27] For all these reasons, the McCone Commission report was hardly regarded by black Americans as the last word on a very controversial subject.

Well before the release of the McCone report in December, it had also become obvious that the rebellion in Watts had transformed the attitudes of millions of white Americans, thereby damaging chances for improvements in race relations. A Gallup poll in September showed that 88 percent of whites, asked how blacks might improve their situations, favored self-improvement, more education, and harder work, as opposed to help from the government.[28] More ominous was a rising white backlash, which was surging to the surface, especially in working-class areas close to black neighborhoods.[29] Hopes that large numbers of whites would continue to engage in interracial cooperation, such as the efforts that had led to the widely applauded Voting Rights Act, seemed doomed.

As Johnson had indicated in his conversation with King, he still hoped that governmental action might alleviate America's racial tensions. "It is not enough," he said in the aftermath of Watts, "simply to decry disorder. We must also strike at the unjust conditions from which disorder largely flows." But the rampaging in Watts continued to discourage him. He told an aide, "I have moved the Negro from D+ to C-. He's still nowhere. He knows it. And that's why he's out on the streets. Hell, I'd be there, too."[30]

Johnson nonetheless lowered his sights. Between mid-August and mid-September he made three moves to indicate he was following a more modest agenda. The first followed on leaks to the public in early August of snippets from Moynihan's in-house report, *The Negro Family: The Case for National Action*, which had been the basis for LBJ's inspirational talk at Howard University. Once leaked, the study became known as the Moynihan Report. Some of the civil rights leaders who read or heard about the document knew that Moynihan, having called for "National Action" to confront race-based economic injustice, was on their side. Others, however, were angry that he had written frankly and unflatteringly about a "tangle of pathology" ensnaring black families in the ghettos. By September many black leaders—and white liberals—were beginning to denounce the report.

LBJ, too, backed away from the report, fearing to associate himself with anything that would further damage his already deteriorating relationships with black leaders. In this spirit—and because he was absorbed by events in Vietnam—LBJ retreated from his promise at Howard University to call a large-scale White House conference in the fall to promote socioeconomic equality for black Americans.[31] Instead, he ordered that the conference be downgraded to a relatively small planning meeting. The larger convocation he had promised would not take place until June 1966. Moynihan, deeply upset, complained of Johnson's coolness: "If my head were sticking on a pike at the South-West Gate to the White House grounds, the impression [of LBJ's hostility] would hardly be greater."[32] Black leaders, worrying that LBJ was abandoning his quest to promote black equality, grew especially discouraged.

LBJ's second move was to humiliate Vice President Humphrey, who until then had served as chief administration liaison with civil rights leaders. Humphrey, he thought, had been too solicitous of black demands. So the president handed the management of important civil rights matters to the Department of Justice and other departments and agencies. He managed the switch with characteristic stealth and swiftness, informing Humphrey of his demotion only after it had been accomplished. He even managed to get Humphrey to sign a memo in which the vice president recommended his own removal. Califano, who had the task of overseeing the reassignment, wrote later that Humphrey was staggered at the news. "He knew he had just been castrated."[33]

The president's third move was to declare a "war on crime." In late September while signing a bill that Congress had just enthusiastically enacted, the Law Enforcement Assistance Act, Johnson declared, "I will not be satisfied until every woman and child in this nation can walk any street, enjoy any park, drive on any highway, and live in any community at any time of the day or night without fear of being harmed." The law resulted in creation of yet another Johnson-era bureaucracy, the Office of Law Enforcement and Assistance, which would gather data and recommend federal responses to the crime issue.

The anticrime act was not a direct result of Watts. Rates of violent crime (thanks in part to the coming-of-age of millions of boomers) had been slowly rising since 1964, and LBJ had called for such a statute in March 1965. But it was evident from the bellicose comments of congressmen, senators, and editorialists, as well as from LBJ's grandiloquent statement, that popular as well as presidential concerns about "crime on the streets" had expanded considerably since the explosion in Watts.[34]

In 1967, Moynihan published a widely noted article, "the President and the Negro: The Moment Lost."[35] As the subtitle indicated, it bewailed the chain of events—highlighted by Watts and negative reactions to his report—that in the late summer of 1965 had transformed the politics of race in the United States. His melancholy was understandable, for the river of progress toward greater racial equality, which had seemed broad and smooth after Johnson's speech at Howard in June, had become choked with obstacles by the fall of 1965.

In hindsight, however, Moynihan's argument needs tweaking. It was far from clear, even before Watts, how America might surmount the barriers that blocked the path toward racial equality. Recognizing how little policymakers knew at the time, Moynihan himself had avoided making specific recommendations in his report. He had hoped that the late 1965 conference of experts and civil rights leaders might begin to come up with answers.

An especially strong barrier to progress for black Americans, of course, was the abiding strength of white racism, highly visible manifestations of which were de facto segregated schools and housing. Another barrier was the high incidence of black out-of-wedlock childbearing that the Moynihan report documented. This incidence skyrocketed within the next few years, rising from 23.6 percent of all black births in 1963 to 38 percent by 1970 and to 70 percent by the 1990s.

A third obstacle—the most widely discussed racial problem—was the high incidence of black unemployment, which continued to be more than twice that of whites, and the level of poverty, which was more than three times as high. In 1965, 45.4 percent of blacks were still living in poverty (compared to 13.2 percent of whites).[36] The linkage of high rates of black poverty and unemployment to a host of social problems afflicting African Americans—fatherless families, dropping out of school, juvenile delinquency, crime, and drug abuse—had a long history, and the connections would persist into the twenty-first century: forty-five years after the Moynihan report, in 2010, the official poverty rate for blacks was 27 percent, roughly three times the 9.9 percent rate for non-Hispanic whites. The black unemployment rate in 2011 was 16.7 percent, for whites 8 percent.

This is a familiar litany of miseries. But as Moynihan and others recognized, the sources of racial inequality were not only deep and enduring but also interrelated in tangled and complicated ways that needed careful and concentrated study. Moreover, neither then nor later have solutions to these ills secured reliable political support.

One solution, often favored by Moynihan, was to establish massive government jobs programs. But these are necessarily very expensive and difficult to set up, and skeptics, including some liberals, have consistently challenged their potential effectiveness. What sort of jobs might be created? Would government-sponsored job training programs, which have also been described as expensive and unproductive, enable ill-educated young people—often school dropouts—to qualify for them? What effect would federal employment programs have on workers and employers in the private marketplace? Many white Americans, having little confidence in the work ethic of low-income black people, wonder why taxpayers should finance programs for a particular group of people they believe were just "sitting around."

Even in 1965, an extraordinarily prosperous year, it was unclear whether the economy was robust enough to enable every able-bodied, decently educated, and ambitious

American to secure living-wage work, especially because huge numbers of boomers were coming of age and moving into the workforce. By the 1970s, when the economy began to slump, it became ever more obvious that the marketplace could not be relied on to provide a good job to everyone who needed one. Troubles besetting America's manufacturing sector, which had historically offered the best-paying jobs for blue-collar folk, became increasingly serious after the mid-1960s.[37]

Efforts to improve the welfare system, another goal on the list of reformers, have also encountered formidable political difficulties. Many Americans have blanched at the thought of using tax money to aid large numbers of women who have one or more children out of wedlock. If the mothers are required to work in order to qualify for assistance (as has normally been the case since a federal welfare "reform" bill that passed in 1996), they are likely, even with training, to be unqualified for anything but very low-paying jobs. And who would pay for child care? For these and other reasons, Califano later grumbled that welfare reform was the "Middle East of domestic politics" in the United States.

A frequently stated answer to the plight of low-income people, including blacks, has been to improve public education. That is why Johnson, a passionate advocate of better schooling, had pushed through the Elementary and Secondary Education Act in April 1965. But it has long since become evident that the cognitive difficulties of lower-class black children—millions of whom grow up in fatherless, poverty-stricken homes and crime-ridden neighborhoods—are large, compared to those of most white children, even before they enter kindergarten. Narrowing the test-score gap between blacks and whites has regularly frustrated reformers.

In short, Moynihan's argument that a "moment" for seriously addressing black problems was "lost" in the summer of 1965 is unverifiable. Still, Watts was a disastrously consequential event in American history. Aside from the escalation in Vietnam, no occurrence that year did more to damage American race relations or to undermine the power of Johnsonian liberalism in the United States. The angry, contentious Sixties were surely arriving.

NOTES

1 Mary Ann Watson, *Defining Visions: Television and the American Experience Since 1945* (Fort Worth: Harcourt Brace College, 1998), 243–244. For analysis of TV coverage of the war, see Chester Pach, "And That's the Way It Was: The Vietnam War on the Nightly News," in *The Sixties: From Memory to History*, ed. David Farber (Chapel Hill: University of North Carolina Press, 1994), 90–118; and Edward P. Morgan, *What Really Happened to the 1960s: How Mass Media Culture Failed American Democracy* (Lawrence: University Press of Kansas, 2010), 133–134.

2   *Newsweek*, Aug. 16, 1965, 30–31.

3   Mark Lytle, *America's Uncivil Wars: The Sixties Era* (New York: Oxford University Press, 2006), 191; Robert Dallek, *Flawed Giant: Lyndon Johnson and His Times, 1961–1973* (New York: Oxford University Press, 1998), 286.

4   *Newsweek*, Aug. 2, 1965, 17.

5   *Herald Tribune* editorial cited in *Time*, Aug. 6, 1965, 52.

6   *Life*, Aug. 13, 1965, 30.

7   See Ethan Rarick, *California Rising: The Life and Times of Pat Brown* (Berkeley: University of California Press, 2005), 314–340; Robert Conot, *Rivers of Blood, Years of Darkness: The Unforgettable Classic Account of the Watts Riot* (New York: William Morrow, 1968); and Nick Kotz, *Judgment Days: Lyndon Johnson, Martin Luther King Jr., and the Laws That Changed America* (Boston: Houghton Mifflin, 2005), 338–341. (The woman wasn't pregnant but was wearing loose clothing.)

8   For damage estimates, see Kotz, *Judgment Days*, 343.

9   *Newsweek*, Aug. 30, 1965, 17.

10 William E. Leuchtenburg, *A Troubled Feast: American Society Since 1945* (Boston: Little, Brown, 1973), 153.

11 Robert Weisbrot, *Freedom Bound: A History of America's Civil Rights Movement* (New York: W. W. Norton, 1990), 159.

12 As Watts was erupting, reviews appeared of an autobiographical book, *Manchild in the Promised Land,* by Claude Brown, a black man. It graphically described the miseries of ghetto life in Harlem and received widespread attention.

13 *Newsweek*, Aug. 30, 1965, 15.

14 Kotz, *Judgment Days*, 343.

15 Lee Rainwater and William Yancey, *The Moynihan Report and the Politics of Controversy* (Cambridge, MA: MIT Press, 1967), 192.

16 Michael Beschloss, ed., *Reaching for Glory: Lyndon Johnson's Secret White House Tapes, 1964–1965* (New York: Simon & Schuster, 2001), 420.

17 Califano, *Triumph and Tragedy*, 59–63. Reagan did run, blasting white liberals for having been permissive in the face of black violence.

18 Dallek, *Flawed Giant*, 223–224.

19 *New York Times*, Aug. 20, 1965.

20 Taylor Branch, *At Canaan's Edge: America in the King Years, 1965–68* (New York: Simon & Schuster, 2006), 306–307.

21 A total of twenty-six black people were killed by police or guardsmen. In addition, a storeowner shot and killed a looter, a white policeman was killed by another policeman who accidentally discharged his gun, a white firefighter lost his life when a wall collapsed on him, and a white deputy sheriff was accidentally killed by rioters. The causes of the other four deaths, of the total of thirty-four, were unexplained. See Charles Silberman, "Beware the Day When They Change Their Minds," *Fortune* (Nov. 1965): 150–154, 255–267.

22 Rarick, *California Rising*, 333; James T. Patterson, *Freedom Is Not Enough: The Moynihan Report and America's Struggle over Black Family Life from LBJ to Obama* (New York: Basic Books, 2010), 68.

23 Silberman, "Beware the Day They Change Their Minds."

24 Patterson, *Freedom Is Not Enough*, 70.

25 Gareth Davies, *From Opportunity to Entitlement: The Transformation and Decline of Great Society Liberalism* (Lawrence: University Press of Kansas, 1996), 100.

26 *Violence in the City: An End or a Beginning?* (McCone Report); "Violence in the City," *Newsweek*, Dec. 13, 1965, 29–32; *Time*, Dec. 17, 1965, 21.

27 For excellent analysis of Watts and of subsequent reports concerning it, see Michael W. Flamm, *Law and Order: Street Crime, Civil Unrest, and the Crisis of Liberalism in the 1960s* (New York: Columbia University Press, 2005), 62–65.

28 Dallek, *Flawed Giant*, 323.

29 Jonathan Rieder, *Canarsie: The Jews and Italians of Brooklyn Against Liberalism* (Cambridge, MA: Harvard University Press, 1985), 102, 254–255.

30 Harvard Sitkoff, *The Struggle for Black Equality, 1954–1992*, rev. ed. (New York: Hill and Wang, 1993), 190.

31 David Carter, *The Music Has Gone Out of the Movement: Civil Rights and the Johnson Administration, 1965–1968* (Chapel Hill: University of North Carolina Press, 2009), and Davies, *From Opportunity to Entitlement*, 94–104.

32 Patterson, *Freedom Is Not Enough*, 76. The 1966 conference, dominated by Johnson loyalists, failed to accomplish anything of substance.

33 Califano, *Triumph and Tragedy*, 64–69; Branch, *At Canaan's Edge*, 333; and Timothy Thurber, *The Politics of Equality: Hubert H. Humphrey and the African American Freedom Struggle* (New York: Columbia University Press, 1999), 181. LBJ had never been close to Humphrey, who had raised questions about his policies in Vietnam. He also thought that Humphrey talked too much. (In December, he complained to Califano that Humphrey had "running-water disease"—"something in the water" in Minnesota rendered him unable to "keep his mouth shut." Califano, *Triumph and Tragedy*, 113–114.)

34 See "CRIME in the Streets," *Newsweek*, Aug. 16, 1965, 20–29; Flamm, *Law and Order*, 51–53.

35 Daniel Patrick Moynihan, "The President and the Negro: The Moment Lost," *Commentary* (February 1967): 31–45.

36 *Statistical Abstract of the United States, 1967* (Washington, DC: US Department of Commerce, Bureau of the Census, 1967), 338.

37 The power of labor unions, significant in the manufacturing sector during the early 1960s, also faded rapidly in later years.

DISCUSSION QUESTIONS

- What were the concerns that the black community in Watts had during the 1960s? What had been their hopes by the mid-1960s, and why did that community perceive that those hopes had not been fulfilled?

- To what extent, if any, did the riots in Watts contribute to the undermining of the Great Society?

- Given that there were both legitimate demands for reform in Watts and for law and order among the authorities, where does the public find a balance that both sides can accept?

CHAPTER XIV

THE PARADOX OF NIXON'S PRESIDENCY

OBJECTIVES

- Analyze the presidency of Richard Nixon.

PREWRITING

- When Nixon was elected president in 1968, how stable was the United States? What were the domestic and foreign problems that the United States faced?

The Paradox of Nixon's Presidency

RONALD K. HUCH

R ichard Nixon's presidency, and his entire political career, is defined by the Watergate scandal that led to his resignation in August, 1974. For many liberals it was the just desserts for a politician they had loathed for more than two decades. That he had built his political success on red-baiting was only one of the reasons for this opprobrium. He was a socially awkward man prone to believe that many, especially the press, were out to "get him." When he exclaimed in 1962 that reporters would not have "Dick Nixon to kick around anymore," he could not have known the worst was yet to come. We must begin with the Watergate story before evaluating the five and a half years of the Nixon Administration.

The saga began on June 17, 1972 as Nixon prepared for his re-election campaign. A mysterious break-in occurred in Democratic headquarters in Washington DC's Watergate office complex. A security guard alerted police that he had observed some tape covering the latch that released the lock on the headquarters' door. This led to the arrest of several men who were still in the office. They had cameras, wire-tapping equipment, and several thousand dollars in cash. It was later learned that G. Gordon Liddy, a former FBI agent, and E. Howard Hunt, a former CIA operative, had organized and led the burglars. Subsequently, it was determined that Liddy and Hunt were working for the Committee to Re-elect the President (CREEP). The burglars became popularly known as "The Plumbers." The purpose of the break-in apparently was to discover what the Democratic National Committee had planned for the upcoming election. Nixon and his supporters were concerned that the Democrats were receiving information from a variety of sources that could be damaging to the president. Nixon was determined to silence his critics by winning the 1972 election in landslide fashion and he instructed his campaign committee to do whatever was necessary to achieve that goal.

By August 1972, the connection between CREEP and The Plumbers had been established, but the Nixon Administration denied any knowledge of what occurred at the Watergate and insisted that it was nothing more than a "simple robbery" attempt. *The Washington Post* reported sporadically on the Watergate events, but there was little national interest at this point. Even after Hunt, Liddy, and five burglars were indicted by a federal grand jury in September, and after John Mitchell, Nixon's campaign chair, admitted that there was a secret fund for spying on Democrats, the American public remained mostly unengaged. In this circumstance, the Watergate story remained largely dormant during the 1972 campaign.

Nixon's re-election was never in doubt. He won in every state except Massachusetts and defeated his Democratic opponent, George McGovern, senator from South Dakota, by a staggering margin. McGovern, once described by conservative philosopher and writer William Buckley as "the most decent man he had ever known," was an anti-war candidate whose campaign theme was "bring America home." McGovern, like all Nixon opponents, encountered a myriad of "dirty tricks" orchestrated by the president's reelection committee. The most prominent of which was to hire people to dress like hippies with long hair and a seemingly drug-addled demeanor to show up at McGovern campaign rallies. The purpose was to convince the American voters that those who supported the Senator were disreputable and un-American. Furthermore, McGovern was relentlessly painted as an extreme liberal.

While Nixon and Agnew celebrated their huge victory, the FBI and, more significantly, *The Washington Post*, were still investigating exactly what happened at the Watergate. The *Post* had assigned two reporters, Bob Woodward and Carl Bernstein, to get to the bottom of what happened and find all who were involved. Their reporting captivated the American public. Using a secret source who stood behind a pillar in a parking garage after midnight, Woodward and Bernstein began to make the connection between the Nixon Administration and the Liddy/Hunt burglars. The secret source became known as "Deep Throat," a reference to a popular pornographic movie at the time. The source remained secret until 2005 when *Vanity Fair* magazine revealed that Mark Felt, a former associate director at the FBI, was Deep Throat. Famously, Felt had told the reporters to "follow the money" and all would become clear. They did, and it led to Nixon's re-election committee.

During the winter and spring, 1973, speculation mounted as to whether or not the president was involved in a plan to cover up the administration's knowledge of, and support for, the Watergate break-in. If he was, then he was guilty of obstructing justice. Nixon continued to insist that he knew nothing of a connection between his administration and any attempt to hide the details of the burglary. Further, he said he would dismiss anyone responsible for such behavior. When White House counsel John Dean told FBI investigators that several of those close to Nixon, including his two top advisors, John Ehrlichman and H.R. Haldeman, were involved, Nixon fired both of them at the end of April. In addition, Nixon demanded the resignations of Dean and Richard Kleindienst, US attorney general. Nixon announced the firings and the resignations in a televised address to the American people. He obviously hoped that this would bring an end to the whole Watergate controversy. Instead, he only heightened interest as to his own involvement in the cover-up.

By this time the Senate Watergate Committee, created to get to the bottom of what actually happened, was preparing to hold public hearings. The hearings began on May 17, 1973, and rivaled the infamous McCarthy hearings of 1954 with regard to the interest of the American people. Broadcast daily on radio and television, the hearings gained a vast audience as one by one the suspects, so often in the news, were brought before the senatorial inquisition. The hoped-for revelations, or perhaps even confessions, did not eventuate. Those who had long despised Nixon were dismayed that the Senate committee could not get any direct evidence that the president was involved. Then, on July 16, everything changed. Testifying before the committee on that day was Alexander Butterfield, a minor, virtually unknown, assistant to the president. In casual fashion he told the senators that everything said in the Oval Office was tape recorded. The stunned reaction was evident for all to see. It meant that conversations among Haldeman, Ehrlichman, Dean, and Nixon were all preserved. Immediately, the Senate Watergate Committee and Archibald Cox, who had been appointed as a special prosecutor to ferret out the cover-up culprits, demanded to hear some of the tapes. Nixon, realizing the devastating affect they would have, claimed executive privilege and refused. On August 15, Nixon again addressed the nation on television saying, "It has become clear that {some senators and commentators} have become increasingly absorbed in an effort to implicate the president personally in the illegal activities that took place." He then went on to state that he had no prior knowledge of CREEP activities and had never taken part in any cover-up. He was right about one thing: there were plenty of people obsessed with linking him to illegal activity.

The Senate Watergate Committee and Archibald Cox issued subpoenas for the tapes, but it would be left to the courts to decide if Nixon had to make them available. Nixon tried valiantly to reach some sort of compromise on the tapes, but all his suggestions were refused by Special Prosecutor Cox. This led the president to order his new attorney general, Elliot Richardson, to fire Cox. Richardson resigned instead. So did the deputy attorney general. Nixon finally found someone, Solicitor General Robert Bork, to carry out his order. The events of the weekend of October 19 became known as the "Saturday Night Massacre."

In the midst of the ongoing dispute over the tapes, the vice president, Spiro Agnew, came under investigation for extortion and taking bribes while he was the governor of Maryland. He was subsequently charged with those crimes as well as tax fraud. He was permitted to plead no contest to failing to report income to the IRS on the condition that he resign as vice president. Clearly, the Nixon government had fallen into complete disarray. In December, 1973, the Senate approved the nomination of Michigan representative, Gerald R. Ford, to finish Agnew's term.

Nixon continued to defend his actions through the remainder of 1973. In a televised press conference in November, he denied that he had ever profited from public service (undoubtedly true) and concluded with a line that would haunt him forever, "I am not a crook." On March 1, 1974, a grand jury indicted the president as a co-conspirator in the Watergate cover-up. Seven other members of his administration were indicted as conspirators. This led to impeachment hearings in the House Judiciary Committee in early May. It was obvious that Nixon would now have a difficult time clinging to office.

In the midst of the turmoil, the president decided to continue with his planned trip to Egypt. It would give him a chance to appear presidential and there is little doubt that he was far more popular in that country than he was in the United States. As it happened, there was also an opportunity for him to solicit sympathy. He had developed phlebitis in one of his legs and the video of him perspiring and struggling to walk up the steps of a pyramid should have resonated with his most fierce opponents. It did not, for it was seen as another of his many tricks to sway public opinion. Nixon returned to find that his position as president was more precarious than ever.

The final blow came on July 24, 1974, when the U.S. Supreme Court ruled that the president could not claim executive privilege with regard to the White House tapes and would have to turn them over to the various parties investigating his role in the Watergate events. The tapes fully revealed the president's involvement in the attempt to obstruct justice. When Republican senators told Nixon that the House would impeach him and that the Senate would convict, he knew the struggle to retain the presidency was over. On August 8, Richard Nixon announced that he would resign as president effective at noon the next day. At that time Gerald Ford became president of the United States. On the morning of August 9, Nixon left the White house by helicopter after giving a rambling, disjointed farewell speech in the presence of his White House staff. From Washington he went to his home state of California. He never faced criminal charges, for President Ford, in an act of compassion and concern for the country, issued a pardon for Nixon on all matters related to Watergate.

NIXON AND VIETNAM

We can now begin our overview of President Nixon's years in office. When he became president in January, 1969 the war in Vietnam raged on and there was no end in sight. During his campaign in 1968, Nixon had promised that he would find a way out of the struggle with honor for the United States. Such an end proved to be elusive.

Soon after taking office, Nixon ordered the bombing of Cambodia and Laos in an effort to disrupt the Ho Chi Minh trail, which was used to supply Communist forces in South Vietnam. It was a massive bombing campaign that aroused even more anti-war sentiment in the United States. The president also continued the use of a controversial herbicide and defoliant known as Agent Orange. Agent Orange had been used since the early 1960s to clear areas of jungle for United States troops. It proved to be a deadly chemical that caused short-range and long-range harm to those who came in contact with it. There was considerable outrage that the United States employed such a chemical and that, coupled with the intense bombing, served to increase the anti-war demonstrations. The polarization of American society over the Vietnam War reached new dimensions.

A significant portion of Americans followed the line that they would support their country "right or wrong." At the same time, those who were well educated came more and more to see their country in a negative way. This led to accusations that the opponents of the war were not "patriotic." Just as folk singers like Joan Baez used her extraordinary popularity to bolster the antiwar cause, the self-claimed patriots had their voices as well. The great country singer Merle Haggard somewhat unwittingly became a hero to those who believed the fabric of U.S. society was being undermined by the drug-abusing, long-haired, privileged, anti-American counter culture. Haggard's 1969 song "Okie from Muskogee" became an anthem for those who felt threatened by what they considered the outrageous behavior of so many young people. As soon as the first bars of this song were recognized at a Haggard concert, the audience would stand and cheer and sing along. None of them used drugs, wore Roman sandals, or "burned draft cards down on Main Street." Haggard followed up with another similar song in 1970 called "Fightin' Side of Me" in which the lines "if you don't love it {United States} leave it" and "when you are running down my country man, you are walking on the fightin side of me" were especially pugnacious.

The potential for significant violence to result from the conflicting views about America's presence in Vietnam, as well as the growing cultural divide, was on display at the Democratic nominating convention in 1968, but it was an event in Ohio in May, 1970, at Kent State University that stunned the country to a much greater extent. A routine anti-war demonstration, likely in response to President Nixon's April 30 announcement that the United States would begin a land invasion of Cambodia, concluded with four students dead and nine others wounded. For reasons that remain unclear, the Ohio National Guard opened fire on the campus and some of those who were shot were simply walking from one class to another. Nixon's immediate reaction was to call the protestors "bums" even though one of those shot was a young woman from a family who strongly supported the president. The effect of the shootings was to cause many in the country to question if the uproar at home was worth continuing a war for which no good ending appeared possible.

After initially expanding America's involvement in the war, Nixon began to sense that his policy of intense bombing and expansion into Cambodia was not producing the results he had hoped. He therefore decided up a plan, recommended to him by some in the military, known as "Vietnamization," whereby South Vietnamese forces would play a bigger role in defending the country. This would allow the United States to gradually withdraw some of its soldiers. At the same time, Nixon continued to press for purposeful peace negotiations with North Vietnamese leaders, but he was never close to finding a resolution. He was further frustrated by his inability to communicate effectively with the South Vietnamese president Nguyen Van Thieu. Moreover, Vietnamization was clearly a failure, as the South Vietnam army was poorly led and organized.

Shortly after the November election in 1972, and before the Watergate scandal caught up with him, Nixon resolved to bring home the remaining U.S. military personnel. He was desperate to end the continuing domestic conflict over the war. He proposed another peace plan to the North Vietnamese, but that too was rejected in December. This led him to order the devastating bombing of Hanoi over the Christmas holidays. This led to North Vietnam agreeing to an armistice that included the release of all prisoners of war. Significantly, it also included the right of the North Vietnam army to remain in South Vietnam. On January 27, 1973, the United States military began to leave Vietnam and by the end of the year, all had returned to the United States. Although Nixon proclaimed that he had preserved the honor of the army and the country, there was no doubt that after twelve years of war and countless casualties, including more than 47,000 U.S. soldiers killed, the war was lost.

The epilogue to the war came quickly. Distracted by the unraveling Watergate scandal, the country and the president now paid little attention to the developments in Vietnam. During 1974 the South Vietnamese army dissolved into chaos and the Communist forces gained in every direction. By the spring of 1975, the North Vietnamese had taken control of South Vietnam as thousands fled from the capital of Saigon. In 1976 a united Vietnam was renamed the Socialist Republic of Vietnam. The North Vietnamese and the Viet Cong carried out a massive revenge on those who had supported the United States.

NIXON IN THE PEOPLE'S REPUBLIC OF CHINA

President Nixon's most remarkable foreign policy achievement was the recognition of the importance of the People's Republic of China (PRC) to the United States. It was remarkable for several reasons; first, Nixon's longstanding reputation as a strident anti-Communist; second, the fact that presidents from Harry Truman through Lyndon Johnson had obstinately held to the absurd notion that the real Chinese government was on the tiny Island of Taiwan; third, the American people had been told again and again that all Communists were alike in their godless perfidy. When Nixon announced in 1971 that he was planning a trip to the PRC in February, 1972, it served to undermine all the usual assumptions about Nixon, China, and Communists in general.

The idea for a reversal of U.S. policy toward the PRC undoubtedly came from Nixon's national security adviser, Henry Kissinger. Kissinger came to the White House as a notable scholar of early 19th-century Europe. He had written a book about Klemens von Metternich, the Austrian statesman who had created the so-called Concert of Europe after the Congress of Vienna in 1815. In the spirit of Metternich, Kissinger no doubt thought of himself as a principled manipulator of United States foreign policy. Kissinger prodded Nixon to the point that Nixon allowed him to visit with Chinese leader Chou en Lai in the summer of 1971. The discussions between Kissinger and Chou led to arranging a visit by the president.

When Nixon arrived in the PRC on February 21, 1972, he was given a rousing welcome as he disembarked from Air Force One. As reporter Charles Burns remembered in the *New York Times* on the fortieth anniversary of Nixon's arrival, the president had on heavy makeup as he shook hands with Chou and stood at attention for the "Star-Spangled Banner." During his seven-day stay in the PRC, Nixon met with Chou, exchanged toasts with Mao Tse Tung, and visited the notable landmarks of China, including the Great Wall. There is no question that it was a triumphant visit for Nixon, and one that only he, as a longstanding antagonist of Communism, could have accomplished. The rapprochement between the PRC and the United States that Nixon and Kissinger brought about would have a long-lasting positive consequence for the economies of both countries. Moreover, it served to disabuse the American public of the contention that Communism was monolithic. It was quite obvious after the 1972 visit that the United States and the PRC were both hostile to the Soviet Union.

Nixon's excursion to China won him high praise from many world leaders. At home, he earned reluctant praise from his legion of detractors, and even more reluctant praise from those who had thought the United States should avoid seeking normal relations with any Communist country. Nixon's ability to take actions that ran against his personal beliefs was never fully understood, or appreciated. It is also true that he had a sense, based upon Kissinger's appraisal, that going to China would bring him political dividends. Furthermore, it gave him an opportunity to tweak those who had maintained that his political career was based upon Red-baiting.

NIXON AND DOMESTIC POLICY

Between the Watergate scandal and his historic reversal of U.S. policy toward Communist China, President Nixon's domestic initiatives were largely overlooked while he was president and for years after he left the White House. Joan Hoff's 1994 book, *Nixon Reconsidered*, redressed a good deal of that neglect. The fact is that Nixon quietly carried forward a liberal agenda nearly as extensive as that associated with Lyndon Johnson and Franklin Roosevelt. One may quibble over his motivation; many liberal commentators have argued that he was fundamentally insincere and contend that his domestic policies simply reflected his awareness of the political winds. Much of this thinking cites the memoirs of his close associate and Watergate conspirator, H.R. Haldeman, whose resentment toward Nixon was obvious after the president dismissed him in April, 1973. It is true that, to some extent, Nixon's domestic policies were a result of public pressure, but this cannot explain the substantial range of his legislation. According to one of his speechwriters, Ben Stein, Nixon's personal prejudices were many, but he was able to submerge these for what he perceived to be the good of the country. Public office holders are supposed to proceed in this fashion, but many simply cannot bring themselves to abandon long-held beliefs. Nixon was able to do this time and time again. It often led to accusations that he reversed himself on many issues simply for political gain. Nixon's opponents always underestimated his intelligence and the fact that he was capable of reflection and sound judgment on matters of policy.

One of the clearest examples of Nixon's ability to change course can be seen in his handling of the economy. He came to the presidency in 1969 holding the traditional economic views long held by Republicans. At the time, the economy appeared strong and there was no reason for concern. But in 1971 a combination of high unemployment and rapidly advancing inflation caused the Nixon Administration to take actions that can only be described as dramatic and unexpected. He declared a wage and price freeze (often considered a socialist policy by Republicans), a reduction of taxes, and a temporary hold on foreign governments' demanding gold for American dollars. Initially, these tactics vastly improved the American economy from late 1971 until the middle of 1973. At that point, oil companies became involved in a conspiracy to drive up oil prices that led to an artificial scarcity of gasoline. A big part of the conspiracy was to convince Americans that oil was in short supply and that oil reserves would likely disappear within twenty to thirty years. The argument, though totally phony, even convinced a number of respected academics and geologists. The Nixon Administration was victimized by the nearly unparalleled greed of American oil companies. As a result, the American economy fell into recession during the time that the president was caught up in the Watergate events.

Although the Republican Party, with the exception of Theodore Roosevelt's administration, had always maintained its belief that small government was the best government, President Nixon greatly expanded the role of the federal government. In 1970, he upset United States industry leaders by signing a law that created the Occupational Safety and Health Administration (OSHA) in an attempt to reduce the number of industrial accidents and deaths. Industry leaders were quick to accuse the president of unnecessarily trying to regulate their business practices. Nixon, however, was only getting started. Within a three-year period from 1971 through 1974, the Nixon Administration created the Environmental Protection Agency (EPA) and the National Oceanic and Atmospheric Administration. This was followed by such legislation as the Marine Mammal Protection Act, the Noise Control Act, the Endangered Species Act, and the Safe Drinking Water Act. The Nixon Administration, much to the annoyance of subsequent Republican leaders, did more to protect and improve the environment than any other in American history. The president recognized that environmental issues had become popular in the United States. What had begun with the publication of Rachel Carson's book *Silent Spring* in 1962, had blossomed into a major national movement by the early and mid-1970s. Though his detractors insisted that Nixon made decisions based upon political gain, his big government agenda seems to have resulted from his realization that the 1970s were not the 1950s. American society had very much changed from the "certainties" most accepted in that decade.

No more evident is Nixon's sensitivity to newly formed American opinion than in his administration's legislation regarding women and black people. In private conversation, Nixon frequently made off-color and offensive references to both. Ben Stein told NPR that the references he heard in the Oval Office were so demeaning that he could never repeat them. Yet, the Nixon government approved more legislation in the interests of women and black Americans than any other administration before or since. When Birch Bayh, Democratic senator from Indiana, and Patsy Mink, Democratic congresswoman from Hawaii, introduced legislation that became known as Title IX, President Nixon quickly endorsed the measure. Title IX established the right of college women to engage in athletic competition on the same basis as men. In introducing the legislation, Bayh had said that the long-held belief that women enrolled in college to find a husband was outdated and detrimental to women advancing in the professions. Nixon agreed. The legislation was to be enforced by the then-Department of Health, Education, and Welfare. Although there was some uncertainty when the law was first passed, Congress eventually made it clear that any college or university that received federal money, directly or indirectly, would come under the terms of the law. The Health, Education, and Welfare Department was divided into two departments during the administration of President Jimmy Carter in 1979: the Department of Health and Human Services and the Department of Education. Under that set-up, the Department of Health and Human Resources is now responsible for assuring compliance with Title IX.

Beyond Title IX, President Nixon demanded that sexual discrimination in the awarding of any educational benefits be immediately abandoned. Most surprisingly perhaps, the president supported the Equal Rights Amendment to the Constitution that promised to guarantee to women all the rights that had traditionally been associated with men. The Equal Rights Amendment ultimately failed to receive sufficient support from state legislatures, but Nixon's endorsement of the proposed amendment did not waver. While feminists argued that Nixon was not doing enough to advance the Equal Rights Amendment, he was actively encouraging government agencies to file sex discrimination lawsuits and even established a National Task Force on Women to focus attention on areas in which it was clear that women were facing discrimination. Finally, Nixon ordered that women should be included under the Affirmative Action policies that had evolved since the 1930s.

Some years after he resigned the presidency, Nixon was asked what he considered to be his most important success on the domestic front. He responded by citing his administration's record in ending school segregation in the South. It was certainly a major lasting achievement of his time in office. Nixon orchestrated the virtual end to all black schools by having federal officials work closely with local officials throughout the South. Even as he hugely extended the role of the federal government in American society, Nixon insisted that most decisions should be left to state and local authorities. His desegregation initiative was one of the few times that local authorities were encouraged to take action that would expand civil rights in the South. With the helpful nudging of the federal government, most of the remarkable desegregation was carried out by local politicians and education administrators.

Although the Republican Party as a whole greatly objected, the president expanded affirmative action legislation to assist blacks. He established that qualified black contractors should be given preference for all government contracts. Though many in his party vilified Nixon for not only endorsing, but also extending, affirmative action laws, he had determined that it was right to redress many of the inequities of the past. In fact, Nixon had always been a supporter of civil rights legislation. In the 1950s, he had spoken strongly in favor of legislation that would enable more black people to vote in the South. He stood firmly against the Southern segregations in the Senate. His record on civil rights matters was far more impressive than that of his Democratic colleague, John F. Kennedy. His private jokes about black people notwithstanding, as president he stands with Lyndon Johnson as the presidents who did the most for civil rights in the twentieth century.

Having been born into a relatively poor family, and having lived his life without the luxuries usually associated with presidential candidates, Nixon was especially attentive to the plight of poor people in the United States. Although some of his proposals to assist the poor, such as dramatically expanding the food stamp program, were turned down by Congress as being too expensive, he was able to implement a number of measures directed toward assisting the poor and elderly. Benefits for those relying on Social Security, Medicare, and Medicaid were significantly enhanced during his years in the White House. In addition, he created the Supplemental Security Income (SSI) for those who were advanced in age or who were disabled. The SSI provided a guaranteed income. Nixon frequently fretted about the indignities faced by those who were at the bottom of the social and economic ladder.

Nixon's views on homosexuality in the United States were not so enlightened. The White House tapes, revealed by the Watergate inquiry, make clear the president's view that accepting homosexuality in any way, shape, or form, would prove disastrous to the country. Using the foul-mouthed language that pervades the tapes, Nixon contended that Greece, Rome, and the Catholic Church all came to grief as a result of homosexuality. It is not surprising that Nixon held this opinion as it is a reflection of what the vast majority of Americans believed in the 1970s. Yet, even in the midst of an anti-homosexual rant, Nixon was careful to say that his objection to homosexuals was not on grounds of morality, but rather the effect their prominence seemed to have on countries and institutions. Had he lived beyond the year 2000, it is probably safe to say that his views about homosexuality would have been much different.

There is no gainsaying that Richard Nixon was perhaps the most complex, fascinating, and unlikely president in the history of the United States. There are many reasons for this. He was not wealthy. He was uncomfortable and rigid in social and political gatherings. He not only did not court the media, he often went out of his way to antagonize reporters and commentators. The dark side of his personality came through in his frequent accusations that many, even in his own party, were out to "get him." His actions were so often in contradiction to what he said he stood for. He contended that he believed in traditional Republican principles, but then, as president, did just about everything that was contrary to those principles. While his substantial foreign and domestic achievements were overshadowed by the Watergate furor, and the devastating end to the Vietnam war, Nixon's legacy should not be that of a "disgraced" president who broke the law and played loose with the Constitution. Rather, he should be honored as the president who accommodated the country's transition to a new era of consciousness about minority rights, women's rights, environmental concerns, and compassion for those often forgotten. Nixon's flaws were abundant, but he was far from a "disgraceful" president.

DISCUSSION QUESTIONS

- Based on the article, was Nixon an effective at managing the troubles of the United States? How was he involved in soothing unrest over civil rights and the Vietnam War, as well as restoring American influence during the Cold War?

- Did Nixon direct his policies for moral and idealistic reasons? Or for realistic reasons?

- To what extent have Nixon's accomplishments been overshadowed by his involvement in the Watergate Scandal?

CHAPTER XV

PROSPERITY AND POVERTY IN AN AGE OF GLOBAL CAPITALISM

OBJECTIVES

- Analyze the economic and social status of the United States after the Cold War.

PREWRITING

- To what extent did the end of the Cold War allow American influence to permeate the world? How did this affect the United States?

Prosperity and Poverty in an Age of Global Capitalism

NINA ESPERANZA SERRIANNE

In 1848, Karl Marx predicted that the global community would become a "universal interdependence of nations." This prediction came to fruition during his lifetime with the first industrial revolution and accelerated throughout the twentieth century as multinational corporations and technology created a deeply integrated world. The new global financial structure of the post–Cold War era was specifically dependent on the American financial system. This codependence ultimately resulted in the world financial crisis of the early 2000s when the "bubble burst." The story of the 1990s in the previous chapter began after the collapse of the Berlin Wall and ended with the terrorist attacks on September 11, 2001; the economic boom and bust of the 1990s followed the same trajectory. Whereas the 1980s is recognized for Reaganomics, trickle-down economic policies, and increasing class stratification, the legacy of the 1990s is one of financial gains for stock market investors and corporations before the second major stock market crash and economic meltdown that followed on the heels of the first in 1987.

In the 1990s, Wall Street made billions of dollars. The stock and bond successes of Wall Street and the Silicon Valley technology boom were contagious and seductive. People wanted to share in the prosperity that the newly wealthy flaunted. Johnson explained in *The Best of Times* that the story of the boom and bust occurred in two parts. The first was the abundant wealth of the 1980s that resulted from technological innovations by young entrepreneurs. The second, in the 1990s, concerned "young computer 'geeks' and 'nerds' enjoying the most luxuriant lifestyles after capitalizing beyond wildest dreams from overnight start-up ventures and initial public offerings that left them, still in their twenties, richer than any American before them, richer than their Gatsbyesque counterparts in the Roaring Twenties, richer than those favored few of the Gilded Age in the 1880s." The number of young "technotimes" tycoons increased daily; according to studies cited by Haynes, sixty-four new millionaires were created daily in Silicon Valley. The wealth and success spread to Wall Street and investors. The U.S. economic booms were greater than those of the Gilded Age or any other era in American history. After a decade of waiting for the trickle-down effect, a new and exclusive generation of Americans lucratively capitalized on the American Dream, the technological revolution, and globalization.

The American markets of the 1990s aggressively redefined the global economy in the post–Cold War era. Under the Reagan and Bush administrations, Americans were becoming poorer as the lower classes waited for economic prosperity to trickle down and the country slid into a series of recessions. As Americans grew tired of Washington's focus on foreign policy, Clinton seized the opportunity and redirected voters to domestic fiscal issues by campaigning on the famous phrase "It's the economy, stupid." The Nobel Prize-winning economist Joseph Stiglitz explained in *The Roaring Nineties: A New History of the World's Most Prosperous Decade* that during the election process and the first years of his presidency, "Clinton invited Americans to use the economy as their presidential scorecard," and they did just that. Americans viewed the boom of the economy following Clinton's election not only as a reflection of post–Cold War markets but, more important, as an indication of the capacity of the executive office. Stiglitz affirmed that the New Economy was a promise of the end of the ups and downs of the economy and business cycles. Owing to new technologies, people believed they had control over their inventories and that they held the power to stay on top of the market.

American investors had the power to mediate the markets in the rest of the world and acquire an abundance of personal wealth. In the 1990s, $1.5 trillion in capital per day was moving through New York's markets. As the stock market continued to grow, so did consumer confidence. The rapidly expanding technology and telecom industries appealed greatly to those investing. Although Clinton was clear in his campaign about many economic issues, deficit reduction was not included in his platform; however, when he assumed office, economic reform, specifically deficit reduction, became one of his primary goals. Both the administration and the international community were still formulating economic and political policies to meet the post–Cold War reality. Within a short time, Clinton's agenda targeted deficit reduction and control. Clinton's policy agenda also focused on the deregulation of Wall Street investment firms. According to Stiglitz, "[investors] wanted the appearance of a fair market, not the reality—and for them there was thus the risk that government regulators would go too far." The economic recovery was generous to a specific class of Americans, particularly investors and politicians.

The unparalleled economic growth of the 1990s resulted in an even greater bust when the bubble popped. The bigger the growth, the bigger the collapse, and this time international markets were integral to one another because of globalization. The bust was devastating not only to the United States but to the world as well. Stiglitz noted that the leadership role assumed by the United States after the Cold War encouraged the belief that Clinton could fix the recession and lead America and the world into a new era of prosperity. Although the United States has experienced eras of great wealth, the nineties was the "high-water mark" for the financial sector.

Before the bust, the new wealth and growth of the economy was due in part to the number of available employment opportunities. One of the greatest legacies of the Clinton administration was the fulfillment of the campaign promise to create new jobs in America. Clinton vowed to return Americans to work after the recession and did so for the duration of the decade. Jobs grew at a rate unparalleled in U.S. history. Between 1993 and 1997 in Clinton's first term in office, ten million jobs were created, and in his second term, an additional eight million jobs were created. The rise of jobs meant the decline of unemployment numbers and in 1994, for the first time in two presidential administrations, unemployment dropped below 6 percent. The trend was set for the rest of the decade as joblessness continued to decline. Setting an all-time low for the first time in three decades, in April 2000 unemployment dropped to under 4 percent. In the last year of the Clinton presidency, not only did job growth show miraculous robustness but the stock market also peaked. In the words of Stiglitz, it was as if the stock market was giving Clinton a final salute.

Many economists argued that although the inevitable bust came at the turn of the twenty-first century, the "boom" of the 1990s lasted significantly longer than the booms of previous decades. Internationally, more people invested in American markets. Foreign investments and interest in the growing economy grew exponentially as the market did. The seemingly overnight wealth earned by investors, specifically in "dot-com" investments, was seductive. Globally, people invested in both the American markets and the market structure being adopted by other countries at the urging of the United States. This ephemeral wealth via rising stock values proved detrimental in the new millennium.

The North American Free Trade Agreement (NAFTA) was created after the fall of the Soviet Union when trade agreements internationally began taking new forms. In the post–Cold War context, countries were free to trade with fewer barriers. Under NAFTA, the new laws allowed businesses from Mexico, Canada, and the United States to invest and import with greater ease. In theory, NAFTA should have equally benefited all of its participants; however, Mexico was slighted compared with the profits of the

United States and Canada. According to the *New York Times*, between 1992 and 2007, Mexico's economy grew only 1.6 percent per capita on average, whereas America's continued to grow at an accelerated rate. The original legislation was a project of the Bush administration but was implemented under Clinton. NAFTA was a contentious issue during the 1992 election between the candidate Ross Perot and the incumbent administration. Whereas Clinton largely supported NAFTA as it was proposed, Perot famously claimed during a 1992 presidential debate that NAFTA would create a "giant sucking sound" as it drained jobs from the U.S. economy "south" to Mexico. However, as president, Clinton continued to support the bill and negotiated two side agreements, the North American Agreement on Labor Cooperation (NAALC) and the North American Agreement of Environmental Cooperation (NAAEC), to change the bill in an effort to accommodate the concerns of (union) labor and environmental groups.

Beginning January 1, 1994, the agreement removed most of the tariffs as well as the trade and investment barriers between the United States, Canada, and Mexico. The elimination of tariffs spurred economic growth in the United States. Conducting operations abroad now appeared far more attractive because of the cheap labor and operating costs, and perhaps too appealing, as corporations and companies began exporting labor. NAFTA supporters contended that the removal of taxes between North American countries would help employees as a result of changes in trade; however, this policy change hurt workers because American companies sent jobs abroad and significantly eliminated domestic jobs, especially factory work.

Some of the preexisting trade provisions were incorporated into NAFTA; for example, the agricultural provisions of the U.S. and Canada Free Trade Agreement. The NAFTA implementation process was given a lengthy timeline. Specifically, all nontariff barriers were eliminated; other tariffs were phased out over the course of five to fifteen years. NAFTA created the largest free-trade market to date globally; according to the Office of the United States Trade Representative, "450 million people producing $17 trillion worth of goods and services" were now linked. Globalization made the world smaller through more interdependent economies, and NAFTA created new interconnectedness in North America.

The argument against NAFTA was that it not only hurt other countries, specifically Mexico, but it also damaged the U.S. economy and its workers. The factory jobs exported abroad impacted every industry, including the manufacture of clothing, cars, electronic software, and parts. Studies since the implementation of NAFTA estimate that jobs lost in the manufacturing sector account for 60.8 percent of all employment lost as a result of the new policy. Supporters of NAFTA have stated that the falling unemployment rate under Clinton in the years after NAFTA was signed was tied to the new trade regulations. There is still debate on whether NAFTA fulfilled its covenant to the United States and other countries. Stiglitz asserted in *The Roaring Nineties* that the promises of NAFTA did not reach Mexico. NAFTA legislation continued to expand despite the arguments against the agreement; in May 2000 the U.S. Congress passed a new extension of NAFTA that included the Caribbean nations. As the international community became smaller because of globalization, the economies of the world became more interreliant. The wealth of the United States was dependent not only on American investors but also on other countries that followed the U.S. economic model, which enhanced American prosperity. However, the interdependence of the financial markets in the post–Cold War era proved detrimental when the "bubble burst" after the world financial crisis of the early 2000s.

For the last three years of the 1990s, each year saw the collapse of economies in a multitude of countries. Because of the interdependence of financial markets, the collapse of one caused a crisis in or the collapse of others. In 1997, the Thai economy began the economic crisis that engulfed the world in a few short years. This was the first indication that the global economy and global capitalism were fallible. The crisis that was originally blamed on the management of the Thai economy quickly proved to be symptomatic of the fiscal structure of the global economy.

The financial crisis spread like an epidemic. Within a few months the economies in Malaysia, Indonesia, the Philippines, South Korea, Hong Kong, and China also collapsed. In a flash, the Asian crisis rattled stock markets around the world. In October 1997, the Dow-Jones industrial average, an index of the relative price of securities, plummeted 554 points, making it the largest points lost in the history of the stock market up to that point. Unfortunately, this would not be the last time in the 1990s that it would plummet hundreds of points in one drop. To cope with the devastation, trading on U.S. stocks was suspended. Despite pushback from nationals, in December South Korea requested a bailout from the International Monetary Fund (IMF). In the hope of ameliorating some damage of the Asian collapse, the IMF approved a $57 billion bailout package. Although the package helped repair the crisis, it was only a matter of time before other world economies collapsed as well. By January, Asia's largest private investment bank in Hong Kong filed for liquidation and the economies of Russia and Brazil were close to collapse.

In June 1998 the Russian stock market crashed. Clinton understood the drastic impact and devastation that the collapse of the Russian economy would have internationally. In an action that was representative of post–Cold War changes, Clinton promised to support the faltering country and its president. Criticisms against communism were still fresh in the United States, but the reality was that Russia was suffering more under global capitalism than it had under communism. The Russian GDP declined 40 percent and poverty increased tenfold. In the capitalist world market, Russia was heavily dependent on taxes and exports, but as the Asian economic crisis quickly spread, the Russian economy became even more subject to rapid change and instability.

In June, Japan announced for the first time in twenty-three years that it was experiencing an economic recession. To protect the American stock market and Wall Street investments, the U.S. Treasury, the Federal Reserve, and the Clinton administration advocated for an intervention to stop the collapse of international markets. In June, the United States invested $6 billion to buy yen in an attempt to strengthen the U.S. economy. With Russia desperately needing assistance as well, a month later President Clinton called on the IMF to support and negotiate emergency loans for Russia. Three days later, the IMF agreed to grant Russia an emergency loan package of $23 billion—only because international lenders utilized an emergency line of credit. Russian stocks rose immediately. Although the Russian economy was smaller than the economy of the Netherlands, the crisis still reverberated around the globe.

In 1999, the economic crises in Asia and Russia spread as the economies of other countries plummeted. Seeing the inevitable trajectory, Brazil began to negotiate an $18 billion loan with the IMF. By January 1999, the country was paralyzed by its financial crisis and the currency was significantly devalued. As the year progressed, the desolation of the world financial markets continued. Largely due to the breakdown of the Brazil and Mexican economies, the market in Argentina fell into a recession. By 2000, the Argentinian recession had not subsided and debt reached 50 percent of the country's GDP. At the end of 2000, Argentina had been approved for an emergency rescue package that included a total of $20 billion ($14 billion in IMF loans and $6 billion from other lenders). As the countries around the globe continued to fall into deep recessions, the boom of the 1990s came to a close.

Starting in 1998, the global stock markets hit all-time lows, which deterred investors from investing because they feared to lose more money. Throughout the collapse of the Asian, Russian, and Latin American economies, the United States felt the effects but remained strong, peaking in the last year of the Clinton presidency. As the new millennium began, the U.S. economy remained at record highs and reflected the prosperity of the decade. Americans spent the 1990s dominating the global economy and obtaining massive wealth. The culture of Wall Street and the profits from Silicon Valley and the tech revolution made many investors feel financially invincible.

The inevitable "bust" as a consequence of the "boom" became even more apparent in 2000 when the peaked U.S. economy quickly ascended. When the stock market plummeted, the value of companies was drastically depleted. According to Stiglitz, in two years, $85 trillion was wiped off the value of the firms in the U.S. stock exchange alone. The prosperity and high employment rate of Americans swiftly spiraled downward. From July 2000 to December 2001, over two million jobs were lost and long-term unemployment more than doubled. Whereas unemployment reached record lows under the Clinton administration, it now rapidly jumped from 3.8 percent to 6 percent. In this short time, the income of 1.3 million Americans fell below the poverty line. This loss of income impacted access to health care and other basic human needs; 1.4 million Americans lost their health insurance within a year. The crash of the economy accelerated as President George W. Bush took office. There has been much scholarly debate over the change in administration and the timeline of the recession. Many economic scholars conclude that it is undeniable that the recession began under Clinton and the policy decisions of the George W. Bush administration added momentum to an already crumbling economy.

It was not long into the new millennium that many of the companies that were fundamental to the technology and financial booms of the 1990s experienced crashing stock values, specifically the dot-com companies. The inflated value of the stocks of the technology sector now quickly plummeted. As explained by Walter LeFeber, stocks previously worth $80 were suddenly worth $5. Most important, the investors who had believed they were millionaires were suddenly unemployed and strapped with a bleak financial portfolio. At the beginning of the century, it was apparent that companies were financially vulnerable; by 2001–2002 the crash of the dot-com companies proved to be detrimental to every sector of the economy.

As the dot-com stocks crashed, unemployment spread rapidly. Within a matter of months, the record-low unemployment rate of the Clinton administration had already increased by 50 percent. This mass loss of jobs changed the narrative of prosperity. The consumer confidence that defined the market for tech growth had vanished, and stocks were plunging. Internet and website-based companies collapsed under their own weight, and so did transnational corporations. AOL Time Warner was forced to take write-offs of $100 billion. As Stiglitz explained in *The Roaring Nineties*, this depreciation of value was especially significant because ten years previously, at the beginning of the 1990s, AOL Time Warner and other companies were not even worth $100 billion, let alone able to handle losing that much in value and still survive financially.

In the 1990s, the story of transnational corporations and the technology sector began with growth at an unparalleled rate, invoking images of Gilded Age America and the first Industrial Revolution. The historically distinct American corporation was modified by changes in globalization. The '90s represented a new era of transnational power wherein the sheer size of the multinational corporations was unprecedented. In *Michael Jordan and the New Global Capitalism*, LaFeber cites statistics from the 1980s showing that of the hundred largest "economic units" in the world, including companies and countries, fifty of them were individual corporations and fifty were nations. Throughout the decade, transnational corporations acquired more power as globalization contributed to their size and wealth.

The first Industrial Revolution and the Gilded Age not only paved the way for advances in technology and machinery but also for business ideologies. The executives running corporations in the 1990s took notes from their predecessors; specifically, Phil

Knight, CEO of Nike, looked to the legendary businessman and philanthropist John D. Rockefeller as he built his empire. One of the differences between the corporate revenue of the Gilded Age and the end of the twentieth century was the immense reliance on new post–Cold War open markets. Unlike post–Civil War era corporations that were sustained by transactions within the United States, LaFeber notes that the Nikes, Coca-Colas, and McDonalds of the world needed global consumerism to maintain profits. In the 1980s, all American corporations received 80 percent of their revenue from overseas production. For example, in 1996 four out of every five Coke bottles were sold outside of the United States. Globalization, and an increased acceptance of Western culture, allowed these corporations to extend their reach.

Since World War I, U.S. dominance over global capital was exacerbated by technology and Wall Street investment firms. When the Soviet Union fell, many scholars viewed the collapse of the Berlin Wall and the Communist government as the last restriction to global capitalism. American markets were now free to reign and influence other international markets. An era of unchecked global capitalism began. Stiglitz referred to this decade as "the Roaring Nineties"—the decade of megadeals and megagrowth; economic growth began to reach new levels that had not been experienced in a decade. During the 1990s, a person's ability to attach to a transnational corporation or the U.S. market was the key to financial success, and this came with a price. The '90s was a new decade, a new economy, a new global era, and a new technological world. This new world became synonymous with the dot-com investment sphere, transnational corporations, and unprecedented wealth for transnational entrepreneurs.

The new open markets, combined with innovative opportunities for marketing through technological advances, allowed for transnational corporations to expand in pioneering ways. A prime example of this throughout the 1990s wand since was Nike, Inc. The idea for Nike began when Phil Knight was attending Stanford Business School during the 1970s. For a class assignment, Knight wrote a paper laying out his vision for a future track-shoe company whose aim was to enhance athletic performance. As described by LaFeber, Knight calculated that the weight of the average running shoe inhibited runners; by reducing the weight of the shoe by one ounce, he could free the runner of 550 pounds during a mile-long run. After graduation, Knight took his ambitious dream to the next level and collaborated with Tiger Shoe, a Japanese shoe company. The fledgling entrepreneur returned to the United States and sold the shoes out of his car under the company name Blue Ribbon Sports. Nike became a brand name when an employee dreamed about Nike, the Greek goddess of victory, and pitched the idea to Knight. Since Knight's Stanford days, he intended for his vision to transform into a global transnational empire. Within a few years, Nike sold half of all running shoes in the world and by the mid-1990s Nike was a $9 billion company.

The rapid success of the brand was attributed to its recognizable advertising. The "swoosh" logo originated in the 1970s when Carolyn Davis, a design student at Portland State University, was paid $35 to create a logo. As the shoe company began to sell internationally, the wordless "swoosh" logo crashed language barriers that challenged most advertisers. Then in 1988, Nike added to its cross-trainer ads the slogan "Just Do It." Two more years and a $60 million campaign later, the three words were internationally recognizable. Nike capitalized on the growth of television audiences and the appeal of television ads. The legendary movie director Spike Lee took Nike advertising in a new direction when he made commercials for Nike featuring the superstar basketball player Michael Jordan. The commercials appealed to the audience by making Jordan's extraordinary talents appear effortless. LaFeber explained that Jordan, much like the "swoosh" logo, was an icon that transcended words. Knight had stated, "It save[d] us a lot of time ... you can't explain much in 60 seconds, but when you show Michael Jordan, you don't have to. People already know about him. It is that simple." By the early '90s, Nike was a transnational corporation whose successes depended on global revenue and mass marketing.

Jordan's international fame epitomized market globalization; the ad campaigns shaped popular culture of the 1990s and brought revenue to his multinational endorsers: his endorsements had a $10 billion dollar impact on the U.S. economy alone. Approximately 5.2 billion in revenue went directly to Nike. Jordan's talent was unprecedented in NBA history. His image in society and in the media transcended race and appealed to people of all ethnicities and classes. At the beginning of Jordan's career, in addition to $3.5 million in Chicago Bulls salary, the star athlete earned $17 million in endorsements. This figure expanded exponentially throughout his career as he collaborated with many name brands and high-profile companies. By the early '90s, Jordan's earnings increased to $25 million a year, though there was little to no increase in his NBA salary. Multinational corporations continued to invest in the iconic player and by 1997 his earnings exceeded $100 million annually. As LaFeber pointed out, the success of Jordan's image and income was a result of the "products of the post-1970s technology." Cable television advertisements allowed Jordan to become a global celebrity and the media impact on U.S. and international popular culture was profound. Companies like Nike came to rely on Jordan's ads to keep their customers loyal to the brand and their profits high.

Although Nike's advertisements were international and appealed to all races and socioeconomic classes, the cost of the shoes was priced for more affluent consumers at $150 or more. In the United States, when new models of the Air Jordans were released people waited in 25-degree weather to purchase a pair. Additionally, there were reports of teens who were killed or had committed murder for a pair of Air Jordans. Within the first four months of 1990, the Atlanta police dealt with fifty robberies pertaining specifically to sports apparel, including shoes. Crimes related to the desire for Air Jordans across the country ranged from robberies to murders of youths. As in other decades, the shoes and clothing were a symbol and barometer of success and financial affluence. As LeFeber explained, upward of 80 percent of the shoes and apparel sold within the United States were not purchased for their "intended purpose" of playing sports; instead, they were purchased for fashion and status.

The wild consumer consumption of Nike athletic apparel and the lengths to which some people were willing to go to obtain them was symptomatic of deeper social issues. The inequality between classes and races created a sense of social exclusion and dissonance for many poor teens as they were flooded with images of expensive athletic apparel that they could not afford. The sociologist Elijah Anderson was quoted in *Sports Illustrated* in 1990 regarding the link between economic disparity, the wave of crimes, and consumerism. Anderson explained that many inner-city kids were not exposed to the same economic opportunities as their white middle-class peers, but held the same desires for these material goods; they were "bombarded with the same cultural apparatus [as the] white middle class." When many young teens and adults found they could not afford the shoes and clothing, they turned to selling illegal drugs to obtain the money, and drug trafficking was complicated by gang-related activity.

Along with the social cost to America, Nike and other multinational corporations' labor choices exacted a price abroad. In the 1990s, a pair of shoes cost Nike approximately $5.60 to make in Asia using native labor and the resell price was anywhere between $70 and $150. The production capacity of the company was enormous. In the early 1990s, Nike produced four million pairs of shoes a year. Five years later, Nike had expanded to ninety-seven international production lines that produced forty-five million pairs of shoes. The following year in 1996, Nike reached a production number of seventy million pairs of shoes. Nike's ability to engage in such intensive production was a result of cheap labor. As LaFeber explained, Nike workers in 1996 were paid $2.23 a day, making Michael Jordan's $20 million endorsement fee from Nike higher than the combined yearly payrolls of all of the Indonesian plants producing the shoes.

The end of the Cold War impacted U.S. and international markets and changed business plans for corporations seeking to employ workers, specifically those in previously Communist countries. The changes in previously Communist governments and state-run economies influenced business contracts. Specifically, Asian countries opened up to employment opportunities sought by capitalist countries, which prompted a shift in many factory jobs from the United States to China. As transnational corporations shifted jobs from the domestic labor force to cheaper foreign labor, Americans lost their positions in U.S. factories. Nike eliminated 65,000 jobs in America. The transference to foreign labor practices allowed the company to pay Asian workers $0.14 an hour. The shift to foreign labor began slowly in the 1980s with non-Soviet countries and expanded when trade embargos against Vietnam were lifted for the first time since the Vietnam War. The wages paid to workers abroad continues to violate labor standards in many counties, particularly in the United States, where the company headquarters are located. Nike paid Vietnam workers $1.60 a day in a country where it cost at least $2.00 a day to eat three meals. Workers faced the dilemma of starving or working the extra hours to be paid closer to the $2.00. Many workers would faint from exhaustion and malnutrition as a result of the working conditions and lack of food.

In the new age of globalization, a venue was created for cultural imperialism to be spread internationally and for labor relocation outside the United States. The use of the word "sweatshop" has become synonymous with poor working conditions, labor abuses, and illegal low-paying jobs. The massive labor abuses of the Gilded Age continued in the United States with the spread of globalization. Although sweatshops existed for the production of a variety of consumer goods, they began as a result of urbanization in the mid-nineteenth century. The sociologist Robert J. S. Ross writes in *Slaves to Fashion* that when ready-to-wear clothing became increasingly popular, the clothing industry underwent high demand for these products, which in turn required more labor. Factory owners remedied the labor shortage by employing sweatshop workers and have continued to do so in the century and a half since.

There are no universally accepted conditions that define the term "sweatshop." According to Ross, it is legally defined in the United Stated by the American apparel industry as "a business that regularly violates both wage or child labor and safety or health laws." This definition is dependent on the Fair Labor Standards Act of 1938 (FLSA), which establishes a minimum wage and requires premium pay for work over forty hours in one week. The FLSA term emerged from an investigation on behalf of then Congressmen, now Senator, Charles Schumer of New York to further explore labor abuses.

As global capitalism has expanded, so has American investment in lower-wage countries. Corporations determine where to employ labor for their companies based on "global scanning," a term coined by Raymond Vernon. As Ross explains, multinational corporations "systematically searched the globe for the most propitious sites on which to place their production facilities and to target their sales effort." The strategic exploitation of workers for cheaper labor draws on the greatest flaws of global capitalism and globalization: companies target areas where unions are weakest and labor protections do not exist or are rarely enforced, and it is easy for workers to be repressed and forced to accept low wages. In the 1990s, company investments in Asian factories became popular because of the lack of regulations in working conditions and wages, unlike European factories. In 1998, garment workers in Burma were paid approximately $0.04 an hour because of the country's abysmal work standards, whereas workers in Italy were paid $12.55 for the same job but were protected by labor laws.

In the 1990s, after the implementation of NAFTA, in order to increase their profits companies stopped investing in developed countries with stricter labor laws.

In 1998, eleven million people worldwide were employed to make clothes. When textile and footwear workers were added to this number, they totaled over twenty-nine million worldwide. The wages of this labor force, as in the example of Nike, are still below the cost of living. A prime example of the abuse and exploitation of workers in the '90s, and now, is the GAP factories in Saipan, one of fourteen islands located in the Commonwealth of Northern Mariana Islands (CNMI). After World War II, the islands became a U.S. territory and later in 1975 they joined as a commonwealth. This commonwealth status placed the islands under U.S. sovereignty and jurisdiction; thus the clothing manufactured there may be labeled "made in the USA" even though the labor practices violate American laws. The island continues to provide an ideal loophole for manufacturers and corporations because it is exempt from many U.S. labor restrictions.

The loophole in labor regulations did not go unnoticed by contractors and corporations around the world. Ross notes that it allowed U.S. markets to exploit "the duty- and quota-free access to the U.S. market." In the 1980s, Korean and Chinese contractors brought workers, specifically young Chinese females, to the islands to work as "guest workers" in the factories. This labor strategy allowed companies to avoid many of the legal issues surrounding the immigration status of the workers; there was an absence of accountability and regulation regarding the immigration status of the workers and worker wages. The manipulation of the laws continued into the new millennium, and as late as 2007 the minimum wage in Saipan was as low as $3.05. Loopholes in the law allowed American companies to utilize and exploit unregulated sources of labor.

From the 1980s to the 1990s, Ross explains, the demographics of the island changed drastically. In the 1980s, there was no garment sector on the island and there were approximately 110 manufacturing employees. By the late 1990s, the island was dominated by the garment-sector factories and the dormitories in which the low-wage workers were housed. According to Ross, in 1999, over forty-seven thousand workers were employed on the island, and of this number, over thirty-five thousand were non-U.S. citizens. The corporations benefitted greatly from the low-wage labor, but not without criticism from human rights advocates.

Changes in U.S. trade policies in the 1990s increased the appeal of sweatshops abroad, but many companies continued to employ sweatshop workers in the United States despite the labor laws. The United States is commonly ignored for its sweatshop labor practices and other human rights abuses. Ross writes that people are not "willing (or able)" to envision the same abuses heaped on contemporary American sweatshop workers, as was the reality with Gilded Age America. The unfortunate reality is that labor abuses are still present. As of 2000, more than 60 percent of the contractor shops in New York City and Los Angeles overtly engaged in sweatshop practices. The U.S. Bureau of Labor Statistics estimated in 2000 that at least 435,000 recorded workers in the United States were vulnerable to sweatshop working conditions in the garment industry. The unrecorded workers laboring in sweatshops can only be estimated, as there is no way to count them precisely. Scholars project that unrecorded workers make up another 20 percent and are primarily sewing machine operators.

It is important to place the domestic employment of sweatshop labor in a global context. Because of U.S. labor laws it is easy to ignore the impact American workers had on the clothing and textile industry. Ross surmised that "if we go back to 1998 employment levels, using the 1998 sweatshop estimate, the United States is the second largest employer of clothing workers in the world (after China). Its 400,000 sweatshop workers, if they were separated in a national economy would be the world's fourth largest mass of clothing workers ... the estimate of 255,000 sweatshop workers for the year 2000 would place the United States' victims of labor abuse as the eighth largest mass of clothing workers in the world." The labor abuses of transnational corporations and companies are frequently overlooked, especially when the laws on the books appear to protect the workers.

Nike and other sweatshop-based brands were criticized in the late 1990s when activists drew attention to the labor abuses behind the products. As quickly as Nike became popular, many human rights groups spoke out against the corporation and its labor practices. Phil Knight once said that "Nike [had] become synonymous with sweat shops." In 1995, one of the most famous celebrity clothing lines criticized for labor abuses was that of Kathy Lee Gifford, the actress and TV personality. Her Wal-Mart clothing line production used child labor in Honduras. However, she denied allegations from the National Labor Committee Education Fund and other human rights and media groups. The accounts of the sweatshop abuses included fifteen-hour workdays in buildings with little ventilation and surrounded by barbed wire and armed guards. Three years after Gifford pledged to end labor abuses in her clothing line production, she was under scrutiny for the same abuses in El Salvador. In response to her alleged abuses, and those of many other companies and corporations, the Clinton administration decided to take action.

The creation of the Fair Labor Association (FLA) and its "code" in 1997 was a direct response to the Kathy Lee Gifford controversy from the Clinton administration's secretary of labor, Robert Reich. L. L. Bean, Reebok, Kathy Lee Gifford, and Nike formed a coalition in collaboration with the Clinton administration to address the issues and created a "code of conduct" for their factories. The negotiations to discuss accountability began on April 14, 1997. The coalition of apparel and footwear companies created the "code" to assuage the concerns of cautious and conscious consumers. Part of the incentive for companies to meet the standards of the "code" was the label the

FLA would place on clothing and consumer goods to restore the faith of the buyers. The participants gathered symbolically at the White House to sign into action the recommendation for employers and workers. The final suggestions included limiting the workweek to sixty hours and maintaining wages at the legal minimum wage of the country in which the factory was located. Additionally, to create external and internal accountability, the organizations publicly agreed to allow external monitors to conduct surprise visits to the factories.

The FLA did not require overtime work to be voluntary, but it did require the employers to pay "at least regular rates." As most workers in the garment workers' industry are commonly paid per piece, this created another loophole for employers and failed to protect the employees. As Ross aptly stated, "if they fail to meet a quota for the day to make minimum wage, they may be (legally or illegally) required by the employers to work extra time without additional pay." Activists slammed this proposal because it was weak on labor abuses. It all proved to be a public-relations stunt when investigators found that workers were still being mentally, physically, and sexually abused and nothing was done to protect them. The only change that occurred after the proposal was to introduce a new loophole for the owners of the factories and the transnational corporations. In many countries the legal payment for work was not equitable to the cost of living.

Because of criticism, corporations began to make changes, not for human rights protections but for long-term stability between the corporation and its factory workers. One example was the women's apparel giant Victoria's Secret. As Thomas Friedman explains in *The Lexus and the Olive Tree*, the pressure from high-profile antisweatshop campaigns resulted in less consumption of goods and forced companies to take a stand. As pressure grew to hold companies accountable, Victoria's Secret, like many other corporations, turned to domestic labor. However, in this case, instead of employing factory workers, they were exploiting prison labor. In an attempt to appear as if they were supporting U.S. jobs, many companies changed their labor investments from overseas labor to cheap domestic prison labor.

A vast number of companies not only took advantage of new trade opportunities through NAFTA and cheap labor abroad but also prison labor at home. The journalist Beth Schwartzapfel, reflecting on the subcontracted labor of the 1990s in a 2009 article in the *Nation*, wrote that "prisoners in the past two decades have packaged or assembled everything from Starbucks coffee beans to Shelby Cobra sports cars, Nintendo Game Boys, Microsoft mice and Eddie Bauer clothing. Inmates manning phone banks have taken airline reservations and even made calls on behalf of political candidates." As will be discussed later, the utilization of prison workers has a long history rooted in slavery and convict leasing and is a current reality rooted in the war on drugs. Prison labor in the United States has been utilized by corporations, business owners, and farmers or plantation owners for almost one hundred nonconsecutive years of American history, regardless of the language of the Thirteenth Amendment: "Neither slavery nor involuntary servitude, except as a punishment for crime whereof the party shall have been duly convicted, shall exist within the United States, or any place subject to their jurisdiction."

Corporations have invested in prison labor since 1979 when Congress passed the Prison Industry Enhancement Certification Program (PIE). According to Schwartzapfel, PIE provided private-sector companies with an incentive to utilize prison labor as a source of employment. Additionally, states offered "free or reduced rent and utilities in exchange for the decreased productivity that comes with bringing materials and supplies in and out of a secured facility and hiring employees who must stop working throughout the day to be counted and who are sometimes unavailable because of facility-wide lockdowns." In the 1990s, post–Cold War elimination of global trade barriers, opportunities domestically for prison labor, and loopholes in labor laws for continental U.S.-based sweatshops permitted companies unprecedented access to cheap labor.

Later in the decade, the backlash from activists raised public awareness. Consequently, beginning in 1998, the sneaker-manufacturing sector of the U.S. economy declined. Although the decline was partially attributed to the hard work of grass-roots activists, it was also largely due to the crash of the international market. In 1999, labor rights activists sued eighteen apparel retailers and manufacturers for human and labor rights violations against workers in the CNMI. The list of violators included GAP, Dayton-Huston (soon to be Target), J. C. Penney, Sears, May, Limited, Jones Appeal, Liz Claiborne, Phillips Van Heusen, Polo Ralph Lauren, and Warnaco. The majority of retailers eventually settled with the plaintiffs for $8.75 million in damages. The money compensated for some of the human rights violations and loss of labor, but did not fix the larger issues.

The growth of the U.S. economy became the template for global capitalism as the American government and market leaders pressured other countries to develop the same policies and structures. The symbiotic and parasitic relationships of the new interdependent world economy were fostered by the new era of merging global capitalism. The post–Cold War economy was built on the concept of promises. Some of these promises were rooted in NAFTA, and other policies presented the hope of new financial and technological expansion. This was especially appealing for the developing countries that struggled to succeed globally with the superpowers: the United States, China, and Europe. As Stiglitz explains, the promise of the new economy quickly gave way to stiff trade barriers and large subsidies, which denied farmers in the Third World access to American markets.

Access to the market was far from egalitarian. From the beginning, developed Western countries were favored and the American economy was the top priority. Stigltiz also notes that there was a strong disconnect between domestic policies in the United States and those designed for Third World countries; they were based on two different economic philosophies. The American government's foreign policy was to put American interests first. This protectionist position was present during the 1990s and was tied to a long history of U.S.-controlled economic and diplomatic relations. The complicated, dependent, and manipulated relationship between global economies, as Stiglitz explains, dated back to the Opium Wars with China. As economies throughout the world collapsed in the second half of the twentieth century, it became evident how codependent the countries had become. The boom and bust cycle was experienced around the world.

In 1995, the structure of world trade mediation created the need for a new organization, the World Trade Organization (WTO). Replacing the General Agreement on Tariffs and Trade (GATT), which had been created in 1948 after World War II, the organization, according to the WTO, "provides a forum for negotiating agreements aimed at reducing obstacles to international trade and ensuring a level playing field for all, thus contributing to economic growth and development. The WTO also provides a legal and institutional framework for the implementation and monitoring of these agreements, as well as for settling disputes arising from their interpretation and application."

The members of the WTO hold the power to enforce trade-rule sanctions and ensure that countries are held accountable and follow the rules. When officials met in Geneva in 1995 and established the WTO, it replaced the seemingly antiquated GATT designed to reduce tariffs and oversee multilateral trading. The most evident difference between the two international organizations was the range over which they had authority. Whereas GATT focused on the regulation of goods and merchandise, the WTO targeted regulation. The technological revolution, along with the growing wealth of Wall Street and the stock market, influenced every area of regulation. The WTO was granted the authority to cover the same scope of activity as GATT, and additionally to cover telecommunications, banking, and intellectual property rights. Initially, at the end of 1994, the same 128 countries that were signed to GATT signed to the WTO; by 2013, the number of countries increased to 158. With a $158 million budget, the WTO was officially in effect on January 1, 1995.

The WTO quickly became a point of contention between labor rights activists or critics of globalization and free trade activists. As stated by the historian Michael Kazin in a *New York Times* editorial, the prosperity of the 1990s convinced many that free-market ideologies and policies could benefit everyone. In reality, the wage inequalities and the collapse of many global markets demonstrated that the promises of globalization were ephemeral. A BBC article concisely listed the four main criticisms of the WTO. First, the organization is too powerful; in effect it can compel sovereign states to change their laws and regulations by declaring them to be in violation of free-trade rules. Second, the WTO is "run by the rich for the rich" and does not provide egalitarian access to trade opportunities. Additionally, the problems facing developing countries are not legitimized. One continuous example is the opening of markets; the developed countries have strategically kept their markets closed to products from poorer countries. Third, the WTO is indifferent to the impact of free trade on a variety of issues such as workers' rights [labor abuses], child labor, and environment and health issues. Last, the WTO lacks democratic accountability. The organization operates so that all hearings and meetings regarding trade disputes are closed to the public and the media. As an opinion piece in the *New York Times* in December 1999 explained, "When one country challenges another's trade practices, for example, the cases are decided by panels of three trade experts whose deliberations are cloaked in secrecy. This is clearly a process that needs to be opened up to public view." This absence of accountability only increased the power of the WTO.

Arguments for the organization typically include the democratic origins of the organization—it is a coalition organization comprised of member countries. However, the reality is that although the organization has democratic roots, it is not egalitarian and some countries have more power and voice than others; specifically, the power of the developed countries overshadows the developing countries. Another common argument in support of the WTO is the impact that it has had on global trade and living standards. The Clinton administration cultivated support for the creation of the WTO, but in the years since has attempted to appease both advocacy groups and the WTO. In his presidency, Clinton promoted an agenda of free trade that was based on the argument that it had supported the boom of the 1990s. However, Clinton later shifted his position because of pressure from activist groups pushing for the enforcement of labor and environmental protections. This attempt to combat labor violations was much like the FLA effort to hold Nike and other corporations accountable: it was simply a political act to quell the contempt.

The arguments for and against the WTO, as well as the dispute over free trade and fair trade, culminated in a protest in Seattle in 1999. The fight between the police and the demonstrators created media images reminiscent of the anti-Vietnam War protests of the 1960s and 1970s. From November 29, 1999 to December 3, 1999, the leaders of the WTO met in Seattle, Washington, to discuss the agenda of the organization and future trading policies. More than fifty thousand protesters gathered to object to the policies. By the morning of the first day of meetings, the dissenters flooded the streets to bring attention to free-trade policies and global injustice.

The chaos was exacerbated by the lack of preparation by the city of Seattle for such a large-scale protest. The city compensated for its absence of a plan with police brutality and restrictions on First Amendment rights. Within hours, the police and the National Guard utilized chemical weapons, pepper spray, rubber bullets, and clubs against those in the area, bystanders included. In response to security concerns regarding the arrival of the president and the escalation of the protest rally and police brutality, Seattle Mayor Paul Schell declared a "civil emergency" and a "no protest zone" in the twenty-five-square block surrounding the Convention Center. The constitutionally guaranteed right to freedom of speech was ignored by the city as it encouraged the Seattle Police Department, the Washington State Patrol, and the National Guard to enforce restrictions on public gatherings and speech.

On the second day of the WTO protest, over five hundred demonstrators were arrested, in violation of their First Amendment right. As the WTO meetings came to a close, the protests were muted. This was in part because most of the protestors were arrested, injured, or both. After the protests were over, on December 6, 1999, Seattle Police Chief Norm Stamper took full responsibility for the events and resigned from his position. The story picks up again in 2007 when, after almost a decade, a federal jury found the City of Seattle "liable for the unlawful arrests of about 175 protesters during the World Trade Organization meeting … in 1999." The jury concluded that the city violated the rights of the protestors, specifically in regard to "unreasonable search and seizure." However, it also decided the city was not liable for violating the right to free speech.

Throughout the 1990s, as trade and investments crossed borders, so too did cultural exchanges. The international financial market that was created by Wall Street in the 1980s and 1990s had permitted American culture and markets to further penetrate the world. Anti-American sentiments were rooted in both the cultural imperialism and economic collapses of the late 1990s. The impact of the fiscal crisis and the Westernization of many cultures fostered resentment in many countries and tension with allies. As Stiglitz describes the "darker side of globalization" in the post–Cold War world, not only were ideas, goods, and services able to move more easily across boarders but violence and terrorism were also able to penetrate. In 1998, terrorist attacks on U.S. embassies reminded U.S. officials just how easily borders could be transcended.

On August 7, 1998, bombs exploded 4 minutes apart at the U.S. embassies in both Kenya and Tanzania. In Nairobi, seventy-four people were killed, eight of whom were Americans, and an additional sixteen hundred people were injured in the blasts. In Dar es Salaam, seven lives were lost and seventy-two people were injured. These deaths were symptomatic of the terrorism that was to follow. The United States blamed the attacks on the terrorist Osama Bin Laden and his terrorist network Al-Qaeda. To retaliate, the United States targeted missiles at what was assumed to be the supply sources for Al-Qaeda in both Afghanistan and Sudan. On September 11, 2001, the most extreme terrorist attack on U.S. soil in recent years reminded Americans of just how easy it had become for terrorism to cross borders.

RECOMMENDED READING

The most comprehensive book on the economy of the 1990s: the Nobel Prizewinning economist Joseph Stiglitz's *The Roaring Nineties: A New History of the World's Most Prosperous Decade* (New York: W. W. Norton, 2003). William LaFeber, *Michael Jordan and the New Global Capitalism* (New York: W. W. Norton, 2002), is an entertaining and engaging analysis of globalization through Michael Jordan and American culture. A specific look at sweatshop abuses is available in Robert J. S. Ross, *Slaves to Fashion: Poverty and Abuse in the New Sweatshops* (Ann Arbor: University of Michigan Press, 2004).

DISCUSSION QUESTIONS

- According to the article, how could the 1990s be compared with the 1920s and the 1950s in terms of consumerism? Is this a fair comparison?
- To what extent did the spread of American commercial influence abroad disrupt the United States? How did the United States attempt to address this?
- To what extent was 1990s American capitalism "democratic"?

CHAPTER XVI

GLOBAL AFTERMATH

OBJECTIVES

- Analyze the political, diplomatic, and military status of the United States after the Cold War.

PREWRITING

- Consider the diplomatic limits on the United States before the end of the Cold War. Without the Soviet Union to act as a check on American influence, in what ways are those limits removed? Or do they remain in other aspects?

- Consider the traditional ways by which the United States has spread its influence around the world in the twentieth century; militarily, economically, and culturally. Are those methods still used today?

Global Aftermath

FRANK NINKOVICH

The half-century period of America's historical singularity began to wind down in 1991 with the downfall of the Soviet empire and the collapse of communism. At first glance, appearances suggested otherwise, as post– Cold War America was dominant on a scale never before seen in world history. Confounding the many predictions of a return to traditional multipolar international politics, there followed instead a "unipolar moment" in which the United States stood out as something unique, an unchallenged global power. In the neologism of the French foreign minister, it was a "hyperpower"; to its critics, it was a global empire; while for those who viewed it more appreciatively, it was a liberal hegemon. Uniting such disparate judgments was a widespread belief that US supremacy was both the culmination of a deep exceptionalist impulse and the beginning of a new phase in which it would seek to perpetuate its supremacy[1].

But far from being the crowning achievement of a historical career that led inexorably to this moment, these years did not mark the entry into the promised land of exceptionalism; they were, instead, a transitional period in which US foreign policy gravitated erratically toward the more modest default position embodied in dollar diplomacy. Extraordinary as it was, America's dominance during these years was only a transient state of affairs that owed much to some highly unusual circumstances: the residual legacy of Cold War military preparedness combined with the historically improbable disappearance of any serious military or ideological competitors. But there were other reasons for thinking that this ascendancy was only temporary. One had to do with hegemony's flimsy grounding in the history of US foreign relations and the absence of a home in a cultural tradition. Hegemony, which was quite new, went against the grain of a half century of policies that had revolved around meaningful international cooperation, and it also broke with an even longer tradition of modest leadership. More importantly, despite the widespread impression that the United States was able to do as it pleased, its power, like that of the Wizard of Oz, was less imposing than it seemed.

* * *

The unprecedented political and military dominance amassed by the United States in the post–Cold War decades was the product of favorable domestic and foreign conditions. One enabling factor was a stupendous military capability inherited from the Cold War. American power was a legacy of its earlier investment in military tech-nologies and the ability to profit from the so-called Revolution in Military Affairs. Once developed, this unique capability took up fixed residence in a welcoming institutional matrix from which it was impossible to evict. Since Eisenhower's farewell address in 1961, the dense network of institutions that formed the military-industrial-scientific complex had become even more parasitically embedded in the American economic and political structure. Though military spending relative to GDP declined during the 1990s, it nevertheless equaled that of the next fifteen powers combined. On the foreign side of the ledger, the disintegration of the USSR and its empire left a Russia that was in every respect a flaccid remnant of its former self. In what had amounted to a historical elimination tournament, America was the only competitor left standing.

With no credible military challenger in sight, and with no significant contraction of military capabilities, the United States stood alone atop the Everest of power while other nations were limited to surveying the world from the foothills. The American military establishment, in one of its habitual misreadings of history, would have liked to keep things that way. "Our first objective is to prevent the re-emergence of a new rival," declared a 1992 draft Defense Planning Guidance. One problem, however, was that the powerful national security state built up over more than four decades was now left without a mission. With the sudden disappearance of a threat that had long warranted the hypertrophied defense establishment's privileged existence, policy makers had difficulty in defining credible new dangers. The best that James Woolsey, President Bill Clinton's CIA director, could do was to suggest that, despite the removal of the most dangerous beast of prey, the jungle was still teeming with "a bewildering variety of poisonous snakes." Woolsey's inability to specify a threat suggests that part of the reason for continued security expenditures on a grand scale lay closer to home. It is close to a sociological law—sometimes called a bureaucratic pathology—that bureaucracies, once established, have a well-documented tendency to perpetuate themselves. In this case, the military bureaucracy was enmeshed within an institutional network so dense and powerful that radically downsizing it was unthinkable.[2]

Nevertheless, despite this military dominance, the earliest signposts of the 1990s pointed toward a diplomatic path whose waypoints had previously been set by dollar diplomacy. Expectations of cooperation had always been disappointed in the past, but President Bush gave voice to some long-suppressed hopes by painting the future in rosy colors. "Now we can see a new world order coming into view," he told Congress, "a world where the United Nations—freed from the Cold War stalemate—is poised to fulfill the historic vision of its founders." This line of thought was given intellectual cachet in the so-called end of history thesis advanced by Francis Fukuyama, in which the future promised an unchallenged resumption of liberal globalization. The most obvious signpost indicating entry into this new New Era was that the prospect of war among the great powers had dwindled to virtually zero, becoming, in John Mueller's words, "sub-rationally unthinkable." As a tangible expression of this sentiment, nuclear disarmament among the powers, hitherto the stuff of pipe dreams, was put on the slow and bumpy road to becoming a reality.[3]

The implausibility of great power war was accompanied by a degree of active collaboration that would have been utterly fanciful only a few years earlier. An uncommonly broad coalition that in 1991 forced Iraq to disgorge its conquest of neighboring Kuwait marked the high point of joint military action, but it was not the sole example. In southeastern Europe, following the breakup of post-Tito Yugoslavia into a bedlam of quarrelsome successor states, NATO and the United States, following some initial bumbling, were able to quell a conflict that threatened to unleash genocidal forces. Farther afield, the war in Afghanistan featured another diverse coalition, including NATO forces that for the first time were fighting "out of theater." Even the much derided "coalition of the willing" used to justify the 2003 invasion of Iraq recognized that the intervention needed to be legitimated by a cloak of multilateralism. The limited NATO engagement in Libya in 2011 that hastened the downfall of strongman Muammar al-Qaddafi temporarily regained some of the lost momentum of cooperation. True, Russia and China often frustrated Security Council action in the UN, but their disapproval centered on proposed actions against troublesome third parties and did not involve life-and-death differences between the great powers.[4]

With great power political tensions at a historical low, for a time in the 1990s economic policy threatened to become high policy. In international affairs as in the domestic policies of the Clinton administration, the refrain might well have been "It's the economy, stupid!" One analyst argued that "under Clinton, foreign policy has become almost synonymous with trade policy." Another commentator identified Clinton's approach with dollar diplomacy, whence the single-minded pursuit of expanded trade would bring security, democracy, and other good things. In truth, the

1990s did bear more than a passing resemblance to the 1920s as a period when the world, for a brief moment, appeared to be on the verge of becoming a liberal utopia. With some troubling exceptions, it was a decade of astounding economic growth as more and more countries entered the club of modernizing nations while others were taxiing for takeoff. Globalization, already a hot scholarly topic, was now on every politician's lips as well. Embracing these changes, Clinton spoke enthusiastically about "our commitment to globalization." His mention of "harnessing the forces of globalization" indicated clearly that international society was once again towing history in its wake.[5]

What happened next lends support to the adage that periods of happiness are the blank pages of history. In the aftermath of the attacks on the twin towers of the World Trade Center in New York City on September 11, 2001, the country veered toward a more pugnacious, unilateralist kind of globalism. Those attacks, it was endlessly repeated afterward, were said to have "changed everything" as the national mood shifted from complacency to crisis. Even the most dangerous moments of the Cold War, perhaps with the momentary exception of the Cuban missile crisis, had failed to incite the kind of deep public fear and anger aroused by the 9/11 attacks. In response to the new national obsession with terrorism, the George W. Bush administration announced a war on terror of indefinite duration. It envisioned using the nation's military superiority to remove the threat and, in the process, to resolve the unfinished business of globalization by installing democratic regimes in a Middle East region overpopulated with authoritarian regimes—"draining the swamp," in the policy speak of the day. In his 2005 inaugural, Bush declared, "The survival of liberty in our land increasingly depends on the success of liberty in other lands. The best hope for peace in our world is the expansion of freedom in all the world."[6]

The United States took the offensive first by invading Afghanistan, which the al-Qaeda network had been using as its base of operations, and more controversially, by invading Iraq in March 2003. The war in Iraq, while hotly debated at home, was wildly unpopular abroad, stirring up accusations of US imperialism and fostering anti-Americanism among people who only two years earlier had expressed deep sympathy for America. But the new American unilateralism ran deeper than Iraq. The Bush administration made no attempt to disguise its disdain for the United Nations, which it considered to be little more than a talking shop. The Senate's refusal to ratify a number of landmark treaties—the Kyoto protocol on climate change, the Rome statute establishing an international criminal court for trial of war crimes, a global ban on land mines, and others—further promoted the image of the nation as a bad citizen of the international community. Ironically, the attempt to make a case against rogue nations and terrorism was instead convincing many that the United States had become a rogue internationalist.[7]

Much of the criticism of the United States assumed, too readily, that the Bush administration had unleashed a deep trait in the American national character. On its face, the unilateralist turn of its global war on terror was the perfect embodiment of an aggressive exceptionalism. For much of the world, the Bush policies reinforced the long-standing stereotype of the United States as a "gunfighter nation," an image that American historians had done much to promote and one that the Texas-bred president sometimes played to, particularly in his "wanted: dead or alive" description of the manhunt for al-Qaeda leader Osama bin Laden. This assertive and trigger-happy America, many were convinced, was not the quirky product of a single administration; rather, it was an outgrowth of deep historical roots that would be around for a long time to come.[8]

Seeking to unearth its sources in the past, some observers sensed a revival of Wilsonianism in this efflorescence of exceptionalist rhetoric. Even before the invasion of Iraq, a writer in the *Wall Street Journal* said of George W. Bush: "The 'W' Stands for Woodrow." While the press and political pundits gnawed away at the Wilsonian theme, scholars preferred to discuss America's new global position in terms of empire. In dozens of works, academic writers sought to compare America's extraordinary position after the end of the Cold War with that of former imperial powers, with classical Rome usually the first analogy to come to mind. Rome's territorial sweep, its overpowering military, its ability to impose a Pax Romana accompanied by Roman citizenship, and its republican heritage all provided fodder for comparison. Another variation on the theme of empire saw the United States as inheritor of the imperial crown worn by Great Britain in the preceding century. This idea had enjoyed brief favor in the late 1940s when Britain's decline first became manifest, but the imperial family resemblance stood out more vividly in the new global circumstances. For some, the British analogy justified American behavior; while for others, the connection with Pax Britannica was an embarrassment in a new era in which imperialism was a dirty word.[9]

These dramatic interpretations made for good stories, but were they good history? Did it make sense to see the United States, formerly the mainstay of a liberal international order, transformed virtually overnight into an overweening power intoxicated with its own might? Was post-9/11 foreign policy the point at which the United States finally fulfilled the destiny that had been foreseen since the founding of the republic? Legions of policy analysts and historians liked to think so. But if there is anything to my narrative, it makes more sense to see the post–Cold War decades as a residual period in which contingent events led to a temporary outburst of interventionism. Then, too, if one brackets the Iraq war and the war on terror, a look at the broader outlines of American policy shows that in most vital respects the United States continued to adhere to the basic vision of internationalism that had sustained it through the century.

The arguments about a revival of Wilsonianism, empire, and abandonment of multilateralism all suffered from fatal flaws. For one thing, these debates lacked policy relevance. Few people except the intellectuals who consulted each other's books took notice of them, and deservedly so, for the comparisons with Rome were far-fetched. One might as well have sought meaningful connections between gladiatorial contests and American football—once one gets past the fact that both wore helmets, the comparison breaks down very quickly. The image of the torch being passed from an exhausted Britain had an initial plausibility to it, but here too the superficial similarities were far outweighed by substantive differences. The displacement of Great Britain as the world's leading power was not a simple casting change in which an ambitious American understudy replaced a fading leading man. It was, rather, a new production entirely in which the United States played a radically different kind of starring role. Whether measured in geopolitical, economic, or cultural terms, the stature and influence of Great Britain at the height of its power differed enormously from that of late twentieth-century America.[10]

Analogies to Wilsonianism were equally misplaced. If there was a connection, President Bush went out of his way not to acknowledge Woodrow Wilson's influence, despite some tailor-made opportunities to do so. Bush's reluctance was traceable to a host of fundamental differences with Wilsonianism that went beyond partisan politics. Most importantly, Wilson had sought the more limited practical goal of making the world safe for democracy rather than unrealistically attempting to spread democracy by force in critical regions. In addition, Wilson's crusade, if that is what it was, placed its faith in collective security and international organization, whereas the Bush administration preferred to hold the UN at arm's length. Most of all, Wilsonianism was largely irrelevant to the world of the twenty-first century. As I pointed out in an earlier chapter, Wilsonianism offered a set of solutions to problems that, by the end of the twentieth century, no longer existed. The most striking resemblance between the two was that both approaches were historical outliers. If one looks beyond the spurious comparisons to Wilsonianism, it is not clear that the Bush administration's democratizing ambitions fit *anywhere* within the ideological boundaries of the history of American foreign relations. Wilson's brand of collective security had defined one extreme that was never again pursued; the Bush administration's justifications bookended another.[11]

In its essential long-term features, American policy in the aftermath of the 9/11 attacks changed hardly at all. Present-minded commentators liked to paint succeeding presidential administrations as polar opposites, but a look at the Clinton-Bush years demonstrated a high degree of continuity. During this period, the United States never deviated from the fundamentals of good citizenship in international society. It continued its membership in NATO, whose members even agreed to participate with the United States in the war in Afghanistan, which for a time was viewed as a good war.

The United States also continued to bear its responsibilities for security in Asia and for governance of the international economy, all the while maintaining its membership in a host of functional international organizations. Even its unilateralism was little different from unpopular interventions during the Cold War, particularly the wars in Korea and Vietnam, which also had been fought as shaky "coalitions of the willing." Then, too, Clinton had advocated preemptive war in certain situations (as had Eisenhower) as well as regime change in Iraq. All of which suggests that the swerves of one presidency were being mistaken for a fundamental change in America's approach to the world.

There were other indications that the crisis was less than it was made out to be. Realist logic predicts that overbearing behavior will be countered by coalitions, thus creating a new balance of power. But the underlying continuity of American policy gave no cause for the formation of an anti-American bloc despite the uproar in world public opinion. The absence of any moves toward such a countermobilization indicated that American hegemony was more an annoyance than a genuine threat to the vital interests of the core states. More positively, it confirmed the widespread understanding, though not screamed from the housetops, that only a dominant America could be counted on to provide the public goods needed by a global society. If this was genuinely the case, then a hegemonic United States remained indispensable to world society's continued well-being. In contradiction to the self-defeating logic of the "security dilemma" of international relations theory and metaphorical accusations of imperialism, the security of the United States continued to rely on the use of preponderant American power to make other nations feel secure.[12]

America's remarkable global influence depended to a significant extent on the legitimate exercise of power as the bulwark of international society. In many cases, American domination had been invited by the dominated, who would have been terrified to see it renounced. But that hard-earned legitimacy, which had enabled the United States to establish its primacy and was equally vital to maintaining it, had the by-product of circumscribing America's military strength. The expectation of cooperation, which the United States had been instrumental in creating, severely hamstrung its ability to exercise its power. To maintain its position, the United States needed to continue to act in the spirit of multilateralism, whereas behaving like a classic hegemon was the surest way to erode or even destroy that hegemony.[13]

But there were solid reasons to think that continuing down the path of unilateralism was unsustainable over the long term. First, the precariousness of the Bush administration's policies was underscored by its highly contingent character. It would have been very easy to lead a consensual international effort against terrorism, especially in light of the extraordinary outpouring of sympathy from abroad—"Nous sommes tous Américains," said a memorable headline from *Le Monde*. But a public opinion that craved action, the availability of a superlative military machine, and the potent presence within the government of a small group of hawkish neoconservatives eager to exploit America's military superiority bent the policy needle in the direction of unilateral military action. Ordinarily, a fringe group of this kind would not have been able to exercise such influence, but in the post-9/11 environment its members were presented with a golden opportunity to leverage their unconventional views. And they did, only to encounter rapidly diminishing returns.

Economic difficulties posed even more serious obstacles to a continuation of unilateralism. By the 2010s, a multitude of domestic problems cast a shadow over the ability of the United States to sustain its extraordinary position. For a time after 9/11, the desirability of having an almighty military was virtually unchallenged. One decade and a trillion dollars later, however, questions of affordability began to set limits on how much military might the United States could effectively wield. Victory could be easily achieved against conventional military opponents, but the costs of fighting open-ended and inconclusive wars in which the United States was hard-pressed to hold its own against substate actors were enormous. In the 1950s, Eisenhower believed that permanent military mobilization would sap the strength of the economy. In the 1980s, Paul Kennedy prematurely predicted that "imperial overstretch" would afflict the United States, as it had so many other great powers in the past. But it became increasingly clear that the prospect of huge budget deficits, coupled with chronic trade imbalances financed by the borrowing of enormous sums from China and other nations, made it impossible to sustain such high levels of military spending. Something, at some point, had to give. So while the power position of the United States was clearly unprecedented, it was approaching the point at which it could no longer sustain that power.[14]

But chronic economic troubles were only the most visible symptoms of a descent from the heights, as a growing inventory of serious domestic problems suggested that hegemony was no longer practically viable. When one looked at societal indicators, lying beneath the surface were some festering domestic ills that increasingly constrained America's options. Ironically, at the very moment that American military power reached heights previously imaginable only in the dreams of would-be world conquerors, the domestic basis of that superiority was being undermined. In the middle of the twentieth century American society and culture had been paramount in many different areas, but the advent of the millennium showed the country receding into the middle of the pack in many sectors. In some ways, American society had regressed to a status reminiscent of the late nineteenth century when the nation had failed to stand out in most head-to-head comparisons to other developed nations. At that time, it had been an economic giant and a military pygmy. Now even its unequaled economic dynamism and productivity, formerly its most compelling claim to distinctiveness, was in process of being eclipsed by a band of energetic upstarts and reinvigorated old-timers.

One writer has pointed to "the other exceptionalism," a long list of fields in which the United States lagged far behind the standards set by other developed countries. The American standard of living, once un-paralleled, was matched or exceeded by a substantial number of countries that boasted higher per capita incomes (In 2011, the UN Human Development Index ranked the United States in twenty-third place.) While the American middle class had stagnated over a stretch of thirty years, other nations passed the United States by. The gap between rich and poor threatened to make America a class society, making it increasingly difficult to view it as the land of opportunity. Some comparative studies even suggested the heretical possibility that Europe offered stronger prospects for social mobility and better life chances. Although higher education remained a bright spot, it was becoming increasingly unaffordable, whereas other nations provided much greater support to their young. In primary education, the situation was execrable, as other countries routinely outperformed American students by wide margins on standardized tests. Scientific education in particular was lagging. To compensate, the United States relied increasingly on the "brain drain" in which foreign-educated scientists and engineers made up the intellectual deficit.[15]

Americans worked longer hours, took fewer vacations, and were less well paid than counterparts abroad. The country spent more per capita on health care than any other country but without corresponding returns to health and life expectancy, whereas other nations did far better with less. The American Constitution was less and less attractive as a model for other democracies. "I would not look to the U.S. Constitution if I were drafting a constitution in the year 2012," said Associate Justice Ruth Bader Ginsburg. In areas where it was in the forefront, such as its incarceration rates, there was no cause for pride. And, in the minds of European critics, the continued resort to capital punishment was semi-barbarous. Similarly, the nation's stingy and porous social welfare safety net struck some foreign observers as a denial of economic human rights. If one compares the United States at the turn of the millennium with Charles W. Eliot's list of American contributions to civilization in the 1890s, America had lost its distinctiveness. Notwithstanding its remarkable ability to successfully integrate large numbers of immigrants, the United States was no longer the trendsetter in international law, standard of living, advances in eliminating war as a method of settling disputes, mass suffrage, religious toleration, and the diffusion of well-being. On top of everything, massive gridlock in Washington suggested that the political system was incapable of addressing the lengthening list of serious national problems.[16]

Given these disturbing trends, the situation was ripe for a return to a more modest policy outlook built atop deeper historical footings. For most of its history since the late nineteenth century, the United States had been content to be among the leading nations, first as follower and later as leader, pursuing a vision of foreign relations as a cooperative enterprise. Even at the height of its Cold War influence, an extraordinary degree of diplomatic effort, perhaps the bulk of it, was expended on tending to relations with allies. The delayed return to normal internationalism began in the administration of President Barack Obama, who, in his words, "made a commitment to change the trajectory of American foreign policy." According to one widely read interpreter, Obama hoped to bring US policy into line with the nation's "core interests," which also happened to be the central concerns of dollar diplomacy, namely, "dealings with the great powers and [the] embrace of larger global issues." His version of internationalism reinstated a central conviction of the 1990s that global society was composed increasingly of like-minded states that would pull together on the major problems facing them. Not surprisingly, the ugly international image of the United States was reversed almost overnight, almost embarrassingly so. The desire to see the United States restored to its former status was transparently evident in the award of the Nobel Peace Prize to Obama, in advance of accomplishments he had yet to record.[17]

Confronted simultaneously with the sharpest economic downturn since the Great Depression, a budgetary crisis, and a rapidly diminishing public appetite for the war on terror, the president planned a withdrawal from Iraq and scheduled a drawdown from Afghanistan. But he also sought to steer American foreign policy away from the unilateralism of the Bush years by pursuing a greater degree of international collaboration. An important instance of this shift was his patient construction of an international coalition to impose effective sanctions against Iran as a way of discouraging the Islamic republic from developing nuclear weapons. Another was the intervention in support of anti-Qaddafi rebel forces in Libya. Rather than rely on American troops, NATO air power provided the bulk of the force while the United States contented itself with supplying indispensable logistical and intelligence support, an approach that some called "leading from behind." There were some failures of cooperation, too, but whatever the outcome it was unlikely that American policy would continue down the byway taken during the Bush years.[18]

In the face of such indicators of American decline, the future of exceptionalism suddenly became a charged issue. "The age of American predominance is over," declared a leading economist who went on to predict that China would take over America's economic role. Younger Americans especially were increasing likely to exhibit "a declining belief in our special virtue as a world power." Obama himself caused a stir and handed Republican politicians a campaign issue when he gave the impression of disavowing American exceptionalism by relativizing it. At a press conference in Strasbourg on April 4, 2009, he stated, "I believe in American exceptionalism, just as I suspect that the Brits believe in British exceptionalism and the Greeks believe in Greek exceptionalism." This touched off a brouhaha back home. "God did not create this country to be a nation of followers. America is not destined to be one of several equally balanced global powers," thundered Republican presidential aspirant Mitt Romney. In response to the political fallout from his statement, Obama retreated somewhat. The most quoted line in his 2012 State of the Union address was "anyone who tells you that America is in decline or that our influence has waned, doesn't know what they're talking about . . . America remains the one indispensable nation in world affairs." But then the next year, he argued for taking action against Syria "with modest effort and risk," concluding, "That's what makes America different. That's what makes us exceptional." To equate the uniqueness of American policy with only modest effort and risk was a significant comedown from US foreign relations at its most ambitious.[19]

Both the requiems and the exceptionalist swagger were intellectually dubious because they were based on a "rise and fall" model of thinking about power that no longer conformed to how the world functioned. Admittedly, if one works from that kind of perspective, then the second half of the twentieth century cannot help but look like the booster stage of America's rise to supremacy. In contrast, the story I have presented in this book portrays these years as a period of extraordinary influence that could not be sustained. It was, moreover, not a record likely to be copied or surpassed by any other power because the international system was no longer about single powers selfishly, and unrealistically, seeking dominance. The story was not about the United States or potential competitors, but about the future of the global society that the United States had been so instrumental in saving and reviving. The more interesting question was whether international cooperation had become institutionally and culturally established among nations to the extent needed to sustain a global society whose continued success was far from certain.

Just as liberal economic theory correctly predicted that America's disproportionate economic superiority in 1945 would wane as other countries recovered and prospered, it was equally foreseeable that the US star would shine less brightly in the firmament of nations. But this was hardly a tragedy. At its inception, the American empire was intended to be temporary, pending the restoration of an international society in which cooperation rather than hegemony would be the norm. In 1941, the publisher Henry Luce wrote an essay in *Life* magazine advocating what he called "the American Century." Luce, with his China missionary origins, envisioned a world that was converted to American ways. Often seen as an imperialist Urtext, it is worth pointing out that he did not envision an Americanization of the globe. "America cannot be responsible for the good behavior of the entire world," said Luce, "but America is responsible, to herself as well as to history, for the world environment in which she lives." Elsewhere, he wrote, "Emphatically our only alternative to isolationism is not to undertake to police the whole world nor to impose democratic institutions on all mankind." The point was to assure the continued operation of global society, not to dominate it.[20]

The American Century, unlike the Third Reich, was not intended to be "the American millennium." Only the twentieth century would be an American century, "our century." And so it was. To an amazing extent, Luce's vision was realized in practice, which helps to explain why it has been so compulsively revisited. Luce did not address the question of what would succeed it, but American policy makers did. From the earliest days of the Cold War, they recognized that the postwar world was not an American creation, and they left open the yet-to-be-realized possibility that the follow-up to the American Century would produce an international environment in which others did their share of the rowing. America's relative decline was consonant with a rapidly globalizing world in which the United States would possess a monopoly of neither virtue nor vice.[21]

Following the half century of American dominance in foreign affairs, then, the post–Cold War years were an anticlimax. After having reached the pinnacle of international power, there was no way for the United States to go but down. The extraordinary character of America' story lay in the journey to the top, not in the flag-planting ceremony at the summit. By itself, this was predictable. Alpinists, after all, do not linger on the peaks that they conquer, for getting to the top is less dangerous than remaining there. After pausing for a few moments to enjoy the view and breathe the rarefied air, they need to start the faster but still fraught descent downward to safety. To think otherwise, as did many chauvinist policy makers and cheerleaders who believed that American hegemony was a natural state of affairs, was to confuse the by-product of the journey with a permanent historical condition.

NOTES

1 Charles Krauthammer, "The Unipolar Moment," *Foreign Affairs* 70 (Winter 1990/1991): 23–33. For the argument that the unchangeable truths of realism still applied, see Kenneth N. Waltz, "Structural Realism after the Cold War," *International Security* 25, no. 1 (Summer 2000): 5–41. A more neutral characterization is Elizabeth Cobbs Hoffman, *American Umpire* (Cambridge, MA: Harvard University Press, 2013).

2 On bureaucratic pathologies, see especially the classic work by Francis E. Rourke, *Bureaucracy and Foreign Policy* (Baltimore: Johns Hopkins University Press, 1972).

3 John Mueller, *Retreat from Doomsday* (New York: Basic Books, 1990), 11, is the locus classicus of the argument that great power war is obsolete. See also Christopher J. Fettweis, "A Revolution in International Relation Theory; Or, What If Mueller Is Right?," *International Studies Review* 8, no. 4 (December 2006): 677–97.

4 Obviously, the leading nations of the world did not sing in perfect harmony. They disagreed on a host of issues—genocide in Rwanda and Sudan's Darfur region, sanctions against Iraq, action against North Korea and Iran, and policy toward the Israeli-Palestinian problem, among others. Russia was an annoyance, but the nation most often identified as a source of renewed great power competition was China, with its amazing economic growth, increasing self-confidence, and burgeoning military capability. However, the dire forecasts of a looming conflict with this new giant neglect the fact that this single-party state, with its mixed economy tilting rapidly toward the capitalist mode of production, was increasingly dependent upon the continued success of an open world economy, and in particular on its close relationship to the United States as consumer of its exports, for sustaining the economic growth upon which the legitimacy of the Communist Party depended. China's continued success, moreover, was dependent on the success of globalization. See Kenneth Lieberthal and Wang Jisi, "Addressing U.S.-China Strategic Distrust," Brookings Center, 2012. (These comments were written before the crisis between Russia and Ukraine erupted early in 2014. Nevertheless, these events have not substantially changed my views.)

5 David L. Marcus, "The New Diplomacy," *Boston Globe Magazine*, June 1, 2007, 17; Lawrence F. Kaplan, "Dollar Diplomacy Returns," *Commentary* 105, no. 2 (February 1998); Clinton, remarks at a dinner for the Conference on Progressive Governance for the 21st Century in Florence, Italy, November 20, 1999; Clinton remarks to business and community leaders in Santiago, Chile, April 16, 1998, PPUS.

6 George W. Bush, inaugural address, January 20, 2005. At the dedication of his presidential library in Dallas on April 27, 1913, Bush repeated the sentiment: "My deepest conviction—the guiding principle of the administration—is that the United States of America must strive to expand the reach of freedom."

7 Clyde Prestowitz, *Rogue Nation: American Unilateralism and the Failure of Good Intentions* (New York: Basic Books, 2003).

8 Policy makers in the early Cold War years had anticipated and rejected a hegemonic policy based on power. In 1950, Paul Nitze, in looking forward to a post–Cold War world, argued that "Pax Americana [here read hegemony] would be contrary to the American ethos, and it would invite enmity and opposition to us on the part of other peoples and nations. Moreover, it was beyond the capacity and will of the United States to enforce." Paul Nitze, *From Hiroshima to Glasnost: At the Center of Decision; A Memoir* (New York: Grove Weidenfeld, 1989), 119.

9 Max Boot, *Wall Street Journal*, July 1, 2002. Some observers offered a structural interpretation of events in which the mere existence of such a superior military force mandated its use. Clinton's secretary of state Madeleine Albright had famously wondered, "What's the point of you saving this superb military for, Colin, if we can't use it?" Madeleine Korbel Albright, *Madam Secretary: A Memoir* (New York: Miramax Books, 2003). For one synoptic effort, see Kimberly Kagan, ed., *The Imperial Moment* (Cambridge, MA: Harvard University Press, 2010). For a review of the recurrent thorny issues that attend debates about empire, see Paul K, MacDonald, "Those Who Forget

Historiography Are Doomed to Republish It: Empire, Imperialism and Contemporary Debates about American Power," *Review of International Studies* 35, no. 1 (January 2009): 45–67.

10 Though Great Britain had been a world power, it was not nearly as influential militarily as the United States. It was not the dominant power in Europe; its responsibilities came nowhere near to matching those of the United States; and it was, quite unashamedly, a colonial empire. Despite many marvelous cultural achievements to its credit, Great Britain's mass democracy never came close to creating the kind of magnetic attraction that American society would generate in the postwar years.

11 Some scholars claimed to find precedents for this action, but their procrustean arguments strained to fit a historical aberration into a pattern that was not there. See especially John Lewis Gaddis, *Surprise, Security, and the American Experience* (Cambridge, MA: Harvard University Press, 2004), and Tony Smith, "The Bush Doctrine as Wilsonianism," in *Wilsonianism in Crisis?*, ed. G. John Ikenberry (Princeton, NJ: Princeton University Press, forthcoming), posted as http://ase.tufts.edu/polsci/faculty/smith/wilsonianism.pdf. For a counterargument, see Frank Ninkovich, "Wilsonianism after the Cold War: Words, Words, Mere Words . . . ," in *Reconsidering Woodrow Wilson*, 299–326.

12 Michael Mandelbaum, *The Case for Goliath: How America Acts as the World's Government in the Twenty-First Century* (New York: Public Affairs, 2005).

13 Edward A. Kolodziej and Roger E. Kanet, eds., *From Superpower to Besieged Global Power: Restoring World Order after the Failure of the Bush Doctrine* (Athens: University of Georgia Press, 2008). For a discussion of the distinction between primacy and hegemony as an exercise of legitimate authority, see Ian Clark, *Hegemony in International Society* (New York: Oxford University Press, 2011).

14 Michael Mandelbaum, *The Frugal Superpower: America's Global Leadership in a Cash-Strapped Era* (New York: Public Affairs, 2010); Joseph S. Nye, "The Dependent Colossus," *Foreign Policy* (2002): 74–77; Joseph S. Nye, *The Paradox of American Power: Why the World's Only Superpower Can't Go It Alone* (Oxford: Oxford University Press 2002); G. John Ikenberry, "Liberalism and Empire: Logics of Order in the American Unipolar Age," *Review of International Studies* 30 (2004): 609–30.

15 Hodgson, *The Myth of American Exceptionalism*, 128–54; "Sustainability and Equity: A Better Future for All," *UN Human Development Report 2011* (New York: Palgrave Macmillan, 2011).

16 January 30, 2012, interview on Al-Hayat TV as cited in Adam Liptak, "'We the People' Loses Appeal with People around the World," *NYT*, February 6, 1912. The US murder rate per 100,000 was actually relatively moderate, though high when compared with western Europe, China, and Japan. It ranked twenty-fourth overall worldwide in 2012.

17 Fareed Zakaria, "The Strategist," *Time* 179, no. 4 (January 30, 2012): 26, 28; G. John Ikenberry, "Liberal Internationalism 3.0: America and the Dilemmas of a Liberal World Order," *Perspectives on Politics* 6, no. 1 (March 2009): 71–87.

18 Fareed Zakaria, *The Post American World* (New York: Norton, 2009).

19 President Obama's address to the nation on Syria, September 10, 2013; Mark Feisenthal, "Economists Foretell of U.S. Decline, China's Ascension," *Reuters*, January 10, 2011. Peter Beinart, "The End of American Exceptionalism," *National Journal Magazine* (Febraury 3, 2014). National Intelligence Council, *Global Trends 2030: Alternative Worlds* (Washington, DC: 2012): "By 2030, no country—whether the US, China, or any other large country—will be a hegemonic power." See also the essays in *The Short American Century*.

20 While advocating an ambitious expansion of American influence throughout the world, Henry R. Luce's famous essay "The American Century" was notable for rejecting geopolitical justifications for American participation in the war. Henry R. Luce, *The American Century* (New York: Farrar and Rinehardt, 1941), 20–24, 32–34. See David M. Kennedy's essay in *The Short American Century*, 15–37.

21 Henry Luce, "The American Century," *Life*, February 17, 1941.

DISCUSSION QUESTIONS

- Consider the "city on a hill" notion from the colonial era. In what ways had the United States lived up to that dream by the 1990s? In what ways did the United States in the 1990s fail to live up to that dream?

- Consider the different approaches of Presidents Theodore Roosevelt, William H. Taft, and Woodrow Wilson in international relations. In what ways did the United States in the 1990s resemble any of those approaches?

- Consider the United States as an example for other democracies. Had that perception shifted by the 1990s? If so, why?

CONCLUSION

To "conclude" a reader on United States history is an impossible undertaking. History is constantly changing and does not end. New facts may be uncovered, new questions may arise, and new interpretations may challenge preconceived notions. Is history, then, something that is only for the present generation to interpret? Do we only embrace the "new" without thought to what came before? What people consider valuable today may change in the future. You will have to decide in the days and years to come if the past is worth remembering as it is today. The present discussion on physical symbols of memory in the United States—monuments, war memorials, and such—is one such example. What one person considers worth remembering may not be an opinion that someone else may share. As historians though, is it ethical to reject anything that can inform us of the past? To paraphrase a common jibe of the historical profession, ask that question in a room of a hundred historians and you will receive a thousand different opinions.

It is thus perhaps more constructive to return to the beginning than to offer a conclusion. Why does one study history? It cannot be replicated in a laboratory. It's interpretative. And those interpretations must be useful. A useful past explains how we arrived where we are today. If you have a clear understanding of the past, you have a good idea where you may be heading in life. The interpretation of that past, however, is yours.

PERSONAL BIO

DR. JACK D. ANDERSEN

A native of San Antonio, Dr. Andersen is a historian with a BA from Texas A&M University, an MA from Texas State University, and a PhD from the University of North Texas. His research focuses own topics related to war and society in American military conflicts since the nineteenth century. He has taught United States history at several institutions in Texas and is an Associate Professor of History at Collin College in McKinney, Texas.

CPSIA information can be obtained
at www.ICGtesting.com
Printed in the USA
LVHW060239030919
629751LV00004B/129/P